W9-DDJ-054

Organizational Communication

BALANCING CREATIVITY AND CONSTRAINT

SECOND EDITION

Organizational Communication

BALANCING CREATIVITY AND CONSTRAINT

SECOND EDITION

ERIC M. EISENBERG
University of South Florida

H. L. GOODALL, JR.
University of North Carolina at Greensboro

Bedford/St. Martin's
Boston ♦ New York

Sponsoring editor: Suzanne Phelps Weir
Managing editor: Patricia Mansfield Phelan
Project editors: Diane Schadoff/Harold Chester
Production supervisor: Scott Lavelle
Art director: Lucy Krikorian
Text and cover design: Evelyn Horovicz
Graphics: MacArt
Cover art: David Bishop

Library of Congress Catalog Card Number: 95–73210

Copyright © 1997 by St. Martin's Press, Inc.

All rights reserved. No part of this book may be reproduced, stored in a retrieval system, or transmitted by any form or by any means, electronic, mechanical, photocopying, recording, or otherwise, except as may be expressly permitted by the applicable copyright statutes or in writing by the Publisher.

Manufactured in the United States of America.

1 0 9
f e d

For information, write:
Bedford/St. Martin's
75 Arlington Street
Boston, MA 02116
(617-426-7440)

ISBN: 0–312–13692–7

Acknowledgments and copyrights can be found at the back of the book on pages 375–376, which constitute an extension of the copyright page.

To Lori and Sandra

Contents

Chapter ❷ Situating Organizational Communication 19

Chapter ❸ Founding Perspectives on Organizations and Communication 52

Chapter ❹ The Systems Perspective on Organizations and Communication   94

Chapter ❺ Cultural Studies of Organizations and Communication   123

Chapter ❻ Critical Approaches to Organizations and Communication 149

Chapter ❼ Postmodern Perspectives on Organizational Communication 171

Chapter ❽ The Experience of Work   193

Chapter ❾ Relational Contexts for Organizational Communication 231

Chapter ⑩ Communicating in Teams and Networks   271

Chapter ⑪ Managing the Total Organization: Strategy, Image, and Communication Technology   305

Chapter ⑫ The Future of Organizational Communication 331

Preface

Both of us were gratified by the success of the first edition of *Organizational Communication: Balancing Creativity and Constraint.* In addition to strong sales and positive reviews, the book received the 1994 Text-book and Academic Authors Association "Texty" award for excellence in communication, education, and performing and visual arts. The text has also figured into a cross-disciplinary conversation about the role of organizational communication studies in liberal education as well as about how textbooks should be written to address the needs of the changing adult college market.

However, as we set out to update the first edition of this book, we realized that, since its publication in 1993, fundamental changes in the world of work would demand that we do much more than mere revision. Therefore, in the second edition of *Organizational Communication,* we have written a new book. Among many other changes, the book now features up-to-date discussions of such topics as global competitiveness, intercultural workplaces, international labor and trade treaties, information technology, communication cultures, the new "social contract" between employers and employees, corporate downsizing and restructuring, and team-based initiatives.

More specifically, the book aims to help students bridge the gap between what they learn in college and what they will experience in the workplace by incorporating many real-life examples from the contemporary business world. In Chapter 7, for instance, students are taken on a tour of BMW's new U.S. plant, a state-of-the-art facility that has been designed to function as a "working theory of postmodern communication." In addition, the text has been extensively rewritten and redesigned in order to improve its readability, layout, and overall appearance. Questions for Discussion now appear at the start of each chapter, numerous new Focus on Ethics boxes ask students to consider how they might resolve various ethical dilemmas posed by today's business world, and nine new case studies that focus on contemporary issues of organizational communication also include thought-provoking assignments.

In addition to writing a new chapter on managing the total organization (Chapter 11), we have extensively rewritten and updated the other eleven chapters in the book.

- Chapter 1, "The Changing World of Work," introduces students to organizational communication in the context of today's new global, intercultural, technological, strategic, and managerial developments. It also discusses how the new reengineered world of work will affect the future of organizations and communication.
- Chapter 2, "Situating Organizational Communication," which covers four theories of organizational communication, has been rewritten to focus on the dialogic approach and to provide more examples.
- Chapters 3 through 5, which cover the historical approaches to organizational communication, now include more discussion of human resources theory and intercultural assumptions (in Chapter 3, "Founding Perspectives on Organizations and Communication"), of Karl Weick's sense-making systems and Peter Senge's learning organizations (in Chapter 4, "The Systems Perspective on Organizations and Communication"), and of the cultural approach to organizational communication (in Chapter 5, "Cultural Studies of Organizations and Communication").
- Chapters 6 and 7, "Critical Approaches to Organizations and Communication" and "Postmodern Perspectives on Organizational Communication," now two chapters instead of one, have been significantly expanded to cover intercultural communication, feminism, alternative organizations, information technology, and the global workplace.
- Chapter 8, "The Experience of Work," now features a discussion of the fastest-growing segment of the new global economy—outsourcers, entrepreneurs, and consultants—and of the new experience of work that many college graduates will encounter as a result.
- Chapters 9 and 10, "Relational Contexts for Organizational Communication" and "Communicating in Teams and Networks," have been rewritten to focus more specifically on intercultural communication, multiculturalism, organizational spirituality, and relationships with customers and suppliers.
- Chapter 11, "Managing the Total Organization: Strategy, Image, and Communication Technology," a new chapter, focuses on the roles of competitive strategy, image, and communication technology. The first of its kind in an organizational communication textbook, this chapter gives students the information they need to put theoretical knowledge into practice.
- Chapter 12, "The Future of Organizational Communication," reviews the major challenges that organizations and communicators will face in the future, discusses how computer technology and biotechnology will affect both workers and consumers, and shows how scenario planning can be used as a tool for thinking about and planning for the future.

A new *Instructor's Manual*, written by one of our colleagues and informed by other users of the first edition, and an audiocassette that reviews key chapter concepts for discussion and exams, supplement the second edition of the text.

Acknowledgments

We would like to thank the many people who have contributed to the making of *Organizational Communication* in various but significant ways. We are especially grateful to our patient and enterprising editor at St. Martin's Press, Suzanne Phelps Weir; to her able assistant, Hanna Shin; and to our excellent copyeditor, Wendy Polhemus-Annibell, for their valuable contributions to the second edition. To the numerous businesspeople who graciously invited us into their companies, we are thankful for the opportunity to learn about the experiences of organizational members firsthand.

We offer special thanks to our colleagues who reviewed the manuscript and offered insightful suggestions for improvement: John Llewellyn, Wake Forest University; Brian Betz, SUNY at Oswego; Fred Steier, University of South Florida; Vernon Miller, Michigan State University; Phil Salem, Southwest Texas State University; John C. Meyer, University of Southern Mississippi; Carey Adams, Southwest Missouri State University; Joann Keyton, University of Memphis; David Walker, Middle Tennessee State University; Brenda Allen, University of Colorado at Boulder; Mark Braun, Gustavus Adolphus College; Joseph Scudder, Indiana University at Bloomington; Judi Brownell, Cornell University; Gary Shulman, Miami University; Gerald Driskell, University of Arkansas; Nick Trujillo, California State University at Sacramento; and James O'Rourke, Notre Dame University.

In addition, we are indebted to a number of colleagues, students, and staff members for their support of this project: Walter Beale, Christine Flood, Pete Kellett, Jody Natalle, Craig Smith, Joyce Ferguson, Lori Lindberg, David Olson, and Janice Enekwechi at the University of North Carolina, Greensboro; Linda Andrews, Art Bochner, Connie Hackworth, Lexa Murphy, Sharon Smith, Paul Stockinger, Linda Timmerman, and Sue Viens at the University of South Florida; Patricia Riley at the University of Southern California; Patricia Geist at San Diego State University; Rita Whillock at Southern Methodist University; Stew Auyash at Ithaca College; Carl Lovitt and Art Young at Clemson University; and Bruce Hyde at St. Cloud State University.

We could not have written this book without the enthusiastic and loving support of members of our immediate families—Lori Roscoe, Evan and Joel Eisenberg, and Sandra and Nic Goodall—as well as of grandparents (especially Martha and Clarence Bray), siblings, and close friends. Finally, we are grateful to those individuals who, despite the intellectual, social, political, economic, and spiritual turmoil of our time, remain committed to continuing the dialogue.

Eric M. Eisenberg
H. L. Goodall, Jr.

The Changing World of Work

Don't be afraid to explore;
*   without exploration there are no discoveries.*
Don't be afraid of partial solutions;
*   without the tentative there is no*
*   accomplishment."*

• Deng Ming-Dao (1992, p. 295)

QUESTIONS

FOR DISCUSSION

- Why study organizational communication?

- Why is learning how to ask good questions necessary to improving communication in organizations?

- What continuities and changes define today's business practices?

- What organizational challenges are associated with globalization?

- How have our changing values influenced the emergence of new issues in organizational communication?

S tudents embarking on careers often harbor misconceptions about the world of work. Many report that they expected their first "real" job to be more serious and orderly and their managers more competent and fair. A similar experience of surprise and disorientation may affect older, more experienced workers with successful careers when they are laid off and unable to find comparable employment (Meyer, 1995). The shock of losing a job after years of success—increasingly associated with global competition and the rapidly changing technological requirements of jobs—affects both individuals and societies.

How can we deal with these changes in the business world? There are no easy answers. Even straightforward questions such as "What is the best way to supervise employees?" or "How can we attract and keep customers?" or "What is effective organizational communication?" require addressing a host of situational and historical factors (Eisenberg & Phillips, 1991). As a result, the definition of effective communication does not remain constant; rather, it varies by company or industry, the people involved, and the culture.

Put another way, answers to questions about organizational communication are highly situated and perishable. The type of communication that works well for a small start-up clothing manufacturer may be inappropriate for a mature film-production company. Patterns of interaction that were effective last year may be outdated today due to changes in jargon, technology, or the nature of the industry. According to management expert Tom Peters (1987), companies that have been doing something the same way for more than ninety days should probably look to initiate change. Those that fail to recognize the need for change may perish. One example from our experience involves a machine shop in California. The general manager, a Marine Corps veteran, models the shop's management systems and structures after the military. While this model may have been effective in the past (and even then, only in selected industries—see Morgan, 1986), it no longer works for the company. Neither the managers nor the employees are comfortable with the rigid hierarchy and intimidating management style. The current business environment requires flexibility. The rapid changes that take place in today's social, economic, and political climates demand speedy, flexible responses. But flexibility is not a strength of the military model. In a recent restructuring, IBM created numerous independent business units to meet the demand for greater flexibility. Similarly, in the 1990s General Electric reconsidered the wisdom of its autocratic management style under CEO Jack Welch, questioning whether the benefits of a top-down approach still outweigh the costs in employee morale, turnover, and productivity.

When we first taught classes in organizational communication more than fifteen years ago, the banking, air transportation, and fast-food industries were considered noncompetitive. Today, however, they are among the most highly competitive industries in the world. The meaning of organizational communication in the business world of even five years ago no longer applies. Therefore, our focus here is on *enabling you to ask good questions about organizations, the answers to which will change over time.* Although we sometimes offer our opinions about what constitutes good organizational communication in many companies most of the time, these are not rigid conclusions. Successful executives, consultants, researchers, managers, and employees know how to ask good questions about organizational communication situations. Over time, their actions are guided by how they see and make sense of such situations, by keeping an open mind to the various ways of interpreting those situations, and by remaining committed to a lifetime of learning. Their flexibility enables them to manage conflict and diversity more effectively and to adapt more readily to a fast-paced business environment. They reinvent themselves and their organizations in response to or in anticipation of changing times.

We pose a number of questions in this book: Why do people work? How can workplaces be improved? Can work be both fun and profitable? Are all workplaces basically the same, or, if not, how do they differ? How can people maintain a healthy relationship between their work and personal lives? What role should communication technology play at work? Should all people have an equal voice in decision making? How can organizations make the most of their diverse memberships? How should an organization present itself? What role do leaders play in promoting organizational effectiveness? And, most important: How can knowledge of communication help us perform better at work? Although the answers to these questions will differ over time and across companies, those who take the time to consider their importance are better able to deal with today's ever-changing business world. These *interpreters* of organizational communication are the designers of our collective future.

New Developments in the World of Work

"Self-managed Work Teams!" "Total Quality Management!" "Reengineering the Corporation!" The business shelves of local bookstores scream with prescriptions for improving organizations. Some books even proclaim "The End of Work" and invite you to consider a "Jobless Future." It is clear from these examples that significant changes face the business world, changes that may mean the end of work as we know it. As we will see, many of these changes have to do with communication.

However, it should be noted that not everything about business is new or changing. For example, success in business continues to be hard to achieve and maintain. Changing technology and customer preferences, ineffective management, and the difficulties associated with keeping a business profitable over a long period of time help to explain why only 4 percent of the businesses operating in 1900 still exist today. Also unchanged is the antagonism that exists between the economic concerns of corporations and the personal concerns of employees. Although companies have shown increased interest in improving the quality of their employees' work life, they are not often willing to sacrifice the good of the company to achieve that goal. In recent years, considerable effort has gone into designing organizations that are both pro-profit and pro-people. But such organizations are by no means commonplace, and the challenge to be profitable while also providing a positive work environment is often too great.

This first chapter focuses on three broad trends facing contemporary organizations—globalization, increased competitive pressure, and the changing relationship between organizations and employees—and their implications for communication.

GLOBALIZATION

In recent years, remarkable changes in global politics—the end of the Cold War, the breakup of the Soviet Union, the destruction of the Berlin Wall in Germany, and the beginnings of a unified European Community—have altered or dissolved divisions that once seemed insurmountable. Regional conflicts throughout the world continue to alter the names and boundary lines of countries. Nowhere has the permeability of national boundaries been clearer than in the business world. Business has moved toward a *global marketplace,* a world economy in which the United States is but one of many participants. More than 100,000 U.S. companies conduct business abroad. In addition, approximately one-third of the profits of U.S. companies and one-sixth of the nation's jobs come from international business (Cascio, 1986; Offerman & Gowing, 1990). While half of Xerox's 110,000 employees work overseas, half of Sony's employees are not Japanese. Musicians such as David Byrne and Paul Simon import world music to the United States, while American music, films, and television command large markets elsewhere.

Three regions will dominate the global marketplace of the twenty-first century: North America, the Pacific Rim, and Europe. Although globalization gives the United States an expanded market for its products and services, it also threatens to erode U.S. business because of increased foreign competition. At one time U.S. consumers could respond by "buying American," but the globalization of business has made that slogan less meaningful. Barnet and Cavanaugh (1994) make this clear in their attempt to identify an "American" car:

> What is an "American" car? A Geo Prizm, which is really a Toyota Corolla made in California? A Geo Metro, marketed by GM but made by Suzuki and Isuzu? What is a "foreign" car? A Jaguar made in England by a wholly owned Ford sub-

sidiary? A Mazda Navaho, which is really a Ford Explorer made in Kentucky? (p. 279)

Similarly, U.S. Labor Secretary Robert Reich (1991) points out the international nature of the purchase of an "American" car:

> When an American buys a Pontiac Le Mans from General Motors, for example, he or she engages unwittingly in an international transaction. Of the $10,000 paid to GM, about $3,000 goes to South Korea for routine labor and assembly operations, $1,850 to Japan for advanced components (engines, transaxles, and electronics), $700 to the former West Germany for styling and design engineering, $400 to Taiwan, Singapore, and Japan for small components, $250 to Britain for advertising and marketing services, and about $50 to Ireland and Barbados for data processing. The rest—less than $4,000—goes to strategists in Detroit, lawyers, bankers in New York, lobbyists in Washington, insurance and health care workers all over the country, and to General Motors shareholders all over the world.

Among the many challenges associated with globalization are those related to questionable labor practices, multicultural management, and communication technology.

Questionable Labor Practices

Different trade policies, import-export quotas, and tariffs among countries in the global marketplace can create problems when certain countries see themselves as victims of unfair global competition. In addition, the emergence of a new world labor market has encouraged businesses to search the globe for the lowest possible labor costs and move jobs overseas. Although such practices have long been commonplace in textiles and other kinds of manufacturing, they were confined almost exclusively to blue-collar jobs. Today, white-collar jobs in most industries are also affected. For example, the U.S. firm Arthur Andersen recently turned to the Philippines for computer software engineers.

Not all prospecting for cheap labor leads to the loss of U.S. jobs, however. In many cases, European and Japanese companies have set up operations in the United States, particularly in the South: "The highest concentration of foreign investment (in the U.S.) is in South Carolina, which is now home to 185 non-U.S. companies. BMW is likely to pay around $12 an hour in South Carolina rather than the $28 it has to pay in Germany" (Barnet & Cavanaugh, 1994, p. 321).

The potential consequences of U.S. jobs being moved overseas were at the center of the debate over the North American Free Trade Agreement (NAFTA). On the one hand, an expanded labor pool makes U.S. companies more competitive by allowing them to hold costs down. In addition, by hiring people from less developed countries, U.S. companies gain new consumers for their products and services. On the other hand, sending work overseas may lead to the destruction of U.S. communities unable to withstand plant closings or massive job losses. Furthermore, the low wages paid to workers in less developed countries—as little as 10–15 percent of comparable U.S. wages—raises questions about exploitation.

The debate also centers on whether employees must always be sacrificed when a company's profits are in jeopardy. Here the standard view that gives primacy to stockholders is being extended by some to a notion involving *stakeholders*. A stakeholder is anyone (including investors, managers, employees, customers, suppliers, or members of the general public) who has a significant interest or stake in the company. From this perspective, organizational decision making does not focus exclusively on maximizing profits or on short-term versus long-term financial returns. Instead, it seeks to satisfy multiple audiences with competing goals. Although protecting shareholder value is still the standard in a capitalist society, profitability as the only criterion for success involves many risks. While it may not be profitable, for example, to recruit and promote physically challenged and minority candidates or to conform to environmental regulations, many companies do so out of a sense of social and moral correctness. A growing number of companies have managed to strike a balance between stakeholder interests and an environment that is both pro-profit and pro-people.

Multicultural Management

Another challenge associated with globalization involves the multicultural management of customers, suppliers, and employees. Globalization is not as a rule a homogeneous process; rather, differences in language and culture remain. One example is Sony's "global localization," which it uses to adapt its products and services to meet various cultural differences in lifestyle, tastes, and values among its global markets. The flavors of foods, the design of automobiles, and the style and size of furniture are other examples of product features that are adapted to meet the demands of a global market. Similarly, while there are McDonald's restaurants all over the world, their menus vary.

Success in global business requires global communication skills. Thus, conducting business across national boundaries means that employees must speak the various languages of their customers and suppliers and, preferably, understand the subtleties of the other cultures. In Finland, for example, which has relied on export markets throughout much of its history, many people speak four or more languages. Similarly, Western countries doing business with Japan have learned much about the Asian tendency to spend a relatively long period of time in planning and developing relationships.

A now-famous example of poor multicultural management is Disneyland Paris (formerly Euro-Disney). After outstanding success with Disneyland in

Japan where the meticulously designed theme park was consistent with the local culture, Disney set out to do the same in France. In this case, however, the theme park was designed in ways that ignored important aspects of French culture and climate. For instance, the expensive American-style hotels that were built around Disneyland Paris and that cost upwards of $300 a night for lodging were not practical for the typical French family that takes a three- to six-week vacation. In addition, when the park first opened, it did not serve alcohol; that policy was soon changed to accommodate the French custom of drinking wine at lunchtime. Perhaps most startlingly of all, the theme park was built in an area that experiences cold winters, at least in contrast to Orlando or Los Angeles.

With the acquisition of global markets, businesses necessarily turn to a more culturally diverse workforce. At a public grade school in Santa Monica, California, 104 languages are spoken. At Vistana Resort, an award-winning hotel in Orlando, Florida, the Environmental Services Department meets regularly to address communication and other issues pertinent to the multiethnic staff. At Kyocera America in San Diego, a Japanese management team struggles to connect with male African American supervisors and female Filipino employees on the line. As these examples show, effective organizational communication today must address a host of multicultural and multinational concerns (see Chapter 5).

Communication Technology

Chapter 11 details the role of communication technology in contemporary organizations. For now, it is important to note that the global business community—and the global markets, economy, and joint ventures implied therein—is in large part made possible by recent advances in communication technology.

Globalization requires companies to communicate in ways that transcend time and space. Computerized communication networks—including those that operate over short distances (called local area networks or LANs) to those that span the globe (such as the Internet and World Wide Web)—allow companies to coordinate production, take and service orders, schedule work, recruit employees, and market their services. Some of the most ingenious applications of communication technology have been in software manufacturing. For example, one such manufacturer has operations in Texas, Ireland, and Indonesia that allow it to conduct business continuously. Before the workday ends in Indonesia, employees forward their work electronically to employees in Ireland, who are just starting the workday. The employees in Ireland, in turn, transmit their work to those in Texas before they sign off.

Communication technology enables businesses to structure themselves in novel ways. Some observers credit the development of the telephone with the creation of the modern skyscraper, which would have been impractical (and unsafe) without the ability to communicate quickly between floors. As we will see in Chapter 11, advances in communication technology both promote global business as well as create new sites for work, such as offices that exist in cyber-space. As a billboard from AT&T proclaims, "The office of the future has no office."

INCREASED COMPETITIVE PRESSURE

In this historic period of global social and economic change, we face novel concerns about how to live and work in a world of real economic, ecological, and personal limits. This is not a temporary or cyclical event. Severe competitive pressures have caused widespread layoffs and plant closings; bankruptcies have become routine. The abuses of credit by government, private industry, consumers, and lending institutions in the 1980s have fostered a conservative lending attitude in the 1990s. Customers, stockholders, and the public have become more cautious about conducting risky business, and venture capitalists have become more conservative about investing in start-up companies. As a result, there is less slack in the system and a slimmer margin for error. The need to develop new ways of dealing with this competitive environment is creating fundamental changes in the structure of organizations, communities, and societies.

Focus on Product Quality and Customer Service

In addition to economic pressures, companies are motivated to reexamine their structures and processes by the customer's increased sophistication and expectation of quality products and services. With few exceptions, U.S. companies are preoccupied with product quality and customer satisfaction, largely the result of foreign competition (particularly from Japan) and the need to compete in a global marketplace. Today, virtually every large workplace has a special program designed to enhance product quality and customer satisfaction based on the ideas of management gurus W. Edwards Deming, Philip Crosby, Karl Albrecht, Peter Senge, Steven Covey, and others. These efforts are often targeted at winning the coveted Baldrige Award for quality (named after former U.S. Secretary of Commerce Malcolm Baldrige).

The current emphasis of U.S. business on customer satisfaction is evident in hospitals and universities as well, which have become, respectively, more patient- and student-focused. Medical residents at Long Beach Memorial Hospital in California, for example, are required to spend one full day as "patients," complete with hospital gowns and intravenous tubes, to help them learn how to empathize with patients. Major changes are under way at Stanford University, which leads the effort to reexamine the basic mission of the university with regard to its primary customers—undergraduate students. Stanford, Yale, and Columbia universities are moving to restructure their operations to respond to economic concerns and better serve the needs of students. In some cases, this has meant staff layoffs and the closing of certain academic departments. Increasingly, hospital and university presidents are using the language of business-people to urge their employees to work toward achieving higher quality services and greater customer satisfaction.

Turbulent Organizational Environments

The environments in which organizations exist vary in terms of their character and complexity. In a classic analysis by Fred Emery and Eric Trist (1965), a weather metaphor is used to describe these variations in environment from turbulent to placid. At one extreme is the *turbulent environment*—dense, complicated, and hard to predict. An organization in such an environment is in constant fear of environmental jolts (or unexpected events that can negatively affect its business) and has difficulty forecasting the consequences of its actions (such as a new marketing strategy, distribution policy, or product feature). At the other extreme is the *placid environment*—uncomplicated, calm, and predictable. A company in a placid environment is less fearful of unexpected events and is better able to deal with the consequences of its actions. Such companies are increasingly rare, however. Public utilities that can make decisions and set policies without fear of significant repercussions are an example.

In contrast, contemporary hospitals exist in a turbulent environment that is profoundly affected by changes in technology, research, demographics, government regulations, and insurance. Consider, for example, how the warm tropical currents that flow periodically through the Gulf of Mexico impact the price of a hospital stay: The storm destroys the Peruvian anchovy crop, which in turn increases the price of gelatin. Composed in large part of anchovy bones, gelatin is a major component of X-ray film. As this example shows, organizations cannot afford to underestimate the complex interconnections that exist within a turbulent environment. Unanticipated consequences are routinely dealt with by effective organizational decision makers. This is what Karl Weick (1979) refers to when he says that managers get into trouble when they fail to "think in circles."

The unpredictable nature of a turbulent environment has led some organizations to focus on rapid retrieval of information about environmental conditions. This may involve such traditional methods as market research and customer feedback or more complex and innovative approaches utilizing computer databases and information systems. Although in recent years many companies have increased their environmental scanning efforts, most firms have not taken full advantage of the available information retrieval capabilities.

Perhaps the simplest, though most often overlooked, way to keep in touch with environmental conditions is through boundary spanners, company employees who have direct contact with the public (Adams, 1980). Bank tellers, telephone receptionists, repair technicians, market researchers, salespeople, and customer service representatives can provide important information about the outside world. According to J. Stacy Adams (1980), boundary spanners serve at least three functions: (1) They can access the opinions of people outside of the organization and use that information to guide organizational decision making; (2) their awareness of subtle trends in the environment can serve as a warning system for environmental jolts; and (3) they serve as important representatives of the organization to its environment.

What does a company do with the information it obtains about its environment? According to Tom Peters (1987), some large companies are unresponsive to such information because of the difficulty of maintaining quality and flexibility in a business that has grown beyond a certain size. The big company is rarely as efficient or innovative as its smaller competitors. Today, successful organizations typically have fewer levels of hierarchy, promote more sharing of power among their employees, are oriented toward niche markets, and are more flexible and responsive in their pursuit of quality products and customer service. Of course, giant businesses benefit from several important advantages: increased financial stability, reduced competition, and strategic mergers and acquisitions. However, there is no truly effective way to manage a company that grows beyond ten thousand employees. This explains why IBM opted to splinter into independent business units and why several Japanese car companies introduced luxury models through separate companies. It also explains why small business employs most working Americans and why it will continue to play a critical role in the economic future of the United States (Drucker, 1992a).

Continuous Learning

Turbulent business environments, increased global competition, and greater customer sophistication mean that companies cannot rely on their past achievements for continued success; rather, they must engage in continuous learning through research and development, environmental scanning, training, and education. By *continuous learning* we mean not only the upgrading of employee skills but also the development of new ways to organize, structure, plan, solve problems, and manage.

But will the future U.S. workforce be prepared to manage these challenges? The illiteracy rate among U.S. workers is as high as 25 percent in some industries. A survey conducted by the Educational Testing Service for the National Assessment of Educational Progress (NAEP) found that only 24 percent of whites, 20 percent of Hispanics, and 8 percent of African Americans aged twenty-one to twenty-five could calculate the tip and change for a two-item restaurant bill. Concerns about the literacy rate and basic skills of today's entry-level workers are compounded by the growing need for highly skilled people. Computer software can check the spellings of words but it cannot proofread for meaning and context. As robots take over routine assembly work, the number of jobs requiring skilled people able to monitor and troubleshoot computerized equipment will increase. This has caused U.S. businesses to spend a record $210 billion on job training and education, an effort about equal in size to public elementary, secondary, and higher education combined (Offerman & Gowing, 1990).

THE CHANGING RELATIONSHIP BETWEEN ORGANIZATIONS AND EMPLOYEES

For the past one hundred years, people left their homes, farms, and communities to work for large companies in exchange for wages. Many worked all their lives for a single company and were rewarded by job stability and a decent pension. This relationship between organizations and employees is quickly becoming a thing of the past. With global competition have come plant closings, company downsizings, and cutbacks, including one million layoffs in 1994 alone. Increasingly, workers are themselves responsible for upgrading their skills. A new term—*corporate anorexia*—has emerged to describe the situation wherein layoffs lead to decreased capacity, which leads to lost business, which leads to more layoffs. But the new employee–company relationship, or "social contract," sends a mixed message, as observer Brian O'Reilly (1994) points out:

> You're expendable. We don't want to fire you, but we will if we have to. Competition is brutal, so we must redesign the way we work to do more with less. Sorry, that's just the way it is. And one more thing—you're invaluable. Your devotion to our customers is the salvation of this company. We're depending on you to be innovative, risk-taking, and committed to our goals. (p. 44)

Shifting Power Bases

In nineteenth-century America, power was measured by a person's tangible assets—land, equipment, oil, and perhaps slaves—and those in control of these resources wielded the greatest power. By the latter half of the twentieth century, however, tangible resources were replaced by less tangible information resources as a measure of power in an information-based society. By the end of the century, over 50 percent of the U.S. labor force was involved in the transfer, reprocessing, or transmittal of information (SCA, 1991). Today, information *is* power, and those who have the quickest access to the best information are the most likely to succeed. Indeed, such companies as TRW and American Airlines cite the information aspects of their business (credit verification and computerized reservations, respectively) as their greatest financial successes (Davis & Davidson, 1991).

Organizational Structure and Employee Well-Being

Workaholic is a term used to describe a person who is unnaturally pre-occupied with work. Typically, a workaholic spends long hours at work, including nights and weekends. Family and friendships are often abandoned in favor of relationships with co-workers or other workaholics. Some workaholics truly enjoy their work, but most worry obsessively about getting unfinished work done. Like in alcoholism, from which the term *workaholism* is derived, the workaholic suffers from a disease that affects the person's quality of life. The dependence, however, is on work rather than on alcohol. Although society has made positive strides toward understanding alcoholism as a disease and the alcoholic as a victim, there is still a tendency to blame the victim for the disease. The same is true of workaholics, who are often viewed as people who *choose* to dedicate themselves to their work at the expense of health, family, and friendships. Some organizations consider the behavior of workaholics desirable—a sign of the employee's dedication to the job and company and a source of increased productivity.

Several organizational theorists propose a new interpretation of workaholism as a *dis-ease,* a condition brought about by the profound influences organizations have over how people define themselves through their work (Alvesson, 1993; Deetz, 1991; Karasek, 1979). In this view, organizational power structures—particularly those inherent in bureaucracies—and the childlike dependence fostered by "rational" employment arrangements may destabilize the employee's personality and produce an unhealthy level of dependency. More specifically, unhealthy work conditions can include:

(continued)

However, some observers argue that having the right information is not sufficient to achieve and maintain power. According to Rosabeth Moss Kanter (1989), informal communication networks are the most dynamic source of power in contemporary organizations because of their role in monitoring a turbulent business environment. In this challenging environment, the formal reporting relationships specified by the organizational chart are too limited to be effective. Increasingly, employees rely on quick, verbal information from trusted co-workers. These informal relationships allow employees to get things done

(continued)

1. authoritarian-style supervision.
2. severe restrictions on the employee's ability to utilize resources.
3. production systems that limit the employee's opportunity to contribute ideas and knowledge.
4. limited opportunities for the employee to influence the planning or organization of tasks.
5. tasks that deprive the employee of the ability to select the method and speed at which he or she will work.
6. tasks that limit human contact.

According to some studies, power structures and working conditions that deny employees the opportunity to participate in decision making while also requiring a high level of performance or output correlate highly with employee depression, irritability, and anxiety (Karasek, 1979; Katz & Kahn, 1978). The causes and symptoms of workaholism are in a sense *ethical* problems. As organizational theorist Stan Deetz argues, "It is wrong to knowingly do physical or psychological harm to others" (1991, p. 38). This raises several ethical questions:

1. Do organizations intentionally reward unhealthy but productive behavior as a way of maximizing employee output?
2. As a manager in a company that rewards workaholic behavior, how could you counteract the problem? What questions would you ask? Who in the company would you consult?
3. As an employee of a company that rewards workaholic behavior, how would you address the problem? Who would you discuss it with?
4. As an employee or manager, would you have an ethical obligation to help a co-worker who is a workaholic (assuming that the person, like an alcoholic, needs first to admit to having the problem)?

across functions within organizations, across organizations, and among business, government, and other stakeholders. The traditional, formal hierarchy is simply too slow.

Some observers object to the idea of informal relationships as power as a restatement of the old cliché, "It's not *what* you know but *who* you know." Others contend that the growing informal basis of power has unfavorable implications for women, minorities, and others who may lack connections with those in power. Although such concerns are not unjustified, a return to the homogeneous, discriminatory workplaces of the past is unlikely. Informal relationships will likely keep much of the power concentrated in traditional hands. But today nearly every company with more than three hundred employees offers workshops in cultural diversity to address the needs of a multicultural workforce.

Finally, under the new social contract, the career ladder has been replaced by the honing of one's own skills and the strategic application of those skills through an expanding web of jobs. As a result, connections and interpersonal relationships have become more important.

New Values and Priorities

As competition increases and managers demand more from employees, new values and priorities about such issues as home and family have emerged. In addition, unlike past generations of workers, today's employees are more likely to seek meaning and involvement in their work life.

> Desire for balance between work and family is increasing among many workers (Hall, 1986). People seek more meaningful, involving work experiences. (London & Strumpf, 1986)

In short, many American workers are changing their definition of success to include not only a career but also family and community (Bellah et al., 1985).

Two primary factors have contributed to this reshifting of priorities. First, with fewer high-paying, unionized manufacturing jobs available in the United States, two-career families have become prevalent. More than 40 percent of the workforce is comprised of dual-earner couples (Zedeck & Mosier, 1990). Second, because grandparents and other members of extended families rarely live nearby, child-care is in high demand (Wolfe, 1991). As a result, family issues have become a part of the national political agenda.

It was not long ago that the model American employee came to work early, stayed late, and was willing to travel anywhere at a moment's notice. Getting ahead meant putting one's job ahead of most everything else. Today's men and women are redefining the work ethic of the past. The motivations of those just entering the workforce are less clear. Some are willing to work as hard as needed to get ahead, while others seek a more balanced life. Businesses are moving to accommodate these needs by providing child care, flexible hours, and parental leave (Moskowitz & Townsend, 1991; Zedeck & Mosier, 1990).

The Meaning of Work

Some of the values being espoused today about work involve not a retreat from it but a transformation of its meaning—from drudgery to a source of personal significance and fulfillment. Employees want to feel that the work they do is worthwhile, rather than only a way to draw a paycheck. However, many misconceptions surround this trend. For example, while white-collar workers and college students tend to view blue-collar workers as motivated primarily by money, job security, and benefits, the most important incentives for workers at all levels include friendly relationships with co-workers and managers. Also important are opportunities to participate in organizational decision making. Without these major determinants of job satisfaction, worker stress and burnout may occur (Miller et al., 1990). Work has considerable social significance for Americans, who usually spend more time on the job than they do with their families.

Worker Identity

Work relationships are more important to people's well-being than they often realize. Retirees, for example, often go through a period of adjustment in which they feel as if they have lost their sense of belonging or identity. Strangely, some even continue driving to work long after they have retired.

The movement to enrich the meaning of work often goes unrecognized when it shows up in the informal connections people make at work, in the strong informal groups that form over long periods of time, and in the desire for input into organizational decision making. For work to be meaningful, employees must feel that their opinions and input are respected; more often than not, however, this is still not the case.

Globalization and the new employee–company relationship make it especially difficult to enhance worker identity and involvement in decision making. Under the new social contract, workers are expendable, temporary, independent contractors. How will this affect the informal networks that enrich worker identity? Will people be able to shift from an identity based on job and organization to one based on their knowledge and skill base? And if so, how will they sustain it? Although the need for intelligent employee input is greater than ever, it usually comes on an as-needed basis. In the near future, however, efforts to make work more meaningful and rewarding will likely become commonplace. We know that the most productive workers are also highly motivated workers. In the short run, broader worker participation in decision making will not be easily achieved, as managers learn the value of consulting employees and employees are encouraged to voice their input freely. In the long run, however, greater worker empowerment may come as a result of economic pressure. As one senior manager of an electronics firm says, "I can't manage this place anymore. Maybe my employees can."

Table 1.1 summarizes the continuities, changes, and new values and priorities affecting organizations today.

TABLE 1.1 Summary of the Continuities, Changes, and New Values and Priorities Affecting the World of Work

Theme: Answers to questions about organizational communication are highly situated and relatively perishable.

CONTINUITIES	CHANGES	NEW VALUES AND PRIORITIES
Success in business has always been hard-won and hard to maintain. (Most businesses fail; only 4% of those in business in 1900 still operate today.)	Increased competitive pressures (there is no room for complacency under market demands for continuously improving quality)	Old answers no longer work (big is not necessarily better; must accomplish more with less)
Persistent antagonism exists between the economic concerns of companies and the personal concerns of employees. (Can a business be both pro-profit and pro-people?)	Focus on quality and customer service (increased stress due to tension between detailed planning and immediacy of responding)	Recovery from "workaholism" (individuals and families seek more balanced lives)
	Turbulent organizational environments (unexpected interdependencies; new reliance on boundary spanners, learning, and information; shifting power bases—not money but what to do with it; power of network relationships; multiculturalism)	Meaning and democracy in the workplace (demand for personally meaningful work experiences and democracy of decision making in organizations)
	Globalization (expanded markets and increased competition; differences in trade policies; *stake*holders replacing *stock*holders; new ethical and moral implications for doing business; inadequately educated labor pool)	Worker identity (work relationships are important to well-being; movement to enrich work experiences is constrained by traditional management styles)

Who Can Afford to Prioritize?

For many people, prioritizing work, family, and other needs may seem like a luxury. "Sure," they say, "I *want* all those things—more input into decisions at work, more time for myself, more time only with family and friends. But most of all I really *need* this job!"

Any discussion of the quality of work life must take into account the many U.S. workers who are unemployed or underemployed and live below the poverty line. As we struggle to make work more meaningful, we must also seek to improve the living and working conditions of those at the bottom of the economic ladder by setting priorities that include everyone.

Why Study Organizational Communication?

We study organizational communication to understand and enhance our role in inventing a better future and to maintain some degree of control over the work environment. More specifically, a knowledge of organizational communication allows us to:

- ask informed questions about everyday business practices.
- develop communication skills that can improve our chances of success.
- improve the quality of our work life.
- develop empathy for others who work at varying levels in different industries.
- apply our knowledge and skill in communication to promoting organizational effectiveness.

SUMMARY

Defining organizational communication in the 1990s means identifying historical continuities; global political, economic, and social changes; and the evolving values and priorities of employees. In this turbulent environment, the traditional ways of communicating and of doing business are no longer effective. Instead, principles of effective organizational communication have become highly situated and perishable.

Communication is the substance of organizational life. To be effective, however, it must contribute to our understanding of how to improve organizational life. As such, it seeks to achieve a productive balance between the employee's need for creativity and the organization's demand for order. In combining theory and application in ways that speak directly about our own experience, the study of organizational communication offers us several opportunities: to learn how to ask informed questions, to develop effective communication skills, to improve the quality of our work life, to develop empathy for other workers, and to promote organizational effectiveness.

Situating Organizational Communication

The world's first bureaucracies—staffed as they were by armies of scribes generating untold thousands of written records—were the administrative organizations established under the pharaohs of ancient Egypt. Especially noteworthy is the fact that the oldest surviving literary work should be a book on communication and human relations in the organizational context: the Precepts of Ptah-hotep.

• W. Charles Redding and Philip Tompkins (1988, p. 8)

QUESTIONS

FOR DISCUSSION

• What are the approaches to communication discussed in this chapter? What insights does each provide?

• How do the concepts of self, other, and context contribute to our understanding of organizational communication? How are these concepts interpreted by the four approaches discussed in this chapter?

• Is "real dialogue" possible in today's organizations? What are its promises and challenges?

Questions about organizational communication are as old as humanity. In the chapter-opening quotation, W. Charles Redding and Philip Tompkins argue that even the issues that most concern communicators today—how and when to speak and listen to others—have changed very little throughout history. James G. March (1965) makes a similar observation: "[When] one reads a treatise on management by a modern-day successful manager, one is frequently struck by the extent to which Aristotle probably said it better and apparently understood it more" (p. xiii).

It is not hard to understand why organizational communication is an important concern. People coordinate their activities—from hunting and gathering to caring for children and building airplanes—to accomplish goals. Unlike other creatures, humans rely on language as a means of relating to and controlling their physical and social environment. Thus, the importance of communication has endured. The approaches to understanding it, however, have changed over time. This chapter traces those changes, beginning with the evolving models of communication as information transfer, transactional process, strategic control, and a balance of creativity and constraint, and concluding with a model of communication as dialogue.

Approaches to Organizational Communication

Hundreds of communication theories have been offered over the years. Many of these attempts to define communication are part of a broader approach or perspective. This chapter discusses four major approaches to understanding organizational communication: communication as (1) information transfer, (2) transactional process, (3) strategic control, and (4) a balance of creativity and constraint.

COMMUNICATION AS INFORMATION TRANSFER

The *information transfer* approach views communication as a metaphorical pipeline through which information is transferred from one person to another (Axley, 1984; Reddy, 1979). Managers thus communicate well when they transfer their knowledge to subordinates and others with minimal spillage (Eisenberg & Phillips, 1991). According to Steven Axley (1984), most communication theories rest on one or more of the following assumptions:

1. Language *transfers* thoughts and feelings from one person to another person.
2. Speakers and writers *insert* thoughts and feelings into words.

3. Words *contain* those thoughts and feelings.
4. Listeners or readers *extract* those thoughts and feelings from the words.

The information transfer approach views communication as a tool that people use to accomplish goals and objectives. Redding and Tompkins (1988) refer to this as the "formulary-prescriptive phase" within the historical development of organizational communication. During this phase, clear, one-way communication was emphasized as a means of impressing and influencing others. In this view, communication is typically defined as "the exchange of information and the transmission of meaning, and . . . the lifeblood of an organization" (Dessler, 1982, p. 94). It is further characterized as "information engineering," wherein information functions as a tool for accomplishing goals but the process of transmission is not seen as problematic; that is, "If I say it and you can hear it, you ought to understand it" (Feldman & March, 1981). Thus miscommunication occurs only when no message is received or when the message that is received is not what the sender intended. Approached this way, typical communication problems include information overload, distortion, and ambiguity.

Information overload occurs when the receiver becomes overwhelmed by the information that needs to be processed. Three factors can contribute to information overload: (1) *amount,* or the absolute quantity of information to be processed; (2) *rate,* or the speed at which the information presents itself; and (3) *complexity,* the amount of work it takes to interpret and process the information (Farace, Monge, & Russell, 1977). Information overload situations can vary in intensity and type. A government worker in a severely understaffed bureaucracy, for example, may have to deal with mountains of simple, steady work. In contrast, a police officer on patrol is faced with varying amounts of complex information that often presents itself at a fast rate.

Distortion refers to the effects of noise on the receiver's ability to process the message. Noise can be *semantic* (i.e., the message has different meanings for sender and receiver), *physical* (e.g., the sound of static on a telephone line or of a jet plane passing overhead), or *contextual* (i.e., the sender and receiver have different perspectives that contribute to the miscommunication).

Finally, *ambiguity* occurs when multiple interpretations of a message cloud the sender's intended meaning. Abstract language and differing connotations are common sources of ambiguity. When a manager asks two employees to work "a little bit harder," for instance, one might put in an extra half-hour a day and the other might work all night.

David Berlo (1960) offers a communication model that reflects the information engineering approach. According to his *SMCR* model, communication occurs when a sender (*S*) transmits a message (*M*) through a channel (*C*) to a receiver (*R*). The sender "encodes" an intended meaning into words and the receiver "decodes" the message when it is received. Keith Davis (1972) offers a similar definition: "Two-way communication has a back-and-forth pattern similar to the exchange of play between tennis players. The speaker sends a message, and the receiver's responses come back to the speaker."

The information transfer model, although somewhat dated, is still useful in explaining certain communication situations in organizations. For example, it can be used to explain how a supervisor gives an employee instructions for doing a specific task. To illustrate a more complex application of the information transfer approach, let's assume that an advertising agency has just received a new account. The senior account representative calls a team meeting and gives assignments to the junior people. One of the team members, however, has difficulty with the assignment. He found the senior representative's presentation confusing and he was distracted by people coming in and out of the room during the team meeting. The deadline arrives and none of the team members' assignments are complete. In this situation, communication is said to have "broken down" because the intended meaning of the sender (the senior representative) did not reach the receivers (the team members).

Critics of the information transfer approach argue that it is overly simple and incomplete, painting a picture of communication as a sequential process (i.e., "I throw you a message, then you throw one back"). In addition, the model assumes that the receiver remains passive and uninvolved in constructing the meaning of the message, and that words mean exactly what the sender wants them to mean—no more or less.

COMMUNICATION AS TRANSACTIONAL PROCESS

Dissatisfaction with the information transfer approach to communication led to the development of the *transactional process* model. It asserts that in actual communication situations, clear distinctions are not made between senders and receivers. Rather, people play both roles, often simultaneously. According to Wenberg and Wilmot (1973), "All persons are engaged in sending (encoding) and receiving (decoding) messages simultaneously. Each person is constantly sharing in the encoding and decoding processes, and each person is affecting the other" (p. 5). The transactional process approach highlights the importance of *feedback,* or information about how a message is received, and particularly nonverbal feedback, which may accompany or substitute for verbal feedback. Consider, for example, the nonverbal messages that students send to instructors during a lecture to indicate their degree of attention and comprehension. The importance of nonverbal communication is captured by Watzlawick, Beavin, and Jackson's (1967) famous axiom, "You cannot not communicate." In other words, a person need not speak to communicate; nonverbal messages are conveyed through a person's silence, facial expressions, body posture, and gestures. As a result, then, any type of behavior is a potential message (Redding, 1972).

The transactional process model differs significantly from the information transfer approach in terms of the presumed location of the meaning of the message. In the information transfer model, the meaning of a message resides with the sender, and the challenge of communication is to transmit that meaning to others. The transactional model rejects this idea in favor of one in which "meanings are in people, not words" (Richards, 1936). It focuses on the person receiving the message and on how the receiver constructs the meaning of that message (Axley, 1984). As a result, says Steven Axley (1984), "Miscommunication is the normal state of affairs in human communication . . . miscommunication and unintentional communication are to be expected, for they are the norm" (p. 432).

One area to which the transactional process model may be effectively applied is leadership. Ideas about leadership have evolved from the simple belief that certain people are born with leadership skills to the acknowledgment that leadership involves a transaction between leaders and followers. Thus, successful leaders are able to mobilize the meanings that followers have for what leaders say or do. In this sense, then, leadership is the transactional management of meaning between leaders and followers.

Many experts criticize the transactional process view for its emphasis on the creation of shared meaning through communication (Bochner, 1982; Eisenberg, 1984; Parks, 1982): "Human communication is the process of constructing shared realities" (Shockley-Zalabak, 1991, p. 29) or communication is "shared meaning created among two or more people through verbal and nonverbal transaction" (Daniels & Spiker, 1991, p. 46). The bias toward clarity, openness, and shared meanings may be based more on ideology than on empirical reality. Moreover, the degree of shared meaning cannot be verified, and organizational communication is more often characterized by ambiguity, deception, and diverse viewpoints (Conrad, 1985; Eisenberg, 1984; Weick, 1979).

COMMUNICATION AS STRATEGIC CONTROL

Unlike the transactional process model, which assumes that effective communicators are clear and open in their efforts to promote understanding and shared meaning, the *strategic control* perspective regards communication as a tool for controlling the environment (Parks, 1982). It recognizes that greater clarity is not always the main goal in interaction due to personal, relational, and political factors. The strategic control perspective sees communicators as having multiple goals in situations. For example, in a performance review, a supervisor might have two primary goals—to be understood and to preserve a positive working relationship (Goodall, Wilson, & Waagen, 1986). Therefore, in this view, a competent communicator is one who chooses strategies appropriate for accomplishing multiple goals.

In addition, the strategic control approach to communication recognizes that although people often have reasons for their behavior, they should not be expected to communicate in an objective or a rational way. Communicative choices are socially, politically, and ethically motivated. We expect others to break the communicative "rules" of clarity and honesty when it is in their own best interests to do so (Conrad, 1985; Okabe, 1983).

The limits of general statements about what constitutes "effective" communication led to a focus on *communication as goal-attainment,* or as a means to accomplish one's ends through adaptation and saying what is appropriate for the situation (Phillips & Wood, 1982; Wood, 1977). Communicators must be "rhetorically sensitive" (Hart & Burks, 1972); they must also be able to recognize the constraints of the situation and to adapt to multiple goals simultaneously, such as being clear, assertive, and respectful of the other person (Tracy & Eisenberg, 1991).

In organizational communication, *strategic ambiguity* describes the ways in which people may communicate unclearly but still accomplish their goals (Eisenberg, 1984). Specifically, strategic ambiguity

1. promotes unified diversity.
2. preserves privileged positions.
3. is deniable.
4. facilitates organizational change.

Strategic ambiguity takes advantage of the diverse meanings that different people can give to the same message. For example, the mission statement "Quality Is Job One" is sufficiently ambiguous to allow all Ford employees to read their own meanings into it. In contrast, the more specific statement "Quality Through Cutting-Edge Engineering" is less inclusive and less likely to inspire unity, particularly in the manufacturing and administrative ranks of the company.

Strategic ambiguity preserves privileged positions by shielding persons with power from close scrutiny. A seasoned diplomat or professor emeritus giving a speech, for example, is traditionally given the benefit of the doubt by supporters who may have to fill in some gaps in understanding. Similarly, by being less than precise, employees can protect confidentiality, avoid conflict, and conceal key information that may afford them a competitive advantage. In this sense, strategic ambiguity is said to be deniable; that is, the words seem to mean one thing, but under pressure they can seem to mean something else.

Finally, strategic ambiguity facilitates organizational change by allowing people the interpretive room to change their activities while appearing to keep those activities consistent. For example, with the advent of air travel, transatlantic ocean liner companies that provided overseas passage by ship were faced with a major challenge to their service. The firms that defined themselves as transportation companies did not survive, whereas those that interpreted their business more broadly (and ambiguously) as entertainment went on to develop vacation or leisure cruise business. Similarly, the commitment of McDonald's to become the "world's community restaurant" is ambiguous.

Organizational Ambiguity in Action

The strategic uses of ambiguity can have positive or negative influences on the quality of organizational life. Viewed positively, strategic ambiguity can encourage employees to define corporate vision statements, objectives, and goals in personal and productive ways. When Ford says "Quality Is Job One," everyone from assembly-line workers to top management is encouraged to take the initiative to ensure a quality product. But ambiguous statements used to define performance objectives can have negative or prejudicial applications. *Quality* is an ambiguous term. When it is left solely to the discretion of managers and employees to define, misunderstandings often result. Similarly, because rewards based on quality attainments are subject to organizational power relationships (see Chapter 6), there is a potential for abuse in the form of favoritism or inequitable application of quality standards.

Strategic ambiguity thus raises important ethical questions. Consider the following scenarios:

1. You are a manager charged with the responsibility of implementing a Total Quality Commitment program in your company. At a preparatory training seminar you learn that successful quality commitment programs leave determinations of quality standards to employees. But you are concerned about the potential differences of opinion among employees regarding quality and how it should be measured. What steps can you take to make strategic use of the ambiguity while also preserving equity among employees? Should the process begin with *your* definition of quality? Why or why not?

2. You work for a company that has just adopted a Total Quality Commitment program. Your supervisor, unhappy about the program, tells you (off the record) of his intentions to sabotage the program by rewarding only employees who work overtime and weekends. You are shocked by his behavior. You also believe that the program will improve the workplace. Do you have an ethical obligation to confront your supervisor? To inform co-workers of his intentions? To report him to superiors? What would you do?

Unlike other models of communication, the strategic control approach is opposed to the idea of shared meaning as the primary basis or motivation for communication. Rather, it holds that shared meaning is an empirically *un*verifiable concept (Krippendorff, 1985) and that the primary goal of communication should be organized action (Donnellon, Gray, & Bougon, 1986; Eisenberg, 1986, 1990; Eisenberg & Riley, 1988). If we accept the idea that the meaning one person creates may not correspond to the meaning that another person gives to the same communication, it is less important that the two people fully understand each other than it is that they act in mutually satisfying ways (Weick, 1995).

Although the strategic control perspective advances our appreciation of the subtleties of communication, it is not without significant problems. First, it minimizes the importance of ethics. While strategic ambiguity is commonplace in organizations, it is often used to escape blame. *Fortune* magazine quotes an executive's definition of effective communication: "All you have to remember is . . . let the language be ambiguous enough [so] that if the job is successfully carried out, all credit can be claimed, and if not, a technical alibi [can] be found" (Whyte, 1948). Another limitation of the strategic control approach is its strong emphasis on the behavior of individuals (or on individuals controlling their environment through communication), often at the expense of the community. As such, it clouds issues related to cooperation, coordination, power and inequality, and the interdependent relationships of individuals and groups. The strategic control model suggests that the world is comprised of independent communicators, each working to control his or her own environment, and that meaning exists only within people's minds. It thus overemphasizes the role and power of individuals in creating meaning through communication.

Table 2.1 summarizes four views of communication—as information transfer, as transactional process, as strategic control, and as balancing creativity and constraint.

COMMUNICATION AS BALANCING CREATIVITY AND CONSTRAINT

The view of communication as *balancing creativity and constraint* is closely linked to sociological theories concerning the individual and society. Since the late 1960s, the central focus of social theorists has been the relationship between individuals and society—or, in our case, between employees and organizations. That relationship is sometimes cast as a tension between macro and micro perspectives. The *macro perspective* sees individuals as molded, controlled, ordered, and constrained by society and social institutions. In contrast, the *micro perspective* sees individuals as creating society and its social systems. While we no doubt conform to social pressures, rules, laws, and standards for behavior, "we are rule and system *users* and rule and system *breakers* as well" (Wentworth, 1980, p. 40). This dichotomy has obvious implications for organizational communication, depending on whether the emphasis is on how employees communicate to create and shape organizations or on the constraints organizations place on that communication.

In their foundational text on the individual and society, *The Social Construction of Reality* (1967), Peter Berger and Thomas Luckmann maintain that societies and organizations are constructed as people act in patterned ways; over time, people take those behavior patterns for granted as "reality." In other words, most of what we take for granted in organizations is created or constructed through people's choices and behavior. Over time, routines develop and members amass a general knowledge of "how things are done." What follows is a tension between the need to maintain order and the need to promote change (Morrill, 1991).

While many writers have contributed significantly to this line of thought (Alexander & Giesen, 1987; Gouldner, 1971; Knorr-Cetina & Cicourel, 1981), Anthony Giddens's (1979) *theory of structuration* is especially relevant to students of organizational communication. In discussing the relationships between individual communication and social systems and structures, Giddens focuses on the *creative* and *constraining* aspects of structure—or what he calls the *duality* of structure. In this view, the designer of a new product advertisement, for example, is both bound by the rules, norms, and expectations of the industry as well as open to the possibility of transcending those structures by designing a creative ad. Similarly, the process of creating a department budget, while limited by the rules and norms of finance, involves creative input as well. In this sense, *creativity* means that social systems are constructed and altered through communication. The communication process is not viewed as what goes on *inside* organizations but as *how people organize* (Barnard, 1968; Farace, Monge, & Russell, 1977; Johnson, 1977). This does not mean that the process is always deliberate or rational; to the contrary, much of what is taken for granted as organizational reality is either unintentional or based on people's perceptions and assumptions (which may or may not be valid). Moreover, people create social reality through communication in an ironic sense—they rarely get the reality they set out to create (Ortner, 1980).

The theory of structuration thus sees human behavior as an unresolvable tension between creativity and constraint. William Wentworth (1980) describes that tension as a conflict between under- and oversocialized images of people. For Wentworth, the idea that people are either inherently constrained *or* inherently creative does not offer a complete characterization of the relationships between individuals and society. Instead, he argues, social life is a *balance of creativity and constraint*—of constructing social reality and being constrained by those constructions—and it is through communication that the balance is achieved.

TABLE
2.1 Organizational Communication: Preliminary Perspectives

COMMUNICATION AS INFORMATION TRANSFER	COMMUNICATION AS TRANSACTIONAL PROCESS	COMMUNICATION AS STRATEGIC CONTROL	COMMUNICATION AS BALANCING CREATIVITY AND CONSTRAINT
Metaphor: Pipeline or conduit; sender transmits a message to a receiver.	*Metaphor:* Process; communication is a process that creates relationships; "You cannot not communicate."	*Metaphor:* Control; individuals attempt to control their environments.	*Metaphor:* Balance; individuals attempt to develop distinct identities while at the same time participating in an organized community.
Assumptions: (1) Language transfers thoughts and feelings from person to person; (2) speakers and writers insert thoughts and feelings into words; (3) words contain the thoughts and feelings; and (4) listeners or readers extract the thoughts and feelings from the words.	*Assumptions:* (1) There are rarely clear distinctions between senders and receivers; (2) nonverbal feedback accompanies or substitutes for verbal messages; (3) meanings are in people, not words.	*Assumptions:* Strategic ambiguity gains control because it (1) promotes unified diversity, (2) preserves privileged positions, (3) is deniable, and (4) facilitates organizational change.	*Assumptions:* All communication accomplishes two things at once; it reflects historical constraints of prior contexts, and it represents individuals' attempts to do something new and creative. This is the duality of social or organizational structure.
Description: Source transmits a message through a channel (air or light) to a receiver; communication is a tool people use to accomplish objectives.	*Description:* Person receiving the message constructs its meaning; idea is for senders to adapt their messages to the needs and expectations of their listeners.	*Description:* Strategic ambiguity takes advantage of the diversity of meanings people often give to the same message; choices of what to say are socially, politically, and ethically motivated; strategies can be selected to accomplish multiple goals.	*Description:* Communication is the moment-to-moment working out of the tension between individual creativity and organizational constraint. Approaching organizations as constructed through communication requires simultaneous attention to the

(continued)

COMMUNICATION AS INFORMATION TRANSFER	COMMUNICATION AS TRANSACTIONAL PROCESS	COMMUNICATION AS STRATEGIC CONTROL	COMMUNICATION AS BALANCING CREATIVITY AND CONSTRAINT
			ways in which groups of people both maintain order through their interactions, and allow individual actors the freedom to accomplish their goals.
Measure of effectiveness: Receiver of communication understands (or does) precisely what the speaker intended.	*Measure of effectiveness:* Shared meaning.	*Measure of effectiveness:* Coordinated actions accomplished through diverse interpretations of meanings.	*Measure of effectiveness:* A balance between satisfied individuals and a coherent community.
Limitations: (1) Overly simplifies communication: treats transmission of the message as linear and unproblematic; (2) sees the receiver as a passive receptor uninvolved with the construction of the meaning of the message; (3) does not account for differences in interpretation between speaker and listener.	*Limitations:* (1) Emphasis on shared meaning is problematic and ultimately unverifiable; (2) bias toward clarity and openness denies political realities; (3) does not account for ambiguity, deception, or diversity in points of view.	*Limitations:* (1) Can minimize the importance of ethics; (2) places strong emphasis on individuals over communities; (3) overemphasizes the role and power of individuals to create meaning through communication.	*Limitations:* Can sometimes be difficult to identify what counts as a constraint; also tends to draw attention away from material economic realities that may threaten the system independent of member behaviors.

Our definition of organizational communication in this text is derived from the perspectives of Wentworth and others. We believe that *communication is the moment-to-moment working out of the tension between individual creativity and organizational constraint.* By the phrase "moment-to-moment working out of the tension" we refer specifically to the balance of creativity (as a strategic response to organizational constraints) and constraints (as the constructions of reality that limit the individual's choice of strategic response).

As an example of how the tension between creativity and constraint is constructed through communication, we can cite the meetings we attended at a company that manufactures hydraulic lifts. These staff meetings were controlled by the company president according to an agenda that he prepared. Most discussions were marked by short briefings on various topics (such as new sales, personnel changes, and capital equipment expenditures) and little actual decision making. Although the executives in attendance were experienced decision makers, they knew the president viewed opposing ideas as a sign of disloyalty. Nicknamed "Little General," the president routinely embarrassed employees who disagreed with him or who attempted independent action. Over time, employee nonconfrontation was taken for granted, and what had started out as a human construction came to be accepted as an organizational reality (Berger & Luckmann, 1967).

In spite of the strong constraints on communication and the norm of nonconfrontation at the company, however, occasionally the urge to be creative emerged during meetings. An employee might, for instance, introduce a topic that was not on the president's agenda or present new data that conflicted with data given by the president. By observing communication in these ways, we saw creativity and constraint in action, as the company's norms were applied or challenged.

Moreover, this balancing act activates creativity as a strategic response to organizational constraints. In our example, the staff members acted on information they already had to guide their choices of when to speak and what to say. Unfortunately, however, the organizational reality of nonconfrontation limited their strategic choices and ability to respond. Because the president seemed unable to respond to their initiatives positively, and because they were unable to alter his construction of reality, the balance was tipped toward constraint and away from creativity. It was this lack of balance that made the staff meetings one-sided affairs and relatively unproductive.

Having reviewed the history of communication theory—communication as information transfer, transactional process, strategic control, and a balance of creativity and constraint—we can use the best concepts from each perspective to develop in detail our own model of *organizations as dialogues*. Figure 2.1 summarizes our progress thus far.

Interpreting Communication through Self, Other, and Context

The idea of "balancing creativity and constraint" may be new to you, but it is useful in understanding our struggle to think and act in social organizations—

Metaphor: Balance

Assumptions

1. The duality of structure: Individuals are molded, controlled, ordered, and shaped by society and social institutions; individuals also create society and social institutions.

2. Communication is the moment-to-moment working out of the tensions between the need to maintain order (constraint) and the need to promote change (creativity). As such, communication is the material manifestation of

   a. institutional constraints.
   b. creative potential.
   c. contexts of interpretation.

Representative Model

Creativity ═══════════△═══════════ Constraint

Communication

Description

Creativity	*Communication*	*Constraints*
Interpretations of meanings; all forms of initiative; new ways of organizing tasks and understanding relationships; resistance to institutional forms of dominance; uses of storytelling and dialogue to alter perceptions; uses of social constructions of reality to forge new agreements and shape coordinated actions at work	Reveals interpretations of contexts; asks questions about resources for creativity and the presence of constraints; suggests the possibility of dialogue	Social and institutional forms, laws, rules, procedures, slogans, and management styles designed to gain compliance and limit dialogue at all costs; top-down decision making and problem solving

FIGURE 2.1
Communication as a Balance of Creativity and Constraint

families, businesses, and other institutions. Social and organizational constraints, however, vary according to a person's life situation and membership in multiple organizations. Two common sources of constraint for working people are family commitments and career or job commitments. In cases involving conflicting constraints, the individual must decide which one is most important based on his or her own priorities. Balancing constraints and opportunities for creativity also depends on how the individual perceives them in a given situation. However, problems may arise when a person's perceived constraints are not well understood by others (such as the celebrity who admits to being insecure about his or her talent). Ultimately, to exercise creativity in communication—to alter what is perceived by others as a "reality"—requires both imagination and an appreciation of the responses others will likely have to one's choices and actions.

Symbolic Interaction

Individuals in organizations interpret their work lives and communicate according to those interpretations. The meanings they have for themselves, their actions, the work they do, their interactions with others, and their companies are shaped by their interpretations. We draw here on an intellectual movement called *symbolic interactionism.* It assumes that life is primarily a search for meaning and that meaning is found in social interaction (Blumer, 1969; Mead, 1934). As we communicate with others at work, at home, or elsewhere, we are engaged in a continuous process of *sense-making* (see Chapter 4). As we make sense of our world, we simultaneously develop an understanding of the elements of communication relationships—ourselves, others, and the contexts in which we interact.

The Elements of Communication Relationships: Self, Others, and Context

Self. The *self* is who we think we are. Our self-concept is formed in part from the social relationships we have with others and from others' responses to what we say and do (Bakhtin, 1981; Blumer, 1969; Jackson, 1989). According to George Herbert Mead (1934), the self consists of two interrelated "stories": (1) the story of "I," or the creative, relatively unpredictable part of a person that is usually kept private, and (2) the story of "me," or the socially constrained, relatively consistent part of a person that is more openly shared with others. The "I" is impulsive, whereas the "me" strives to fit into society's rules and norms. The creative aspect of the self (the "I") desires meaningful action with others. The constraining aspect of the self (the "me") guides this action by anticipating responses and applying social rules of behavior.

At the heart of our working definition of organizational communication as a balance of creativity and constraint is how the self interacts with others. The balance is achieved in part by giving voice to our experiences. This means that we can see—and respond to—our own self just as we do to others. We hold internal conversations—sometimes called *intrapersonal communication*—with our self; we "feel" good or bad about who we are and we try to balance our desire for self-determination (e.g., adventure or romance) with our concern for organizational and social constraints (e.g., the relevant social codes of conduct). As one observer notes, "at the heart of all modes of understanding . . . lies the need to assure ourselves that the world . . . is coherent and built on a scale which is compatible with and manageable by us. Only then can we enter into a relationship with it; only then can our sense of self be stabilized" (Jackson, 1989, p. 36).

Our definition of the self has important implications for interpreting organizational communication. Because the self is constructed out of our need to balance creativity and constraint in our experiences with others, the self is necessarily *dialogic*, or made in concert with others (Bakhtin, 1981; Goodall, 1991; Holquist, 1990). At work we engage in conversations that affect our perceptions of ourselves and others. We retell stories that were told to us by others, and we use and comment on others' opinions of who we are (Blumer, 1969; Laing, 1965). We make use of both real and imagined characters and relationships (Goodall, 1996). The voice of our experience, therefore, carries with it the perceptions, memories, stories, fantasies, and actions of the many people who shape our lives—co-workers, family members, friends, teachers, students, enemies, celebrities, heroes, and villains (Conquergood, 1991). In other words, our identity only makes sense in relationship to others.

Others. If the first guideline for effective communication requires that we give voice to our experience, the second is that we be open to alternative interpretations. This requires that we take communication with *others* seriously, in terms of its influence on our sense of self. Racist or sexist talk, for example, has negative consequences on a person's sense of self. How we talk *about* others also says a lot about the self. We construct the other in relation to our conception of self. People who consistently speak badly about others often reveal their own negative self-concept. Conversely, people who generally speak well of others usually have a positive self-concept.

Our construction of others is not entirely of our own making. It is constrained by the self's culture, race, gender, and subconscious. How we learn to see and respond to the presence, actions, and meanings of others is shaped by many influences. In this sense, then, the self's symbolic construction of the other is also always complex and dialogic.

Especially interesting is the role of others in our understanding of organizations. As noted earlier in the chapter, the information transfer, transactional process, and strategic control models of communication focus on how the sender (self) acts toward the receivers (others). Usually the sender is viewed as a manager and the receiver as a subordinate, reflecting the managerial bias of these theories (Putnam, 1982). Employees are viewed as "others" to be acted upon, communicated to, ordered, and controlled, rather than as partners in the organizational dialogue. This concept of others as partners to the dialogue contains the important idea of plurality. *Plurality* refers to the fact that the self and others mutually construct the meanings they have for contexts and for each other. It also encompasses the idea that multiple interpretations of a context are possible, and that neither the self nor the others alone can control those interpretations.

Context. *Context* refers to where communication occurs (i.e., the physical setting) and the interpretive frameworks used to make sense of the communicative exchange. Context is vital to our understanding of organizational communication. For one thing, it shapes our interpretations. In addition, multiple contexts are always available for sense-making, and the concept of context tells us much about organizational dialogue.

There can be no meaning without context (Bateson, 1972). If we think of a message as a text, the *con-text* is information that goes with and helps make sense of the text. For example, if you overhear a friend call someone you don't know an "idiot," how would you make sense of the comment? You would need to know more about the relationship between your friend and the other person as well as about what happened just before your friend made the comment. You might even need to know where the comment was made. *Relationship* and *situation,* two basic aspects of context, would affect your interpretation. If your friend and the other person had been teasing each other all day, the comment might be interpreted as a sign of friendship.

The role of context is always complex. We cannot fully understand the meaning of a message without first examining the relationship, its history, and the immediate situation for clues. This is especially true in organizations, where lines of authority, personal relationships, politics, the business situation, and other factors affect the interpretation of communicative exchanges. Because it is impossible to communicate in isolation, people necessarily communicate in contexts. But contexts are not stable. According to the *Oxford English Dictionary,* the word *context* originated as a *verb* meaning "to weave together, interweave, join together, compose." We favor this older definition because it highlights context as "a verbal process aimed at the manufacture of something . . . the seaming together of otherwise disparate elements, perceptions, fabrics or words, the piecing together of a whole out of the sum of its parts" (Goodall, 1991a, p. 64). Thus, when we say that individuals communicate in contexts, we use that term to refer to (1) how a person defines a situation at any given moment and (2) the process of altering that definition over time. Note also that our definition of context reflects the duality of structure: People both *create* contexts through communication and are *constrained* by those contexts once they are created (e.g., my decision to tell off my boss will constrain future interactions with my boss). As Linda Putnam (1985) puts it, "people establish the context, use the context to interpret messages, and use the messages to change the context" (p. 152). Over time, what we define as context becomes the constructed reality that we take for granted. Therefore, when we say that individuals communicate in context, we mean that they communicate in accord with their constructions of reality, or their interpretations of the evolving situation.

We are, in a sense, redefining what it means to work in an organization. Rather than viewing employees as the product of a corporate culture, we believe that a great deal of work is the interpretation of contexts. While most obvious in white-collar jobs, this applies to blue-collar work as well. How people think and talk about their work and how they feel about the relationships they maintain at work and the company itself all have a significant impact on their behavior choices and, ultimately, on the performance of the organization.

Ben Hamper's *Rivethead* (1991) provides some stark examples of how differences in interpretation can affect people's behavior. In recounting life at a General Motors factory in Flint, Michigan, the book gives us a glimpse into the lives of factory workers, many of whom view the plant, their work, and the company in different ways. There are tough-talking bigoted men who work hard and follow the rules, even harder-working family men and women who drink too much after work, and Hamper who tries to beat the system by maintaining a psychological distance from work. The message is clear: There is no single definition of work; instead, each person brings his or her own context for interpretation, which in turn informs and shapes the person's behavior. Naturally, there are limits to the kinds of interpretations that any one individual can construct. Organizations are made up of collections of individuals who strive to create meanings but who are constrained by meanings constructed in part by other individuals also engaged in sense-making. Interpretation is what allows us as individuals to connect to the larger world. It is a never-ending quest to make sense of who we are and what we do for a living, but it is always constrained in part by other interpreters.

Suppose, for example, that you are a supervisor in a large bank and that during lunchtime you discover one of your employees sobbing in the restroom. What would you do or say? Your first challenge would be to interpret the situation and the context, for human communication makes sense only in context. What do you know about this employee that could help you make sense of his behavior? Might personal problems, layoffs at work, or stress play a role? Recalling that the employee's mother had been ill, you inquire about the situation and discover that his mother's illness has become life threatening. This is the context; it makes sense of the employee's behavior and it allows you to offer an appropriate response. Furthermore, your interaction with the employee in the restroom will affect your future interactions in ways that will depend on how you and the employee interpret the situation. Thus, your relationship might become more aloof or more friendly as a result. Not only is context necessary to make sense of the initial communication, that communication will, in turn, construct the context for making sense of future interactions.

Multiple Contexts and the Situated Individual

Multiple contexts exist for interpreting communication. What are *multiple contexts?* Consider this definition provided by Goran Ahrne (1990):

> From birth every human being is affiliated to a family and a nation-state. Children's first experiences of the exercise of power occur within the family. After some years all children will have to yield to the power of the nation-state in the form of school. Growing up, children will slowly get to know the world outside the family and the school. Gradually the everyday world will be larger, adolescence being the typical time for activities in groups or gangs of various kinds . . . . Having married and settled down and started to work, people fill their everyday lives with organizational affiliations. In the course of their lives individuals orient themselves within the existing organizations in the social landscape. Every individual attempts to establish a domain within this landscape, balancing between different organizational influences and leaving some unorganized space. (p. 72)

In other words, we grow up and learn about life in multiple contexts, each of which has its own constraints—or rules, norms, and expected understandings—that make it unique. These constraints play two roles: (1) they limit creativity and individual freedom and (2) they suggest particular constructions of reality that assist in interpretation. For example, if a co-worker leans over and kisses you (against your wishes), it would be clear from the business context that such behavior is inappropriate and that a strong negative reaction on your part is warranted. But if a family member does the same thing, the meaning would be entirely different, as would your response.

Consider also how interpretation is complicated by multiple contexts in the typical family business or when husband and wife work together in the same company. You can imagine the conversations—"Dad, you can talk to me that way at home, but not here in front of the other employees!" or "How could *you,* my spouse, vote against me at the meeting!" Different contexts suggest different rules for action and interpretation. Even within a small organization, multiple contexts are always available for interpretation.

In conducting performance appraisals, how tough should supervisors be on marginal performers? Seen in the context of the business as a financial entity accountable primarily to shareholders, the supervisor should be direct and tough. In a relational context that emphasizes the supervisor–employee relationship, however, the supervisor could justify being more understanding. Interpreting and communicating in multiple contexts is the stuff of organizational life.

This brings us to another key point: All individuals are situated in multiple contexts. In a broad sense, this means that behavior is both guided and constrained by the types of organizations with which we affiliate, whether they be capitalist enterprises, voluntary associations, nation-states, or families (Ahrne, 1990). More specifically, all behavior is situated in smaller, or more local, contexts:

> The situated individual is a person who is constructing the everyday business of the maintenance and construction of the social realities in which we live. The situated individual is connected to others through a network of shared, mutually negotiated, and maintained meanings. These meanings provide location, identity, action, and purpose to the individual. They tell me where I am, who I am, what I am doing, how to do it, and why . . . . The network of meanings is not independent of the situated individual. It is the product of the interaction among situated individuals. (Anderson, 1987, p. 268)

Difficulty is encountered when the multiple contexts impinging on an individual suggest inconsistent or conflicting communication or behavior. For years, the top management of some U.S. companies cultivated close relationships with their employees that resulted in company success and employee commitment. Recently, however, management is being encouraged by economic concerns to fire or lay off long-standing employees. A manager in this situation faces conflicting contexts—the business context and a more personal context—and no communication is likely to satisfy the demands of both.

A study of Disneyland's corporate culture provides a detailed example of multiple conflicting contexts for interpretation (Smith & Eisenberg, 1987). In the early days of the theme park, employees used two metaphors, "the show" and the Disney "family," which were keyed to larger contexts. The first metaphor—of Disneyland as a show—suggested that employees were actors who played important roles. They could thus be told by the "director" to act in particular ways because of "box office concerns" (e.g., to smile more or style their hair). The other metaphor—Disneyland as a family—however, suggested a different and sometimes opposing context in which management, like a concerned parent, took care of its employees and provided a nurturing environment. These two conflicting contexts for interpretation contributed significantly to the decision of Disneyland employees to go on strike in the mid-1980s. Recent reports (Van Maanen, 1991) suggest that the drama metaphor won out. The *situated individual* model of organizational communication may be summarized as follows:

1. The individual is an actor whose actions and communication are based on the interpretation of contexts.
2. More than one context always exists to guide the individual's actions and interpretations.
3. Communication is the sum of action and interpretation; as such, it can reveal sources of creativity, constraint, meaning, interpretation, and context.

An example can clarify this notion of the situated individual. One of the authors of this textbook became involved with a problem facing a customer service manager at a large travel agency. The manager (we'll call her Laura) sought to convince management of her need for a full-time accountant to manage the recordkeeping of customer service billings. Although Laura's initial request was met with assurances from her boss that the accountant would be hired, management's sudden decision to deny her request followed. The problem, then, was how to interpret the denial and what, if anything, to do about it. But there were various possible ways to make sense of (or contextualize) the situation. From Laura's point of view, the problem centered on a lack of expertise in her department and the need to address it by hiring the accountant. The finance department saw the situation differently: Because it had sought for several years to hire its own accountant, it strongly resisted the idea that one might now be hired in customer service. As a result, rumors surfaced among the finance department staff about Laura's competency as a manager, suggesting that she would not need the new position if she was doing her job properly. Still another view of the situation came from the general manager of the travel agency: He resisted the new hiring simply because none of the companies he had worked for in the past had an accountant in customer service. The board of directors based its disapproval on economic concerns: Any new hires in a recession would not please shareholders. Finally, Laura's peers perceived her as aloof and a loner, rather than as a team player. Consequently, no informal group within the company was inclined to support Laura's agenda to hire an accountant. Laura might not have faced this problem if she had been more involved in informal communication networks.

Keep in mind that this is a *simple* example of how multiple contexts can inform the interpretation of selves, others, and action. Although the facts remain the same—whether to hire an accountant in customer service—the *meanings* of those facts are constructed differently depending on which context is applied. Because no one individual has access to all potential contexts, each individual's interpretation is based on a limited understanding of the reality being constructed. The information drawn on to build a context for interpretation is varied, multiple, and always limited. Furthermore, this is as good as it gets. All interpretations, therefore, are partial, partisan, and problematic (see Chapter 3). Fortunately, however, the limitations of one person's interpretations are usually offset by others' perspectives. Because sense-making is a social activity, more than one person is always involved in the construction of reality. When individuals work to coordinate their contexts, interpretations, communication, and actions, they are said to be *organizing*. One way of viewing this organizing process is as a dialogue.

Organizations as Dialogues

We are both social and private beings. As such, we establish a sense of self that is *apart from* the outside world (an *identity*) that engages in a lifelong dialogue with another sense of self that is a *part of* the outside world (*a member of a com-*

munity). If we could somehow construct reality on our own—as a monologue—we would then be totally alone. Conversely, if our contexts for interpretation came entirely from others, we would lose our identity. The critical issues, then, revolve around these concepts of identity and community, or self and other (Buber, 1985). One way to address them may be in dialogue.

DEFINITIONS OF DIALOGUE

In our working definition of communication as a balance of creativity and constraint, we maintain that *dialogue* is balanced communication, or communication in which each individual has a chance to speak and be heard. Dialogue also has three levels: dialogue as (1) equitable transaction, (2) empathic conversation, and (3) real meeting. (See Table 2.2.)

Dialogue as Equitable Transaction

In defining dialogue as *equitable transaction,* we call attention to the fact that not everyone in an organization has an equal say in making decisions or in interpreting events. In the traditional organization of the early twentieth century, people in low-level jobs were discouraged from "interact[ing] with anybody in the organization unless [they] got permission from the supervisor, and then he wanted to know what [they] were going to talk about. So there's this notion in an organization that talking to people is not what your job is, that talking to people [means] interfering with . . . productivity" (Evered & Tannenbaum, 1992, p. 48). Even in some of the most advanced companies today, certain peoples' voices are valued more highly than others'. These people are said to have *power* because they can back up what they say with rewards or sanctions. But the extent to which one person's remarks carry more weight than another's is not always obvious to the casual observer because a deeper exercise of power is applied to the shaping or defining of context. That is, determinations of whose voice counts most are either well established before the observer arrives on the scene or are created by those who define what is addressed. Numerous contextual factors—the structure of rooms, arrangement of furniture, differences in dress and appearance, length of time scheduled for meetings, who is invited (or not invited) to attend meetings, and norms derived from prior communication situations—affect how much weight is given to the points of view of certain people. Once we are in a situation we can try to speak *as if* from a position of power, but this is difficult given the numerous contextual factors involved.

One good way to learn about how individuals participate in organizational dialogues is to ask questions about who does and does not get to speak on organizational issues and to pay close attention to when, where, and for how long individuals speak. Organizations marked by dictatorship or traditional bureau-

TABLE
2.2 **Balancing Creativity and Constraint through Interpretation
of Contexts: A Summary**

CONTEXT AND INTERPRETATION	MULTIPLE CONTEXTS AND THE SITUATED INDIVIDUAL	ORGANIZATIONS AS DIALOGUES
Assumptions: (1) There is no meaning without context; (2) relationship and situation shape context; (3) organizations are collectivities of contexts.	*Assumptions:* (1) There is always more than one context for interpreting the meaning of communication; (2) interpretations of meanings are shaped by constraints that (3) suggest a particular construction of reality; and (4) multiple contexts suggest multiple interpretations of reality.	*Assumptions:* (1) Humans are neither entirely social nor entirely private; (2) humans establish a sense of self as well as a sense of membership in a community; (3) the accomplishment of both selfhood and community is accomplished through dialogue with others.
Definitions: Context is the information that goes with and helps make sense of the text.	*Definitions:* The situated individual communicates in contexts and assists in the construction of contexts.	*Definitions:* A dialogue is balanced communication in which participating individuals and groups each have a chance to speak and to be heard.
Feature: (1) Contexts are not stable; (2) contexts reveal the duality of structure; (3) contexts redefine work in organizations as interpretation of contexts.	*Features:* (1) The individual is an actor whose actions and communication are based on interpretations of contexts; (2) there is always more than one context that can be used to guide action or interpretation; (3) communication is the sum of action and interpretation and as such it can reveal sources of creativity, constraint, meaning, interpretation, and context.	*Features:* Three senses of dialogue apply to communication in organizations: (1) dialogue as equitable transaction; (2) dialogue as empathic conversation; and (3) dialogue as real meeting.

cracy function more like monologues than dialogues because one person or an elite group controls the context for communication.

Voice manifests itself in the ability of an individual or group to participate in the ongoing organizational dialogue. In most organizations, a few voices are loud and clear (e.g., those of the owners or senior managers) while others are muted or suppressed (e.g., those of the janitorial and clerical staff). In the literature on organizations, voice has a more specific meaning: It refers to an employee's decision to speak up against the status quo, rather than keeping quiet and staying (loyalty) or giving up and leaving (exit) (Hirschman, 1970). In an ideal world, voice is the preferred option because it raises important issues and encourages creativity and commitment. In most companies, however, many barriers to voice exist. The suppression of employee voice within organizations can lead to *whistle-blowing,* wherein frustrated employees take their concerns to the media, the courts, or others outside of the organization (Redding, 1985a). In extreme cases of repressed employee voice the results may include sabotage and violence in the workplace (Goodall, 1995).

At a minimum, then, dialogue requires that communicators be afforded equitable opportunities to speak. While the notion of dialogue as equitable transaction is a good starting point for thinking about organizational communication, it does not address the quality of that communication.

Dialogue as Empathic Conversation

In defining dialogue as *empathic conversation,* we refer to the ability to understand or imagine the world as another person understands or imagines it. Achieving empathy is difficult for people who believe that their view of reality is the only correct view and that others' perceptions are misinformed or misguided. Indeed, Western communication is largely based on assumptions of what is "right." As a result, it becomes much more difficult to accept the validity of a different perspective, especially a radically different one. However, empathy is crucial in organizations. It promotes understanding among different departments, makes managing diversity possible, and acknowledges that while individuals and groups have different perspectives on the organization, no single perspective is inherently better than others. The challenge is in accepting differences in interpretation without feeling pressured to achieve total agreement. Put differently: "Can I recognize the value of your [perspective]. . . without us having to somehow merge into something that's less rich than the community of differences?" (Evered & Tannenbaum, 1992, p. 52).

Researchers at the Massachusetts Institute of Technology (MIT) take a similar view of organizational dialogue in their efforts to create learning communities (Senge, 1991; Senge et al., 1994). Building on the work of physicist David Bohm, the researchers define dialogue as a kind of "collective mindfulness" in which the interactants are more concerned about group process than about individual ego or position. From this perspective, dialogue affords new opportunities for people in organizations to work together. Not merely a set of techniques, dialogue requires that people "learn how to think together—not just in the sense of analyzing a shared problem or creating new pieces of shared knowledge, but [also] in the sense of occupying a collective sensibility, in which the thoughts, emotions, and resulting actions belong not to one individual, but to all of them together" (Isaacs, 1994, p. 358). The MIT dialogue project has attracted the attention of business because it links holistic thinking with dialogue, flirting with the idea that our relationships with others can possess a spiritual quality. We know that treating people like objects is inappropriate. But are understanding and empathy enough? These questions recall the work of contemporary philosophers Martin Buber and Mikhail Bakhtin, whose critique of empathy as the ideal of dialogue leads us to yet another definition of dialogue.

Dialogue as Real Meeting

In defining dialogue as *real meeting,* we mean that through communication, a genuine communion can take place between people that transcends differences in role or perspective and recognizes all parties' common humanity. The notion of dialogue as empathic conversation is insufficient because it assumes that one individual experiences the other as a kind of object, rather than as a fellow interpreter. In other words, even empathic communicators, once the conversation has ended, may continue to view the dialogue as mainly instrumental in accomplishing their personal and professional goals. Therefore, one's performance of empathy may be false or even a means to a personal strategic end.

Certain types of dialogues are valuable in and of themselves. Buber distinguishes between *interhuman* dialogue, which has inherent value, and *social* dialogue, which has value as a route to self-realization and fulfillment. According to Buber, "we are answerable neither to ourselves alone nor to society apart from ourselves but to that very bond between ourselves and others through which we again and again discover the direction in which we can authenticate our existence" (qtd. in Friedman, 1992, p. 6). Consider also this quote from Bakhtin:

> A single consciousness is a contradiction in terms. Consciousness is essentially multiple . . . . I am conscious of myself and become myself only when revealing myself for another, through another and with the help of another . . . . The very being of man [*sic*] is the *deepest* communion. To be means to communicate. . . to be means to be for another, and through the other, for oneself (qtd. in Emerson, 1983).

From this perspective, since life exists only in communion with other humans, dialogue is a fundamental human activity. But how do meetings in organizations resemble Buber's ideal? Buber sees it as a relationship between "I and Thou," wherein two individuals acknowledge that each is an interpreter and neither reduces the other to an object of interpretation within a context that has already been constructed.

Seeking dialogue because it has value for itself can sometimes result in positive consequences for the organization:

> [Dialogue] is one of the richest activities that human beings can engage in. It is the thing that gives meaning to life, it's the sharing of humanity, it's creating something. And there is this magical thing in an organization, or in a team, or a group, where you get unrestricted interaction, unrestricted dialogue, and this synergy happening that results in more productivity, and satisfaction, and seemingly magical levels of output from a team. (Evered & Tannenbaum, 1992, p. 48)

This definition of dialogue combines the abstract or spiritual with the more practical aspects of how we communicate. Are we open to the voices of others? Do we recognize that all views are partial and that each of us has the right to speak? Are we open to the possibility of maintaining mutual respect and openness of spirit through organizational communication? Such questions are not easily answered by people in organizations today. Although people may desire to maintain an open dialogue, they may be constrained by learned behaviors that guard against intimate disclosure, by the social, professional, and political consequences of those disclosures, and by the habit of separating emotions from work.

To establish dialogue as real meeting, we must learn to interpret communication as a dialogic process that occurs between and among individuals, rather than as something we do *to* one another. Both parties are responsible for the dialogue as well as for the risks taken; only together can they make progress. We engage in dialogue to learn more about the self in context with others. Dialogue helps us attain new appreciations for the multilayered dimensions of every context: "The crucial point is to go into a dialogue with the stance that there is something that I don't already know, with a mutual *openness* to learn. Through dialogue we can learn, not merely receive information, but revise the way we see something. Something about the dialogue honors *inquiry* and learning from the inquiry" (Evered & Tannenbaum, 1992, p. 45). Authentic dialogue also provides a practical communication skill that is invaluable: We learn to speak *from* experience and to listen *for* experience. By sharing and risking the truth of our experience, we discover important questions that can guide our interpretations of contexts, of others, and of ourselves. We gain access to the shaping forces of our own and other's experiences. These forces guide our individual and collective constructions of reality, teach us about what counts as knowledge as well as how to value it, and influence how our evaluations of persons and things are generated.

Dialogue as real meeting is difficult to attain, which is why it does not characterize most relationships in and outside of organizations. Most organizations readily acknowledge the importance of equitable transactions and may settle for increased empathy across hierarchical levels and professional groups. Still, dialogue as real meeting is an important communicative goal because it can transform organizations into energetic and dynamic workplaces. Such organizations are both effective and enjoyable because they encourage the kinds of communication required for real human connection. In William Torbert's (1991) words, we should strive to create "liberating structures" through the "power of balance" (p. 97).

Table 2.3 summarizes the advantages and limitations of promoting dialogue in organizations.

Ⓢummary

This chapter defines four theories of communication in organizations: communication as information transfer, as transactional process, as strategic control, and as a balance of creativity and constraint. It also defines such terms as *meaning, context, self,* and *other,* culminating in our proposed model of organizations as dialogues. Central to our discussion is the idea that, in our pursuit of identity and community, we constantly strive to make sense of the world; the meaning we find is both ever-changing and constructed in communication with others. This process is inherently undemocratic, since some people have more clout than others. However, most interesting from a communication perspective are (1) that some people's ideas prevail in dialogue and (2) that this balance of power may be altered. Dialogue is not only an abstract concept. Theories of organizational communication are increasingly focused on orchestrating diverse voices through more effective communication.

Our personal context affects not only our interpretations but also our communication with others. For example, if an employee has children and the boss does not, the differences in their family lives and responsibilities will become part of the employee's consciousness and communication at work. What the employee and supervisor can share will be limited by the differences in their personal contexts for meaning. The same can be said for differences in religion, ethnicity, cultural background, gender, and affluence, among others. The point is that who we are in our personal lives strongly affects who we are and how we communicate at work.

There are advantages and limitations associated with promoting dialogue in organizations. It can increase employee satisfaction and commitment, reduce turnover rates, and lead to greater innovation and flexibility within the organization. But it is also time-consuming, requiring that issues be screened in terms of the amount of dialogue they do or do not warrant. Although certain people will possess the power to decide which issues are most important, this is necessary in a turbulent business environment. In addition, promoting dialogue may lead communicators to assume that their ideas and opinions will be implemented. Although there may be an equitable distribution of power and voice in the group, within a capitalist system the owners and their agents make the final decisions. Recent moves to develop employee-owned companies are beginning

TABLE
2.3
**Summary of the Advantages and Limitations
of Promoting Dialogue in Organizations**

ADVANTAGES	LIMITATIONS
For the individual	*For the individual*
Opens possibilities for creativity.	Is difficult to attain and therefore may act as a constraint on relationships.
Enables one to deal productively with instabilities of organizational life through the faculty of forgiveness.	May promote instabilities caused by unilateral risk-taking in relationships.
Enables one to deal productively with miscommunication through making and keeping promises.	May promote miscommunication caused by failure to keep promises or unwillingness to make them.
Values speaking about personal experiences.	Personal experiences may be hard to talk about.
Provides rich contextual details about how interpretations are made.	Information overload.
Individual transformation may lead to organizational transformation.	Seeking transformation may conflict with individual and organizational objectives.
For the organization	*For the organization*
Greater individual satisfaction with and commitment to the organization.	May sacrifice timing for communication and reduce decision-making effectiveness.
Reduced turnover rates due to enriched job and communication experiences.	May set up expectations that ideas and opinions will be binding or will be implemented.
Greater opportunities for innovation and flexibility.	May lead to a lack of closure or the feeling that there is no "right" answer.

to address this concern. Finally, dialogue may lead to a lack of closure or to the feeling that "no right answer" can be found. This problem is related in part to Western society, in which people expect definitive answers about science, medicine, politics, and technology, for example. But in organizational communication it may be more appropriate to focus on practical guidelines for action.

We conclude this chapter with two important questions. The first question asks: Is dialogue possible in organizations? Our experiences lead us to believe that dialogue *is* possible in organizations. But it is also rare. More common is

TABLE
2.4
Summary of the Principles of Existential Philosophy Informing the Situated Individual Model

1. Our search is for a vocabulary that will serve as the basis for a dialogue across cultures, not a search for universal truths or essences.

2. Human "being" is dispersed into the world in the form of human relationships, intentions, and projects. In seeking to understand that world, we situate ourselves squarely within it rather than taking up a vantage point outside it.

3. We do not privilege any vocabulary as representing the truth or essence of things; instead, we offer a way of interrogating lived experiences from everyday life. To ask questions about lived experiences seems wiser than to make universal claims about which there must always be exceptions to the rule.

4. Existentialism reveals a common preoccupation with our human struggle between yielding to the brute facts of existence—the sense of being abandoned or thrown into a world made by others at other times—and the necessity of appropriating, addressing, and experiencing that world as something for which we are responsible, something we bring into being, something we choose.

5. In sum, existentialism places social facts within an ontological perspective. Accordingly, we neither presume scientific status for our worldviews to give them authority and legitimacy, nor deign to label the worldviews of others "folk" as a sign of their epistemological inadequacy. "Our" worldviews are placed on a par with "theirs" and seen not as true accounts of external reality but as ways of coping with life, of making the world make sense.

Source: Adapted from Michael Jackson, *Paths toward a Clearing* (Bloomington: Indiana University Press, 1989), pp. 49–50.

communication that creates barriers to real meeting by attempting to convince others that their perceptions are faulty—"Management shouldn't think that way," "That idea will never fly," and "I know my people aren't dissatisfied." However, limited dialogue is also evident in this communication, and much may be gained by expanding the current interest in coordinating the diverse voices in business.

Our second question is more difficult to answer: What role can the situated individual play in constructing organizational reality through communication? Some observers, most notably postmodernists, take exception with the concept of the situated individual. They argue that it simply restates the idea that a person has a political ideology in favor of free will and capitalism (Grossberg, 1991). In their view, most choices are so constrained that decisions are virtually made for us, and what we believe to be free or motivated action is actually the force of the world acting through us. Other observers, however, are less willing to underestimate the experiences of the situated individual (Jackson, 1989). In this view, we are born into a society that expects us to act out a balance of individual and social responsibilities. We are expected to make decisions about ourselves and about how our actions may influence and be influenced by others. Ultimately, however, the responsibility for those actions is our own. Thus, for example, if someone commits a serious crime, society may be implicated but it is the criminal who goes to jail.

Finally, the situated individual model of organizational communication as dialogue suggests a connection to a broader worldview, one that is characterized by existentialism but modified by what we have learned about phenomenology, cultural anthropology, social theories, communication theories, spirituality, and economics (Sartre, 1973). Why existentialism? As you consider the answer to that question, think about the statements listed in Table 2.4. Then construct your own account of how the situated individual model of organizations as dialogues derives important premises from existential philosophy.

THE MANY ROBERT SMITHS

JASON, THE JANITOR

"Smith is a tidy man. I pass by his desk at night when I'm cleaning up, and his area is the only one that's perfect. *Nothing* is *ever* out of place. I've made a kind of study out of it. You know, paid lots of attention to it on account of it being so unusual. So I've noticed things.

"I'd say Smith must be a single man. There are no pictures of family on his desk or on the walls. Most people leave keys to their personal life in the office—photographs, items they picked up during vacations, stickers with funny sayings on them. But not Smith. In Smith's area, there is no trace of anything personal. Just some books and the computer. The books never change positions, which tells me he never has to look things up. So I think Smith must be a smart man, too.

"I've never met him. Or if I did, I never knew it. But I see him in my mind as a tall, thin guy with glasses who doesn't smile too often. He may be shy, too. Fastidious people are often shy. Maybe he's an accountant or a computer programmer. It's hard to say. But Smith makes my job interesting. I look at his desk every night to see if anything has changed."

CATHERINE, THE RECEPTIONIST

"Smith is okay, a little shy maybe. He says 'hello' to me every morning. Just a 'hello,' though—nothing more, not even my name. I didn't know his name for months. But then, I didn't say much to him either.

"Then one afternoon he had a visitor. It was a woman—a beautiful woman in her late twenties or early thirties. She asked to speak to Bobby. 'Bobby who?' I asked. She looked confused; then she smiled and said, 'Bobby Smith, I thought everyone knew.' Well, this was interesting. I mean, I suddenly realized Smith had a first name—Robert. I had never thought of him as anyone's 'Bobby' before.

"I paged Smith and he came downstairs. When he saw the woman visitor, his face turned white like he'd seen a ghost. She called his name, and he stood still. I thought he was about to cry or something, but instead he just shook his head, as if to say, 'No.' He didn't *say* anything. Just shook his head. Then he turned and walked back upstairs, slowly.

The woman just watched him. Then she turned around and walked out. I never saw her again. I don't know if she was a girlfriend, sister, or friend. Smith never said anything about her.

"In this job, I meet all kinds of people. I've learned a lot about people while working here as a receptionist. But Smith is still a mystery to me. I don't know much about him. All I know is that his first name is Robert but that some people call him Bobby, that he says 'hello' to me every morning like clockwork, and that there was once a beautiful woman in his life. Oh yeah, and he's about 5 feet, 7 inches tall, has short hair and a big moustache, wears an earring, and obviously works out a lot."

WILSON, THE BOSS

"Smith is a strange guy, but a good worker. He never misses a day, even willing to work nights or weekends to get the job done. His work is always neat and well organized. Personally, I wish he would get rid of his earring and moustache, but that's just him I guess.

"I hired him five years ago as an entry-level accountant. His work in that position was good. He was promoted to a senior accountant position very quickly, as if someone up there in the company ranks was watching out for him. Usually it takes the best accountant five to seven years to make it to senior status; Smith made it in three. Last fall I asked him to take charge of a major audit, and he's been diligently working on that project ever since.

"Smith never talks about his life outside of work. And I never ask him. He seems to like it that way. But from the way he is built, I'd say he spends a lot of time working out at a gym. He drives a vintage black Porsche, a speedster, and it is always clean. He leaves it open during the day with a pair of Ray-Bans on the dash, always in the same position.

"I figure he comes from a wealthy family. He graduated from Stanford. But he doesn't talk like a Texan. I'd say he's from Pittsburgh. I don't know why I say that.

"Actually, to be honest, Smith scares me a little bit. I don't know anyone who's as calm and collected and perfect as Smith is. In movies it's always the mass murderer who's like that. Not that I think Smith is that way. But I wouldn't be surprised, either. I wish his starched shirts would just one time come back with a rip in them or something. I know that sounds small. I can't help it. Smith does that to me."

FELICIA, A CO-WORKER

"Robert is my good friend. He's a warm, sensitive person with a heart of gold. He and I have talked a lot over the past couple of years. Mostly about our dreams. We both want to work hard, save a lot of money, and be able to do something else with our lives while we are still young enough to enjoy it.

"Robert came from a poor family. He grew up moving around from town to town while his mother looked for work in construction. He had two brothers and a sister, all older. He was the baby. His father was killed in the Vietnam War. His older brothers are both in the military and don't have much in common with Robert, and his sister is a successful lawyer in Washington. Robert showed me a picture of her once; she's a beautiful woman. They had a big argument a while back. He wouldn't say much about it, except that he hasn't seen her since. His mother died of lung cancer two years ago.

"Robert worked hard in school but won an athletic scholarship to Stanford. He was a gymnast. Or still is, because he spends two or three nights a week working with underprivileged kids downtown teaching them gymnastics. And he is big in Adult Children of Alcoholics, which I took him to. That's a whole story in itself. He has a lot of hobbies, which, when he does them, aren't exactly hobbies anymore. He is such a perfectionist! Like that car of his, for instance. He built it himself, out of a kit. And you should see his apartment."

JENKINS, THE RETIRED CEO

"Robert Smith is one of the company's finest employees. And he is an exceptional young man. I recruited him at Stanford when I was teaching there right after I retired. Since then, I've followed his career. I asked him not to say much about our relationship, because a lot of people could get the wrong idea. I want him to make it on his own, which he has. I put in a good word for him here and there, but never anything too pushy.

"I knew his father in Vietnam. He served in my command and was a good soldier. He was due to be shipped home later in the week when he was killed. It was sad. I wrote the letter to his family myself. When I got out of the Army I moved over into the private sector. You can imagine how odd it was for me to walk into that accounting class at Stanford and see Robert Smith, who looks just like his dad except for the moustache and earring, sitting in the front row. I couldn't believe it. Still can't.

"In a way, I feel related to Robert. He still comes to visit us on the holidays. I like that."

ASSIGNMENTS

1. You are the executive recruiter (or headhunter) who compiled the preceding information about Smith from interviews with his colleagues. You also have Smith's resumé and performance appraisal reports to supplement the interviews. Your job is to prepare a personality profile of Smith for a firm that may be interested in hiring him. What would you write? How would you explain the different perspectives on Smith? If you were Robert Smith, what would you say about the interview statements?

2. We live complex (and often contradictory) lives as situated individuals in organizations. This should make us sensitive to the various ways in which meanings are constructed through communication. Construct an investigation of yourself using interview statements used by others to describe who you are. Supplement these statements with your own resumé. What do the statements tell you about yourself? About your construction of others? About yourself as a situated individual in an organization? About the complexities of interpreting meaning?

3. As a student of communication, you are interested in finding ways to improve your own and others' interpretations of meanings. Review the case study as if you are the communication consultant working with the executive recruiter. Your job is to help the headhunter construct better follow-up questions and produce a complete report on Smith. What questions would help explain the different views of Smith?

CHAPTER 3

Founding Perspectives on Organizations and Communication

A well-designed machine . . . consists of a coherent bringing together of all parts toward the highest possible efficiency of the functioning whole . . . .The machine is [the] . . . total rationalization of a field of action and of total organization. This is perhaps even more quickly evident in that larger machine, the assembly line.

• John William Ward (1990)

QUESTIONS FOR DISCUSSION

- Why is all communication partial, partisan, and problematic?

- What is the classical management approach? What does the machine metaphor imply about communication in organizations based on classical management?

- Why study the principles of the human relations and the human resources approaches to organizational communication?

- Is it appropriate to think of all organizations as fundamentally the same? How might this assumption influence how we study communication in organizations?

S ome forms of communicating and organizing have existed as long as humanity. Speculations about how we communicate and organize also have a long history. Our focus here is on the history of organizational communication theory. This chapter addresses theories associated with three general approaches: classical management, human relations, and human resources.

Why Focus on Theory?

Definitions of communication theory run the gamut from someone else's good ideas to formal systems of hypotheses that aim to explain, predict, and control. But all theories share two features: they are *historical* and *metaphorical*. Any theory of organizational communication is historical in that it is a product of the time in which it emerged, reflecting the concerns and interests of the culture that produced it. A theory is metaphorical in that it suggests, through language, enlightening comparisons between organizational communication and other processes. Scientific management theory compares organizations and machines, for instance.

Our approach to the role of theories in understanding organizations begins with a practical outlook. As students of organizational communication, we choose to participate in a particular *discourse community,* which in this case is made up of individuals who share an interest in organizations and communication. Communication theorist Kenneth Burke (1989) likens participation in a discourse community to entering a room in which conversation is already in progress. We wander around for a while, listen, and occasionally join in the talk. Sooner or later we find ourselves engaged in conversation that seems important at the time. As time passes, we have many such conversations. Eventually, we notice that the hour is late and it is time to leave. The conversation continues without us. For each of us, active participation in the discourse community requires detailed attention to the talk that preceded our entry into the room.

Theories function as resources in that they enhance our ability to explain and act on a wide variety of practical issues, such as where the idea of organization originated and what motivates people to work. The way we talk about an issue or problem influences the solutions we can propose. Theories of organizations and communication enhance our ability to deal with practical issues. They are also historical narratives, or goal-oriented stories told for the purpose of explanation. Theories may offer a creative integration of disparate issues—how organizations can be both pro-profit and pro-people or why communication and efficiency are linked—or they may provide a complete explication of a narrow topic—how to lead an effective decision-making group or relieve employee stress. In either case, theories reflect unique historical circumstances and diverse cultural and political interests.

Because organizational communication theories are evolving episodes in an ongoing historical narrative, we should not strive to choose one theory over another. Instead, we should learn to see each theory as a participant in a larger, ongoing dialogue. Consequently, our interest in theories goes beyond what they help us to explain. We are also interested in the position of theories in the general stream of events, in their relationship to other theories, in their unique properties, in their strengths and limitations, in the interests they represent or exclude, and in the effects of retelling them on our conversation and the world.

Organizational Communication Theories as Historical Narratives: The Three P's

The three *P's* of historical writing—*partiality, partisanship,* and *problematic*—both provide an important perspective on communication and reveal the limitations of any account. All talk is partial, partisan, and problematic, and theories are no exception. The kinds of questions we raise about our reading of theory add to our understanding of organizational communication.

PARTIALITY

An argument could be made that any attempt to trace the history of organizational communication would be incomplete and, therefore, misleading. Obviously, we have chosen to write this chapter anyway. Our primary condition is *partiality: Our account contains only part of the story.* However, the inability to articulate a complete account of the history of organizational communication is not unique to our field, nor is it disabling. As French philosopher Jacques Derrida (1972) notes, all thought is inscribed in language, and language is rooted in an inescapable paradox: There is no point of absolute meaning outside of language from which to view—or to prescribe—the truth of the world. Because all language is partial, there can be no absolute history, no full account, no complete story of organizational communication. Therefore, from this perspective, our account is necessarily partial.

PARTISANSHIP

We write this chapter, and indeed this book, under the limitation of *partisanship: The story we tell is one that we favor.* The history of organizational communication typically emphasizes the interpretations of dominant white males in Western culture, with little attention given to how members of oppressed, marginalized, or subjugated groups such as women and minorities would tell the story. Consider, for example, how a Native American might interpret the nineteenth-century expansion of railroads, mining, and manufacturing interests across the Great Plains. Depending on one's interests, or partisanship, this story would be seen as one of tragedy or opportunity. As this example illustrates, to reinterpret any account assumes a familiarity with what has come before. Therefore, scholars and practitioners may disagree about how the story gets told and who should tell it, but they would likely agree on at least some of the story's events and characters. Everyone agrees that Native Americans considered the Great Plains their natural hunting grounds and that westward expansion by white settlers took place. Partisanship, then, is not so much about identifying facts but about interpreting their possible meanings.

All thought is partisan. Knowledge is shaped by the theories and interpretations we use to make sense of the world, or to create what we call a worldview. If we think of each theory as a kind of mini-worldview, then we see clearly that one theory cannot explain everything. No one partisan view can comprehend all the interests of all people over all time. When we read about theories, then, it is useful to think of each theory as telling a particular story. Because each story represents the interests of the storyteller, it is a partisan perspective on the broader, more complex stories about the world. In this sense, many theories contribute to the complex story of organizational communication.

This principle can be directly applied to routine episodes of communication at work. For example, let's assume that Deon makes this announcement at a team meeting: "I just talked to Beth about our project, and she thinks we ought to go with the approach I suggested last week." His comment may be viewed as partisan on several accounts. The other team members might consider whether Deon's interpretation of his conversation with Beth was influenced by what he wants to happen. Or perhaps Deon influenced Beth's opinion. The key point here is not that Deon has intentionally misrepresented Beth's opinion at the team meeting, but that all talk is partisan. When we speak, we tend to represent our views of situations in ways that favor our interests and goals.

PROBLEMATIC

Finally, we write this chapter on the condition that the story itself will be *problematic: Our account asks more questions than it can answer, and the answers it does provide are based on what is currently known rather than on all that could be known.* In admitting the problematic nature of our narrative, we also invite dialogue, asking our readers to bring to our account their experiences and understandings. Consider how this concept can inform our understanding of everyday organizational communication. Rather than making ultimate statements, it encourages us to ask more questions and thereby to invite others into the dialogue. Rather than assuming that we know the whole truth about any issue, it encourages us to ask for the input of others who may hold different perspectives.

The Classical Management Approach

The underlying metaphor of the *classical management approach* is that organizations should be modeled after efficient machines (Ginsberg, 1982; Morgan, 1986). Most contemporary histories of organizations and communication begin with the advent of the Industrial Revolution in the late 1800s. Although organizations and communication existed prior to the steamboat, railroad, and cotton gin, it was not until the Industrial Revolution that modern machinery and methods of production emerged, with the accompanying rise of the factory bureaucracy (Perrow, 1986).

HISTORICAL AND CULTURAL BACKGROUND

The rise of the modern factory during the industrial period was an extension of a more widespread social (and racial) class structure, which sought to stabilize power relations among people by controlling the means of production and consumption in society (Foucault, 1972, 1979). Before the Industrial Revolution, only rarely did anyone work for someone else in exchange for wages. Today, in contrast, "only about 15 percent of our working population is able to get by without working for someone else. High schools, colleges, and universities train us to accept wage slavery" (Perrow, 1986, p. 50). It was the Industrial Revolution that marked the beginning of this important shift. (Interestingly, as we discuss in Chapter 8, this trend may now be reversing, as businesses downsize, restructure, or move operations overseas and more people are becoming self-employed providers of goods and services.)

The organization of work and communication in the early factories was highly influenced by the then-emerging concepts of division of labor and hierarchy. *Division of labor* refers to the separation of tasks into discrete units, and *hierarchy* to the vertical arrangement of power and authority that distinguishes managers from employees. These concepts formed the foundation of the modern organization. But they originated in an affluent, class-conscious view of social control in which the rise of the middle class was seen as a threat to the upper class. The rationale was that the work institution should mirror the organization of the ideal society. This may help explain why prisons and factories were modeled on the same architectural principles, and why the behavior of inmates and workers was monitored and controlled in similar ways (Sennett, 1978). Another clue about why organization and order were linked to hierarchy may be found in Kenneth Burke's work on purposive—or rhetorical—language. Burke states that people are symbol-users (and abusers) "goaded by the spirit of hierarchy," or moved to a sense of order (1989, p. 69). From this perspective, then, language is a symbolic construction of order that is based on hierarchies used to "perfect" nature. In our construction of language-based realities, we create rules for organizing sentences (grammar) and arguments (logic) and for cooperating with audiences through symbols (rhetoric). It is no wonder, then, that hierarchical (or purposive) forms of organization mirror the hierarchical nature of language.

The relationships among class consciousness, purposive language, and social control developed simultaneously with the rise of science. With science came much more than a highly ordered method of explaining phenomena: From explanation emerged the ability to predict, and from the ability to predict came the potential to control. Thus, the underlying theme of the classical management approach to organization is the scientific rationalization of control. Organizations are viewed as the primary vehicle through which our lives are rationalized—"planned, articulated, scientized, made more efficient and orderly, and managed by experts" (Scott, 1981, p. 5). Moreover, the principle means for deciding what is or is not "rational" derive from applications of the scientific method to the organization of work.

FROM EMPIRE TO HIERARCHY

From the eighteenth to the early twentieth centuries, organizations functioned much like empires. Corporations were viewed as extensions of governments in that they expanded trade, provided employment for the masses, and contributed to economic and social development (Rose, 1989). Cities in the New World were mapped according to the appropriation of territories by organizations. Even today we can still see the close relationship between homes and factories in some regions, as well as how wealth and status allow a family to move farther away from the site of production. The closer a house is to a factory, the less material power and social status the family living in that dwelling tends to have. Thus, social control is effectively produced in part by the relationship between the location of industry to neighborhoods.

In the mid-eighteenth century, Benjamin Franklin (1706–90) popularized the early notions of empire and pragmatism in his *Poor Richard's Almanac*. It is primarily a collection of parables and quotations that elevate hard work (called industry), independence (the accumulation of wealth on individual, corporate, and national levels), and the virtues of planning, organizing, and controlling one's life through work. Here are some examples from *The Complete Poor Richard's Almanac* (1970):

> Industry need not wish—There are no Gains without Pains.
> God gives all things to industry.
> God helps them that help themselves.
> Sloth makes all things difficult, but industry all easy.
> Early to Bed, early to rise, makes a Man healthy, wealthy, and wise.

Although Franklin was not the only writer to express these ideas (similar sentiments are found in Japanese and Chinese proverbs, the Old Testament, and the Talmud), he was the first to popularize them as the foundation for an American work culture. Moreover, the proverbs were influential precisely because they fit neatly into the wisdom of older narratives used in churches, schools, and business.

During this same period, Frederick the Great (1740–86) organized his armies on the principles of mechanics: ranks, uniforms, regulations, task specialization, standardized equipment, command language, and drill instruction (Morgan, 1986). His success served as a model for organizational action, one based on the division of labor and machinelike efficiency. Given this historical background, it is perhaps no surprise that inventor Eli Whitney's (1765–1825) ground-breaking demonstration of mass production in 1801 was based on standardized parts and divisions of labor in the production of guns, whose purpose was to maintain order and extend the power of empires.

Adam Smith (1723–90), a philosopher of economics and politics, published *A Wealth of Nations* in 1776, which praises the divisions of labor evident in factory production. As Karl Marx (1818–83) would demonstrate in the mid-nineteenth century, division of labor was essential to organizing corporations and societies along class lines. By 1832, a blueprint for such an organizational form had emerged (see Figure 3.1). Characterized by strict divisions of labor and hierarchy, it would later be called the classical theory of management (Fayol, 1949). Notice in the figure that the classic bureaucratic organization privileges a top–down or management-oriented approach. Two assumptions of this perspective are worth noting. First, the emphasis on developing scientific methods for production is politically and socially linked to providing that information only to managers and supervisors, who in turn use it to organize and control workers. Second, the model endorses the need to foster a passive audience in the workplace. In other words, workers are viewed as silent receptors of management information, incapable of responding, interpreting, arguing, or counteracting this subtle but persuasive form of control. Thus, effective communication in the nineteenth century meant giving orders and emphasized the downward transmission of information.

The top–down flow of information in hierarchies also led to the emergence of *domination narratives,* which ascribed particular readings of how truth,

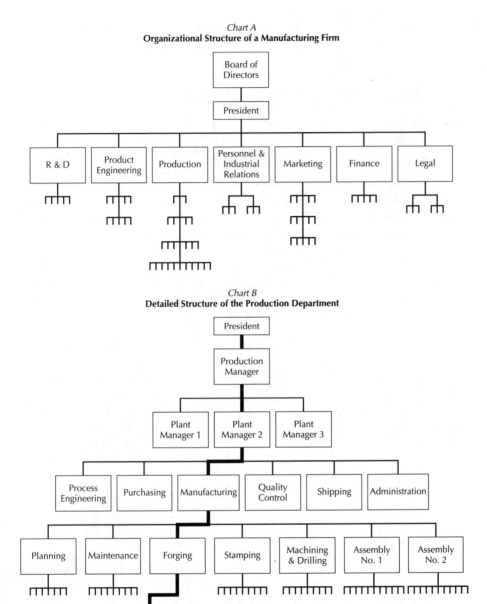

FIGURE 3.1
Organization Chart Illustrating the Principles of Classical Management Theory and Bureaucratic Organization

Source: Gareth Morgan, *Images of Organization* (Newbury Park, Calif.: Sage, 1986). Reprinted by permission of Sage Publications, Inc.

power, and control were constituted in everyday conversation. Table 3.1 summarizes the communication values of domination narratives.

FROM RESISTANCE TO DOMINATION

The rapid expansion of industrialization in nineteenth-century northern Europe and North America created the need to organize and manage labor in ways that mirrored dominant social and political values. In the United States, slavery both supplied the laborers for agricultural work in the South and mirrored a view of hierarchy that was based on the racial divisions sanctioned by white slaveholders. One result of the deep divisions between ways of organizing labor and the social values that supported them was the Civil War (1861–65). The outcome of that war is an interesting, but often overlooked, part of the history of organizations and communication in this country. It can be viewed as a struggle between social values that coincided with the hierarchical division of organized labor and the different interpretations of how hierarchies should be determined (i.e., by race or by social class). As such, the Civil War provides a broad lens for understanding the role of hierarchical organization in the development of U.S. industry.

Where differences exist in the type of work that people do, there will also be differences in how that work is done, evaluated, valued, and compensated. Those in power control the interpretation of such differences: the story they tell favors their interests. For white slaveholders in the South, slavery was justified on economic and moral grounds. They believed they had a right to a cheap source of labor to farm their lands, and that their accumulation of wealth was at the heart of Calvinist moral advancement (Raban, 1991). From their perspective, then, slavery was necessary for the productive accomplishment of work that would grant them entry to a Protestant heaven. This partisan view of racial division and moral order gave slaveholders the power to control both the daily lives of slaves as well as the means of resolving conflict. Thus, any slave attempt to challenge white authority was viewed as a challenge to the moral order. As a result, communication between slaveholder and slave was one-sided, unequivocally favoring the slaveholder's interests.

One feature of societal dialogue helps us understand organizational dialogue: *resistance to domination.* In addition to the domination narratives discussed earlier in the chapter, all societies have narratives of resistance. These are the narratives of the less powerful and the powerless, of those who ordinarily have little or no voice in organizational and societal dialogue. They provide different accounts of events and the meanings those events had for the participants (Friere, 1968). Unless the domination is eventually overturned, these stories only rarely make it into textbooks. Slave narratives are an example.

James Scott (1990) points out how the accounts of the powerless can func-

TABLE
3.1

Summary of Communication Values Found in Domination Narratives

WHAT IS TRUTH?	WHAT IS POWER?	HOW IS CONTROL POSSIBLE?
Absolute; based on dominant ideology, received wisdom, established doctrine, procedural dogma, or consensus account that favors the authority of the power-holders and legitimates the subservience of those defined as subordinates.	Control over vocabulary, including the ability to define key terms for understanding the truth in all situations, strict divisions of all sources of conflict into binary opposites (e.g., black/white, us/them, right/wrong), and the use of *either/or* reasoning (e.g., "Either you are with us or against us"); also the ability to exercise discipline or punishment for failure to adhere to the dominant narrative.	Unified (often through causal linkages) integration and presentation of all explanatory narratives.
Communication practices: Use of representative anecdotes that embody the principle; reification of processes into concrete definitions and formulas; evaluation of the status quo or the "way things have always been."	*Communication practices:* Use of referent authority (tradition, rules, religion, science, law); simplistic extensions of authority to specific cases; reduction of complex issues into "essences" that can be explained by dominant narratives; use of categorical generalizations and rhetorical syllogisms.	*Communication practices:* Vehement distrust of change; rigid adherence to dominant narratives, definitions, and accounts; dismissal of all competing narratives by relegating them to the status of hearsay, falsity, improbability, or outright absurdity.
Representative story: "Great companies have always relied on rational ways of organizing work, which is why bureaucracy is the most rational form of organization. It is the way things have always been—there's no point in questioning it."	*Representative account:* "It is a well-known scientific fact that managers are supposed to do the thinking, and workers are supposed to do the working. I am a manager and I do the thinking; you are the employee and therefore you do what I say."	*Representative explanation:* "Flattening the chain of command is crazy and the result will be chaos."

tion as "hidden transcripts" of the other side of the story. Narratives of resistance gave slaves a way to express their outrage among others in the same situation. Their stories reversed the order of things, placing slaveholders in inferior intellectual, moral, and performance positions. In this "world turned upside down" (Scott, 1990; Stallybrass & White, 1986), those without power could take control of the story and use it as a "performative space for the full-throated acting out of everything that must be choked back in public" (Conquergood, 1992, p. 91). By looking at the dominant narrative alongside the slave narrative we get a sense of the potential dialogue that might have occurred between the two groups. Unfortunately, however, that dialogue remained mostly implicit because the dominant group's narrative was told in public and the slave's narrative in private.

In addition to slave narratives, other forms of resistance to domination came with the slave songs, ditties, and dirges that would later become known as "the Blues." This, in turn, would lead to two other musical forms of resistance to domination: rock and roll and rap music (Goodall, 1991a). Similarly, there are accounts of resistance to domination from those who were once among the dominant and powerful. Perhaps the best known of these accounts is the gospel hymn "Amazing Grace," which combines the rhythms and sensibilities of a slave song with words penned by a former slave trader turned English minister, John Newton (1791):

> *Amazing Grace, how sweet the sound,*
> *Amazing Grace, how sweet the sound,*
> *That saved a wretch like me.*
> *I once was lost, but now I'm found,*
> *Was blind, but now I see.*

Newton's diaries also contain evidence of the values of hierarchy, empire, and scientific management in the operation of slave ships (Moyers, 1989). Dramatic testimony is found in Newton's drawings of how chained slaves were "scientifically organized" for the long voyage between Africa and the New World (see Figure 3.2). Like cattle or dry goods, slaves were kept in tight, straight lines to minimize wasted space in the ship's hull. Meager food and water were dispensed according to a rigid schedule. Management took the form of absolute tyranny and utilized scientific principles of cost efficiency and production.

Although in later decades many economic and technical advances would attest to the benefits of rational approaches to organization, the scientific management that was applied to slave ships shows how it can be abused in cases of absolute power. In the twentieth century, the Holocaust provides another example of the abuse of classical principles of organization. Similar practices exist today in businesses throughout the world. Hierarchically ordered systems of domination and abuses of power persist in areas under severe political and military occupation as well as in illegal sweatshops employing immigrant laborers the world over (Lavie, 1990; Scott, 1990).

Yet, where there is domination, there is always some form of resistance.

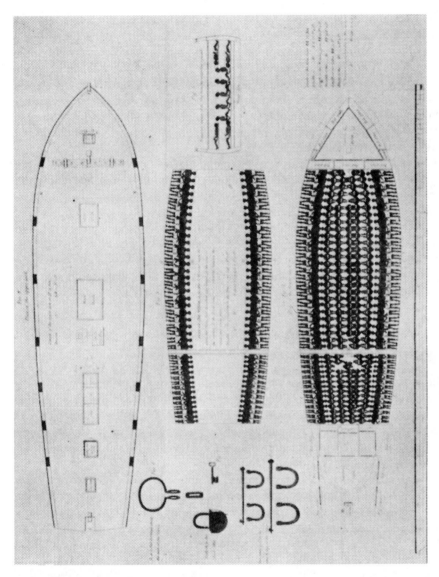

FIGURE 3.2
Diagram showing how slaves were stowed on ships

Source: Reproduced from *Slave Ships and Slaving* (1969), p. 159

Table 3.2 summarizes the communication values found in resistance narratives. Such narratives reveal that, even under extreme conditions of servitude or denial of basic human rights, dominated groups find ways to engage in conflict with power-holders. They challenge the elite's interpretations of reality through voices that are rarely spoken in public for fear of repercussions. Rumors, gossip, songs, private jokes, gestures, and stories express the interests of workers in ways that organizational power-holders would not endorse. Narratives of resistance thus have broad applications to contemporary organizational cultures, subcultures, and countercultures (see Chapter 5).

The end of the Civil War brought an end to slavery, but hierarchies in society and organizations continued. Some observers argue that the Civil War brought the triumph of one region's views about division of labor over another's, with social class rather than race serving as the primary organizing principle. Others see the end of the war as marking the birth of a democracy, in which people could advance on the basis of ability despite their social class, race, religion, or creed. Still others point out that even though slavery was abolished, widespread racial prejudice was not. The economically disadvantaged blacks who had overcome slavery in the South would encounter prejudice in a different form in northern cities and factories.

SCIENTIFIC MANAGEMENT

The years 1880 to 1920 were characterized not only by significant racial and class prejudice but also by unprecedented economic expansion in the United States. With massive industrialization came ruthless treatment of workers by owners who subscribed to a "survival of the fittest" mentality. Those employees who succeeded were deemed morally strong; those who failed were deemed unworthy of success (Bendix, 1956).

Born in this era was the middle-class engineer Frederick Taylor (1856–1915), a pioneer in the development of scientific management. His classic book, *Principles of Scientific Management* (1913), is based on the assumption that management is a true science resting on clearly defined laws, rules, and principles. Taylor's time and motion studies led to improved organizational efficiency through the mechanization of labor and the authority of the clock. Work was divided into discrete units that were measured by how long it took a competent worker to accomplish them. This principle was then used to plan factory outcomes, to evaluate worker efficiency, and to train less skilled workers. The production system thus required divisions of labor, carefully developed chains of command, and limited communication (e.g., orders and instructions).

Taylor's goal was to transform the nature of both work and management. He hoped that cooperation between managers and employees would bring a new era of industrial peace: "Under scientific management, arbitrary power, arbitrary

TABLE
3.2 **Summary of Communication Values Found in Resistance Narratives**

WHAT IS TRUTH?	WHERE IS POWER?	HOW IS TRANSCENDENCE POSSIBLE?
Depends on the relationship of the story to the position of power held by the storyteller.	In the resistance tactic of countering a dominant strategy; in the performance of "a world turned upside down"; in the retelling of the resistance account.	Off-stage performances of resistance narratives organize and inform opposition to power-holders.
Communication practices: Saving face, indirect confrontation, disguise, artful misinterpretation of instructions, use of secrets, portrayal of dominant elites as immoral, unethical, stupid, or fallible; appearing to comply with domination while actively pursuing tactics of insubordination.	*Communication practices:* Resistance narratives, songs, humor, gossip, theatrical performances, dramatic gestures, and asides.	*Communication practices:* Occupy territory controlled by the dominant interests and use it to stage resistance narratives.
Representative story: "There is an Indian story . . . about an Englishman who, having been told that the world rested on a platform which rested on the back of an elephant which rested in turn on the back of a turtle, asked . . . what did the turtle rest on? [The Indian's response:] Another turtle. [The Indian:] Ah, Sahib, after that it is turtles all the way down" (Geertz, 1973, pp. 28–29).	*Representative explanation:* "[A] tactic is a calculated action . . . a maneuver 'within the enemy's field of vision,' . . . and within enemy territory. . . . It operates in isolated actions, blow by blow. It takes advantage of opportunities and depends on them. . . . It must vigilantly make use of the cracks that particular conjunctions open in the surveillance of proprietary powers. It poaches in them. It creates surprise in them. . . . It is a guileful ruse" (de Certeau, 1984, p. 37).	*Representative explanation:* Power-holders legitimate their stories of truth, justice, and rationality through control of territory and property and they use surveillance (from the idea of surveying one's property) to keep tabs on how "their" places are being used. By contrast, the powerless "appropriate" or "poach" space within the power-holder's place, and they use these spaces for performances of resistance that demonstrate what they "know" as well as their hope for the future (see de Certeau, 1984).

Source: Adapted from Dwight Conquergood, "Ethnography, Rhetoric, and Performance," *Quarterly Journal of Speech* 78 (1992): 80–97.

dictation, ceases; and every single subject, large and small, becomes the question for scientific investigation, for reduction to law" (Taylor, 1947, p. 211). But things didn't work out that way; although Taylor believed he was developing his ideas to help the working person, by the end of his life he was cursed by labor unions as "the enemy of the working man" (Morgan, 1986). Even so, Taylor's work ushered in a new focus on the relationship between managers and employees as a key to organizational productivity.

Scientific management, then, is a management-oriented, production-centered view of organizations and communication. Its ideal, the efficient machine, holds that humans function as components or parts. It also assumes a fundamental distinction between managers and employees: Managers think, workers work (Morgan, 1986). But the ideal of scientific management can be realized only in task situations that are straightforward, that require no flexibility in responding to contingencies, and that offer no opportunities for initiative. This description of an organization does not take into account human motivations for working, personal work relationships, and the flexibility required by the turbulent nature of organizational environments. Moreover, efforts to improve efficiency by raising production levels often alienate workers, as in Henry Ford's automobile plant, which experienced a turnover rate of 280 percent under scientific management (Morgan, 1986).

FAYOL'S CLASSICAL MANAGEMENT

At roughly the same time Taylor was working on scientific management in the United States, the French industrialist Henri Fayol (1949–) was developing his influential theory of "administrative science," or classical management. A highly successful director of a French mining company, Fayol's management principles became popular in the United States and elsewhere in the late 1940s. He is perhaps best known for articulating the five elements of classical management—*planning, organizing, commanding* (goal-setting), *coordinating,* and *controlling* (evaluating). He was even more specific in detailing *how* this work ought to be done.

Katherine Miller (1995) groups Fayol's principles into four categories: structure, power, reward, and attitude. Regarding *structure,* Fayol prescribed a strict hierarchy with a clear vertical chain of command; he called this the "scalar principle." He believed that each employee should have only one boss and be accountable to only one plan. Like Taylor, Fayol advocated division of labor through departmentalization (the grouping of similar activities together). The resulting organizational structure is the classic hierarchical pyramid.

In terms of *power,* Fayol advocated the centralization of decision making and respect for authority. He held that authority accrues from a person's position *and* character, and that discipline and obedience could only be expected if both were present. Moreover, he viewed discipline as a respect for standing agreements, not only a respect for position.

Regarding *rewards,* and mirroring Taylor, Fayol advocated fair remuneration for well-directed efforts, thereby foreshadowing the potential of profit-sharing as a compensation system (Tompkins, 1984). Most concerned about the employee's perception of equity in pay and other issues, Fayol believed in the value of a stable workforce. He was thus a proponent of stable tenure for employees as a means of avoiding high turnover rates and recruitment costs.

Finally, regarding organizational *attitude,* Fayol held that employees should subordinate their personal interests to those of the organization. He also saw rational enforcement of agreements through fair supervision as the method for ensuring this organizational attitude. At the same time, Fayol encouraged employee initiative, or the capacity to see a plan through to completion, and believed that supervisors should work hard to foster positive employee morale.

Fayol intended to develop a set of guidelines for organizational administration that would be useful across a variety of situations. Some of his principles, most notably those related to standing agreements, unity of command, and centralization, target issues of organizational communication (Tompkins, 1984). However, as Fayol cautioned, "there is nothing rigid or absolute in management affairs, it is all a question of proportion. Seldom do we have to apply the same principle twice in identical conditions; allowances must be made for different changing circumstances" (1949, p. 19).

BUREAUCRACY

In the harsh working conditions of the early 1900s, job security did not exist, young children worked long hours for meager wages, and workers were hired and fired for reasons that had to do with their race, religion, sex, attitude, or relationship to the boss. This method of dealing with employees, called *particularism,* was expedient for owners and managers but had dire consequences for employees. Particularism also presented an ideological conflict in the United States: "On the one hand, democracy stressed liberty and equality for all. On the other hand, large masses of workers and nonsalaried personnel had to submit to apparently arbitrary authority, backed up by local and national police forces and legal powers, for ten to twelve hours a day, six days a week" (Perrow, 1986, p. 53).

It was this conflict between ideology and practice that gave rise to what we now call *bureaucracy.* According to Scott (1981), organizational bureaucracy has the following characteristics:

1. A fixed division of labor among participants;
2. A hierarchy of offices;

3. A set of general rules that govern performances;
4. A separation of personal from official property and rights;
5. Selection of personnel on the basis of technical qualifications [and] equal treatment of all employees; and
6. Employment viewed as a career by participants; tenure protects against unfair arbitrary dismissal.

The well-known German scholar, Max Weber (1864–1920) was not a blind advocate of bureaucracy; rather, his cultural pessimism led him to conclude that bureaucracy would prevail (Clegg, 1990). Although Weber (1946) was skeptical of bureaucracy, he saw it as technically superior to all other forms of organization. Table 3.3 summarizes Weber's principles of bureaucratic organizations.

Most people today associate bureaucracy with the red tape and inflexibility of public agencies. However, these may not be the necessary results of a bureaucratic approach. In his famous defense of bureaucracy, Charles Perrow (1986) argues that the machine itself ought not be blamed, but rather the people who misuse it as a personal tool.

It is useful to examine bureaucracy in terms of both what came before it—particularism—and Weber's goal of "universalism," which sought to introduce standards of fair treatment in the workplace. Even today, managers struggle to hold on to the powers to hire, fire, promote, and discipline employees at will. Pre-bureaucratic decision making is viewed by managers as easier and more expedient than decision making in a bureaucracy. The latter makes decisions harder to implement at the same time that it protects employees from abuse.

However, the ideal bureaucracy cannot be fully realized for several reasons: (1) It is not possible to rid organizations of all extraorganizational influences on member behavior; (2) bureaucracy does not deal well with nonroutine tasks; and (3) people vary in terms of rationality (Perrow, 1986). These inadequacies of bureaucracy became the basis for other theories. Sociological studies of bureaucracy found Weber's claim of its inevitability overstated (Clegg, 1990; Hage & Aiken, 1970). Alternative forms of organizing were proposed that loosened the rigid assumptions of classical management theory, thus paving the way for new insights into human organization.

IMPLICATIONS FOR ORGANIZATIONAL COMMUNICATION

The classical management approach views communication as nonproblematic. In organizations, communication is simply a tool for issuing orders, coordinating work efforts, and gaining employee compliance. Moreover, in a hierarchical world, the primary function of communication is the transfer of information through the proper channels. This approach raises several ethical questions, some of which are addressed by Focus on Ethics 3.1.

TABLE
3.3
Max Weber's Principles of Bureaucratic Organizations

STRUCTURE AND FUNCTION OF ORGANIZATIONS	MEANS OF REWARDING EFFORT IN ORGANIZATIONS	PROTECTIONS FOR THE INDIVIDUALS WHO DO THE WORK
Business must be conducted continuously.	Officials must consider their offices as their sole or primary occupation for which they receive fixed salaries, graded by rank.	It is necessary to protect the rights of individuals to ensure a source of personnel and to prevent arbitrary use of power in the service of nonorganizational or anti-organizational goals.
Hierarchy of offices, with each office under the control of a higher one.	Officials do not own the means of production or administration.	Officials serve voluntarily and are appointed.
Systematic division of labor based on training and expertise; specific areas of responsibility and action clearly understood.	Officials cannot appropriate their offices and must render an accounting of their use of organizational property.	Service constitutes a career with promotions according to seniority or achievement.
Performance of duties governed by written rules and records of actions and decisions already taken.	Officials must separate their private affairs and property from the organization's affairs and property.	Obedience is owed the office-holder, not the person.
Benefits: (1) Provides mechanisms for control over performance of individuals and (2) provides means for specialization and expertise and means of coordinating roles to prevent them from interfering with each other.	*Benefits:* (1) Salary rather than other forms of compensation or reward limits potential for abuse; (2) legitimate rather than charismatic leadership (although charismatic still exists in bureaucracies).	*Benefits:* (1) Officials are subject to authority only with respect to their duties; (2) there is the right to appeal decisions and grievances.

Source: Charles Perrow, *Complex Organizations: A Critical Essay,* 3rd ed. (New York: Random House, 1986).

Rank Has Its Privileges: The Influences of the Bureaucratic Organization on Home and Family Life

Among the world's largest bureaucracies is the U.S. military. Character-ized by principles of scientific rationality, the military is organized ac-cording to hierarchies or ranks and relies on standardized procedures for behavioral control. Viewed from the perspective of classical scientific management, then, the military operates as an efficient machine.

Often neglected in studies of bureaucracy are its influence on em-ployees' home and family life. How do those who work for bureaucra-cies make the daily transition from a highly controlled work life to a more loosely organized home life? Does the bureaucracy have an effect on home and family management?

In the following excerpt from Mary Truscott's *Brats: Children of the American Military Speak Out* (1989), the narrator explains how growing up in the military deeply affected childhood learning and family life.

> *I learned to snap off a salute before I learned to ride a bike. There were plenty of role models for me to imitate; people who were always saluting my father. It didn't seem unusual. Some men saluted, and others were saluted.*
>
> *The military jargon that was so pervasive on the post and in our household included many rank-related qualifiers. The size and location of our houses were based on rank. We lived on "Colonel's Row" in stately three-story duplexes with full maid's quarters in the basement, but we had done our time in apart-ments before my father made colonel. My father had "his men," the men under his command. My mother came home from the Officers' Wives Club functions and frequently told my father about the "little captain's wife" or "little major's wife" she had met. Too young to remember when my father had been a lowly major, I developed a mental image of a community of Lillipu-tian people, captains and majors and their families, inhabiting the smaller and, I knew, inferior housing on the other side of the post.*
>
> *The ascending rank was always part of a family name. I answered the telephone with "Colonel Truscott's quarters, Mary speaking." I addressed all adults with their surname and current*

(continued)

(continued)

rank. I never knew many men who were "mister," with the exception of school principals.

We lived on the post for the most part, only minutes away from my father's office, but I had no idea of what my father did at work. My dad was in the Army; other men were businessmen, doctors, lawyers, Indian chiefs. In his study at home he had a framed poster from a lecture he had given that had his picture on it and the caption THE NATION'S FOREMOST EXPERT ON RADIOACTIVE FALLOUT. *Whatever it was that my dad did at work, I felt certain that if we were bombed and fallout came raining out of the sky, my father would lead us to the designated fallout shelters on the post and we would survive, no matter how awful the blast, because he was "The Nation's Foremost Expert."*

We visited my father's office a few times, and it was remarkably devoid of any sign or indication of his work. The walls in his office were pale green, with perhaps a flag and a strictly functional map or two to break the monotony. His desk was typical Army issue, either wood or metal, and the chairs had convex seats covered with slippery green vinyl that made it impossible to sit still. The Army seemed to be a serious, boring place to work . . . .

Rank truly had its privileges. The written and unwritten rules that established the chain of command for the men in uniform also applied to their families. Rank created a virtual caste system, and life on a military post had no uncertainties. There were stripes and insignia on uniforms, stickers on cars, and name-plates on houses. Families were segregated, by rank, in separate and not necessarily equal enclaves, and there were separate club facilities for officers and enlisted men. Post housing was the most obvious indicator of rank.

The privileges accorded by rank were highly visible, but the social taboos on the post were often not apparent or even official. The officers' children tended to cross the lines of rank without compunction, but the children of enlisted men were conscious of the rules that forbade their fathers from fraternizing with officers and kept to themselves for the most part . . . .

Regardless of who the father was and what he did, rank was either a source of pride and status or an embarrassing label that put the military brat on the wrong side of the tracks. And all

(continued)

(continued)

> *military brats, no matter where their father had fit in the hierar-*
> *chy of rank, emphasized, over and over, that rank was pervasive*
> *and clearly defined.*

Ethical questions can be thought of as sources of creativity or constraint. On the basis of the preceding narrative, how would you respond to the following questions?

1. What ethical issues surround the notion that "rank has its privileges"? Do those privileges extend beyond the duties and responsibilities of work?
2. How does hierarchical thinking influence the narrator's view of the world? How does this type of thinking contribute to our understanding of social divisions in class, race, age, and gender?
3. Is the integration of home and work as described by the narrator necessary to the survival of all bureaucracies or only the military? Explain.

The Human Relations Approach

Kenneth Burke was once asked how he became interested in the study of human communication. Burke replied: "People weren't treating each other very well. I wanted to help find a way to make relationships better" (qtd. in Goodall, 1984, p. 134). Burke's comment was made during the 1930s, a time of unparalleled economic depression when models of bureaucracy were questioned and theories of human relations emerged.

HISTORICAL AND CULTURAL BACKGROUND

Three major events—the Great Depression, World War II, and a new way of understanding human behavior—came at a time when the perceived limitations of scientific management were at their peak. The Great Depression (1929–40) created economic and social hardships for millions of people and led to major changes in government policies regarding Social Security, public assistance, and funding of public improvement projects. The Depression also contributed to major migrations of workers—from the drought-ridden central farming states to the West Coast, and from the impoverished rural South to northern cities—as people went in search of jobs to support themselves and their families. But a surplus of available workers and a lack of employment opportunities meant keen competition for jobs and widespread abuse of workers by employers. It is not

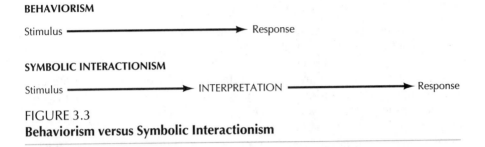

BEHAVIORISM

Stimulus ⟶ Response

SYMBOLIC INTERACTIONISM

Stimulus ⟶ INTERPRETATION ⟶ Response

FIGURE 3.3
Behaviorism versus Symbolic Interactionism

surprising, then, that this period was also marked by the expansion of powerful labor unions. These organizations advocated human rights, fair wages, and improved working conditions for the labor force.

Although divisions between managers and workers had existed since the Industrial Revolution, they became more intense during the Depression. Demands for improved working conditions were accommodated only when the improvements increased productivity and profits. Wages were determined by factory output, but increased output tended to increase the number of incidences of work-related injury, illness, or death. In addition, the typical twelve-hour workday, six days a week, with one half-hour break for a meal contributed to the strained relationship between workers and managers.

With World War II, however, came an enormous expansion of new jobs in both the military and private sector. The war also contributed to the emerging human relations movement by placing academic researchers, managers, and military personnel in direct communication with each other. W. Charles Redding (1985a), a pioneer of organizational communication and one of its leading historians, refers to this threesome as "the Triple Alliance." He argues that through the alliance, managers and military officers benefited from new ideas about organizing work and developing trust among workers, while academic researchers benefited from their access to industrial plants and their involvement in training workers, military personnel, and managers. The effects of this war-formed alliance would have a lasting impact, particularly on the subdiscipline that was created out of that alliance—organizational communication (Redding, 1985a).

Finally, the period is marked by a new approach to understanding human relationships and behavior, which Herbert Blumer (1905–89) would later call *symbolic interactionism*. Symbolic interactionism draws on the pragmatism of Charles Pierce, William James, and John Dewey; the social philosophy of George Herbert Mead; and the Freudian interpretation of the symbolic realms of experience. According to Blumer (1969), symbolic interactionism is a simple but revolutionary alternative to behaviorism: Humans respond to the meanings they have for things. A *meaning-centered* rather than a *behavior-centered* approach to understanding human action was thus born (see Figure 3.3).

WHAT IS HUMAN RELATIONS?

Although Taylor had hoped to emphasize the importance of cooperative relationships between managers and employees, his methods did little to contribute to the quality of those interactions in the early twentieth century. It was not until the 1930s that Elton Mayo and Chester Barnard would examine the employee–manager relationship in an entirely new way. Their work would provide the foundation for the human relations approach as well as become a precursor of contemporary thinking about management. Their perspective marked a clean break from earlier points of view: "People are tractable, docile, gullible, uncritical—and want to be led. But far more than this is deeply true of them. They want to feel united, tied, bound to something, some cause, bigger than they, commanding them yet worthy of them, summoning them to significance in living" (Bendix, 1956, p. 296).

Elton Mayo (1880–1949), a Harvard professor, set out to critique and extend scientific management. But Mayo did not share Taylor's view of organizations as comprised of wage-maximizing individuals. Instead, Mayo stressed the limits of individual rationality and the importance of interpersonal relations. In contrast to scientific management, Mayo (1945) held that

1. society is comprised of groups, not isolated individuals;
2. individuals are swayed by group norms and do not act alone in accord with self-interests; and
3. individual decisions are not entirely rational; they are also influenced by emotions.

Chester Barnard, a chief executive at Bell Telephone in New Jersey and the author of the influential book *The Functions of the Executive* (1938), asserted the importance of cooperation in organizations: "Organizations by their very nature are cooperative systems and cannot fail to be so" (Perrow, 1986, p. 63). The key to cooperation, he argued, lay in persuading individuals to accept a common purpose, from which all else would follow. Unlike Taylor's emphasis on economic inducements, for Barnard the role of management was largely communicative and persuasive. Effective managers thus strived to communicate in ways that encouraged workers to identify with the organization. Barnard also valued the contributions of informal contacts to overall organizational effectiveness. For the first time, then, the purpose of management was seen as more interpersonal than economic.

THE HAWTHORNE STUDIES

While Barnard was running New Jersey Bell, a landmark event was taking place at another subsidiary of AT&T, the Hawthorne plant of Western Electric in Cicero, Illinois. Mayo and F. J. Roethlisberger (also a Harvard professor) were called into the Hawthorne plant by W. J. Dickson, a manager and industrial engineer, and others concerned about widespread employee dissatisfaction, high turnover rates, and reduced plant efficiency. Previous efforts to correct these problems by using principles of scientific management had failed. Perrow (1986) picks up the story:

> The researchers at Western Electric took two groups of workers doing the same kinds of jobs, put them in separate rooms, and kept careful records of their productivity. One group (the test group) had the intensity of its lighting increased. Its productivity went up. For the other group (the control group), there was no change in lighting. But, to the amazement of the researchers, its productivity went up also. Even more puzzling, when the degree of illumination in the test group was gradually lowered back to the original level, it was found that output still continued to go up. Output also continued to increase in the control group. The researchers continued to drop the illumination of the test group, but it was not until the workers were working under conditions of bright moonlight that productivity stopped rising and fell off sharply. (pp. 79–80)

Over time, Mayo and his colleagues realized that the productivity improvements they had measured had little to do with degree of illumination or other physical conditions in the plant. Instead, they found that the increased attention given to the workers by management and researchers was the key to increased productivity. This finding—that increased attention raises productivity—has come to be known as the *Hawthorne effect*.

Further research supported Mayo's critique of scientific management. A prominent finding of the Hawthorne studies was drawn from an experiment in the bank-wiring observation room, where it was found that even under poor working conditions, supportive informal group norms could have a positive effect on productivity. For the first time, then, it was shown that individual workers were complex beings, sensitive to group norms and possessing multiple motives, values, and emotions. "At the social psychological level, the Hawthorne studies pointed to a more complex model of worker motivation based on a social-psychological rather than an economic conception of [human beings]; and at the structural level, the . . . studies discovered . . . the importance of informal organization" (Scott, 1981, p. 87).

REFLECTIONS ON HUMAN RELATIONS

It is difficult to criticize the primary goal of the human relations approach—to restore whole human beings and quality interpersonal relationships to their rightful place in what had become an overly rational view of organizations. In this spirit, the work of Chris Argyris has been most influential. According to Argyris (1957), the principles of formal organization, such as hierarchy and task specialization, are incongruent with the developmental needs of healthy adults. But do real alternatives exist? Critics have labeled Argyris and others who share

TABLE

3.4

Summary of Historical and Cultural Influences on the Classical Management and Human Relations Approaches to Organizations and Communication

CLASSICAL MANAGEMENT	HUMAN RELATIONS
Theme: Scientific rationality leads to improved efficiency and productivity	*Theme:* Improved human relations leads to improved efficiency and productivity
Enlightenment ideals	Romantic ideals
Industrial Revolution	Development of psychology
Scientific methods	Social scientific methods
Dominant metaphor: Organization as an efficient machine	*Dominant metaphor:* Organization as the sum of relationships
Supporting principles: *Ideal form of society* is authoritarian and values hierarchical organization	*Supporting principles:* *Ideal form of society* is democratic and values open and honest relationships
Divisions of labor/social classes/races/sexes/nations; if "the rules" were applied equally to everyone, individuals who worked hard and obeyed instructions could better themselves	*Divisions* of labor/management honored; negotiation of differences through open communication valued
Conflict based on divisions; dialectical relationships between management and labor based on power and money	*Conflict* based on lack of shared understanding; dialogic model of relationships between management and labor based on trust, openness, honesty, and power
Application of the principles of mechanics to organizations and communication led to operationalizing the machine metaphor (e.g., "This business runs like clockwork.")	*Application* of humanistic and behavioral psychology to organizations and communication led to operationalizing "relational metaphors" (e.g., "This business is like a family.")
Communication—top-down and procedurally oriented; following "the rules" is valued, and opposing them calls into question the whole moral order	*Communication*—relational and needs-oriented; self-actualization is valued if it occurs through work
Dominant form of organizing: Bureaucracy	*Dominant form of organizing:* Teams or groups within bureaucracies
Stability best obtained through adherence to procedural forms of order	Stability best obtained through relational and personal happiness
Limitations: Too constraining; encourages mindless adherence to details and procedures and discourages creativity	*Limitations:* False openness, abuse of trust and/or honesty; equation of employee happiness with efficiency or productivity

his views "romantics," arguing that alienation is an inherent part of organizational life (Drucker, 1974; Tompkins, 1984).

Indeed, there is little empirical evidence to support the effectiveness of the human relations approach, particularly the claim that positive employee morale fosters productivity (Miller & Form, 1951). Nevertheless, the approach, reflecting the romantic ideals of the time, has played an important role in further research on organizational behavior. (See Table 3.4 for a summary of the move from classical management to human relations in the study of organizations and communication.) Generally, however, research that applies human relations thinking to the relationship between management and organizational effectiveness has been inconclusive and disappointing. Its underlying ideology has been interpreted as an unacceptable willingness to trade profitability for employee well-being. William Whyte, in his classic critique *The Organization Man* (1969), criticizes the human relations approach for attempting to replace the Protestant work ethic and entrepreneurialism with a social ethic of complacency that emphasizes dressing well, acting nice, and "fitting in." Another critic has referred to human relations as "cow sociology": "Just as contented cows [are] alleged to produce more milk, satisfied workers [are] expected to produce more output" (Scott, 1981, p. 90).

A similar critique of a simplistic connection between good feeling and organizational effectiveness has been offered by communication scholars (Eisenberg & Witten, 1987). Although we would all like to believe that openness, self-disclosure, and supportive relationships have positive effects on organizational productivity, research does not support that contention. Instead, models of employee motivation have become increasingly complex, refining what is meant by good leadership and the conditions under which a focus on interpersonal relations may be desirable. But the applicability of these contingency models is limited to specific situations, resulting in a body of research with no clear implications for practice:

> The practitioner who wants to apply the human relations approach has no clear directive as to what to do—and this is true not only of the findings on size of immediate work group, the character of informal work group solidarity, degree of identification with company goals, and type of leadership style as related to productivity; it also applies to the findings on the relation of "morale" (i.e., satisfaction with job and with company) to all of these variables. The evidence is typically inconclusive, the interpretations sometimes contradictory. (Wilensky, 1967, p. 34)

BEYOND HUMAN RELATIONS

The foundational work in human relations led to three very different lines of research (see Table 3.5). The first sought to investigate the effects of *leadership style* on worker productivity. The second line of research, typically associated with Herbert Simon and built on Mayo's critique of Taylor's wage-maximizing model of individuals, sought to identify the *limitations of decision making* in organizations. Finally, the *institutional school* extends Barnard's ideas about executives by focusing on the communication between senior managers and the organizational environment.

Leadership Style

From World War II through the 1960s, numerous studies were conducted on the relationship between leadership style and worker productivity in response to a fundamental shift in thinking about worker performance. No longer ascribed to the unmotivated worker, poor performance was now seen as a result of poor management. Thus, increasing worker productivity became the job of management, and the search for ways to lead, manage, and supervise people began. No other problem in the history of organizations would prove as challenging.

A ten-year study of leadership characteristics at Ohio State University began in 1945. It attempted to identify leadership traits associated with work group productivity. The research team isolated two factors—*initiating structure* and *consideration*—to describe leaders. A person "high" in initiating structure was active in planning, communicating, scheduling, and organizing, while a person high in consideration showed concern for the feelings of subordinates, promoted mutual trust, and fostered two-way communication. A leader could score high on one or both accounts (Perrow, 1986). The study's major finding was that the traditional management skills associated with initiating structure were as important as the interpersonal skills in promoting worker productivity.

In a similar research effort conducted at the University of Michigan at about the same time, leaders were classified along a continuum ranging from employee-oriented to production-oriented, but the study provided no definitive conclusions about effective management skills. Later research offered more complex models of managerial behaviors that could be applied to certain situations. Frederick Herzberg's (1966) *two-factor theory of job satisfaction,* for instance, assumes that people have two independent sets of needs—to avoid pain and to grow psychologically—and that management strategies need to be tailored to address each set of needs. Therefore, improving working conditions or increasing salaries (what Herzberg calls "hygiene factors") would be expected to reduce dissatisfaction, but it would not necessarily promote satisfaction. Changing the design of the work to make it more rewarding would most likely increase satisfaction. In order to motivate worker performance, according to Herzberg, managers need to maintain a clear distinction between the two sets of needs because changes in hygiene factors are not likely to affect productivity or morale.

TABLE
3.5 **The Legacy of Human Relations:**
Three Research Traditions

TRADITION: LEADERSHIP STYLE

Key Assumption: Supportive communication positively affects productivity and morale

Findings and Implications for Organizational Communication
- Effective leader behavior can be classified as employee-oriented or production-oriented.
- Effective leadership style varies so much by situation that clear, practical conclusions are rare.
- The desire for open, supportive communication by leaders is motivated more by ideology (what people wish were true) than by research evidence.

TRADITION: SIMON'S DECISION-MAKING MODEL

Key Assumption: Individual decision making is only intended to be rational.

Findings and Implications for Organizational Communication
- Individuals in organizations are never fully rational in their decision making.
- Decision making is limited by decision premises, which are constructed largely through communication.
- Organizations can exert unobtrusive control over employees through the control of decision premises.

TRADITION: INSTITUTIONAL SCHOOL

Key Assumption: Organizations are dependent on their social environments for legitimacy and survival

Findings and Implications for Organizational Communication
- There are important differences among organizations.
- Organizations have a life of their own apart from individual members or groups.
- Organizational statespersons must manage relationship with environment.
- Institutions limit certain kinds of communication to shield their technical core from evaluation.

Similarly, Fred Fiedler's (1967) *contingency theory of leadership* maintains that different leadership styles are appropriate for different situations. For example, when a group is either extremely favorable or unfavorable toward a leader, a task-oriented style of management is considered most effective, whereas in less extreme cases an interpersonal style may be effectively applied. Contingency theories of management continue to enjoy popularity today.

Simon's Decision-Making Model

In Herbert Simon's (1957) decision-making model of individuals in organizations, people attempt to make rational decisions, but their ability to do so is hindered by both the situation and their limited processing ability. Specifically, people lack knowledge not only of the consequences of their actions, but also of the alternative courses of action and of the criteria on which to judge the choices available. Rather than attempting to maximize all factors in decision making, the best we can do, according to Simon, is to "satisfice." Satisficing means that people tend to "settle for acceptable as opposed to optimal solutions, to attend to problems sequentially rather than simultaneously, and to utilize existing repertoires of action programs rather than develop novel responses for each situation" (Scott, 1981, p. 75). Communication is thus critical in Simon's model; it establishes the definition or interpretation of the situation, which, in turn, guides individual decision making:

> This definition of the situation . . . is built out of past experience (it includes prejudices and stereotypes) and highly particularized, selective views of present stimuli. Most of the individual's responses are "routine"; they invoke solutions . . . used before. Sometimes [individuals] must engage in problem-solving. When they do, they conduct a limited search for alternatives along familiar and well-worn paths, selecting the first satisfactory one that comes along. They do not consider all possible alternatives, nor do they keep searching for the optimum one. Rather, they "satisfice" or select the first satisfactory solution. Their very standards for satisfactory solutions are a part of the definition of the situation . . . . The organization can control these standards . . . only to a limited extent are they up to individuals. (Perrow, 1986, p. 122)

Simon's decision-making model is further refined in his collaborative work with James G. March, *Organizations* (March & Simon, 1958). The writers detail the ways in which organizations control individuals by controlling their definition of the situation, or by actively shaping their assumptions and decision premises. The more isolated an individual is in an organization, the more the leader's communication resembles monologue and the more constrained the individual member's decision premises become. In contrast, the more sources of information in an organization, the greater the likelihood of divergent opinions, interpretations, definitions of the situation, and dialogue.

According to March and Simon (1958), then, organizations can exert *unobtrusive* (or hidden) *control* over members by limiting alternatives and shaping decision premises. From one perspective, such controls as division of labor, job titles, a formal hierarchy, and key rules and regulations are necessary to Barnard's ideal of cooperation. From another perspective, however, such controls represent the triumph of owners and managers over workers. When decision premises are controlled, individuals *voluntarily* restrict their own behavior according to what they perceive as possible, given their definition of the situation. This latter realization is the driving force behind critical theory (see Chapter 6).

The Institutional School

Like Simon's decision-making model, Philip Selznick's (1948, 1957) *institutional* view of organizations is counter-rational. But unlike Simon's focus on the individual, the institutional approach is more interested in the total organization, which is viewed as having a life of its own. Specifically, the institutional perspective is based on the following major assumptions:

1. *The differences among organizations are important:* A case study method is used to expose the ways organizations differ from one another and to identify their unique characteristics (foreshadowing the organizational culture approach discussed in Chapter 5).
2. *Organizations are not the sum of individual actions; rather, they take on lives of their own that no single individual can control:* This assumption reinforces the idea from Chapter 2 that meanings are co-constructed in dialogue and foreshadows key aspects of systems theory discussed in Chapter 4.
3. *The relationship between an organization and its environment is a key to its survival:* Earlier theories focused almost exclusively on the inner workings of an organization, primarily because environments were relatively stable. As environmental turbulence has increased, its impact on organizations has become more important.

However, the institutional approach does not apply to all organizations. Only some organizations become institutions, in that society prizes them more for the values they embody than for any particular service or level of performance. Examples include libraries, universities, and medical centers. People identify with institutions, associating them with what it means to live well in a good society. Institutions thus become invested with community values, and the managers of institutions must be skilled in communicating with the public (Perrow, 1986). The institution's survival depends on the public's image of it, not on performance, productivity, or effectiveness.

John Meyer and Brian Rowan (1977) describe how the institutionalization process works in hospitals and schools. To protect their legitimacy, the leaders of these organizations must communicate effectively with the community while also shielding data about technical performance from outside scrutiny. Thus a college or university has numerous and complex requirements for awarding a degree or for majoring in a particular field of study. But similar quantification is rarely, if ever, applied to the supposed technical output of the university—student learning. Professors are not evaluated on the basis of how much their students have learned in their courses. Until only recently, hospitals were not scrutinized in terms of the quality of their patient care.

Today, however, the legitimacy of institutions is being questioned more than ever before. Schools and hospitals are being pressured to account for the effectiveness of their technical work. The results will likely be dramatic. In a study of the California state mental health system, J. Rounds (1984) notes that after the traditional decision premises of the institution were questioned (in this case, rules about who could be categorized as mentally ill), pandemonium ensued as different groups with various degrees of technical expertise scrambled to participate in an increasingly frustrating dialogue. The collapse of an institution's legitimacy both opens the possibility for positive change and enormously complicates further action by the institution.

The institutional school emphasizes the relationship between organizational environment and communication and redefines the role of at least some senior managers to that of political statesperson. It also provides further evidence for the importance of communication, not only in the area of information transfer but also in defining situations and creating organizational reality. Finally, it emphasizes that limiting communication about certain issues (e.g., technical evaluations) can preserve legitimacy and the status quo.

The Human Resources Approach

From a communication perspective, the contributions of the human relations approach include its critique of the rational, individualistic model of organizations, and its advancement of an alternative view of individuals situated in social situations that are constituted through communication. However, while human relations recognizes that individual decision making is limited by organizations, it does little to suggest a solution. It took a move toward what is now called the *human resources approach* to value the role of upward communication and the employee's voice in decision making. While incorporating most of the assumptions of human relations, the human resources approach is more concerned with the total organizational climate as well as with how an organization can encourage employee participation and dialogue. Three theorists best capture the spirit of the original human resources movement: Abraham Maslow, Douglas McGregor, and Rensis Likert.

MASLOW'S HIERARCHY OF NEEDS

According to Abraham Maslow's *hierarchy of needs,* people's basic needs for food, shelter, and belonging must be satisfied before they can move toward achieving their full human potential, or what Maslow calls "self-actualization" (see Figure 3.4).

Writing in *Eupsychian Management* (1965), Maslow poses the question, "What kinds of management and what kinds of reward or pay will help human nature to grow healthily into its fuller and fullest stature?" He concludes that the

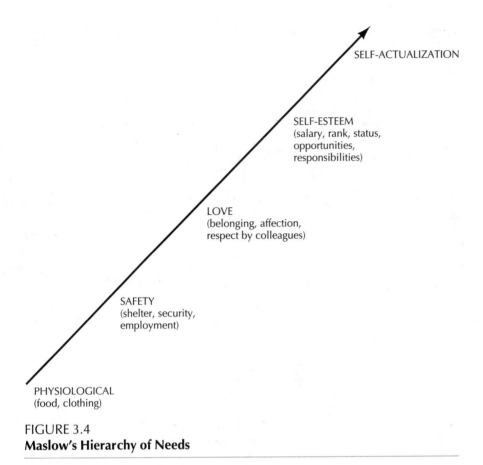

SELF-ACTUALIZATION

SELF-ESTEEM
(salary, rank, status,
opportunities,
responsibilities)

LOVE
(belonging, affection,
respect by colleagues)

SAFETY
(shelter, security,
employment)

PHYSIOLOGICAL
(food, clothing)

FIGURE 3.4
Maslow's Hierarchy of Needs

conditions that foster individual health are often surprisingly good for the prosperity of the organization as well. He thus defines the problem of management as that of setting up social conditions in the organization so that the goals of the individual merge with those of the organization. In many ways, Maslow's work paved the way for more recent theories of performance, including Mihalyi Csikszentmihalyi's (1990) theory of flow (see Chapter 8).

MCGREGOR'S THEORY Y MANAGEMENT

Sharing Maslow's critical view of classical management theory, Douglas McGregor (1960) argued that scientific management is based in part on an assumption that the average employee dislikes work and avoids responsibility in the absence of close control. He calls the control-oriented, bureaucratic style of management *theory X,* which he summarizes as follows:

1. The average human being has an inherent dislike of work and will avoid it if he [or she] can.
2. Because of [their] . . . dislike of work, most people must be coerced, controlled, directed, [or] threatened with punishment to get them to put forth adequate effort toward the achievement of organizational objectives.
3. The average human being prefers to be directed, wishes to avoid responsibility, has relatively little ambition, and wants security above all. (pp. 33–34)

Although theory X may seem quite limited, it helps identify some of the implicit and explicit assumptions of the traditional organization.

McGregor (1960) advances an alternative set of assumptions or principles in his *theory Y:*

1. The expenditure of physical and mental effort in work is as natural as play or rest.
2. External control and threat of punishment are not the only means for bringing about effort toward organizational objectives. [People] will exercise self-direction and self-control in the service of objectives to which [they are] committed.
3. Commitment to objectives is a function of the rewards associated with their achievement (including the reward of self-actualization).
4. The average human being learns, under proper conditions, not only to accept but [also] to seek responsibility.
5. The capacity to exercise . . . relatively high degree[s] of imagination, ingenuity, and creativity in the solution of organizational problems is widely, not narrowly, distributed in the population.
6. Under the conditions of modern industrial life, the intellectual potential . . . of the average [person is] only partially utilized. (pp. 47–48)

In theory Y, McGregor builds on the best of the human relations approach to offer fundamentally different views of employees and of their relationship with management. Employees are viewed as possessing a high capacity for autonomy, responsibility, and innovation. Unlike the Theory X manager, the Theory Y manager has a more participative and facilitative management style and treats employees as valued human resources. Optimistic about incorporating the individual's desires in an organizational framework, McGregor argues that "the essential task of management is to arrange things so people achieve their own goals by accomplishing those of the organization" (Perrow, 1986, p. 99). In contrast to the scalar principle of classical management in which decision-making ability is centralized within management, McGregor offers the principle of integration wherein employees are self-directed as a result of their commitment to organizational goals.

LIKERT'S PRINCIPLE OF SUPPORTIVE RELATIONSHIPS

Continuing the trend toward employee participation in decision making, the work of University of Michigan professor Rensis Likert has contributed to our understanding of high-involvement organizations. Likert's (1961) *principle of supportive relationships* holds that all interactions within an organization should be supportive of individual self-worth and importance, with a particular emphasis on the supportive relationships within work groups and the degree of open communication among groups.

Likert divides organizations into four types or "systems," according to degree of participation: System I—exploitative/authoritative, System II—benevolent/authoritative, System III—consultative, and System IV—participative. The principle of supportive relationships considers open communication as among the most important aspects of management. It also favors general supervision over close supervision and emphasizes the role of the supportive peer group in fostering productivity. Therefore, Likert's principle supports System IV, *participative management.*

However, research on Likert's systems has been inconclusive (Perrow, 1986). Many studies have shown that good classical changes in organizations (e.g., improved work procedures and plans) are as important as participation in increasing organizational effectiveness. The human resources approach continues the human relations tendency to treat all organizations as similar, which opponents in the institutional school and the cultural approach (see Chapter 5) view as inappropriate. Moreover, while human resources emphasizes employee participation in organizational decision making, it does not explain the pragmatics or the politics involved in establishing such a voice for employees. As a result, its prescriptions for participation tend to have limited practical use. Nevertheless, the quest for effective forms of participative decision making continues today (Miller & Monge, 1986).

Focus on Ethics 3.2 considers an ethical dilemma inherent in the politics of management under the influence of human resources.

SUMMARY

This chapter discusses the communication theories associated with three general approaches: classical management, human relations, and human resources. All historical narratives and all human communication exhibit the three *P*'s: partiality, partisanship, and problematic.

The classical management approach emerged during the Industrial Revolution, a period characterized by a quest to adapt the lessons of science and tech-

The Politics of Middle Management

A key assumption of the human resources approach is that happy employees are also productive employees. But in the act of defining happiness, there is the potential for tyranny. Consider this ethical dilemma in relation to the role of the middle manager in human resources (Shorris, 1984, pp. 17–34):

1. "The most insidious power is the power to define happiness." Happiness cannot be described, and what cannot be described cannot be attained. So it is that we create imagined happiness as the opposite of what we can describe—dissatisfaction.
2. All leaders must have the ability to define happiness. In the absence of absolute happiness, we content ourselves with relative happiness.
3. There are three ways in which capitalism and the bureaucratic society conspire to use happiness as a source of fear and reward:

   a. *The merchant* offers happiness in the immediate future. Commodity purchases offer material rewards; failure to consume commodities suggests material poverty and, therefore, a lack of relative happiness.
   b. *The manager* offers happiness in the future. According to human relations theory, his or her power is largely symbolic (kind words, generous deeds, a pat on the back). But because being in management is a source of symbolic attainment in our society, the manager represents what the rest of us aspire to. As such, the manager is the enforcer of our moral code.
   c. *The despot* offers happiness in the historical future. By making prophetic claims about the historical future, he or she is like a secular god and only lacks immortality to be a god. The despot combines displays of material and symbolic happiness, and suggests that others may attain them only if they do as they are commanded.

4. When work becomes rationalized and bureaucratized, the resulting order symbolizes levels of happiness. The manager has the

power to define happiness as the next step up the career ladder. The manager's definition of happiness creates the moral system in which white-collar workers and some managers live, but the despot's definition, with its ultimate promises and religious demands, has a greater effect on the middle manager's life. In return for happiness, middle managers agree to the abolition of their freedom, thereby becoming a part of the organization and accepting the notion that any sin against the organization may cast them out of heaven and into the limbo of the unemployed.

Given these insights, consider how you would handle the following situations:

1. Your supervisor explains that you will be promoted if you can find ways to cut costs by one-third in your department. You know this will mean cuts in personnel, even though your boss never says so directly. But you are already working with a limited staff, and stress is high among employees as a result of the heavy workload. In addition, you fear that any further reduction in staff may affect employee morale and perhaps lower productivity in your department. At the same time, you are heavily in debt and in need of the promotion to make ends meet. Should you gain some happiness at the expense of others'? Is the short-term gain of a promotion worth the long-term risks of negative morale and reduced productivity? How will you handle the situation?

2. You are a midlevel manager privy to information about your company's intent to restructure and downsize its operations. You know this will put you in intense competition with other midlevel managers to keep your job. The vice president of personnel, whom you have long considered an ally, has asked you to keep this information to yourself. She has also asked you to prepare a speech on "Working Your Way up the Ladder" to be delivered to members of the supervisory training group, most of whom will lose their jobs in the downsizing of the company. You are faced with an ethical dilemma. What will you write for the speech? Will you use the opportunity to help project your own job or to address broader issues? How will you handle the situation?

nology to making perfect machines. These early organizations were thus built on the model of the efficient machine, and management was characterized by a machinelike dependence on hierarchy, divisions of labor, strict rules for communication between management and workers, and formal routines. The term *bureaucracy* is often used to describe the structure of these early organizations. In some industries, these attempts to rationalize organizations continue today.

Communication in the image of the ideal machine is what happens before the machine is turned on, such as when a manager explains how to operate the machine to the workers responsible for the labor. Communication that occurs during work tends to slow down production. Therefore, informal talk is considered unnecessary and costly. Morgan (1986) suggests that the machine metaphor is useful for organizing work that is straightforward and repetitive in nature and that is performed in a stable environment by compliant workers. He attributes the limitations of this approach to its narrow focus on efficiency: It does not adapt well to changing circumstances, and it can have a dehumanizing effect on employees. When opportunities for dialogue do not exist, employees' resentment may be expressed as resistance, leading to work slowdowns or sabotage.

In the classical management approach, any attempt at achieving a balance between individual creativity and organizational constraint through dialogue will tilt in favor of constraint. The individual needs of workers are largely ignored, communication is limited to the giving of orders, and the strict imposition of rules and routines seeks to maintain order above all else. When such strict adherence to hierarchical power remains in place for too long, underground opposition or resistance is likely to emerge. During the latter stages of the Industrial Revolution, for example, slavery was abolished and labor unions became more prevalent.

The human relations approach to organizations and communication emerged against the cultural and economic background of the Great Depression. Studies demonstrating a positive correlation between managers who paid attention to workers and improved productivity led to new theories about the role of communication at work. The balance in the organizational dialogue thus tipped back toward a concern for individual creativity and the satisfaction of needs. But critics argued that the balance had tipped back too far, and that making workers happy did not necessarily make them more productive. They saw the new social ethic as a threat to the Protestant work ethic and its emphasis on achievement and entrepreneurship.

Refinements in human relations theory led to the human resources approach. Through this approach, advances were made in our understanding of the relationship between individual needs for creativity and organizational structures. In the period following World War II, studies of leadership style, decision making, and organizations as institutions served to redefine the individual in organizations as socially situated and rational only within limits.

This highly contingent and dynamic view of the individual suggests a new role for communication: the construction of definitions of the situation, or decision premises, which shape individual behavior. It also suggests a new view of employee motivation and performance: The employee's motivation is derived from his or her interests, which constitute the individual's definition of the situation. Hence, situations are symbolic constructions of reality, which are individualized according to personal needs, desires, and interests. This suggests that many employees are motivated as much by symbolic rewards (e.g., identification with the organization, quality of information, praise, satisfying relationships with co-workers) as they are by their paychecks.

The human resources movement is a precursor of many of today's most common management practices. Most firms have given the personnel department a new name—the human resources department—and an increasing number of companies emphasize respect in their relationships with employees. As a result, employees are given more freedom to construct organizational reality through opportunities for dialogue. Their increased involvement, however, has also meant greater responsibility and accountability for their actions and decisions. Of all the approaches to management that we have observed in action, participative management is the most difficult to implement and understand. But when applied successfully, it fosters more satisfied, committed employees and more productive organizations.

Two extremes of thought on organization and management—tightly controlled formal bureaucracies versus a looser, more empathic view of employees as valuable human resources—are at the opposite ends of our theoretical continuum for understanding organizational communication. At the far right is bureaucracy, which holds that formal structure and communication that respect the chain of command ensure productivity and stability. At the far left is the human resources approach, which holds that open communication between managers and employees ensures creativity, adaptability to change, and satisfaction of the individual's needs and motivations. In this chapter, we have seen the problems associated with an organizational dialogue that is tipped too far in favor of either approach. In the following chapters, we will examine new theories that propose solutions to these problems.

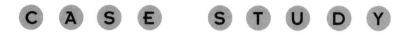

RIVERSIDE STATE HOSPITAL

BACKGROUND

Riverside State Hospital is a five-hundred-bed state-supported psychiatric facility located along the scenic banks of the Tennessee River. Admission to the facility requires a physician or court referral. The hospital staff consists of physicians, psychologists, psychiatrists, nurses, dieticians, pharmacists, therapists, technicians, and general housekeeping and groundskeeping personnel, all of whom are state employees. The hospital is run primarily as a bureaucracy, with levels of authority and salary based on seniority and rank.

All employees hold a government service (GS) rank, the lowest being GS-1 (groundskeeping trainee) and the highest GS-15 (administrator or CEO). In addition, within each rank are seven to ten steps, which are determined by seniority and achievement. Performance reviews are conducted annually, at which time promotions in steps or in GS rank may occur. Employees are given annual salary adjustments for inflation or cost-of-living increases. Full state government benefits are provided to all workers.

Riverside employees work an eight-hour shift. Employees below rank GS-12 (head or chief) take a thirty-minute lunch break and two 15-minute breaks during their shift. The professional staff (physicians, nurses, pharmacists, and the like) works on a three-shift schedule: 7 A.M. to 3 P.M., 3 P.M. to 11 P.M., and 11 P.M. to 7 A.M. The hospital operates year-round.

THE PROBLEM

A few days ago a resident patient at Riverside Hospital was killed when part of the wall next to his bed collapsed. Horris James Wilcox, Jr., was fifty-six years old when he died. He had no family and had been a resident at the hospital for three years. He suffered from traumatic amnesia and scored in the borderline range on intelligence tests. He was otherwise in good health. He was also well liked and seemed to be responding to treatment.

In a statement made to state investigators and the news media, hospital administrators called the accident a "tragedy." They also explained that "there had been no indication that the wall was weak, or that Wilcox was in any danger."

You are the private investigator retained by Wilcox's insurance company. Your job is to determine whether any evidence exists that would make Riverside Hospital liable for Wilcox's death. If such evidence can be found, your employer may not be held financially liable to pay Wilcox's death and burial benefits.

THE INVESTIGATION

You learn from your investigation that Wilcox was a quiet man who tended to keep to himself, although he did join the other patients on the ward for scheduled games and activities. During these times, he talked a lot about current news events. Watching the cable news channel was his favorite source of entertainment. He was known among the staff as the most informed patient on the ward.

Your investigation also reveals that Wilcox's amnesia was complicated by his belief that he was directly affected by whatever he saw on television. News events—particularly family tragedies—affected him deeply. The hospital staff had tried reducing his television viewing time to prevent further complications, but the patient became depressed. His television privileges were restored as a result, and the staff tried instead to use the emotions he displayed about news shows in his therapy. Perhaps, they reasoned, some family tragedy had produced the traumatic amnesia.

In addition, for the past month Mr. Wilcox had repeatedly exclaimed "The sky is falling," especially when he was confined to his bed at night and in the mornings upon awakening. He would also point at the ceiling and walls of his room and cry out, "there is trouble here, trouble from the sky." On several such occasions he had to be physically restrained and calmed with drugs. During this same month, the space shuttle *Challenger* had exploded in the sky over Cape Canaveral, and videotaped replays of that event had appeared frequently on the television news. Given Wilcox's past history of responding emotionally to tragedies reported in the news, the staff linked his most recent behavior to the *Challenger* disaster. But you think there may be more to it. Considering Wilcox's unwillingness to go to bed at night, his complaints about an impending tragedy may have had an altogether different meaning: perhaps "the sky" was a reference to perceived structural defects in the walls and ceiling of his room. You wonder whether Wilcox was trying to direct attention to the actual physical deterioration of his room. Moreover, his psychiatric history may have led those in charge of his care to dismiss his allegations.

Upon further investigation, you learn that the walls and ceiling in Wilcox's room had been repainted three times during the past twelve months due to stains from a leaking water pipe. You think the leak may have seriously weakened the wall, and you feel that hospital personnel should have followed up on this warning. But you also discover that state funding for maintenance had been cut back severely during the previous summer, and while there was structural damage to the wall, there was no indication that it was unsafe. From the hospital administrators' perspective, then, the culprits were an aging building and insufficient state funding to repair it. Even so, they maintain that the collapse of the wall was "an unforeseeable accident."

You obtain copies of the building inspection reports for the past three years. You note that in the past year, state inspectors recorded the deteriorating condition of the wall and ceiling area that eventually collapsed. These forms are signed by Hillary Hanks, the head of resident life.

In an interview with Hanks, you discover that while her signature appears on the state inspection forms, she did not actually sign them. She explains that her secretary, Nancy Ellis, regularly signs her name on state forms to save time. She adds: "There are so many forms to sign that if I signed them all, I wouldn't get any real work done." When you speak to Ellis, she confirms Hanks's story. Furthermore, Ellis is annoyed because the man who delivered the forms to her was supposed to point out any problems that required attention. The problem with the walls and ceiling in Wilcox's room had not been reported verbally to Ellis, and, therefore, she didn't notify Hanks. Now Hanks is in trouble with her superior, and that means Ellis will lose her chance at a promotion. Any trouble for Hanks generally means trouble for Ellis, too. Ellis admits that she regularly avoids telling her boss any bad news for exactly that reason. But this time, Ellis claims, she was unaware of the bad news. You ask Ellis what she did with the inspection report. She points to the overstuffed filing cabinet behind her. "That's where I put it," she says, "along with all the other paperwork that never gets read around here."

You find out that the report was prepared by state inspector Blake Barrymore, who gave it to a groundskeeper for delivery to the appropriate hospital administrator because "it was raining that day and I was late for another inspection." He adds that it is not his official responsibility to deliver the report himself or to follow up on it. You discover that the inspection report was delivered by Jack Handy, a reliable and well-liked groundskeeper. But you also discover that Handy is illiterate. He did not know what the forms contained because he could not read them. He did not report any problems with the walls or ceiling because Barrymore didn't tell him there were any problems. Besides, Handy added, "Nobody listens to a groundskeeper anyway. I could tell the administrators that there was a bomb in the hospital and because I'm just a groundskeeper, they'd let it pass. So I just do what I'm told to do."

You file your report. The insurance company claims that gross negligence on the part of Riverside Hospital indirectly caused the death of Horris James Wilcox, Jr. At a press conference, the hospital spokesperson places the blame for Wilcox's death on Nancy Ellis, claiming it was her responsibility to report the problem to her superior, Hillary Hanks. The spokesperson adds that Hanks has been "reassigned" to other duties and is unavailable for comment. In a final statement, the spokesperson says: "The hospital deeply regrets this tragic accident, and reminds the state legislature that until the requested funds for structural repairs are made available, the hospital administration cannot be held accountable for structural defects that are beyond its control."

ASSIGNMENTS

1. Apply what you have learned in this chapter to the case study and its outcome. Should Ellis be held responsible for Wilcox's death? Why or why not? In what ways did the hospital's organizational structure contribute to his accidental death?

2. What recommendations would you propose to help Riverside Hospital avoid similar occurrences in the future? How can organizational communication be improved?

The Systems Perspective on Organizations and Communication

The human being experiences himself . . . as something separated from the rest—a kind of optical delusion of [the] consciousness. This delusion is a kind of prison for us, restricting us to our personal desires and to affection for a few persons nearest to us. Our task must be to free ourselves from this prison by widening our circle of compassion to embrace all living creatures and the whole of nature in its beauty.
  ● Albert Einstein, *Relativity: The Special and General Theory* (1921)

In life, the issue is not control, but dynamic connectedness.
  ● Erich Jantsch, *The Self-Organizing Universe* (1980)

QUESTIONS

FOR DISCUSSION

- How has the information revolution influenced the development of systems theory?

- How are biological systems and organizational communication systems similar and different?

- In what ways is organizational learning connected to the processes associated with systems thinking?

- How has the sense-making model reinvigorated the application of systems theory to organizational communication?

In this and the following chapter, we continue our story of organizations and communication by considering two dominant metaphors—*systems* and *cultures*—for thinking about the contemporary world. According to one observer, "the unhealthiness of our world today is in direct proportion to our inability to see it as a whole" (Senge, 1990, p. 168). But by thinking in terms of systems and cultures, we find ways of thinking about wholes, which in this era of environmental and economic limitations may be essential to our very survival. Unlike the machine metaphor of classical management theory, the focus of the systems and cultural approaches is not so much on individual parts or people as it is on relationships, or on "the pattern that connects" (Bateson, 1972). As such, these approaches give emphasis to communication; that is, to the development of meaning through human interaction.

We begin, then, with the systems approach. It broadens our way of looking at organizations by borrowing concepts from other, seemingly unrelated areas of study, including engineering, biology, chemistry, physics, and sociology. Associated with the nature of a system are such components as environment, interdependence, goals, feedback, and order. In addition, the systems approach has important implications for the situated individual striving to balance creativity and constraint.

The Systems Approach

A recent advertisement for BMW poses this question: "What makes the BMW the *ultimate driving machine?*" Might it be the car's superb handling and braking? Aerodynamic design? Powerful engine? According to the advertisement, no single feature makes the BMW special; rather, the car is unique in the way that all of its qualities work together as a whole to create "the ultimate driving machine."

The message behind this advertisement is at the heart of the *systems approach,* which emphasizes the important difference between a collection of parts versus *a collection of parts that work together to create a functional whole.* That functional whole is called a *system,* and in a system the whole is greater than the sum of its parts. Sociologist Walter Buckley (1967) translates the latter expression as follows: "The 'more than' points to the fact of *organization,* which imparts to the aggregate characteristics that are not only *different from,* but [also] often *not found in* the components alone; and the 'sum of the parts' must be taken to mean, not their numerical addition, but their unorganized aggregation" (p. 42). In other words, organization makes a social system more than just its components. In a marriage, family, team, or business, the relationships that exist among people are what make the group a system.

Historical and Cultural Background

Unlike the classical management, human relations, and human resources perspectives on organization (see Chapter 3), which emerged in response to the Industrial Revolution and concerns about improving worker productivity and quality of life, the systems approach has its roots in the information revolution.

THE INFORMATION REVOLUTION

The *information revolution,* which emerged in the late 1950s as new thinking about fundamental principles of the universe took hold, would have a dramatic impact on organizations and communication. Albert Einstein's theories of relativity provided the initial impetus for the revolution. Beforehand, Newtonian concepts of the universe had prevailed, wherein space and time were viewed as distinct entities operating "in a fixed arena in which events took place, but which was not affected by what happened in it . . . . Bodies moved, forces attracted and repelled, but time and space simply continued, unaffected" (Hawking, 1988, p. 33). Scientific management thus relied heavily on time and motion studies (whose principles were drawn from Newtonian physics) to provide data to managers about worker productivity.

But a new way of thinking brought new questions: What if time and space are not fixed but relative? If, as Einstein's general theory of relativity suggests, time runs slower nearer the earth due to the influence of its gravitational pull, does this imply that observations of what appears to be a fixed reality are skewed by the observer's position? For example, if things happening at the bottom of a mountain appear to take longer when observed from the top of the mountain, is there something fundamentally wrong with the fixed notion of order or reality in the universe? Theories of relativity explain what may be wrong:

> Space and time are . . . dynamic quantities: when a body moves, or a force acts, it affects the curvature of space and time—and in turn the structure of space-time affects the way in which bodies move and forces act. Space and time not only affect but also are affected by everything that happens in the universe. (Hawking, 1988, p. 33)

In other words, rather than conceptualizing time and motion studies within the limited framework of a specific task, the interpretation of the task is expanded to include how it functions as part of a dynamic interdependent system. Appropriate questions might include: What are the intended and unintended consequences of increased or decreased efficiency? How do pressures to reduce time and eliminate unnecessary motion impact employee morale, absenteeism, commitment, and turnover? How, in turn, do these factors affect productivity in important but potentially unexpected ways?

This major shift in our understanding of the laws of the universe does more than simply call into question the rationality of time and motion studies. It brings to the forefront of our understanding the idea of *dynamic systems of interacting components,* whose relationships and interactions point to a new kind of order based on *pattern* of interaction. The ideas of dynamic systems have been applied to atomic physics, navigational science, aerospace, and electronics, but it was not until after World War II that a general systems paradigm emerged with applications to organizations. The radical shift in interpretation, from substance to dynamic pattern, required a new vocabulary for talking about social collectivities as systems. Not surprisingly, then, it took time for this complex vocabulary to develop and even more time for it to gain acceptance.

In addition to the theoretical advances in physics, new technologies have been spawned by industries capitalizing on scientific advances. Primarily an outgrowth of transistors and, later, the microchip, communication technologies such as television, satellites, and computers have contributed to the emergence of what Marshall McLuhan calls the *global information society* (1964). McLuhan's idea is simple but profound. The instantaneous transfer of information across cultural boundaries means that our perceptions of reality, of cultural differences, of political and social events, and of what constitutes the news cease to be mediated by fixed notions of space or time. Because information now connects us in ways not possible before, the world has become—in McLuhan's words—a "global village."

For example, one application of information technology has contributed to the writing of this textbook. Because we (the authors) live in different regions of the country, we could not meet face to face. But we communicated daily and instantaneously through the Internet. This same computer network also permits us to communicate with other colleagues worldwide. As a result, what once took years to get into print can now be communicated with a keystroke.

Indeed, we don't have to look far to see the impact of systems theory on the field of communication. Consider some of the terms we now routinely use to describe communication: *sender, message, channel, receiver,* and *feedback.* Prior to 1948, the vocabulary of communication developed by the ancient Greeks was still in use (e.g., *speech, speaker, audience, ethos, pathos,* and *logos*). Since then, our language about communication processes has been transformed by the information revolution. As Stuart Clegg (1990) puts it, "Systems ideas are now so much a part of the modernist consciousness that they barely require elaborate iteration" (p. 51). Table 4.1 contrasts the vocabulary and assumptions of systems theory and scientific management theory.

TABLE
4.1 **The Evolution of Scientific Management into Systems Theory**

Scientific management did not simply disappear with the advent of the human relations and human resources approaches. There was still a strong desire among managers, owners, and academics to apply social science to the problems of organization and communication. Part of the initial appeal of systems theory was its ability to capitalize on the complexities of human relationships within a scientific framework while still allowing for description, prediction, and control. This evolution is represented by the following series of advances.

SCIENTIFIC MANAGEMENT	SYSTEMS THEORIES
Metaphor: Machines	*Metaphor:* Biological organisms
Theme: Efficiency: A machine is the sum of its parts.	*Theme:* Rhizome complexity: A system is greater than the sum of its parts.
Influences Industrial Revolution, modernity, capitalism, and empire; assembly-line production and management; division of labor, interchangeable parts, coordination of many small, skilled jobs	*Influences* Einstein's theory of relativity; McLuhan's global information society; J. G. Miller's biological systems; Ludwig von Bertalanffy's general systems; Shannon and Weaver's telephone model of communication
Focus of management principles "The only things that count are the finished product and the bottom line": time and motion studies	*Focus of management principles* "Everything counts": studies of interdependent processes, information flows and feedback, environments and contingencies
Management of individuals as interchangeable parts	Management of relationships among components; focus on groups and networks
Planning the work, working the plan	Planning the work, using feedback to correct the plan
Motivation by fear and money	Motivation by needs and contingencies

(continued)

TABLE
4.1
The Evolution of Scientific Management into Systems Theory
(continued)

SCIENTIFIC MANAGEMENT	SYSTEMS THEORIES
Theory of communication	*Theory of communication*

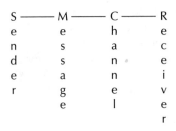

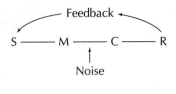

(Linear, Top–Down Model)	(Environments)

Theory of leadership: Trait (tall, white males with blonde hair and blue eyes, who come from strong moral backgrounds)

Theory of leadership: Adaptive (rhetorical contingency): Anyone can learn the skills of leading by attending to the requirements of behavioral flexibility

Limitations: Humans are more complex than machines; encourages individual boredom and deep divisions between managers and employees; discourages communication, individual needs, job initiative, task innovation, personal responsibility, and empowerment

Limitations: Humans are symbolic as well as biological; encourages mathematical complexities that are difficult to put into everyday practices; communication is equated with information

BIOLOGY AND GENERAL SYSTEMS THEORY

Within the broad context of the information revolution there emerged a more specific contributor to systems theory—the life sciences, especially biology. It is easy to see why. A system is alive not because of any particular component or component process (e.g., a respiratory or digestive system), but because of the relationships and interchanges among processes. Within any system there are subsystems, and it is the connections between subsystems (e.g., how oxygen gets from the lungs into the blood, then into the muscles and synapses) that define the characteristics of biological or living organisms. To take a holistic approach means to consider the properties of systems that come out of the relationships among their parts.

Biologists Ludwig von Bertalanffy (1968) and J. G. Miller (1978) are credited with advancing the study of living systems, and von Bertalanffy with pioneering the development of *general systems theory* in particular. It applies the properties of living systems, such as input, output, boundaries, homeostasis, and equifinality, to a dazzling array of social phenomena. (See Table 4.2 for an overview of the hierarchy of general systems theory.) As biologist Lewis Thomas explains in his landmark work, *The Lives of a Cell* (1975):

> Although we are by all odds the most social of all social animals—more interdependent, more attached to each other, more inseparable in our behavior than bees—we do not often feel our conjoined intelligence. Perhaps it is in this respect that language differs most sharply from biological systems for communication. Ambiguity seems to be an essential, indispensable element for the transfer of information from one place to another by words, where matters of real importance are concerned. It is often necessary, for meaning to come through, that there be an almost vague sense of strangeness and askewness. Speechless animals and cells cannot do this. . . . Only the human mind is designed to work this way, programmed to drift away in the presence of locked-on information, straying from each point in the hunt for a better, different point. (pp. 89–94)

In other words, the ambiguity of language makes the interdependencies between members of a social system (i.e., among people) looser than those found in biology or those that connect the parts of a car. "Social organizations, in contrast to physical or mechanical structures, are *loosely coupled* systems" (Scott, 1981, p. 103).

Thus, with the advent of relativity and the initiation of analogies between organic systems and human societies, the concept of dynamic systems was born, offering innovative ways of understanding the relationships among functioning components in space and time. But applying systems theory to human language and the ability to communicate symbolically and ambiguously would prove to be challenging. The work of chemist Ilya Prigogine (1980) has helped to expand the potential application of systems thinking to social organization. By studying

TABLE
4.2 The Hierarchy of General Systems Theory

LEVEL	DESCRIPTION AND EXAMPLES	THEORY AND MODELS
Static structures	Atoms, molecules, crystals, biological structures from the electron microscope to the macroscopic level	Structural formulas of chemistry; crystallography; anatomical descriptions
Clockworks	Clocks, conventional machines in general, solar systems	Conventional physics, such as the laws of mechanics (Newton and Einstein)
Control mechanisms	Thermostat, servomechanisms, homeostatic mechanism in organisms	Cybernetics; feedback and information theory
Open systems	Flame, cells, and organisms in general	Expansion of physical theory to systems maintaining themselves in flow of matter (metabolism); information storage in genetic code (DNA)
Lower organisms	Plantlike organisms: Increasing differentiation of system (so-called division of labor in the organism); distinction of reproduction and functional individual ("germ track and soma")	Theory and models most lacking
Animals	Increasing importance of traffic in information (evolution of receptors, nervous systems); learning; beginnings of consciousness	Beginnings in automata theory (stimulus-response relations), feedback (regulatory phenomena), autonomous behavior (relaxation oscillations)
Humans	Symbolism; past and future, self and world, self-awareness as consequences; communication by language	Incipient theory of symbolism
Sociocultural systems	Populations of organisms (humans included); symbol-determined communities (cultures) in humans only	Statistical and possibly dynamic laws in population dynamics, sociology, economics, possibly history; beginnings of a cultural systems theory
Symbolic systems	Language, logic, mathematics, sciences, arts, morals	Algorithms of symbols (e.g., mathematics, grammar); "rules of the game," such as in visual arts and music

Source: Ludwig von Bertalanffy, *General Systems Theory* (New York: George Braziller, 1968), pp. 28–29.

chemical reactions, Prigogine found that in open systems (i.e., those that must interact with their environments to survive), a movement toward disorder often precedes the emergence of a new order. In contrast to the Newtonian vision of a universe constantly falling apart, Prigogine's findings suggest that both living and nonliving systems have the potential for self-organization or self-renewal in the face of environmental change, and that disorder is a natural part of this process.

FROM BIOLOGY TO ORGANIZATIONAL COMMUNICATION

Academic disciplines whose traditional focus had been on complex processes of information exchange instead embraced systems theory. Sociologist Albion Small (1905) used concepts of systems theory in his influential work at the University of Chicago, and other prominent social theorists, such as Talcott Parsons (1951) and George Homans (1961), followed suit. Similarly, the initial popularity of the systems approach to organizational communication studies was enormous. Daniel Katz and Robert Kahn's *The Social Psychology of Organizations* (1966), a landmark application of systems theory to organizations, argues that organizations are fundamentally open systems in which people are bonded together by symbolic and behavioral responses to their environments. Sociologist W. Richard Scott, in *Organizations* (1981), reviews the history of organizational studies from three perspectives—rational, natural, and open systems—and maintains that each one contributes useful information about the nature of organizing. In the field of organizational communication, then, systems theory provided a new connection between communicating and organizing. After all, symbolic interactionism (Mead, 1934) maintains that meaning only exists in relationships, and that the individual can develop only through interaction.

Enthusiastic about the potential of this approach, Richard Farace, Peter Monge, and Hamish Russell devote an organizational communication textbook to the systems approach—*Communicating and Organizing* (1977), thereby endorsing the now commonly heard statement, "Communication *is* the process of organizing." This means that only through communication can organizations come into being and continue to exist. In addition, communication is *not* inside, outside, or tangential to the organization; rather, it *is* the organization. (Table 4.3 provides a summary of this groundbreaking use of systems theory.)

What Is a System?

A *system* is a complex set of relationships among interdependent parts or components. In the study of organizational communication, we are concerned with the nature of those components in organizations and with the relationships among them. Table 4.4 summarizes the strengths and weaknesses of five such components of systems theory.

ENVIRONMENT AND OPEN SYSTEMS

According to systems theory, organizations do not exist as entities isolated from the rest of the world. Rather, organizations exist in increasingly turbulent *environments,* which provide inputs to the organization and receive outputs in the form of products and services. For a company to succeed today, some of its members must spend a significant amount of time engaged in *environmental scanning,* the careful monitoring of competitors, suppliers, government legislation, global economics, and consumer preferences. Failure to do so leaves an organization open to unexpected *environmental jolts,* which can have disastrous consequences. In most successful companies, environmental scanning is done by *boundary spanners;* these employees usually have the greatest opportunity for interaction with people outside of the company.

An organization's relationship with its environment, however, is not limited to scanning. As *open systems,* organizations must also work with their environments to be successful (e.g., by establishing joint ventures and strategic partnerships). The analogy between organizations and living organisms helps to explain the concept of open systems. Organisms are open systems in that they rely on exchanges with their environment to survive (human beings, for example, need food, air, and sunlight to live). Similarly, organizations rely on communication with their environments to survive. As Walter Buckley (1967) explains, "That a system is *open* means, not simply that it engages in interchanges with the environment, but that this interchange is an *essential factor* underlying the system's viability, its reproductive ability or continuity, and its ability to change" (p. 50). Therefore, an open system that interacts productively with its environment might be called "negentropic," in that it tends to create structure or, more simply, to organize, whereas in a closed system there is little or no interaction with the environment and the organization may approach entropy or disorder (see Focus on Ethics 4.1 for an example).

INTERDEPENDENCE

Another essential quality of a system, *interdependence* refers to the wholeness of the system and its environment, and to the interrelationships of individuals within the system. These relationships can vary in terms of their degree of interdependence. For example, a student's refusal to acknowledge the legitimacy of a particular instructor would have a negative effect on the student's performance in the course but only a minimal effect on the instructor because of the student–teacher relationship: The student is dependent on the instructor but the instruc-

TABLE
4.3
The Structural-Functional Use of Systems Theory

Theme: Communication processes in organizations include gathering, processing, storing, and disseminating information.

ORGANIZATION

Definition: "Five key elements: (1) two or more individuals (2) who recognize that some of their goals can be more readily achieved through interdependent (cooperative) actions, even though disagreement (conflict) may be present; (3) who take in materials, energy, and information from the environment in which they exist; (4) who develop coordinative and control relationships to capitalize on their interdependence while operating on these inputs; (5) and who return the modified inputs to the environments, in an attempt to accomplish the goals that interdependence was meant to make possible" (Farace, Monge, & Russell, 1977, p. 16).

Or: Size, interdependence, input, throughput, and output

Features
1. As size increases, longer time periods are required for messages and materials to move within the organization; therefore, growth poses many problems, including integrating new members into the organization.

2. Without interdependence, organization (and hence, larger

INFORMATION

Definition: "One of the primary ingredients in the concept of information is the discernment of pattern in the matter/energy flows that reach an individual" (Farace, Monge, & Russell, 1977, p. 22).

Or: Pattern discernment that reduces uncertainty in a situation

Features

Einstein showed that matter/energy are interchangeable; this

COMMUNICATION

Definition: "Communication refers to the exchange of symbols that are commonly shared by the individuals involved, and that evoke quite similar symbol-referent relationships in each individual" (Farace, Monge, & Russell, 1977, p. 26).

Or: Shared symbol systems

Features

Symbols have real-world referents; to the extent that persons

(continued)

TABLE
4.3   The Structural-Functional Use of Systems Theory *(continued)*

ORGANIZATION	INFORMATION	COMMUNICATION
goal achievement) is impossible.	means that until a pattern is discerned, there is no information, just matter/energy.	use the same symbol systems, effective communication is likely; when they differ markedly, communication is impeded or made impossible.
3. Organizations have boundaries that separate them from the outside world; inputs originate outside the organization and enter the organization through openings in the boundary.	Discerned patterns *differ* from individual to individual; there is no objective pattern that exists apart from at least one individual recognizing it.	From Ackoff (1957): "We shall say that a communication which changes the probabilities of choice, *informs;* one that changes the value of the outcomes, *motivates;* and one that changes the efficiencies of the course of action, *instructs.*"
4. *Throughputs* are the activities performed by organizational members—the passage of materials, energy, and information from point to point within the organization, to its exit. *Control processes* are established to govern and regulate throughput activity; *coordination* attempts to make every member and every activity operate in harmony.	Patterning and information are *not* synonymous. Patterns may be random; hence, *uncertainty* refers to how confident you are about something.	*Noise* and *distortion* can interfere with communication; *redundancy* minimizes the negative effects of noise and distortion.
5. *Output activities* describe the return to the environment of the materials, energy, and information that have been processed and the rewards or goals sought are reaped.	*Uncertainty* is a measurement based on (1) the number of alternative patterns identified in the situation, and (2) the probabilities of occurrence for each alternative. The greater the number of patterns, the greater the uncertainty. The more uncertainty present in a situation, the more information value a pattern has when it appears.	

Source: Adapted from Richard V. Farace, Peter R. Monge, and Hamish M. Russell, *Communicating and Organizing* (Reading, Mass.: Addison-Wesley Publishing Co., 1977).

TABLE
4.4
Summary of the Systems Approach

COMPONENTS	STRENGTHS	WEAKNESSES
Environment and open systems	Creates new ways of identifying communication problems as problems in relationships or networks, rather than in individuals	Communication network systems research has failed to focus on issues of communication content or social construction of meaning
Interdependence	Represents a major conceptual advance that takes advantage of Einsteinian physics; as such, it represents an attempt to connect theories of organization to theories of order	Expectations for what systems theory can do have not been easily met owing to difficulties of translating concepts into real theory or real research
Goals	Sensitizes our study of multiple political agendas and the fact that a goal at one system level may undermine or support goals at other levels	May focus too much on natural evolutionary change, and not enough on intuitive, breakthrough thinking
Processes and feedback	Enriches the study of communication and organizations through a vocabulary that focuses on the complexities and relationships of human structures and functions	Structural-functionalism is very mechanistic
Openness, order, and contingency	Fosters an appreciation for the contingent and relative nature of organizations and communication	
	Models of systems are amenable to sophisticated statistical measurements	

tor is only minimally *inter*dependent. In contrast, because most marriages are characterized by a high degree of interdependence, the decision of one partner to withdraw emotionally from the relationship would put the whole system at risk. In systems theory, then, the interdependent relationships between people not only give an organization its character, but they are also established and maintained through communication.

The failure to recognize interdependence in dynamic systems leads to what ecologist Garrett Hardin (1968) calls the "Tragedy of the Commons." It takes place when a group of people with access to a common resource use it in ways that focus on personal needs rather than on the needs of the whole, leading to such tragedies as the destruction of rainforests, the exploitation of grazing land, and the pollution of major waterways. While each individual's actions may make sense from his or her perspective, the failure to recognize the interdependency and consequences of one's actions can be devastating to both the individual and the collectivity.

In organizations, the division of labor can cloud the interdependent nature of people's work. For example, when we toured a company that manufactures high-technology radio transmitters, we asked employees to describe the various kinds of jobs available in the company and whether they had considered cross-training or moving to a different department. We found that most employees in the company were unaware of the nature of their co-workers' jobs. Although familiar with the processes they controlled directly, they were not aware of the origin of their work materials or the destination of their finished products. Even employees within the same work group had little awareness of each other's jobs despite their daily contacts. One employee, who for fifteen years had been handing over his finished parts to a co-worker (through a small window in an interior wall), had no idea what the co-worker did with the parts. Representing a worst-case scenario from a systems perspective, the company's employees did not see themselves as part of an interdependent system because of the strict division of labor. In an interdependent system, no part of the system can stand alone but relies on the other parts to do its job effectively. Furthermore, difficulty at any point in the system can eventually affect the whole.

A popular concept in the business press today, *reengineering* is based on the argument that it is often too difficult (and thereby ineffective) to respond to environmental challenges by making incremental improvements in the organization (Hammer & Champy, 1993). Since most organizations are still structured according to hierarchies and departments, they cannot accommodate the flexibility or diversity of functions needed to satisfy today's customer. Consequently, the process of reengineering begins with the question, Who needs to be connected to whom to get this work done? Often new communication technology is used in reengineering efforts to provide instantaneous connections between suppliers and employees within different areas of expertise.

GOALS

Organizational *goals* are defined in various ways by theories of organization and communication. Particularly in the twentieth century, there has been much disagreement on the existence and importance of goals in organizations. From a scientific management perspective, goals are central and both individual and

The Addictive Organizational System

Organizational systems are not always open, nor do they always foster openness. An addictive system encourages individuals to become dependent on the system and to shut out external influences. As a result, employees may become addicted to their work, overworking, covering up, and striving to please the boss. As Anne Wilson Schaef and Diane Fassel (1988) explain:

> The addictive system operates from the same characteristics that individual addicts have routinely exhibited. The major defense mechanism of the addictive system is denial, which supports a closed system. If something does not exist, it simply does not have to be considered. Corporations frequently say, "We have a minor problem, but certainly not a major one." "We are having a sales slump, but it is only temporary." The alcoholic says, "I am not an alcoholic. I may have a small drinking problem, and I may overdo it a bit on weekends or under stress, but I do not have a severe problem." (p. 62)

In addition, an addictive (or closed) organizational system has the following characteristics:

1. *Confusion:* prevents us from taking responsibility and therefore helps us remain powerless over our addiction.
2. *Self-centeredness:* allows the addict to interpret all actions of others as either "for" or "against" them; also reduces the complexities of living to whatever is necessary to get the "fix."
3. *Dishonesty:* Addicts are master liars and have perfected the "con." Addicts lie to themselves, to people around them, and to the world at large.

(continued)

organizational action is directed at goal-attainment. From an institutional perspective, organizations and their members may espouse goals, but rarely do their goals guide their behavior (Scott, 1981, p. 21). In the open systems perspective, goals are negotiated among interdependent factions in the organization and are heavily influenced by its environment.

(continued)

4. *Perfectionism:* Addicts are obsessed with not being good enough and compensate by trying to never make mistakes. This gives them the illusion of control (Schaef & Fassel, 1988).

The results of addictive organizational systems raise ethical concerns. Consider how you would deal with the following situations:

1. You work for an organization that is proud of its strong culture and work ethic. You and your co-workers enjoy the benefits of working for a highly successful company and feel very much a part of the dominant culture. But you routinely give up your evenings and weekends to participate in work-related activities for no additional pay or recognition, and your family life has suffered as a result. For the past two years, your family vacationed without you while you stayed home and worked. You love your job and the people you work with, but you feel estranged from life outside of the organization and you want to improve your family life. What can you do to address the situation? Quit your job? Redefine your relationship with the company? Speak to co-workers about your dilemma? In particular, think about the ethical issues raised by your participation in an addictive organization.

2. Your supervisor is a perfectionist, though she denies it. You think you do your job well, but your supervisor is not satisfied with your output. She often points out "small areas that need improvement" and has suggested that you give up some of your spare time to improve the quality of your work. You believe your supervisor is addicted to the organization. But she is viewed as a highly valued member of the company, and her work habits are the standard for all employees. You respect your supervisor, but you resent her implication that you do not contribute enough to the company that employs you. You are concerned about an ethical issue: How much personal sacrifice should a company expect from its employees? What might systems theory suggest as a remedy to your situation?

Michael Keeley (1980) makes an important distinction regarding organizational goals. Examining the traditional view of organizations as mobilized around common goals, he distinguishes between *the goals of individuals,* which are personal and highly variable, and the *goals individuals have for their organization,* which are more likely to be shared by others.

Goals can also differ across systems levels. For example, a unit at one level within a large corporation may seek the goal of profitability. At the next level, however, the corporation may be under pressure from stakeholders to raise cash; this corporate goal may cause it to try to sell the business unit (a decision that is unfavorable to the unit). At the same time, the other unit's goal of profitability may conflict with the individual goals of workers or managers within the unit, who may advocate such goals as improving product quality or focusing on strategic products at the expense of others. Thus, systems theory emphasizes that what is good for one level of the system may not be good for the other levels.

PROCESSES AND FEEDBACK

A system is not simply an interdependent set of components; it is also an inter-dependent collection of *processes* that interact over time. For instance, in order to sell radio transmitters, we would not only have to submit the orders to engineering or manufacturing, but we would also have to do so in a timely fashion to avoid inefficiency and other workflow-related problems. Engineering, in turn, would need to deliver accurate drawings to manufacturing on schedule, and manufacturing would be required to meet the customer's quality standards and delivery date. The reengineering approach is often directed at minimizing the time it takes to execute these processes.

Suppose, however, that the customer is dissatisfied with the radio transmitters and calls to cancel future orders. Or suppose the customer is generally pleased with the product but requests changes in its design. These are examples of *feedback,* which can be defined as a system of "loops" that connect communication and action. Individuals provide messages to others, who then respond to those messages in some way. The response closes the loop, providing communicators with information about how their messages were received. In other words, feedback contains information about the influence of a particular message or action, and it is usually expressed as a deviation from what the sender intended.

Feedback thus controls systems of communication by regulating the flow and interpretation of messages. In systems theory, there are two main types of feedback: negative and positive. *Negative* or *deviation-counteracting feedback* is illustrated by the customer's complaint about the radio transmitters. The negative feedback seeks to reestablish the goals or quality levels that were initially established for the product. (This type of feedback is sometimes referred to as *morphostasis* or *cybernetics,* after the Greek "steersman" who used his oars to stay on course.) The other type of feedback, *positive* or *deviation-amplifying feedback,* is illustrated by the customer who requests changes in product design. It seeks to find new avenues of growth and development. Positive feedback is often referred to generally as *second cybernetics* (or *morphogenesis*) (Maruyama,

1963). (Other, more complex forms of feedback, such as causal loops and cause maps, are discussed later in the chapter.)

Chris Argyris and Donald Schon (1978) assert in their work on learning organizations that today's businesses need both deviation-counteracting and deviation-amplifying feedback in order to achieve success. While deviation-countering feedback ensures adherence to an established strategy or course of action, deviation-amplifying feedback ensures that alternative strategies or courses of action are considered. Argyris terms the latter practice "double-loop learning," or the ability to "learn how to learn" by reexamining established assumptions and decision premises.

OPENNESS, ORDER, AND CONTINGENCY

Systems theory evokes the image of a complex, interdependent organization that operates within a dynamic environment and is engaged in an ongoing struggle to create order in the face of unpredictability (Clegg, 1990; Thompson, 1967). In retrospect, it is surprising that classical management theories of bureaucracy paid so little attention to an organization's environment, focusing instead on treating all organizations equally and directing management to conduct careful studies of the one best way to accomplish work within the boundaries of the organization. Ideas about environments or global economics were considered irrelevant or misplaced.

In contrast, today's open systems are less reassuring and more unpredictable. But *openness* helps organizations see themselves as part of a dynamic system of intricate interdependencies and relationships. Openness in the organization–environment relationship also has implications for some of the prescriptive aspects of organizational theory. The existence of diverse environments across industries, companies, and even geographical regions means that the same organizing principles and solutions cannot be applied in all situations; rather, they are *contingent* on various contextual and environmental factors. In systems theory, the term "equifinality" means that the same goal may be reached in multiple ways. Jay Galbraith (1973) summarizes the principles of contingency theory as follows:

1. There is no one best way to organize.
2. Any way of organizing is not equally effective.

These principles imply not only that the forms of organizing that will work best depend on the environment, but also that the match between certain organizational approaches and specific environments should be explored because some approaches will work better than others. Organizations that exist in complex and highly turbulent environments require different forms of leadership, interpersonal communication, decision making, and organizational structure than those in relatively predictable environments (Emery & Trist, 1965; Lawrence & Lorsch, 1967).

Much of the research that adopts a systems perspective on organizational communication focuses on the relationships and interdependencies among individuals. One prevalent approach operationalizes these interdependencies as linkages within communication networks (see Chapter 9). Another application focuses on the relationships among whole organizations. Howard Aldrich and Jeffrey Pfeffer (1976) explain two variations of this approach: *natural selection*, which examines an interorganizational field over time to determine the kinds of organizations that are most fit to survive, and *resource dependency*, which focuses on the proactive ways in which organizations can establish key interdependencies with others in the field as a means of strategic adaptation to and survival in certain environments. However, neither of these approaches pays much attention to the role of communication.

The Appeal of Systems Theory for Organizational Communication

Systems theory appeals to students of organizational communication because it highlights the importance of communication processes in organizing. In addition, it is theoretically capable of capturing much of the complexity of these processes. While experience tells us that communication is complex and takes place over time, earlier theories were based on the simple idea that communication involved the sending and receiving of messages.

Systems theory has also been disappointing in two respects. First, its expectations have not been easily met. In general, researchers have had difficulty translating the concepts of systems theory into research findings. Scholars unable to create dynamic systems theories of communication often lacked the methodological tools needed to analyze complex systems of communication and feedback. Systems theories are ideally tested using statistical methods that accommodate multiple factors interacting over time. Since both theories and methods for dealing with complex processes are rare, systems theory has often been characterized as an appealing but abstract set of concepts with little applicability to actual theory or research (Poole, 1996).

Second, the potential of two applications of systems theory to communication—structural-functionalism and communication network analysis—has not been realized. The structural-functionalism application involves the step-by-step identification of inputs, outputs, mechanisms, and traits. Communication network analysis, developed by researchers at Michigan State University and the

State University of New York at Buffalo, maps the connections between parts of a system (or between people in organizations). But neither application focuses specifically on issues of communication content and the social construction of *meaning*. This in itself is not a weakness, but it has a strong impact on the kinds of questions to which systems theory can be applied. While broad questions about structure and process can be addressed, other questions regarding the nature, meaning, and interpretation of messages are less easily addressed.

However, recent efforts to reinvigorate systems theory in ways that are compatible with organizational communication have been made by Margaret Wheatley, Peter Senge, and Karl Weick.

WHEATLEY'S NEW SCIENCE OF LEADERSHIP

Management professor Margaret Wheatley (1992) has received a great deal of attention for her attempt to bring to management the principles and aesthetics of what she calls the *new science*—a combination of quantum physics, self-organizing systems theory, and chaos theory. "In new science, the underlying currents are a movement toward holism, toward understanding the system as a system and giving primacy to the relationships that exist among seemingly discrete parts" (p. 9). In this regard, Wheatley's critique of the machine metaphor of organizations is consistent with our argument thus far. She relies heavily on Prigogine's (1980) theory of "dissipative structures," which views disorder as "a full partner" in the search for order. Just as Frederick Taylor's (1947) first "scientific management" required what he called a "mental revolution," so too does Wheatley's new science depend on major changes in the way we think about the world. Regarding the new science, Wheatley argues the following points:

1. There are no "things" in themselves; even particles of matter are "intermediate states in a network of interactions." This is true for people as well as for organizations. Information is the creative energy of the universe.
2. All living things are naturally engaged in self-renewal, and organizations do this by making creative use of their environments.
3. The search for machine-like control by management is counterproductive. "The more freedom in self-organization, the more order" (Jantsch, 1980, p. 40).
4. What we would call disorder is part of the natural process of order-making.
5. The desire to make meaning is the "strange attractor" that keeps human beings in a constant tendency toward self-organization.

The major implication of Wheatley's approach is that people in organizations—especially leaders—must take a different attitude than they had previously toward order and control. She suggests that positive outcomes are more likely to occur in an atmosphere that fosters collaboration, experimentation, and self-renewal than in one characterized by regulation and top–down control. In addition, communication is critical to the organization's ability to organize. Further research in this area includes Contractor's (1992) work on chaos theory and Steier and Smith's (1992) study of self-organizing systems.

SENGE'S LEARNING ORGANIZATION

Management theorist Peter Senge (1990) has been especially successful at bringing systems thinking to those who actually manage corporations. Like Wheatley, he is both concerned with holism and inclined to use scientific terminology. But Senge focuses on the distinction between what he calls *learning organizations* and organizations that have a *learning disability* or a lack of understanding about how they function as systems. *Learning organizations* practice these five disciplines:

1. *Systems thinking.* Combining holism and interdependence, this holds that for any one member to succeed, all members must succeed.
2. *Personal mastery.* All members share a personal commitment to learning and self-reflection.
3. *Mental models.* Because learning is a kind of self-renewal, it must begin with self-reflection, particularly reflection on the "mental models" that shape and limit an individual's interpretations and actions.
4. *A shared vision.* Tight hierarchical control is replaced by "concertive control" (Tompkins & Cheney, 1993), whereby members act in concert because they share a common organizational vision and understand how their own work helps to build on that shared vision.
5. *Team learning.* Team members communicate in ways that lead the team toward intelligent decisions, with an emphasis on dialogue as the key to team learning.

According to Senge (1990), developing a learning organization requires a major "shift of mind," one that is consistent with our argument thus far in this book. In addition to revitalizing systems theory, Senge's discussion of mental models is reminiscent of theories of selective perception, wherein all perception is limited. What one does with differences in mental models—and how one moves on to team learning—is critical to Senge's approach and our interest in it.

Senge and his colleagues (Senge et al., 1995) at the MIT Dialogue Project build on the work of physicist David Bohm (1980) on the role of consciousness in communication problems. That is, our tendency to see ourselves as separate from the world affects our dealings with others. Bohm argues that the result is *discussion* or "participative openness," wherein we advocate our opinions, but because we are unwilling to suspend our certainty about our own worldview, no real learning takes place. In contrast, *dialogue* or "reflective openness" "starts with the willingness to challenge our own thinking, to recognize that any certainty we have is, at best, a hypothesis about the world" (Senge, 1990, p. 277). From this point, dialogue progresses through a combination of advocacy and inquiry, wherein we collectively offer and expose our ideas to tough scrutiny by others. The primary distinction between dialogue and the typical problem-solving meeting in business is that the former places more value on the communication process, and group members are thereby more willing to distance themselves from their own opinions and ideas.

Although Senge's dialogic approach to learning organizations has been criticized for its lack of attention to earlier studies of communication, it nonetheless contributes to systems theory. Specifically, it points to an explicit link between systems thinking and actual communicative processes, and it emphasizes that the sharing of opinions and perspectives is, at best, a degenerative form of dialogue. Hence, we learn that effective communication in organizations, if it is to lead us beyond polarized points of view and political debates, involves a commitment to changing how we communicate with and relate to others.

WEICK'S SENSE-MAKING MODEL

Karl Weick's exploration of sense-making, developed in his books *The Social Psychology of Organizing* (1979) and *Sensemaking in Organizations* (1995), has influenced the field of organizational behavior and communication. In particular, his work has reinvigorated systems theory by connecting it with issues of sense-making, meaning, and communication, while also providing a bridge for the development of cultural studies of organizations (see Chapter 5).

According to Weick (1979), organizations exist in highly complex and unpredictable environments. The job of organizing involves making sense of the uncertainties in environments through interaction, a process that Weick calls "equivocality reduction." Thus, in the process of identifying the meaning of a given situation or event, the same facts can be interpreted in various ways by different observers. How the members of an organization communicate to make sense of equivocal situations is central to Weick's approach.

As illustrated in Figure 4.1, Weick's (1979) model of organizing has three parts: enactment, selection, and retention. In *enactment,* organizational members create enacted environments through their actions and patterns of attention, and these environments can vary in terms of their perceived degree of equivocality or uncertainty. Once an environment is enacted, the organizing process requires the participants to select from among a number of possible interpretations the best explanation of the environment's meaning. In *selection,* then, collective sense-making is accomplished through communication.

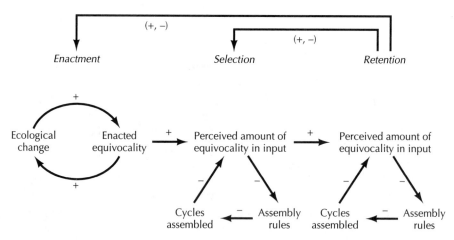

FIGURE 4.1
Weick's Model of Organizing

Source: Karl Weick, *The Social Psychology of Organizing* (New York: Random House, 1979).
Reprinted by permission.

Finally, in *retention,* the best interpretations are retained for future use. Retained interpretations also influence future selection processes, as indicated by the feedback arrow in Figure 4.1. Sense-making is thus represented by Weick as a set of interdependent processes that interact with and provide feedback to each other. In this sense, his model connects systems thinking with interpretation.

Perhaps Weick's (1979) most revolutionary concept is that of the *enacted environment.* Unlike theories of species evolution, in which degrees of environmental variation are determined objectively, in organizational environments people look for clues to threats or opportunities. Their perception is highly selective and dependent on their interests, motives, background, behavior, and other characteristics. Therefore, a company dominated by engineers would focus on changes in science and technology, whereas an organization made up mainly of accountants would focus on financial markets and global economic trends. This concept of the enacted environment is especially important in today's business world, wherein environmental scanning is crucial to an organization's survival. Among the most critical but often overlooked keys to organizational success involves keeping in touch with current issues through reading relevant articles in newspapers and journals and maintaining contacts with others. Many times businesspeople overlook the importance of environmental scanning and miss articles that have a direct bearing on the success of their company. But because the enacted environment is always limited by subjective perception, organizational success requires an ongoing examination of current issues.

Weick extends his model of organizing through three important concepts: retrospective sense-making, loose coupling, and partial inclusion.

Retrospective Sense-Making

An underlying assumption in Weick's model is that decision making is largely *retrospective.* In other words, although people in organizations *think* they plan first and then act according to a plan, Weick argues that people really act first and later examine their actions in an attempt to explain their meaning. He sums this up in what he calls a "recipe": "How can I know what I think until I see what I say?" (1979). Weick (1995) goes on to identify seven "properties of sense-making" as follows:

1. *Identity construction:* The recipe is a question about who I am as indicated by [the] discovery of how and what I think.
2. *Retrospect:* To learn what I think, I look back over what I said earlier.
3. *Enactment:* I create the object to be seen and inspected when I say or do something.
4. *Social:* What I say and single out and conclude are determined by who socialized me and how I was socialized, as well as by the audience I anticipate will audit the conclusions I reach.
5. *Ongoing:* My talking is spread across time, competes for attention with other ongoing projects, and is reflected on after it is finished, which means my interests may already have changed.
6. *Extracted cues:* The "what" that I single out and embellish as the content of the thought is only a small portion of the utterance that becomes salient because of the context and personal dispositions.
7. *Plausibility:* I need to know enough about what I think to get on with my projects, but no more, which means sufficiency and plausibility take precedence over accuracy. (pp. 61–62)

The close fit between the recipe and the seven properties remains when we change the pronouns in the recipe to reflect a collective actor (e.g., "How can *we* know what *we* think until *we* see what *we* say?").

However, Weick's theory of retrospective sense-making does not take into account that some people do act first and interpret later, while others strive to act only in accordance with predetermined plans. Perhaps both processes are always at work. But the important point in Weick's argument is that the balance between planned and unplanned behavior is often the reverse of what we assume it to be. Thus, Weick takes Herbert Simon's (1976) contention that members of an organization are only "intentedly rational" to its logical extreme (see Chapter 3). Such challenges to common-sense beliefs have been called "counter-rational" approaches to organizational theory. Weick pushes this position to the limit, even arguing that random decision-making processes may be superior to rational methods of decision making and planning. His work in this area further unravels the scientific approach to management, wherein communication serves only as a conduit for the one best way of doing things. In contrast, the manager in Weick's model is a manipulator of symbols who motivates employees to make sense of their work life. Interaction is thus emphasized over reflection, with an accompanying bias for action. According to Weick, employees do not need common goals to work well together, nor do they need to know precisely what decisions they will make before they make them. More important, according to Weick, is a willingness to engage in coordinated action aimed at reducing equivocality, which over time may lead employees to discover (in retrospect) the meaning of the course of action that emerges.

Loose Coupling

At the same time that Weick stresses the importance of communication at work, he also points out that, unlike the connections among biological systems, the communication connections among people in organizations vary in intensity and are often loose or weak. Weick's (1976) concept of *loosely coupled systems* has had a major impact on our understanding of organizations as communication systems.

Consider, for example, the typical college or university, in which a great deal of interaction occurs *within* departments but not *across* departments in the various fields of study. The activities of the history department have little effect on those of the engineering department. Similarly, loose or weak connections usually exist among the university's nonacademic units (staff, administration, and faculty) as well. The university is a classic example of a loosely coupled system.

Whereas rational approaches maintain that loose connections tend to deter people from working together to achieve a common goal, Weick (1979) argues that such connections can be advantageous. The multiple goals of an organization can be coordinated without extensive communication or consensus (Eisenberg, 1984, 1986, 1990, 1995). In addition, a loosely coupled system is better able to withstand environmental jolts. In a system of close or tight connections, environmental jolts can affect the entire system, whereas in a loosely coupled system the whole is less affected because of the weak connections among units. Although it is subject to redundancy and inefficiency, a loosely coupled system may still be effective in the long term.

Partial Inclusion

In analyzing the balance between work and other activities, Weick (1979) uses his theory of *partial inclusion* to explain why certain strategies for motivating employees are ineffective. He holds that employees are only partially included in the workplace; that is, at work we see some but not all of their behaviors. An unmotivated employee at work may be a church leader or a model parent, whereas the top performer at a company may engage in few outside activities. In either case, simple theories of organizational behavior are limited when they fail to consider the employee's activities, roles, and interests outside of the workplace.

Weick (1979) clearly differentiates himself from those who value profitability above all else. He sees organizations as communities or social settings in which we choose to spend most of our adult lives. As such, organizations provide opportunities for storytelling and socializing; according to Weick, "they haven't anything else to give" (p. 264). A closer analysis of organizations as communities is the primary goal of the cultural approach, our focus in Chapter 5.

SUMMARY

The broad term *systems approach* encompasses many theories with various assumptions and implications for action. In contrast to earlier organizational theories (many of which can be classified according to their underlying view of the goals of organizing and of workers), systems theory is more open-ended. Adopting a systems approach requires acknowledging the openness and complexity of social organizations as well as the importance of relationships among individuals over time.

In practice, however, a systems approach can either help or hinder situated individuals. It can help individuals better understand overall workings of the organization. It emphasizes the importance of relationships and networks of contacts in allowing groups and organizations to achieve goals that are greater than those of the individual. A systems perspective can also reveal important interdependencies, particularly the connections with organizational environments that can affect an organization's survival. Despite its focus on communication and relationships, however, systems theory does not help to explain the meanings constructed by interactions. It can identify the potential participants in a productive organizational dialogue, but it cannot tell us about the content of that dialogue. It is in this area that Weick augments systems theory with issues related to sense-making, the key process of organizing.

However, systems theory may also be applied in a way that elevates the whole and ignores or dehumanizes individuals. Any recognition of the role of whole systems must be accompanied by an understanding of how individuals create, refine, and destroy them. In the following passage, one of the founders of systems theory admits to its limited applicability to the individual in social organizations:

> [A human being] is not only a political animal, he [or she] is, . . . above all, an individual. The real values of humanity are not those it shares with biological entities, the function of an organism or a community of animals, but those which stem from the individual mind. Human society is not a community of ants or termites, governed by inherited instinct and controlled by laws of the superordinate whole; it is based on the achievements of the individual and is doomed if the individual is made a cog in the social machine. This, I believe, is the ultimate precept a theory of organization can give: not a manual for dictators of any denomination to more efficiently subjugate human beings by the scientific application of iron laws, but a warning that the Leviathan of organization must not swallow the individual without sealing its own inevitable doom. (Von Bertalanffy, 1968, pp. 52–53)

Systems theory is likely to continue to exert significant influence on the field of organizational communication. Particularly in organizations that produce complex products or provide complex services, systems theory is evident in discussions of workflow analysis, internal customers, and cross-functional work groups, as well as in the use of control charts and process maps. Finally, businesses are increasingly recognizing the critical role of markets and environments in their survival. The long-term impact of systems theory on organizations will inevitably lead to further research.

STARGAZERS[1]

Hobbyscope, a midsized manufacturer of hobby telescopes, microscopes, binoculars, and other optical equipment, employs approximately 1,500 employees. Lyn, the manager of the Jr. Scientist product line, has been slow in bringing to Hobbyscope some of the team-based management techniques she learned in her previous job at Astroshock (which manufactures shock absorbers for use in space shuttles). Because most employees at Hobbyscope have been with the company for over twenty years and have well-defined ideas about how to do their jobs, Lyn has proceeded cautiously. In addition, the Jr. Scientist products have changed little during the past decade.

Ray Radar, the president and sole owner of Hobbyscope, recently added a new line of telescopes—Stargazers—designed for astronomy courses at the large state university system. The agreement with the state university system's purchasing department specifies that the telescopes must be delivered in bulk to each campus's bookstore at the start of each quarter. The order has required a major shift in Hobbyscope's production process, given the large quantity and multiple delivery peaks. In the past, Hobbyscope built up its inventory during most of the year in anticipation of the Christmas–New Year's shutdown.

The new line of Stargazer telescopes was initially set up by the owner's son, Roger Radar. It has increased the company's annual sales volume by 800 percent and opened negotiations for other equipment needed by the university system. Just after the first fall quarter delivery date, however, Roger was moved upstairs to help manage the company's newest venture into medical optical equipment. Mr. Radar, impressed with Lyn's performance on the Jr. Scientist line, has promoted her to manager of Stargazers.

After only two weeks in her new position, Lyn has encountered numerous problems. The sales department has been flooded with complaints about the Stargazers' flawed lenses and other damaged parts, all

(continued)

[1]Thanks to Dr. Patricia Riley for this case study.

marked as approved by Inspector 12. Students unable to complete assignments and bookstore purchasing managers have phoned Hobbyscope to request immediate refunds or replacements for their defective telescopes.

Lyn has discovered that the large order was handled by traditional Hobbyscope methods, which lack production process controls. She has also discovered that "Inspector 12" is not an employee but merely an inspection sticker that Roger thought would be good advertising. In addition, Lyn has been unable to track the defective telescopes to a line or shift due to missing serial numbers and haphazard documentation. (When department employees were behind schedule, Roger had told them it was more important to produce the telescopes than to keep accurate records.) Although some of the units may have been damaged in shipping and handling, Lyn's initial review suggests that the main problem was the faulty manufacturing process.

The state purchasing agent who approved Hobbyscope as the sole provider of the telescopes is scheduled to tour the plant and meet with the Stargazer team later in the week. Lyn has scheduled an emergency staff meeting to plan a strategy for dealing with the Stargazer manufacturing problems as well as an agenda for the upcoming meeting with the state purchasing agent. In attendance at the staff meeting are Lyn, Mary (vice president of marketing), Alex (sales manager), Spencer (vice president of product design), Wen-shu (manufacturing supervisor, day shift), and Jaime (vice president of public relations).

ASSIGNMENTS

1. What must be accomplished at the staff meeting before the team can meet with the state purchasing manager?
2. Create an agenda for the upcoming meeting. Determine how the team can best approach the problem, and prepare an opening statement to the state purchasing agent.
3. If the state purchasing agent asks to meet "Inspector 12," how should the team respond?
4. What other issues must the team address?

Cultural Studies of Organizations and Communication

The value of fiction lies in its consequences.
> • Michael Jackson, *Paths Toward a Clearing* (1989)

FOR DISCUSSION

- Why are symbolic action and metaphor central to the study of organizational cultures?
- What historical, political, and social trends contributed to the development of cultural studies of organizations?
- Which of the many different approaches to organizational culture are most useful?
- What major questions are posed by viewing organizations as cultures?
- What are the advantages and limitations of studying organizations as cultures?

123

This chapter introduces the idea of organizations as cultures. The *cultural approach* contradicts the more rational and formal approaches that preceded it, bringing a new focus on the language of the workplace, the routine versus dramatic performance of managers and employees, and the formal and informal practices that mark an organization's character, such as rites and rituals and the display of meaningful artifacts (e.g., architecture, interior design, and furniture). In addition, the chapter traces the history of the cultural approach; the social, methodological, and practical reasons for its popularity; and some of the ways it has been applied by researchers and managers. Finally, a communication view of organizational culture is outlined to show how an organization's unique patterns of interaction and sense-making represent its culture.

The Cultural Approach

Human beings have developed elaborate social cultures as guides to behavior (Eisenberg & Riley, in press; Geertz, 1973). People make sense of themselves in the context of a specific culture (or cultures), yet all cultures are created through people's thoughts and actions.

But what is *culture?* Anthropologist Marshall Sahlins (1976) defines culture as "meaningful orders of persons and things." By "meaningful orders" he means the complex processes and relationships within a culture that are revealed through the culture's symbols. He refers to "persons and things" as interdependent resources for interpreting the meanings of a culture and its symbols. Thus, we learn about a culture not only by what its members say about the culture, but also by the tools they use to create the culture, by the values they display in cultural artifacts, and by their development and possession of things.

A culture is also like a religion. According to T. S. Eliot (1949), "no culture has appeared or developed except together with a religion . . . [and] the culture will appear to be the product of the religion, or the religion the product of the culture" (p. 13). A culture is thereby created by locating a set of common beliefs and values that prescribes a general view of *order* (the way things are) and *explanation* (why things are that way). The tie between religion and culture is important to organizational studies because it indicates how the search for order and explanation compels beliefs.

However, not all members of a culture accept or practice those beliefs in the same way. Like religions, most cultures include various sects or subcultures that share the common order but whose ways of understanding or carrying out the beliefs differ. This point underscores the importance of approaching an organization's culture(s) as a dialogue with many different voices.

CULTURES AS SYMBOLIC CONSTRUCTIONS

The term *culture* is a symbol. It represents the actions, practices, stories (monologues and dialogues), and artifacts that characterize a culture. Similarly, we study the culture of an organization through its symbolic environment (e.g., its organized activities represent the search for meaningful orders) as well as through its uses of symbols (i.e., its actions, practices, stories, and artifacts). The study of organizational cultures thereby involves interpreting the meanings of these *symbolic constructions.*

Viewing organizations as symbols is useful for several reasons. First, all cultural studies begin with a fundamental appreciation of how human conceptions are formed in language. In this sense, then, language creates organizations as well as our understandings of them. Our search for meaningful orders of persons and things begins with what people *say* to each other about the *meanings* of things.

In addition, viewing organizations as symbolic constructions involves defining human beings as symbol-using and symbol-abusing animals, as Kenneth Burke does in his classic essay, "Definition of Man" (1966). (Table 5.1 summarizes the terms of his definition.) Burke's view helps us understand why symbols both *represent* or stand for other things and *evoke* other symbolic powers. For example, an organizational chart simultaneously provides information about hierarchy and relationships and suggests ways of behaving in the future. That is, symbols do not only stand for other things; they also shape our understandings of those things and help us to identify their meanings and uses. As such, symbols are instruments of human understanding and action. A company anticipating being sold, for example, begins to "talk" differently to itself, and these new ways of communicating in turn affect action, as a culture of apathy or cynicism may develop. The culture of an organization induces its members to think, act, and behave in particular ways. For example, the homogeneous organizational cultures of Pepsico and Disney are symbolically constructed by their individual members and serve as constraints on their members' actions and views.

Furthermore, symbol-using and symbol-abusing are inherently human activities. As Kenneth Burke (1982) points out, "All animals eat, but we are the only [animals] who gossip about restaurants or exchange recipes." Similarly, cultures are human constructions of reality. Only human beings both make languages out of symbols and make cultures out of languages. Therefore, studying how and why we make cultures out of symbols and languages tells us much about ourselves.

TABLE
5.1 **Burke's Definition of Humans as Symbol-Users**

Humans are:

1. Symbol-using (and symbol-abusing) animals	Symbols are shorthand terms for situations (how we talk about an event reveals how we understand it).
	Symbols contain motives for actions (the words we use induce us to behave in particular ways).
2. Inventors of the negative	Thou shalt not (we know what to do, in part, because of what we cannot or should not do).
	Dramatic *action* involves character, which involves *choice* (choice assumes alternatives that construct opposites).
	To act is to choose.
3. Separated from their natural conditions by instruments of their own making	Language separates us from nature; the Phoenician alphabet was the first technology.
	Culture is made out of the technologies of language, and culture further separates us from nature.
	Progress is the symbol that motivates technologies.
4. Goaded by the spirit of hierarchy (or moved by a sense of order)	Just as language separates us from nature, it also induces us to separate members of our culture from each other.
	Divisions among social classes, divisions of labor, and divisions of race, age, or gender are first divisions in language and then divisions in how we act toward each other.
	Those "Up" are guilty of not being "Down," and those "Down" are guilty of not being "Up."
	Guilt produces conflict and cooperation, both of which are necessary to maintain hierarchy.
5. Rotten with perfection	We strive toward absolutes: what we name as "right," "progress," "good," "beautiful," or "true."
	Perfection is the ultimate symbol of redemption born out of guilt.
	We are rotten in the sense that we inherited the burden of original sin (guilt about eating the forbidden apple), which in turn made us rely on language to make sense out of what had happened and to dedicate our lives to work that would, hopefully, lead us into a more perfect understanding or place.

Source: Kenneth Burke, *Language as Symbolic Action* (Berkeley: University of California Press, 1966).

Historical and Cultural Background

The first known reference to organizational culture appeared in a 1979 article by Andrew Pettigrew published in *Administrative Science Quarterly.* The concept became immediately popular for a variety of reasons.

FACTORS CONTRIBUTING TO THE RISE OF ORGANIZATIONAL CULTURE

Social Trends

The economic framework of the United States following World War II contributed to the popularity of the cultural approach to organizations. As sociologist Todd Gitlin (1987) explains:

> By 1945, the United States found itself an economic lord set far above the destroyed powers, its once and future competitors among both Allies and Axis powers. Inflation was negligible, so the increase in available dollars was actually buying more goods. Natural resources seemed plentiful, their supplies stable. . . . The Depression was over. And so were the deprivations of World War II, which also brought relative blessings: While European and Japanese factories were being pulverized, new American factories were being built and old ones were back at work, shrinking unemployment to relatively negligible proportions. Once the war was over, consumer demand was a dynamo. Science was mobilized by industry, and capital was channeled by government as never before. The boom was on, and the cornucopia seemed all the more impressive because the miseries of the Depression and war were near enough to suffuse the present with a sense of relief. (p. 13)

But as Gitlin also points out, these sources of renewal and promise were balanced by powerful threats of nuclear holocaust in an atomic age. The tension created by these opposing influences helped to shape the values of the new generation. Social, ethnic, racial, political, sexual, and economic tensions contributed to the complexity of the post–World War II climate, as did the new role of science in society, industry, and ideology. Since the Enlightenment, science had delivered on its promise of creating a more progressive and rational society. But in the twentieth century, science demonstrated a new ability to create weapons that could destroy human society in an instant. In industry, which since the Industrial Revolution had delivered the products and services that made life easier and more humane, inequalities between women and men and among ethnic and racial groups were being sanctioned and fierce competition for scarce natural resources and commodity markets contributed to worldwide tension. Similarly, new information technologies such as radios, stereos, televisions, and satellites made information more accessible as well as more open to commentary. Ideological battles among capitalism, socialism, and communism threatened world peace and led to the Cold War. Moral complexities and ambiguities were also prominent in the post–World War II period.

The political landscape changed as well. The mid-1960s are commonly referred to by anthropologists, historians, and literary critics as the end of Western colonialism (Greenblatt, 1990; Said, 1978, 1984). With the end of colonialism came a loss of cultural differentiation as well as a growing awareness of the role of Western interests in the political and economic subordination of Third World countries (Bhabha, 1990; Clifford & Marcus, 1985; Marcus and Fischer, 1986; Minh-Ha, 1991). Anthropologists were regarded as important resources for understanding the origin of cultures as well as their distinguishing characteristics and destinies.

The end of the colonial period also brought new global economic and political concerns that would increase critical scrutiny of organizations. The emergence of multinational firms and a world economy dominated by capitalism and dependent on cheap labor in Third World countries exposed global problems and inequities. Managing cultural differences in the workplace became important to firms doing business in other countries. Finding ways to improve cross-cultural understandings and communication skills was an integral component of the cultural approach to organizational communication.

In this turbulent social environment, new questions about organizations addressed such topics as power, participation, domination, and resistance in the workplace. For example, men exerted power over women by defining "real work" as that which was done outside of the home by men and "housework" as less worthy of attention or respect. It was not valued for its major contributions to the ideals of family and society. As a result, housework brought women less status than men received for performing "real work." When women began to assert their right to work outside of the home and to assume positions of responsibility in the workforce (in secretarial, food preparation, elementary school teaching, and custodial jobs), they encountered widespread opposition by men. Women's movement into the then-dominated male workforce was viewed as a threat to the long-standing patriarchal culture.

Similarly, in the 1950s to 1970s, members of minority groups posed challenges to the social institutions that had long controlled their access to equality. These groups included people whose racial, ethnic, or religious heritage distinguished them from the dominant white majority, people with physical and mental disabilities, people who had served in the armed forces, and the elderly. They protested against unfair social and professional practices, discrimination, and oppression.

The social climate in which cultural studies of organizations emerged, then, was characterized by increased participation, globalization, diversity, and resistance to domination on the part of minority groups. The popularity of the cultural approach was thus tied to its focus on cultural differences within an organization or a society.

Methodology

The new focus on organizational cultures required a new vocabulary and new approaches for analyzing organizations and communication. Previously, the dominant vocabulary, derived from the fields of psychology, sociology, communication, and management, covered everything from performance, motivation, and rewards to work units, hierarchies, and the outcomes of group problem solving, decision making, and leadership. Our knowledge about organizations and communication was thus symbolically structured out of the theories, methods, and findings of the social sciences.

However, the anthropological vocabulary of the cultural approach gave organizational researchers, managers, and members new ways of viewing organizations (see Table 5.2). Today, this language is commonly used by people in large corporations. It has both broadened the scope of what is considered important about organizations and communication and complicated our thinking about organizational communication processes. For example, the study of an organization's values is no longer limited to the domain of verbal messages; those values may also be found in artifacts and cartoons, in the arrangement of work space, even in the arrangement of cars in the employee parking lot (Goodall, 1989, 1990b).

But how does one analyze organizational culture in a systematic way? The most common methodology has its roots in anthropology, and it is called *ethnography*. Because anthropologists have long studied cultures, researchers sought to integrate anthropological research methods into cultural studies of organizations and communication (Geertz, 1973; Goodall, 1989, 1991a; Van Maanen, 1979, 1988). Ethnography, or the writing of culture (Clifford & Marcus, 1985), recounts the researcher's reflections on the experiences of members of the culture. For example, in writing an ethnographic account of Disneyland, Van Maanen (1991) relies on his recollections of working there while he was a student as well as his more recent observations of and interactions with employees and guests. Unlike traditional research methods in the social sciences, in which the researcher maintains distance from the group under study, ethnography requires the researcher to experience the culture firsthand. Van Maanen (1988) identifies three general types of ethnography: the realist tale, which conveys the basic realities of the culture; the impressionist tale, which presents the research experience along with the findings, often in creative ways; and the confessional tale, which focuses on the emotional experience of the ethnographer in the cultural setting.

Organizational ethnography provides rich descriptions of organizational life, often capturing subtle points of view that are overlooked by traditional re-

TABLE
5.2 **Cultural Terms Applied to Organizational Communication Studies**

SYMBOLS	LANGUAGE	METAPHORS

Words/actions	In-Group Speech
	  Technical terms
	  Jargon
	  Jokes
	  Gossip
	  Rumors
	  Gendered usage
		Determined by use within the
		culture

Artifacts
  Objects
  Cartoons
	Arrangement of the physical
	work space
	Personal meanings
	Humor in the workplace
	Social/political commentary
		Power/status
		Irony/contrast
		Resistance to domination

ROUTINES	**RITUALS/RITES**	**COMMUNITIES**
Repetitive behaviors	Individual performances Group performances New employee orientation Acceptance into group Promotions Annual celebrations Shunning/exclusion Retirement/layoffs	Continuity Acculturation Difference
USE OF OBJECTS	**EMPLOYEE HANDBOOKS**	**REPRESENTATION**
	Company brochures Annual reports	
Logos Awards	Identification Reward	Symbolic unity Enhancement

search methods. In this sense, ethnography becomes a stimulus for cultural dialogue by exposing sources of power and resistance and revealing values and beliefs that may otherwise be taken for granted. Moreover, organizational ethnography encourages us to look beyond the managerial and profitability aspects of organizations and toward a definition of the workplace as a *community*. Office parties, softball games, provocative E-mail, rumors, and jokes can reveal much about the nature and potential success of an organization as a business and as a community.

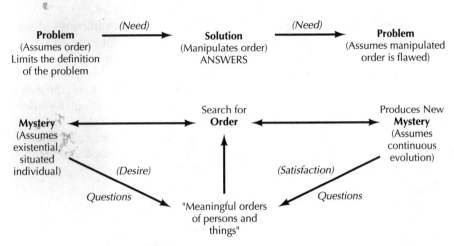

FIGURE 5.1
Seeing an Issue as a "Problem" or "Mystery"

The cultural approach attempts to bring communication research in line with developments in the philosophy of science. As physicists were altering their narratives about the universe based on Einstein's relativity theories and, later, Heisenberg's uncertainty principle, the social sciences were struggling for legitimacy. Measurements of human behavior were modeled on the Newtonian notion of physics and mathematics, as social scientists remained loyal to the model of theoretical physics that science had demonstrated as flawed (Smith, 1972). Relativity and uncertainty had yet to be incorporated into the new interpretive approach of the social sciences (Rabinow & Sullivan, 1986).

One way to understand the distinction between scientific and interpretive approaches to organizational communication is to think of relevant research questions as problems or mysteries (see Figure 5.1). Traditional social science research is based on the problem-solution method: Name a problem, and then work to solve it. But this assumes that a known order already exists, or that the framework for understanding and making sense of an issue is already in place. The perception of a problem produces the need for a solution to the problem, and achieving a solution requires manipulating persons or things within the existing order. These manipulations produce findings (the effects of the manipulations) and, it is hoped, solutions to the problem. In turn, the solutions to existing problems tend to produce new problems that call for new solutions. Thus, while the solutions tend to solve part of the puzzle, they also create new puzzles. Some researchers find fault with the problem-solution framework, arguing that the order being manipulated may not be representative of the actual order.

In contrast, cultural studies of organizations, particularly ethnographies, tend to assume that the puzzle is the search for order. Researchers accept ambiguity, rather than try to resolve it. Furthermore, symbolic constructions of reality are mysteries containing clues for reading the culture. Mystery produces the desire for order—that is, for ways to question meaningful orders, for ways to make stories out of questions, and for ways to appreciate the critical terms of the ongoing dialogue. In turn, cultural studies of organizations tend to produce new mysteries about the meanings of orders, the functions of stories about the orders, and the relationship of orders to a greater order.

Goodall (1989) conducted a long-term study of a computer software company in an attempt to discover the secret of its culture. One employee summed up the experience of his culture this way:

> *It looks like a three-dimensional spider's web,*
> *The beauty of the thing is how it changes,*
> *to accommodate new information,*
> *to become the environment,*
> *to meet the total needs of the user.*
> *It looks like a three-dimensional spider's web,*
> *all of that mysterious calculus,*
> *all of those prize soft numbers,*
> *I don't know.*
> *I made it,*
> *and I don't even know all*
> *of what it is.*
> (Goodall, 1989, p. 39)

While there are many ways to conduct interpretive research, the best studies capture the spirit and diversity of an organization's values and practices by using evocative vocabulary or metaphor. For example, John Van Maanen (1991) uses the metaphor of a "smile factory" in his cultural study of Disneyland. The image of smiles (friendly, fun, courteous) being manufactured (e.g., the products of a rigid assembly-line factory) establishes the tensions of a cultural dialogue among Disneyland employees. By using this language, Van Maanen delineates the interplays of a staged performance: employees are "members of a cast" who wear "costumes," not uniforms, and who exhibit on-stage, off-stage, and backstage behaviors. He also uses the image of the factory to discuss the production of smiles: formal rules about informal behaviors, and the prevalence of supervisory spies who note every infraction. The result is an account of a strong culture whose everyday use of language constructs a metaphor that, in turn, becomes its unique sense of place.

In other words, organizational culture is the result of the cumulative learning of a group of people, and that learning manifests itself as culture at a number of levels. According to Edgar Schein (1991), culture is defined by six formal properties: (1) shared basic assumptions that are (2) invented, discovered, or developed by a given group as it (3) learns to cope with its problems of external adaptation and internal integration in ways that (4) have worked well enough to be considered valid, and, therefore, (5) can be taught to new members of the group as the (6) correct way to perceive, think, and feel in relation to those problems.

Practicality

Organizational culture developed mainly in response to global changes in society and to new developments in science and social research. But contributing to its widespread popularity was the business climate of the 1970s. As noted in Chapter 1, this period was characterized by a significant increase in global competition that highlighted productivity problems in the United States. Although for many years the United States had been the world leader in many industries, it suddenly found itself eclipsed by other nations, most notably Japan. In many industries, Japanese manufacturing techniques threatened to prevail, and many wondered what made them so successful.

William Ouchi (1981) developed what he calls *theory Z* to describe Japanese management. As noted in Chapter 3, McGregor's (1960) theories X and Y distinguish between the assumptions of classical management and human resources concerning individuals in organizations. Ouchi's theory Z holds that the survival and prosperity of organizations depends heavily on their ability to adapt to their surrounding cultures. He uses the term *culture* to refer to national standards of organizational performance, and in comparing those standards in the United States and Japan he found seven major differences (see Table 5.3). Ouchi thus proposed a theory Z type of organization that would integrate individual achievement and advancement while also developing a sense of community in the workplace. A theory Z organization would be capable of reducing negative influences and segmented decision making by incorporating new cultural values into the work environment.

By the mid-1980s, many traditional organizations were failing financially or in danger of doing so. The old prescriptions—"management by objectives," "quality circles"—were no longer effective, and it became clear that radical changes were required for companies to remain competitive. As business leaders began speaking of organizational change—in attitudes, values, and practices—they also began thinking about a holistic transformation in terms of organizational culture. One of the authors of this textbook received a phone call in 1983 from a CEO in search of someone who could "install a new culture" at his company. Managers were attracted to the idea even without much knowledge of how culture develops, much less how it could be altered. But many questions remained: What types of cultures are most productive? What aspects of culture are most closely associated with business success? Some tentative an-

TABLE
5.3
Ouchi's Comparison of Japanese and U.S. Organizational Cultures

U.S. (TYPE A)	JAPANESE (TYPE J)
Short-term employment	Long-term employment
Individual decision making	Consensus (group) decision making
Individual responsibility	Collective responsibility
Expectations of rapid promotion	Slow advancement
Formal organizational control	Informal peer control
Specialized career paths	Generalized career paths
Localized concerns for well-being	Holistic concerns for the organization's well-being

Source: William Ouchi, *Theory Z* (Reading, Mass.: Addison-Wesley, 1981).

swers were provided in two successful books, both sponsored by the McKinsey Corporation, a management consulting firm. The first, Terrence Deal and Allen Kennedy's *Corporate Cultures: The Rites and Rituals of Corporate Life* (1982), defined the elements of strong cultures as a supportive business environment, dedication to a shared vision and values, well-known corporate heroes, effective rites and rituals, and formal and informal communication networks. The other book, *In Search of Excellence* (1982) by Tom Peters and Robert Waterman, made the *New York Times* best-seller list for nonfiction. Its authors studied sixty-two top-performing companies that had been defined as "excellent" by their employees and external analysts and found eight common characteristics of their cultures:

1. *A bias for action:* Top-performing companies are characterized by active decision making; they are not characterized by thinking about decisions for long periods of time or relying on a lot of information to make decisions. If a change occurs in the business environment, they act. This emphasis echoes Karl Weick's work.
2. *Close relations to the customer:* Top-performing companies never forget who makes them successful—their customers. One of the basics of excellence is to remember that service, reliability, innovation, and a constant concern for the customer are vital to any organization.
3. *Autonomy and entrepreneurship:* Top-performing companies empower their employees by encouraging risk-taking, responsibility for the decisions they

make and the actions they perform, and innovation. If an organization is too tightly controlled and the worker's performance is too tightly monitored, initiative, creativity, and willingness to take responsibility all tend to decay.

4. *Productivity through people:* A quality product depends on quality workers throughout the organization. Good customer relations depend on valuing service throughout the organization. Top-performing companies recognize these factors and rally against we/them or management/labor divisions.

5. *Hands-on, value-driven:* Top-performing companies are characterized by strong core values that are widely shared among employees and by an overall vision—a management philosophy—that guides everyday practices. Achievement is dependent on performance, and performance is dependent on values.

6. *Stick to the knitting:* Top-performing companies tend to be strictly focused on their source of product and service excellence. They tend not to diversify by going into other product or service fields. They expand their organization and profits by sticking to what they do best.

7. *Simple form, lean staff:* Top-performing companies are characterized by a lack of complicated hierarchies and divisions of labor. None of the companies surveyed maintained a typical bureaucratic form of organizing. Many of them employed fewer than one hundred persons.

8. *Simultaneous loose-tight properties:* Top-performing companies are difficult to categorize. They encourage individual action and responsibility and yet retain strong core values; they encourage individual and group decision making. They are neither centralized nor decentralized in management style because they adapt to new situations with whatever is needed to get the job done.

By 1990, however, many of the companies identified as excellent had failed, and even Peters and Waterman agreed that many of the rules for success in business had changed. Peters has since written a number of successful books that advise managers on how to do business in chaotic times.

Academic ethnographers also have a lot to say about the failures of strong corporate cultures. In 1993, Gideon Kunda published an ethnographic study on the applications of ideological power to workers' lives in a high-tech engineering firm that challenges many of the assumptions of Deal and Kennedy (1982) and Peters and Waterman (1982). From interviews, observations, and a close reading of the culture's everyday activities, Kunda concludes that the control and commitment features of strong cultures are the most problematic. Specifically, attempts to "engineer culture" are flawed. As a result, workers may internalize ambiguity and question the authenticity of any emotions and beliefs associated with the company. Moreover, workers may learn the lessons of strong cultural performances so well that they seem driven to make irony "the dominant mode of their everyday existence" (Kunda, 1993, p. 216).

The Politics of Interpreting Culture

Critical ethnographers (Conquergood, 1991; Thomas, 1993) often ask the question: "Who gets to speak for whom?" In studies of organizations, this question targets fundamental communication problems: Who owns the right to speak for a company's culture? Do employees own that right, and if so, at what level is the correct interpretation of meaning found? At the senior executive level? Middle manager? Staff? Customer and supplier? Some combination of these levels? Or does the right to speak for the culture reside with academic researchers and other nonmembers of the culture?

Within these issues lie many challenges to researchers. Every act of communication is partial, partisan, and problematic; this is true of interpretation as well. The issues also speak to an ethical challenge: What are the consequences of making statements about an organization's culture? This challenge often divides researchers into two ideologically split camps. On the left are those who assert that Marxist, feminist, and critical theories of the "production and consumption of culture" provide the appropriate frameworks for the interpretations of cultures (see Chapter 6). On the right are those who assert that what gets lost in leftists' critiques about production and consumption is a literature that can be appreciated for its inspiration and poetry.

While this debate rages on campuses and in academic journals, organizations struggle to survive in the increasingly competitive nature of a global marketplace. Academic studies of organizational culture, particularly those derived from liberal sympathies, often seem unnecessarily tedious. While we have learned that culture is important to the success of a business, seldom do these studies present clear findings that can be applied to all organizations. As a result, the gulf between academic and business interests has widened.

For example, let's assume that as a young scholar you are interested in conducting a cultural analysis of an organization. What ethical issues would you address? How would your ideological commitments shape your study? Why do a cultural analysis of an organization? Who would benefit? Who would you speak for? How has culture itself affected your style of seeing, observing, talking about, writing about, and thinking about cultural issues? What directs your critical attention to particular interpretations of meanings?

Five Views of Organizational Culture

As we have seen, various social, methodological, and practical concerns have contributed to the rise of the cultural approach. Research on organizational culture has focused on five major areas of study: comparative management, corporate culture, organizational cognition, organizational symbolism, and critical and postmodern perspectives.

COMPARATIVE MANAGEMENT

The *comparative management* view of organizational culture treats culture as some "thing" imported into organizations through the national, regional, and ethnic affiliations of employees. It looks at companies operating in various parts of the world to show how differences in national and local culture are revealed in the workplace. Among the best-known researchers in this area of study, Grete Hofstede (1983, 1990) found that at IBM offices, which are located all over the world, there is no uniform culture; instead, versions of the company's culture are adapted to local ways of life. In a more recent study of comparative management, Erez and Earley (1993) define organizational culture as a set of mental programs that control behavior. They determine that these programs vary among countries due to differences in national cultures.

A fascinating example of the comparative management approach is Hedrick Smith's (1995) work on global capitalism. According to Smith, the vast differences among organizations in the United States, Japan, and Germany are largely tied to aspects of their national cultures. U.S. organizations tend to develop cultures that value individual achievement rather than team recognition and reward. In contrast, Japanese organizational cultures place a high value on teamwork and community and tend not to tolerate creative individuals who are disconnected from the community. In Germany, workers are both individually and communally oriented, define creativity as precision, and expect to be led by a strong national government.

The comparative management view of culture is not limited to the comparison of whole countries; regional differences can also influence organizational cultures. For example, a brokerage house with offices in Mississippi and New York can expect differences in how employees at the two offices relate to deadlines and schedules.

Despite these interesting contrasts, the comparative management view of culture may become less useful as global economics turns many organizations and their employees into travelers and differences among national cultures dissolve (Clifford, 1992). The homogenization of global culture bears directly on the tension between creativity and constraint. As large multinational organizations pursue global markets, corporate colonization threatens to minimize local differences.

CORPORATE CULTURE

The *corporate culture* view sees culture as something that an organization possesses, manages, and exploits to enhance productivity. Culture is "a rational instrument designed by top management to shape the behavior of the employees in purposive ways" (Ouchi & Wilkins, 1985, p. 462). Pepsico, McDonald's, Microsoft, and Disney, for example, are noted for their strong corporate cultures. Each invests tens of millions of dollars annually in the selection and indoctrination of employees into the company's culture or way of doing things. Companies with strong corporate cultures can be highly successful. They also tend to encourage a strong sense of identity among their employees. But such companies may require employees to give up significant freedoms (even in the area of personal appearance) in exchange for membership.

Not all companies with strong corporate cultures place strict limitations on employees, however. Most successful companies today are in the process of replacing hierarchical management processes with management that is driven by a vision of the future and a set of corporate values. Leadership's main role is helping employees understand and work according to the organization's vision and values. When this approach succeeds, the result is an organizational culture characterized by employees' supervision of their own behavior.

We are presently involved with a restaurant chain that for many years limited significant decision making to the top three officers of the company. Recently, the officers asked the organizational development staff to survey employees about company values that could guide positive behavior. The values they identified were continuous improvement, customer focus, involvement in decision making, and quality of work life. The company has gone to great lengths to explain this set of values to employees, and the results have been extremely positive.

Similarly, in a multisite study relating corporate culture to performance, Kotter and Heskett (1992) found that value consensus can enhance organizational performance under certain circumstances:

1. When people agree on the importance of adapting to a changing environment (i.e., continuous learning or improvement).
2. When a strong entrepreneur is present who also adapts well to change.
3. When an effective business strategy is in place to supplement the organization's vision and values.

Despite sustained criticism of the corporate culture view (Alvesson, 1993;

Smircich & Calas, 1987), it continues to be applied alongside efforts to implement total quality management, reengineering, and self-directed work teams, for example. In these efforts, it helps to focus managers' attention on communication practices and the human side of business. However, its view of culture as something that can be managed and controlled has been the subject of much criticism.

ORGANIZATIONAL COGNITION

The *organizational cognition* perspective defines culture as a way of thinking that is shared by members of an organization. As such, it is implicit in discussions of shared meaning, shared values, and shared rules. LeVine (1984) points out the value of cognition with respect to human communities in general:

> Every human community functions with a group consensus about the meanings of symbols used in the communications that constitute their social life, however variable their behavior and attitudes in other respects, because such a consensus is as necessary for encoding and decoding messages in social communication in general as agreement about speech rules is to encoding and decoding in linguistic mode. (p. 69)

Many other observers have applied organizational cognition to the study of organizations. For example, Mohan (1993) examines cultural "penetration," or the degree to which an organization's members share similar meanings for things. Similarly, Sackmann (1991) asserts that "a collection of people [is] a cultural grouping [because] the people hold the same cognitions in common" (p. 40). In a test of Schall's (1983) communication rules approach to culture, Shockley-Zalabak & Morley's (1994) analysis of shared values in a computer company demonstrates a strong relationship between the values of the company's founders and new employees that persists over time.

The organizational cognition view of culture is appealing in part because it reflects how most people think about communication and relationships—that people have ideas, and that through communication they can share meaning with one another. But no precise method exists for verifying whether two or more people actually share meanings of values or rules. These determinations are made only on the basis of what people say and do. For this reason, many critics of organizational cognition argue that culture is more closely tied to coordinated practices than to cognitive alignment. Although the sense-making process contributes to the development of culture, that process is viewed as occurring between people rather than within people (such that social reality is co-constructed in communication). Therefore, while culture is still related to "the meaningful orders of persons and things," meaning is viewed as public or social, not private, and the importance of cognition as dependent on its relationship to ongoing actions and behaviors.

ORGANIZATIONAL SYMBOLISM

According to *organizational symbolism,* interpreting culture involves paying close attention to the language, stories, nonverbal messages, and communicative exchanges that characterize an organization. Although management scholars have long limited their use of the term *symbolism* to refer to the underlying meanings of such things as corporate logos and value statements, more recent scholars focus on a broader view of symbolism in organizations. Perhaps most important in this regard initially was the Alta Conference on Interpretive Approaches to Organizational Communication organized by Linda Putnam and Michael Pacanowsky. The papers presented at the early conferences are published in the book *Communication and Organizations: An Interpretive Approach* (1983), which chronicles the diverse roles of communication in the construction of organizational cultures. In addition, an influential article by Pacanowsky and Nick O'Donnell-Trujillo (1983) published in *Communication Monographs* helped to establish the view of organizational communication as cultural performance.

More recently, David Boje (1991, 1995), an organizational researcher, has suggested that organizations are storytelling systems. The stories or narratives about the organization's culture convey information about its current state of affairs, and as such the stories serve as resources for everyday sense-making (Wilkins, 1984). As noted in Chapter 4, when an organization is viewed as a system—in this case, a storytelling system—modifications to the stories represent feedback. Paying attention to stories and feedback is important for employees and managers alike (Mitroff & Kilmann, 1975).

Organizational stories may be found in speeches and casual conversations, as well as in employee newsletters, company brochures, strategic planning statements, corporate advertisements, fund-raising campaigns, and training videos (Goodall, 1989; Pacanowsky, 1988). These forums provide opportunities for the organization to talk about its values and aspirations. However, different stories about the organization are told by different storytellers. The corporate or official story about the organization may be told by advertising agents working in conjunction with high-level managers and stockholders. The inside stories are told by employees of the organization, who may offer different accounts. In two recent investigations into the working conditions of fruit pickers, and employees of manufacturing plants in the Carolinas, the accounts given by the business owners and managers differed greatly from the accounts given by the employees. The story told by the owners and managers focused on the number of people employed by the companies, product quality, and reasonable cost to consumers. In contrast, the story told by employees focused on low wages (sometimes paid in the form of crack cocaine or alcohol) and unsafe workplaces (where the average safety inspection occurred once every seventy-five years). In both cases, federal investigations and congressional hearings followed.

Clearly, organizational stories represent the interests and values of the storytellers. In the preceding example, neither side's narrative captured the whole story. Usually, multiple stories or interpretations are needed to describe an organization's culture. These competing stories represent different voices as well as potential dialogues among individuals and groups within the organization. Therefore, we can think of an organization's culture as a potential dialogue of subcultures or as a many-sided story (Boje, 1995).

In a recent attempt to advance organizational symbolism, Charles Bantz (1993) describes the organizational communication culture (OCC) technique for analyzing messages and their interpretations. Using the OCC method, one can analyze important aspects of vocabulary, identify key themes, and infer norms, motives, and interpretations that characterize a particular organization's culture. However, there is a risk associated with making inferences about an organization's culture from its members' use of symbols in that the use and meaning of symbols change over time. A recent study by Hatch (1993) attempts to deal with this issue by extending Schein's (1988) definition of culture as Hatch demonstrates that, over time, people's assumptions develop into values, those values become realized as artifacts, and the artifacts take on meaning through symbols.

Despite the lack of agreement on how to define symbolism, this approach to understanding culture has shifted our focus toward how people communicate together and create meaning in dialogue. But symbolic displays must be considered in practical contexts, not as isolated events. Just as a joke, story, choice of words, or ritual can be misleading out of context, symbols should be studied in ways that link them to the realities of work (Alvesson, 1993). In so doing, this view of culture gives us access to the social construction of meaning as well as its consequences.

CRITICAL AND POSTMODERN VIEWS

Research on organizational culture has moved significantly in the direction of the *critical* and *postmodern* views (which is why Chapters 6 and 7 are devoted to more detailed discussions of these topics). Stanley Deetz, Dwight Conquergood, and Joanne Martin have made significant contributions to this line of research.

Deetz and others (Atkouf, 1992; Smircich & Calas, 1987) argue that the managerial bias in culture research reinforces the "corporate colonization of the life-world" in which the interests of corporations frame all aspects of daily living (Deetz, 1991). These critics call for organizational ethnographers to look at issues of power and domination associated with the development, maintenance, or transformation of a particular culture. They believe the transcripts chronicling the lives of those with less power in organizations should be exposed and read, so that alternatives to the dominant culture can be considered. Dennis Mumby and Linda Putnam's (1993) work on "bounded emotionality," for instance, reframes organizational culture and challenges accepted worldviews.

According to Conquergood (1991), cultures are composed of ongoing dialogues that are variously "complicit" or "engaged." A dialogue is *complicit* when the participants accept or go along with the dominant interpretation of meaning. In contrast, a dialogue is *engaged* when the participants challenge the dominant interpretation with an alternative explanation. Both types of dialogue exist in most organizations. As a result, an organization's culture is characterized by multiple conflicting meanings and a constant struggle for interpretive control.

Conquergood's (1991) ethnographic work, which focuses on Chicago street gangs, Hmong refugees, and Palestinians, calls for a radical rethinking of cultural study. His critique moves us toward a more critical perspective on issues of power and a more postmodern perspective on the research process. He outlines four themes in the critical rethinking of cultural study: (1) the return of the body; (2) boundaries and borderlands; (3) the rise of performance; and (4) rhetorical reflexivity.

In the first, the *return of the body,* Conquergood (1991) calls for the physical immersion of the researcher in the organization. While participant observation has always been an integral part of ethnographic study, Conquergood's version of it is more radical and based on the idea that closeness brings the ethnographer in touch with more than the visual aspects of a culture (Stoller, 1989).

> This rethinking of ethnography is primarily about speaking and listening, instead of observing. . . . Sight and surveillance depend on detachment and distance. . . . Metaphors of sound, on the other hand, privilege temporal processes, proximity, and incorporation. Listening is an interiorizing experience . . . whereas observation sizes up exteriors. . . . The return of the body . . . shifts the emphasis from space to time, from sight and vision to sound and voice, from text to performance, from authority to vulnerability. (Conquergood, 1991, p. 183)

In discussing *boundaries and borderlands,* Conquergood (1991) reinforces the idea that "pure" cultures are an endangered species, as formerly isolated organizations dissolve their boundaries through strategic alliances, joint ventures, and international marketing. As employees increasingly see themselves as self-

TABLE
5.4 **Defining Characteristics of Postmodern Perspectives on Organizational Culture**

	PERSPECTIVE		
Features	*Integration*	*Differentiation*	*Fragmentation*
Orientation to consensus	Organization-wide	Subcultural consensus	Lack of consensus
Relation among manifestations	Consistency	Inconsistency	Not clearly consistent or inconsistent
Orientation to ambiguity	Exclude ambiguity	Channel ambiguity outside subcultures	Acknowledge ambiguity

employed providers of skills under the new social contract (see Chapter 1), cultures may come to exist between organizations as well as within them.

By *the rise of performance,* Conquergood focuses our attention on behaviors, practices, and other nonverbal modes of communication within cultures. "Issues and attitudes are expressed and contexted in dance, music, gesture, food, ritual, artifact, symbolic action, as well as words" (Conquergood, 1991, p. 189).

Finally, *rhetorical reflexivity* refers to the realization that there is no one authoritative account of a culture. Instead, organizational ethnographies reflect as much the writer's biases and worldview as they do the place and people under study. Therefore, multiple studies of an organization's culture need not agree to be useful; each ethnography adds dimensions and voices that the others may have missed. It is this attitude toward knowledge and truth as never final and best found in speaking and listening that characterizes the postmodern approach to organizational culture.

Martin (1992) has contributed significantly to the development of a taxonomy of perspectives on organizational culture that takes into account the movement toward a postmodern view. According to Martin, perspectives on culture can be classified as integration, differentiation, or fragmentation (see Table 5.4). Although most studies of organizations focus on one dominant perspective, most organizations reveal all three. Each perspective reveals a different orientation to three key features of cultural study: orientation to consensus, relation among manifestations, and orientation to ambiguity.

Integration

The *integration* perspective portrays culture in terms of consistency and clarity. Cultural members agree about what they are to do and why they do it. In this there is no room for ambiguity. In addition, an organization's culture is portrayed as a monologue, not a dialogue (May, 1988). This tradition in the cultural study of organizations is evident in Peters and Waterman's (1982) descriptions of excellent companies with strong cultures that adhere to a narrow set of shared values, meanings, and interpretations. Similarly, studies that analyze the influence of the organization's founder (Barley, 1983; Pacanowsky, 1988; Schein, 1991) tend to trace those influences throughout the organization, sometimes to the neglect of competing values within the company (McDonald, 1988).

Indeed, the integration perspective typically favors the story of those in power over other competing stories. A general neglect of marginalized groups within organizations can lead to crises and reduced productivity. Although knowledge of the influence of a founder or a dominant set of values may be useful, the organization's culture is made up of many other interpretations of meaning.

Differentiation

The *differentiation* perspective portrays cultural manifestations as predominantly inconsistent with each other (such as when a formal policy is undermined by contradictory informal norms). Furthermore, when consensus does emerge, it does so only within the boundaries of a subculture. At the organizational level of analysis, differentiated subcultures may coexist in harmony, conflict, or indifference to each other. These subcultures are viewed as islands of clarity, and ambiguity is channeled outside of their boundaries (Frost et al., 1991).

In addition, the differentiation perspective sees organizational cultures as contested political domains in which the potential for genuine dialogue is often impaired. The various subcultures may seldom speak to each other, instead reinforcing their own accounts of organizational meanings without seeking external validation. As a result, they do not actively participate in the broader interests of the organization.

In a recent study, for example, it was discovered that a computer software firm had created barriers to its subcultures' communication when it moved to a new location (Goodall, 1990a). Work groups were physically separated from each other, promoting competition for resources among them. In another study, a conflict between managers and employees over a pay freeze was masked at an annual breakfast by group of speakers hired to create a story that favored management's position (Rosen, 1985). The ploy was unsuccessful and deepened the division between the two groups. Divisions among classes of employees often occupy the interests of subcultures, and the differentiation perspective can show how conflict among subcultures may be avoided, masked, or neglected.

Fragmentation

In the *fragmentation* perspective, ambiguity is an inevitable and pervasive aspect of contemporary life. Studies in this area focus on the experience and expression of ambiguity within organizational cultures, wherein consensus and dissensus coexist in a constantly fluctuating pattern of change. Any cultural manifestation can be interpreted in a myriad of ways because clear consensus among organizational subcultures cannot be attained.

Consistent with postmodern theories of organizations and society (see Chapter 7), the fragmentation perspective replaces certainty with ambiguity as a model for interpretation. Furthermore, ambiguity can be manipulated by management to support its interests and by disempowered employees to cope with those interests (Eisenberg, 1984; Meyerson, 1991). Its application to organizational communication has been varied. For example, ambiguity has been used to explain the divergent accounts of an airline disaster given by eyewitnesses (Weick, 1990), the writing of noninfluential policy statements by analysts with vested interests in writing influential statements (Feldman, 1991), and the ways in which urban dwellers interpret the meanings of living space in cities and parks (de Certeau, 1984).

The meaning of ambiguity for our concept of organizational cultures as dialogue depends on how we define dialogue. If dialogue is viewed as a means of generating consensus, then ambiguity makes dialogue unlikely. Conversely, if dialogue is thought of as embodying a respect for diversity—and perhaps a form of consensus based on acknowledgment of differences—then ambiguity is a necessary component of dialogue. Furthermore, unlike ambiguity about shared meanings or interpretations of culture, multiple meanings are inevitably found in ambiguities about shared practices. Recall that in the interpretive perspective, shared practices and multiple interpretations of meaning for those practices are highly valued. For us, then, ambiguity is a necessary component of dialogue. Indeed, genuine dialogue probably would not exist without ambiguity, for if everything was clearly understood, there would not be much left to talk about (Boje, 1995).

Martin's (1992) allegiance to the fragmentation perspective (or at least to a general postmodern approach) is echoed by Linda Smircich and Marta Calas (1987) in their contention that the "truth" or "falsity" of any account of an organizational culture always has implications for power. Martin's own dissatisfaction with her "imperialist" taxonomy of integration, differentiation, and fragmentation is revealed in her plea to readers to suggest alternatives. Her open-ended approach to thinking about organizational culture is thoroughly postmodern. At the same time, Martin endorses others' subjective and impressionistic studies of organizations (e.g., Van Maanen, 1988; Conquergood, 1991; Goodall, 1989, 1991b, 1996).

A Communication Perspective on Organizational Culture

Reviewing the body of research on organizational culture is a tantalizing and confusing task. Just about anything is regarded as culture, and studies purporting to study culture do so in dramatically different ways. As a result, no consistent treatment of communication has emerged in the culture literature.

For this reason, we propose the following view of communication and organizational culture. In this perspective, organizational culture has the following characteristics:

1. It views communication as the core process by which culture is formed and transformed, and culture as patterns of behavior and their interpretation.
2. It acknowledges the importance of everyday communication as well as more notable symbolic expressions.
3. It encompasses not only words and actions but also all types of nonverbal communication (such as machinery, artifacts, and work processes).
4. It includes broad patterns of interaction in society at large and examines how they are played out in the workplace. Therefore, it views each organization's culture as a cultural nexus of national, local, familial, and other forces outside of the organization (Martin, 1992).
5. It acknowledges the legitimacy of multiple motives for researching culture, from improving corporate performance to overthrowing existing power structures.

Summary

Cultural studies of organizations and communication emerged in response to a variety of social, historical, and political issues. These studies focus on the meaningful orders of persons and things and are usually written as ethnographies. The ethnographic format has been the focus of much controversy, such as whether the ethnographer's perspectives can be generalized and translated into practical managerial strategies. Studies of organizational cultures also tend to use the research methods and vocabulary of cultural anthropology. References to rituals, rites, cultural performances, symbols, languages, values, and artifacts are used to discuss the meanings of individuals and groups in organizational cultures. Researchers tend to classify cultures as integrated, differentiated, or fragmented and to use these distinctions in discussions of consensus, values, and conflict. Some researchers look beyond these categories toward a postmodern account of culture that is based on immersion in the organization.

Although the cultural approach to organizations and communication yields interesting and informative accounts of everyday work life, questions about how much trust we can place in the accounts and what we can productively do with them have emerged. However, these limitations are not unique to the cultural approach; the systems, human relations, human resources, scientific management, critical, and postmodern approaches also share the potential for misunderstanding, misapplication, and abuse. But unlike these other approaches, the cultural approach relies on literary narratives about personal experiences and meanings. It is this characteristic of the cultural approach that has been criticized by researchers, managers, and employees who favor the more traditional social science methods of explanation, prediction, and control.

Changes in the world of work will inevitably affect the usefulness of the cultural approach to organizations. As the relationships between employers and employees change from long-term to shorter-term commitments, organizational cultures may become more homogeneous or less well defined. In addition, communication technology is likely to affect organizational cultures as interaction via computers continues to take the place of face-to-face communication. The smaller cultural networks created by electronic communication may eventually replace identification with a corporate culture.

What role does the cultural approach play in achieving a balance between individual creativity and institutional constraint? While scientific management had tipped the scale toward institutional constraints and human relations and human resources had tipped it back toward individual creativity, the same equation does not apply to systems and cultures. These perspectives complicate both our thinking about organizational communication as well as issues of creativity and constraint. Once viewed simply as creativity *versus* constraint, now we are faced with such complex issues as the ambiguities of symbols used to construct and interpret potential meanings for creativity or constraint.

The cultural approach places value on meaningful orders derived from symbolic constructions. But further research is needed to determine whether those meaningful orders are limited to what appears on the surface of a culture or whether clues to deeper structures of power, status, or personality exist. In conclusion, then, we offer the following thoughts on organizational culture and research:

> A culture—any culture—is like an ocean. There are many wonderful things and creatures in it that we may never understand; they change and so do we, regardless of the depth or perspective of our study. But the ocean is also made up of waves that are as regular as the cycles of the moon, and just as mysteriously musical, powerful, and enchanting. The top millimeter of the ocean is a world

unto itself, and a vital one, in which the broader secrets of biological and evolutionary life . . . are contained. But even their meanings must be read in a vocabulary that is separate and distant. . . . So it is that within that millimeter, among those waves, we find clear and recurring themes. Like the great questions about culture that we pursue, those themes are always with us and not yet fully understood. (Goodall, 1990a, p. 97)

C A S E   S T U D Y

THE CULTURE OF MEETINGS

Helen Schwartzman asserts in *Ethnography in Organizations* (1993), that "nothing could be more commonplace than meetings in organizations," yet most studies of organizational cultures fail to look closely at the exchanges of talk at those meetings (p. 38). She argues that close readings of those exchanges can tell us much about various aspects of a company's culture: power; domination; resistance to domination; gender, race, and class divisions; concepts of time and money; and regional differences, among others. Her argument is compelling.

ASSIGNMENT

As a student of organizational communication and a member of an organization (your class, college, or place of employment), you are likely intrigued by the idea that meetings hold important clues to organizational cultures. For this case study, you will immerse yourself in a culture in order to understand, analyze, and write about it in the form of an ethnography. You will collect the data to be analyzed and then write about it using what you have learned in this and other chapters. You should also address the issues raised in Focus on Ethics 5.1. Here are some other guidelines for conducting your cultural study:

1. Record and transcribe the exchanges between members of the group, team, or organization at one or more of its meetings.
2. Decide how you will analyze the data based on your reading in this and other chapters.
3. Perform your analysis.
4. Prepare your ethnography and share it with your class.

Critical Approaches to Organizations and Communication

Viewing organization as a mode of domination . . . forces . . . us to appreciate the wisdom of Max Weber's insight that the pursuit of rationality can itself be a mode of domination. . . . We should always be asking the question "Rational for whom?"
● Gareth Morgan, *Images of Organization* (1986)

My job as a feminist is twofold. First, it is to critique and question fundamental assumptions and social structures, being alert to implicit patterns of gender and power relations, and being aware when they devalue women. . . . Second, I engage in re-vision of female characteristics. For me, this especially means not rejecting the heritage we have . . . but looking for the functional and creative potential of female, and male, patterns of being.
● Judi Marshall, "Viewing Organizational Communication from a Feminist Perspective" (1993)

QUESTIONS

FOR DISCUSSION

● What are the advantages and disadvantages of viewing organizational communication in terms of power?

● How does ideology influence and constrain communication in organizations?

● What roles do metaphors, myths, and stories play in maintaining and transforming existing power relations?

● What are the main characteristics of the feminist approach to organizational communication?

● What can workplace democracy do to address some of the abuses of power by organizational members?

The various approaches to organizations discussed in the preceding chapters pose questions from *within* the dominant frameworks of Western capitalism, behavioral science, and modern organizational studies, but they do not *challenge* those frameworks. They are also largely evolutionary, not revolutionary. Recent cultural approaches have been more critical (Conquergood, 1991; Goodall, 1991a, 1995b; Martin, 1992), blurring the distinction between cultural and critical approaches and providing a theoretical bridge between evolutionary and revolutionary approaches. But more subversive approaches exist.

The perspectives considered in this and the next chapter examine and oppose the assumptions of the dominant frameworks. Critical organizational theory, which we address in this chapter, reveals the often hidden but pervasive power that organizations have over individuals, while also challenging the assumed superiority of market capitalism. Critical approaches, as we will see, pose important questions about power.

Critical Theory

HISTORICAL AND CULTURAL BACKGROUND

When we think of people as "critical," we often imagine them challenging some action or decision they consider inappropriate or unfair. This is precisely what *critical approaches* to organizations do: They are concerned mainly with the exercise and abuse of *power*. Critical theory thus emerged in response to power issues inherent in the capitalist system of the Victorian period. This was an abusive system of low wages, squalid working conditions, and wealthy business owners (Mead, 1991). In addition, child labor was common, particularism was the rule, and employees had no protection from the whims of their employers. Women and minorities were paid substantially less than white men for performing the same work, and their views about how work should be done or how workplaces could be improved were largely ignored (Banta, 1993). Therefore, the powers of scientific management were based on the separation of managers and workers, rich and poor, genders, and races.

It was under these circumstances of exploitive capitalism that critical theory found its earliest expression in the work of Karl Marx (1818–83). He viewed the division between business owners and employees as misguided and unfair, and he believed it would eventually lead to a violent overthrow of the owners. The world has since witnessed many practical and theoretical adaptations of Marx's ideas (the former Soviet Union, for one), far too many to consider here. But one particular adaptation merits our attention: that of a group of professors from the University of Frankfurt, referred to collectively as the *Frankfurt school,* who used some of Marx's ideas to develop what is now known as *critical theory* (Adorno and Horkheimer, 1972).

THE RISE OF CRITICAL THEORY IN THE UNITED STATES

Critical theory gained considerable popularity in the United States during the 1980s (Strine, 1991). Practical and intellectual reasons account for the current interest in critical theory.

At the turn of the twentieth century, U.S. industrialists broke from traditional capitalism to go in a new direction. For the first time, a clear connection was made between the wages paid to employees and their ability to be active consumers. At Ford Motor Company in the 1920s, for example, workers were paid the then-high wage of $5 a day. Ford reasoned that in order to sell his cars to the masses, workers had to earn enough to buy them. This strategy, known as *progressive capitalism,* dominated U.S. industry from the Industrial Revolution until the early 1970s, when the average, inflation-corrected weekly wage of Americans reached its peak. Throughout this period, both individuals and corporations experienced enormous increases in economic well-being (Mead, 1991). In addition, for the first time in human history, more individuals worked for someone else than for themselves.

However, these decades of progressive capitalism gave way to revolutionary changes in the world of work. With globalization, employers now had the option of hiring lower-wage workers overseas. Although this practice was reminiscent of the earlier abuses of capitalism, it occurred far enough away from home to be ignored. At the same time, a worldwide movement began to make people aware of the earth's limited resources. Moreover, elected leaders of both the United States and England adopted an economic philosophy in opposition to progressive capitalism. In this new approach, more resources were given to big business (e.g., tax exemptions and reduced regulatory fines and controls) in the hope that increased profits would "trickle down" to the average individual. But instead of a sharing of wealth, the typical employee's wages, benefits, and standard of living declined.

In addition, new information technologies offered companies new opportunities to rethink the relationships between global communication and local organization. One major result of this rethinking has been the downsized or reengineered organization, in which traditional communication hierarchies have been replaced by a team-based organization that can respond faster and with greater flexibility to worldwide economic patterns. Finally, as U.S. scholarship became more international, European studies in critical theory were discovered and imported back to the United States. Given the economic climate at the time, the European studies helped to generate interest in applying the questions and lessons of critical theory to organizations and communication in the United States.

Together, these changes have had a *revolutionary* impact on our lives. When the world of work changes fundamentally, every institution in society is challenged. And at the very core of this challenge are questions about power.

THE CENTRALITY OF POWER

Early attempts to define *power* are based on the assumption that it is something a person or group possesses and can exercise through actions. In their classic article, French and Raven (1968) propose five types of social power, following the assumption that person A has power over person B when A has control over some outcome B wants.

1. *Reward power:* Person A has reward power over person B when A can give some formal or informal reward in exchange for B's compliance, such as a bonus or award.
2. *Coercive power:* Person A has coercive power over person B when B perceives that certain behaviors on his or her part will lead to punishments from A, such as poor work assignments, relocation, or demotion.
3. *Referent power:* Person A has referent power over person B when B is willing to do what A asks in order to be like A. Mentors and charismatic leaders, for example, often have referent power.
4. *Expert power:* Person A has expert power over person B when B is willing to do what A says because B respects A's expert knowledge.
5. *Legitimate power:* Person A has legitimate power over person B when B complies with A's wishes because A holds a high-level position, such as division head, in the hierarchy.

French and Raven's approach to power is reflected in much of the research on compliance-gaining (Kipnis, Schmidt, & Wilkinson, 1980); and on behavior altering techniques (Richmond et al., 1984). Examples include research on how supervisors can persuade subordinates to do undesirable tasks, how employees can persuade supervisors and co-workers to give them desired resources, and even how teachers can encourage students to complete assignments.

But this approach to understanding power is incomplete. By focusing on the overt or surface exercise of power by individuals, we learn little about the more covert structures of power (Conrad, 1983). Unlike *overt power,* which is easy to spot and can in principle be resisted (though often at great costs), *covert* or *hidden power* is more insidious. Critical theory focuses on the control of employers over employees (Clegg, 1989) wherein power "resembles a loose coalition of interests more than a unified front. Critical theory is committed to unveiling the political stakes that anchor cultural practices" (Conquergood, 1991, p. 179).

Consider, for example, just how much invisible power is exerted over your choice of major, or for that matter, of being in school. Since the Industrial Revolution, nations have created "public schools" to educate society's young as a way of preparing them for a lifetime of work in organizations. Pennsylvania State University's motto, for instance, says the purpose of the university is "to educate the sons and daughters of the working classes in the agricultural and mechanical arts and sciences." A closer look at that sentence reveals evidence of a nineteenth-century separation of the "managerial" and "working" classes (wherein the rich attend "private" schools) alongside the belief that education should serve practical, state-mandated needs (in this case, those related to agriculture and engineering). Despite fiery debates among ideologically opposed camps, today's educational reforms are largely evolutionary: the question everyone shares is how best to educate students for our high-tech, networked world of work. As we will see, one challenge posed by critical approaches is that our system of education—and our assumptions of lifetime employment with a company—may be in need of reform in our rapidly changing world.

Power and Ideology

Ideology is used to describe bases of power, however and wherever they are expressed. Ideology also consists of our basic, often unexamined, assumptions about how things are or, in some cases, how they should be. During the era of classical management, for example, the dominant ideology about work was based on various assumptions: that men (especially, white men) were better suited to assembly lines than were women; that white men could learn faster than women and minorities and, therefore, should hold supervisory positions; that the U.S. system of work was second to none in the world; that Americans had a right to use the world's natural resources to build their cities, roads, and systems of commerce and industry; and that the American form of government was superior to all other forms (Banta, 1993).

Ideology touches every aspect of everyday life and is manifested in our words, actions, and practices. The existence of ideology encourages us to understand that power is not confined to government or politics, nor is it always overt or easy to spot. Because it structures our thoughts and controls our interpretations of reality, it is often beneath our awareness. It seems "natural," and it makes what we think and do seem "right." According to Michel Foucault (1979), ideological power is a widespread, intangible network of forces that weaves itself into subtle gestures and intimate utterances. As such, ideology does not reside in things but "in a network of relationships which are systematically connected" (Burrell, 1988, p. 227). Ideology exists in the practices of everyday life.

Moreover, ideology is never neutral. It is associated with the interests of dominant individuals and groups, and it is often exercised unconsciously. The pervasive powers of a group, at least from the perspective of people outside of the group, rest within its ideology. In this sense, ideology is always something the other person has. According to Jurgen Habermas (1972), most people think along these lines: "I view things as they really are, you squint at them through a tunnel vision imposed by some extraneous system of doctrine."

Among the recent efforts to investigate the relationship between ideology and organizational practices is Patricia Geist and Jennifer Dreyer's (1993) critique of the dominant model for health care. They explore this model's ability to define and control—through the routine doctor–patient interview—what is considered appropriate, professional, or ordinary health-care communication in ways that often give less weight to the patient's input. Using dialogic theory (Bakhtin, 1986), Geist and Dreyer propose an alternative model for communication encounters between health-care providers and their patients. By refocusing the dialogic encounter on what is *created* in communication (as opposed to what is *given* through scientific authority), Geist and Dreyer aim to empower those who seek medical treatment. Hence, two major challenges to the power of received ideology are present in their research agenda: (1) the power of the traditional medical model of scientific information gathering, and (2) the power of traditional models that distance researchers—and research practices—from the people they study.

Again, the powerful influences of ideology are linked to everyday organizational and research practices in ways that complicate our understanding of what happens in organizations and of the role researchers and their theories should play in those happenings. Before we extend the latter argument, however, we need to examine some of the sources of the hidden powers of ideological control.

THE HIDDEN POWER OF CULTURES: NATIVE ASSUMPTIONS

Ideology operates locally, regionally, nationally, and internationally. For example, ideology can operate internationally in our reactions to other cultures. Iris Varner and Linda Beamer (1995) identify three reactions that we typically have to persons who do not share our native culture:

1. *Assumptions of superiority:* Many cultures assume that their own values and practices are superior to those of others in the world. Hence, when cultural differences in understanding or in ways of doing things exist, English-speaking people tend to ideologically code those differences as primitive or backward, reserving for their own practices a culturally superior position that they assume is "normal." One example is our Western view that

the possession of advanced technologies—computers, fax machines, telephones, televisions—is equated with being educated or knowledgeable. However, many of the so-called Third World or underdeveloped countries of the world have better systems for handling conflict and sustaining marriages and families.

2. *Ethnocentrism:* There is a tendency among people of a culture to view their culture as the "right" one. This leads to complacency in our dealings with others who do not share our culture or its assumptions. American businesses, for example, have attempted to apply to their business dealings overseas the same assumptions they apply at home, often with disastrous results. Adapting to another's culture requires an openness to different ways of doing things, but ideology often makes this difficult.

3. *Assumptions of universality:* People often mistakenly assume that beneath differences in dress and behavior, all people are basically alike. This assumption can lead to misunderstanding and conflict among people from different cultures, who interpret and understand the world from different perspectives. The key is to find ways for people who think differently to work together.

Ideology exists at the surface of cultures. A German manufacturer, for example, recently told us that he had learned that "Americans are like peaches, while Germans are like coconuts." When asked to explain this statement, he added that "Americans like to present a soft, warm, and appealing surface to others, but at their very core is something very hard and impenetrable. Germans, on the other hand, present the world with a hard exterior, often perceived as cold, distant, difficult to crack, but inside they are the ones who are truly soft and warm." His statement is about ideology as much as it is about perception, and his delineation of cultural differences is much deeper than simple labels suggest. Abstract ideological terms such as *conservative* and *liberal* often obscure important individual differences and similarities. Consider also the many differences among those of us who call ourselves "college-educated Americans" or "IBM (or Mac) users." Ideology is pervasive and complex.

THE HIDDEN POWER OF IDEOLOGY: MANUFACTURED CONSENT

The hidden power of organizational systems and structures has been a central focus of critical theory. Jurgen Habermas (1972), a major proponent of modern critical theory, argues that social legitimation plays a major role in holding contemporary organizations together. According to Habermas, capitalist societies are characterized by the *manufacture of consent,* in which employees at all levels willingly adopt and enforce the legitimate power of the organization, society, or system of capitalism. Furthermore, only when this perceived legitimate power is challenged might the basic order face a crisis.

Manufactured consent is evident when an employee says "I'm just doing my job" in an attempt to justify some decision or action. As Mumby (1987) points out, "domination involves getting people to organize their behavior around a particular rule system." The system, not individual managers or actors, can then be blamed—but not held accountable—for actions taken in its name (p. 115). A recent law aimed at correcting this situation makes the senior management of large corporations personally responsible for any criminal actions taken on behalf of the company. Similarly, both Exxon and Union Carbide were held (somewhat) financially accountable for the environmental disasters, respectively, in Valdez, Alaska, and in Bhopal, India.

THE HIDDEN POWER OF COMMUNICATION: MYTHS, METAPHORS, AND STORIES

Myths contribute to the strength of a culture's ideology and its sources of power. These narratives often reveal the beliefs and values of a culture as they tell the stories of legendary heroes, of good and evil, and of origins and exits. In myths we find evidence of basic metaphors that structure "our" view of things. For example, both Goodall (1995a) and Rushing (1993) suggest that, in the West, there is a dominant mythic narrative that describes the origins of order and power and that features three main characters: (1) *power,* the expression of a sovereign, rational, unified, or modern self; (2) *other,* the force that resists the domination of the self by glorifying its opposites; and (3) *spirit,* a mysterious force that is capable (at least narratively) of resolving the differences between, and therefore uniting, power and other.

Organizational narratives, metaphors, and stories are important sources of power and ideology. Indeed, critical theory seeks to understand why organizational practices that maintain strong controls over employees are considered legitimate and, hence, not resisted (McPhee, 1985). Conrad argues persuasively that this kind of legitimation is maintained through such symbolic forms as metaphors, myths, and stories. At Ben and Jerry's Ice Cream, for instance, a theme of "social consciousness" is employed to justify managerial decisions regarding hiring, firing, promotions, and raises. Employees generally accept these controls as part of the "story" that distinguishes the organization and its culture. Over time, such myths, metaphors, and stories can come to define appropriate behavior and suspend employees' critical thinking (see Focus on Ethics 6.1).

Cultural stories about power tend to acquire not only the status of legend but also the influence of myth. A story circulating at a large consulting firm tells of a senior consultant rushing to meet a client, ignoring traffic laws, driving through

Metaphors Can Suspend Critical Thinking

"Family" is a common metaphor used by companies in the United States. For some companies, such as Disney, the metaphor has been very useful. The ideal family includes a warm, wholesome, caring, mutually supportive set of interdependent relationships characterized by open and honest communication. Viewed in this way, family is a positive metaphor for any firm.

But not all families conform to this ideal. Do the terms for describing the ideal family sometimes obscure dysfunctional power relationships between parents and children, among siblings, and with relatives? Should all families strive to achieve the same ideals? Are all successful businesses alike? Consider these questions in your response to the following situations:

1. You dislike your supervisor's frequent use of the family metaphor to explain his behavior (e.g., "Yes, I yelled at you about that report, but even in the best families that sometimes happens" and "We're all family here, so if you have personal problems you can tell me about them"). You believe your supervisor uses the family metaphor as an excuse for his irrational behavior as well as to gain unwarranted access to employees' private lives. What should you do?

2. Your company has just announced that at its annual holiday party, skits will be performed by employee work teams. Your team has been asked to write, produce, and perform a skit that portrays the company as a family. You view this as an opportunity to reveal both the positive and negative aspects of the organization's use of power and informal relationships. But two members of your team argue against your proposal; they agree with your ideas, but they fear management's response to the negative portrayals. You cite their objections as evidence of the company's problems. You strongly believe that the skit will provide a good opportunity to address those issues in a nonthreatening way. How will you argue your case at the next team meeting?

3. What other metaphors may be used to describe and to organize work relationships? Describe those metaphors and their ethical dimensions.

fences and onto sidewalks, and speeding the wrong way down one-way streets, while the new junior consultant sits white-knuckled in the passenger seat. They make it to the meeting on time. Afterward, the junior consultant confronts her boss: "Why did you drive like that? If we had been a few minutes late, the client would have understood!" Later that day, the junior consultant is told to clean out her desk.

The moral of this story is twofold: (1) Do what you must to accommodate a client and (2) do not challenge the judgment of superiors (or you will be fired). The story—despite its truth or falsity—reinforces existing power relations in the consulting firm.

THE HIDDEN POWER OF ORGANIZATIONAL COMMUNICATION: POLITICS

Dennis K. Mumby (1993) reminds us of a principal tenet of critical theory: "that organizations are not neutral sites of sensemaking; rather, they are created in the context of struggles between competing interest groups and systems of representation" (p. 21). Although researchers attempt to show how such struggles are carried out in organizations, they seem less attuned to the roles of *internal politics* and *ideologies* in their own explanatory systems.

Mumby goes on to suggest three ways to improve organizational communication research:

1. *Connect the political to the poetic.* Most research in organizations takes place behind the scenes; employees and managers are observed rather than engaged by the researcher and their behaviors and practices are analyzed on the basis of critical, cultural, or other theories. Researchers should more actively engage their subjects and turn the critical lens back upon themselves and their methods of study (see Goodall, 1991b, 1989).

2. *Conduct more participatory research.* In order "to break down the bifurcation between researchers and those being studied," academics should engage themselves in the types of work they investigate (Mumby, 1993, p. 20). Participatory research would help researchers identify sources of authority beyond the usual realm of academic theory (or at least reexamine the privileged position of current theory), as well as bring to workplaces the insights of those theories. As a result, the research process would encompass not only a search for knowledge, but also mobilization.

3. *Conduct more critically oriented empirical research.* Empirical researchers often do not incorporate critical theories into their studies. A closer alliance between empirical and critical theories would be beneficial to both lines of research. In particular, more attention should be paid to the relationships among specific communicative practices as well as to structures of power and domination (see Conrad, 1988; Rosen, 1985).

Mumby's (1993) suggestions target the general need to challenge the assumptions, definitions, and research methods of organizational communication.

THE HIDDEN POWER OF SOCIETY: HEGEMONY

Antonio Gramsci (1971) uses the term *hegemony* (pronounced "heh-jeh'-moh-nee") to describe the hidden power of society. It encompasses the power of rules, standard operating procedures, and routines. At a public swimming pool, for example, we abide by the posted rules, such as "No running or jumping." Rarely do we question those rules or seek to find out who posted them (in this case, most likely the person holding the insurance policy for the pool).

Similarly, managers of organizations work hard to achieve routine. This occurs when employees come to believe that their behavior is controlled not by other people but by the rules of the company. A subtle transformation takes place—from "This is how we've decided to do things" to "This is the way things are done." Only rarely does the latter situation remain negotiable. In most cases, members are not given the opportunity to redefine the situation.

Another example of hegemony is evident in our musical preferences. Although we think we have the freedom to choose our taste in music, the choices are narrowed by various sociopolitical and economic forces. The types of music we listen to and which musicians write and perform them are decided for us by the recording industry. Our ethnic background, social class, and gender also affect the kinds of music we are exposed to and, therefore, our choices.

Critical Theories of Power

FEMINIST THEORY

Feminist theory focuses on the oppression and exploitation of women in the workplace and on giving women more power and voice in organizational dialogue.

Research on women in organizations has followed closely the view of power described thus far in this chapter. Early studies sought only to identify strategies and behaviors women needed to succeed at work. *Games Your Mother Never Taught You: Corporate Gamesmanship for Women* (Harrigan, 1977) and *The New Executive Woman: A Guide to Business Success* (Williams, 1977), for example, did not challenge the status quo in organizations. Instead, they adopted a deficiency model of women, claiming that women needed to learn certain behaviors to succeed in organizations. This approach corresponds to the examination of overt power strategies generally.

Rosabeth Moss Kanter's *Men and Women of the Corporation* (1977) marked a turning point in the history of thinking about women in organizations. In particular, her discussion of *tokenism*—the promotion of a few women into highly visible positions—argues that increased publicity and attention result in greater pressure to perform and an increased likelihood of failure. Kanter also argues that the responsibility for change should be at the system level because individuals working alone are likely to fail. Other researchers adopt a more radical critique of definitions of organization. Focusing on the underlying assumptions and ideologies of a male-dominated society, they identify hidden aspects of patriarchal organizations that can lead to discrimination against women (Blair et al., 1995; Bullis & Glaser, 1992; Calvert & Ramsey, 1992; Ferguson, 1984).

Implicit in the feminist approach is the assumption that women have distinct ways of seeing the world and of constructing meanings for it. Consequently, organizational dialogues may be transformed by women's voices. According to the feminist critique, however, most corporations are still structured on the basis of outdated societal norms and fail to account for women's needs, such as day care (Freeman, 1990). One of the most significant differences between the feminist worldview and the male-dominated organization has to do with *hierarchy.* While most contemporary organizations are hierarchical, women in general tend to think of organizations in terms of networks or webs of relationships, with leadership at the center of the web, rather than on top of a pyramid (Helgeson, 1990).

In contrast to traditional models, narratives by and about women tend to value

1. fluid boundaries between personal life and work life;
2. relational aspects of work;
3. a balanced lifestyle;
4. a nurturant approach to co-workers;
5. a network of relationships outside the organization;
6. leadership as a web, not a hierarchy;
7. a service orientation to clients; and
8. work as a means of developing personal identity (Grossman & Chester, 1990; Helgeson, 1990; Lunneborg, 1990).

Valuing women's voices in organizations means opening the dialogue to a different set of assumptions: Can we define competition as "doing excellently" instead of "excelling over" (Calas & Smircich, 1990; Lugones & Spelman, 1987)? Can we define power as a way to enhance, rather than diminish, the power of everyone (Miller, 1982)? Can we value and even seek diversity in organizations? Can we view organizations as being responsible for social change (Marshall, 1984)? Can hierarchies be abandoned or revisioned as networks (Ferguson, 1984)?

Judi Marshall (1993) suggests that viewing an organization from a feminist perspective encourages us to examine four differences regarding power and in-terpretation:

1. *Male and female values:* In what is usually conceived of as an "archetypal polarity" (Marshall, 1993, p. 124), men are associated with *agency* whereas women are associated with *communion.* From an Eastern perspective, this relationship forms the *yin* and *yang.* Male values are associated with "self-assertion, separation, independence, control, competition, focused percep-tion, rationality, analysis, clarity, discrimination, and activity. Underlying themes are a self-assertive tendency, control of the environment, and focus on personal and interpersonal processes" (Marshall, 1993, p. 124). Female values are associated with "interdependence, cooperation, receptivity, merging, acceptance, awareness of patterns, wholes and contexts, emo-tional tone, personalistic perception, being, intuition, and synthesizing. Un-derlying themes are openness to the environment, interconnection, and mutual development" (Marshall, 1993, p. 124). Although these polarities have been used to point to differences between men and women, Marshall sees "male and female values as qualities to which both sexes have access, rather than the exclusive properties of men and women, respectively" (1993, p. 125). She argues that "unmasking and contradicting the male pos-itive/female negative values of this world has been a major feminist en-deavor. . . . At times, the values have become reversed; female becomes all positive and male all negative" (p. 126).

2. *Male-dominated cultures:* Marshall (1993) argues that "male forms are the norm to which organizational members adapt. Women copy these in order to gain acceptance and succeed in their careers" (p. 126). Women workers are typically judged according to male standards for job performance and are denied legitimacy for their home lives. Male dominance is viewed as a hidden power because it is perceived as the norm, goes largely unrecog-nized and tends to be relatively stable and enduring. Language and imagery in business tend to reinforce and reflect this pattern.

3. *Male-dominated organizations are high-context cultures:* Marshall (1993) draws on Edward T. Hall's (1973) distinction between high- and low-context cultures to characterize women's experiences in male-dominated organizations: Women "do not share much of the contexting that makes communication understandable. Nor do they have equal rights to engage in defining meaning within the patterns of communication that are ex-perienced by men as low context because of their (women's) subordinate social position" (p. 127). Men transmit messages that carry implicit (male-associated) meanings that women try to adapt to and understand. Women are required to learn to read the culture through a male-dominated, high-context lens, and to monitor their communication and behavior accord-ingly.

4. *Women as communication:* According to Gregory Bateson (1972), "being a woman is 'information,' in that it is 'a difference that makes a difference'". Marshall (1993) uses his descriptor to detail the following core issues of "women as information" in organizations:

tensions about status: Women generally have less tension about status, which allows the male-dominated culture to read "female managers as secretaries, and so on" (p. 130). Women in nontraditional jobs disturb the hierarchy by "challeng[ing] people to innovate and to remodel old routines" (p. 130).

public employment versus the private home: Here "men are largely identified with the public world and women with the private" (Marshall, 1993, p. 130).

man-made language: Terms associated with women are devaluing (Mumby and Putnam, 1993), and "women are often stereotyped and put in their place" (Marshall, 1993, p. 131).

gender-differentiated discourse: Women tend to speak less often, less lengthily, and less loudly than men do, and their communication is evaluated on the basis of a male model.

exclusion from men's informal networks and communication: Women in powerful positions are most often excluded, which has "significant impacts on their contributions to decision making and their abilities both to understand and to influence organizational cultures" (Marshall, 1993, p. 131).

different patterns of thinking and valuing: Women tend to be more relational, contextual, and personal than men, all of which have major implications for the norms of speaking and listening in organizations.

Feminist critical theory shows how exploited groups can challenge the hegemony of a dominant ideology by proposing different assumptions and definitions. Marshall (1993) suggests strategies for resisting the gendering of organizations. Derived from a dialogic model of organizational communication, the strategies are aimed at gaining voice, adapting to context, translating and screening out male-dominated forms of power, and challenging male assumptions about organizational communication.

WORK-HATE NARRATIVES

"I hate my job. But I lay awake at night worried that I'll lose it. The company downsized and restructured. We went to teams, and I was 'redefined' (they changed my job title). I'm no longer a manager. Now I'm a team member who shares facilitator responsibilities with other members of the team. I hate the job, but I feel powerless to change it. And given the economy, I'm not likely to find another job that pays as well. So I just grin and bear it."

"The company I work for was bought by a Japanese conglomerate. I figured I might learn something new about manufacturing efficiency, and I did. I also kept my job, which was important. But no matter how hard I work I'll never advance to management. In America, if you work hard you are supposed to get ahead."

"I hate this company for what it's done to me and my family."

In a world where work is often associated with one's identity and where making a living is a key to social status, sudden changes that negatively affect one's work status can be devastating. As companies downsize and redefine the roles of their employees, many people fear the loss of their jobs in an uncertain future. The preceding examples of *work-hate narratives* point to an insidious form of hegemony: a narrowly defined but pervasively enforced system that defines rational responses to circumstances beyond our control. In short, we are expected—or trained—to surrender unconditionally to organizational changes.

Indeed, we are educated and socialized largely to accept the conditions of work life, which require us to exchange our well-being for a steady paycheck. Leaving school to go to work for a company (at least since the Industrial Revolution) is also a form of control. Most of us willingly accepted these trade-offs when jobs were plentiful and middle-class society was relatively prosperous. Our hopes for ourselves and our children were rooted in the promises of progress—advancing up the company ladder and improving our way of life through work. But these assumptions are becoming less valid as the terms of a new social contract are worked out. At the same time, middle-class people are losing jobs as the U.S. workforce expands at the low end of the economic sector (Aronowitz & DiFazio, 1994; Rifkin, 1995). Job competition is intense, and people are expected to work harder to keep the (often multiple) jobs they have. In addition, advancement opportunities are more likely to be lateral in nature as the metaphor of "climbing the corporate ladder" continues to dissolve. As a result, a clear distinction between the haves and the have-nots exists in almost every community in North America. Even more pronounced are worldwide divisions between a Global North (of haves) and a Global South (of have-nots) (Barnet & Cavanaugh, 1994).

As levels of organizational authority and control increase, the likelihood of worker resistance also increases. Forms of resistance range from work-hate narratives (Goodall, 1995) to violence in the workplace. The work-hate narrative tells the story of the alienated, displaced, downsized, or angry worker. It can function as a therapeutic tool for relieving job pressure, assessing work-related situations, and regaining control over emotions. Work-hate narratives typically have two stages. In the first stage, the narrator's shock and surprise upon learning of the organization's changes combines with a lost sense of identity. Consider, for example, the following narrative of a middle-aged executive who was downsized:

> The first thing I felt [when] . . . I was fired was surprise—bone-rattling shock at finding myself, for the first time since the week I graduated from grade school, without a place in the world of work. My luck had been so good for so many years that I'd learned to think of it as something I had earned [or] . . . was owed. The idea that it could turn bad so abruptly was, for a while, impossible to absorb. I walked the streets in an almost trancelike state, as if I were on the bottom of the sea, cut off from everything, not like other people anymore. I started to daydream about walking through my front door . . . and seeing dozens of people—old bosses, old colleagues, the very people who had done this to me—leap out from behind the furniture and yell "Surprise! Surprise!" In my daydream they're wearing party hats. They explain how the whole thing had been part of some experiment, and how sorry they were to have had to put me through it. Ah well, I say with a smile, all's well that ends well. But each time I come home, they are not there. (Meyer, 1995, p. 39)

In the second stage of the work-hate narrative, the narrator is more accepting of the new circumstances, but often expresses self-blame. In addition, intense envy of co-workers unaffected by the changes is common at this stage. Consider the following example:

> I am ashamed of . . . my feelings: murderous rage, envy, fear, and mostly, shame itself. . . . I am ashamed of myself for being out of work, for getting my family into such a fix, for allowing myself to become an "executive" in the first place and then letting the whole thing go so wrong. I am ashamed of myself for losing. . . .
>
> Yet I'm jealous of anybody who still has the kind of job I used to have, of almost anybody who has a job, period. . . .
>
> Calm down, I tell myself. Stop pacing. Find something sensible to do.
>
> But I find that I can't do any such thing. (Meyer, 1995, p. 39)

We can imagine how this executive's narrative may turn out. On the one hand, if positive results come from the loss of identity and self-blame brought on by the changed circumstances, the story may become one of renewal or of "finding a new life." On the other hand, if the narrator's envy of others and internal rage are not balanced by hopes of a productive future, some other sort of outcome is likely.

Remedies for these tales of woe brought on by sudden changes in people's work identity are part of the growing literature on managing organizational change (Noer, 1993). But work-hate narratives and, in extreme cases, workplace violence, are evidence of the high stakes involved in organizational change—takeovers, restructuring, job redefinition, and downsizing.

Pro-People or Pro-Profits?

The critical approach to organizational communication favors the individual or class of individuals and is, therefore, pro-people. It is often criticized for not taking a pro-profits stance and for underestimating the need for companies to remain profitable in an increasingly competitive global market. But according to Stanley Deetz (1991, 1995), we need to defend individual freedom from corporate domination. He argues that corporate domination in U.S. society runs deeper than most of us recognize, and that corporations have replaced governments as the main controlling force in people's lives.

Recall that the keys to control are: (1) it is hidden and (2) people believe they have freedom of choice even though their options are actually quite limited. Thus, according to Deetz (1991), we believe U.S. society is democratic because we vote to elect our leaders, but there is little democracy or participation in the decisions that are made for us by corporations even though the issues profoundly affect our lives. Deetz calls this form of control the "corporate colonization of the life world" and he believes it will lead to the eventual breakdown of families, schools, and other social institutions. Such issues as childbirth, fashion, education, and even morality have been removed from the domain of the family and turned into externally purchased goods and services (Lukes, 1986). People's decisions about where to live and when to have children are increasingly based on career-related concerns. Alienation and loss of identity result when people can no longer turn to the social institutions that once fostered a sense of belonging to a family or community. Modern education, increasingly concerned with training students for occupations, thereby reinforces the notion that corporate domination is both practical and acceptable. According to Deetz (1991):

> With such institutional domination in place, every other institution subsidizes or pays its dues for the integration given by the corporate structure, and by so doing reduces its own institutional role. The state developed for *public good* interprets that as the need for order and economic growth. The family that provided *values and identity* transforms that to emotional support and standard of living. The educational institution fostering *autonomy and critical thought* trains for occupational success. (p. 17)

Despite his sobering analysis, Deetz and others see positive change as possible in the current business world. Peter Block (1993), for example, argues that the ideal of *stewardship* should replace current notions of self-interest in workplace management. Workplaces could thereby operate democratically as places where employees make decisions together and share accountability for the outcomes of those decisions.

Similarly, Deetz (1995) outlines what he calls the "multiple stakeholder model" for balancing the corporation's profitability needs with society's needs for well-adjusted citizens (see Figure 6.1). In this model, Deetz identifies "stakeholder groups" as including not only consumers, workers, investors, and suppliers, but also host communities, general society, and the worldwide ecological community. Echoing Paul Hawken's (1993) "ecology of commerce," Deetz aims to demonstrate how business decisions influence all aspects of society and ecology. He thus assesses the worth of a business not only in terms of its profitability, but also in terms of how it uses resources (natural, human, technological, and so on) and affects the human community. In democratic societies, the public charter of private corporations gives people the right to perform such analyses. It also gives people the responsibility of ensuring that companies do not take from the collective welfare more than they give back in the forms of products, services, and taxes. These "outcome interests," Deetz argues, must be balanced with stakeholder interests through a coordination of "workplace management." In other words, corporate managers and owners, employees, and citizens must all act responsibly to ensure that bottom-line concerns in corporations do not negatively affect society and the ecology of the planet.

Deetz's (1995) multiple stakeholder model attempts to balance global economic competition with a respect for the well-being of the planet and its citizens. As such, it raises critical questions about the potential consequences of a powerful economic elite and of decision making in the hands of multinational corporate and governmental ladders. But how can this model be applied? Deetz (1995) outlines four steps toward workplace democracy in which shared decision making among stakeholders is crucial.

1. *Create a workplace in which every member thinks and acts like an owner.* The point of business is to be of service; this is best accomplished when every stakeholder becomes responsible for decision making and accountable for the outcomes of those decisions both to the business and to the relationship of the business to society.

2. *The management of work must be reintegrated with the doing of work.* The cost of people watching other people work for the purpose of controlling what gets done and how it is done can no longer be seen as economically efficient. Moreover, it leads to bad decisions (i.e., decisions about how to do work are best made by those who actually perform it and will be rewarded by its outcomes), and to less accountability (i.e., "watched" persons tend to resist domination by finding ways to slow down work processes or "goof-off" on the job).

STAKEHOLDER GROUPS	MANAGING PROCESS	OUTCOME INTERESTS
Consumers		Goods and services
Workers		Income distribution
Investors	Coordination ⟶	Use of resources
Suppliers		Environment effects
Host communities		Economic stability
General society		Labor force development
World ecological community		Lifestyles
		Profits
		Personal identities
		Childrearing practices

FIGURE 6.1
Multiple Stakeholder Model of the Corporation in Society

Source: Stanley Deetz, *Transforming Communication, Transforming Business* (Cresskill, N.J.: Hampton Press, 1995), p. 50.

3. *Quality information must be widely distributed.* In order to fully empower workers and the societies they serve, the current system of filling up the day with mostly meaningless memos, letters, faxes, and newsletters that only encourage control and domination, should be replaced by bringing to the attention of workers "real" information about what is impacting the business and how the business is impacting society and the planet.
4. *Social structure should grow from the bottom rather than be reinforced from the top.* If the basic idea of a participative democratic workplace values the consent of the governed in the governance of everyday affairs, everything from routine office policies to limiting the terms of managers should be accomplished by ongoing negotiations among the multiple stakeholders. (pp. 170–71)

Although theoretically radical and practically difficult to implement, Deetz's suggestions move us toward a more democratic dialogue, or what he calls "constitutive codetermination" (p. 174). Similar strategies have been implemented by some companies in their new plants, such as Saturn Corporation and BMW North America. Indeed, Deetz's model may be easier to implement in new companies than in existing corporate and governmental structures.

Another limitation of critical theory's revision of existing practices is inherent in the suggestion that democracies are improved when power and decision making are more equally distributed. However, there is no position that is not ideological. Hence, one group's view of the necessity for change tends to be countered by another group's belief that change is unnecessary. To assert the inherent "rightness" of one position is, by the very questions critical theorists have taught us to raise, at best naive and at worst elitist.

Critical Theory and Organizational Communication Research

In many respects, research from a critical perspective is similar to that of the cultural approach (see Chapter 5). In order to discover the deep structures of power, the investigator must look for details not only about *what happens* in the organization but also *why it happens.* From a critical perspective, the cultural approach moves in the right direction by focusing on meaning and sense-making. But it neglects to ask *in whose interest* certain meanings and interpretations lie. A critical theorist, then, gathers interpretive cultural data about language, motives, and actions, and makes judgments about the power relationships that exist in the organization. This is a very subjective enterprise; not only can critical theorists be criticized for all of the same faults as cultural researchers (e.g., narrow samples and bias in selecting participants and events), but they can also be called elitists.

Critical theorists have been classified as elitists because, in practice, they must be willing to argue that certain individuals or groups are oppressed but remain unaware of the oppression. This is the most serious problem with asserting the existence of hegemony. In a marked departure from the cultural approach, critical theorists often maintain that people do not know their own minds (Clegg, 1989).

SUMMARY

Critical theory favors individual creativity over constraints on behavior. It seeks to expose corporate colonization, wherein corporations—particularly multinational ones—unobtrusively control much of our lives, from economies to systems of education and training. Similarly, feminism and hegemony reveal the cultural difficulties associated with opening up the organizational dialogue to diverse voices, as well as the potential gains in new organizing methods that might come from such a dialogue. Work-hate narratives, which reveal how individuals are affected by changes in organizations, underscore critical theory's emphasis on everyday practices as a source for understanding power and its consequences.

Until recently, critical theory has been less than successful at advancing alternative organizational arrangements for liberating employees from domination and allowing organizations to survive in the current economic system. While critiques of capitalism have value, critical theory is often criticized for not seeking a middle ground, one that would allow people in organizations to incrementally improve their lives (Carey, 1992). Focused on macroeconomic issues, critical theories lack an applied approach to the complex contours of organizational life. In this sense, most early attempts to apply critical theories to organizations have not led to real improvements. For example, in explaining how and why work-hate narratives occur, critical theory addresses neither remedies for them nor the hegemonic interests that contribute to and shape them.

Despite its limitations, however, critical theory plays three important roles in organizational communication studies. First, it reminds us that meaning is always inherently political. There are no neutral interpretations and no "right" ideology. Second, critical theory points out that the greatest challenge to the hegemony of international corporate power is rooted in democratic alternatives to workplace design and participation. Given Barnet and Cavanaugh's (1994), Rifkin's (1995), and Aronowitz and DiFazio's (1994) bleak visions of our multinational, "megacorporation-controlled" future, we should actively pursue alternative models for promoting diverse participation in an open dialogue. Finally, the new questions about organizing posed by critical theory has encouraged theorists and practitioners to seek ways of creating participative workplaces. Their work aims to transform the controlling and potentially alienating work environment into a more democratic and more profitable environment through the multiple stakeholder model.

The critical approach to organizing and communicating represents an important transition from the *modern* to the *postmodern* organization. Questions about the legitimacy of power tend to lead to other questions about the social order on which that legitimacy is based. In Chapter 7, we consider postmodern perspectives on organizational communication.

C   E

THE BRILLIANT ENGINEER

Carl McKnight is an electrical engineer with twenty-seven years of experience at a major aerospace firm in California. During his long career, Carl has played many pivotal roles in the company, particularly in its development of the space program. He is well respected by his peers and has received a number of awards from both the company and government agencies for his work.

Other than reading scientific journals and attending an occasional convention, Carl does not need to do much else to stay current in his field. He came to it as an electrical genius. Even in college he did not have to work as hard as other students to succeed.

Recently, however, Carl has sensed that his technical expertise seems to carry less weight. In the past, his colleagues regarded his role in designing a new satellite or spacecraft as crucial. Now, however, his comments are often met with groans. Carl is not sure what to make of this change, but he suspects that it may be related to changes in what customers are looking for in electrical and aerospace design. Carl feels that the customers are too willing to forgo cutting-edge design in exchange for lower cost. He is also offended because his expertise, in a sense, has become irrelevant.

ASSIGNMENT

Apply what you have learned in this chapter about critical theory and related concepts to envision a future for Carl McKnight. In responding to the following questions, make sure to address the connections among sources of expertise, sources of overt and hidden power, and processes of overt and covert communication.

1. From his manager's point of view, what plans should be made for Carl's future? How can he best be made a part of the changing situation?
2. From his peers' perspective, what is the best possible future for Carl?
3. From Carl's point of view, what has happened and what should happen next?

CHAPTER 7

Postmodern Perspectives on Organizations and Communication

Reality isn't what it used to be.
• Steiner Kvale, cited in *The Truth About the Truth* (1995)

Postmodernism: Does it exist at all and, if so, what does it mean? Is it a concept or a practice, a matter of local style or a . . . new period or economic phase? . . . Are we truly beyond the modern, truly in (say) a postindustrial age?
• Hal Foster, *The Anti-Aesthetic* (1984)

QUESTIONS

FOR DISCUSSION

• What ideas comprise the postmodern approach to organizations and communication?

• Why does BMW North America define itself as "an information-processing and communications company"?

• What makes the *Nordstrom Employee Handbook* a postmodern document?

• What do postmodernists mean by "work is reframed as interpretation"?

In this chapter, we continue our exploration of organizational communication theories that challenge fundamental assumptions about the world of work. Our focus here is on the postmodern approach. While all chapters in this book aim to prepare you for the transition from school to work, this chapter is especially important in that regard. It discusses what you are most likely to confront when you enter the world of work: a postmodern organization.

We begin our discussion of postmodernism first by defining its primary characteristics and then by way of an example of a postmodern organization: BMW's plant in Spartanburg, South Carolina. We take you on a tour of the plant, pointing out instances of postmodernism as we proceed. After our tour, we examine the historical underpinnings of postmodern theory as well as critics' objections to this perspective on organizing.

What Is Postmodern Theory?

The *postmodern approach* encompasses a social, aesthetic, and political movement whose themes challenge all forms of modern knowledge and the forms of organizing that result from them (Best & Kellner, 1991; Harvey, 1989). Unlike the classical management, human relations, and systems approaches, which envision a progressive, well-ordered society that values rational, cognitive, self-interested, and structural themes, the postmodern approach values counter-rational, reflexive, other-oriented, global, and networked models for order and for organizational study.

Walter Truett Anderson (1995) observes that the transition to a postmodern approach "doesn't lend itself to simple summaries" (p. 10); rather, it is best introduced by way of its four primary assumptions:

1. *Self-concept:* Identity or self-concept (i.e., our ideas about who we are) is not "found" in fixed social roles or traditions but "made" or constructed out of popular culture (e.g., the media's portrayals of work and family on television and in films serve as resources for understanding the self).
2. *Moral and ethical discourse:* Morality is not "found" in a particular culture or religious heritage but "made" or forged out of dialogue and choice.
3. *Art and culture:* No one style dominates; instead, there are endless improvisations and variations on themes, filled with parody and playfulness. Traditional stories are told in new ways and genres are merged (e.g., rap songs with country music lyrics). As a result, previously separate activities and approaches come to lose their distinctiveness.
4. *Globalization:* For the first time in human history, a truly global civilization characterized by rapid information exchange and unprecedented mobility

exists. At the same time, globalization has led to confusion, blurred bound-aries, and endless possibilities for reinventing ourselves.

When the first edition of this textbook was published in 1993, only a few leading organizations had made the postmodern turn. Most companies were still struggling with what postmodern concepts had to do with business. Even today, not all organizations have been affected by postmodern changes. But change is occurring rapidly, and the chances are good that after you graduate you will en-ter a *postmodern organization.* It is characterized by team-based organizing, minimal hierarchies, computer-aided technology and global networks, and project-based (rather than career-oriented) jobs.

A Tour of a Postmodern Organization

We begin our exploration with a tour of a new American automobile plant built on postmodern themes and dedicated to state-of-the-art organizational com-munication. BMW, a well-known German automaker, recently opened its first U.S. plant in Spartanburg, South Carolina. The decision to do so was based on many factors, including lower labor costs, improved access to systems of trans-portation, tax incentives offered by the state of South Carolina, a local pool of skilled manufacturing workers and supporting industries, and access to nearby educational institutions. This state-of-the-art plant was constructed on schedule, workers were hired and trained, and production of BMW automobiles began during 1994.

BMW's Spartanburg plant is an interesting experiment in postmodern orga-nizing. As Walt Benkhe, BMW North America's communication manager, puts it, "We built this plant as a theory of postmodern communication. We know we built it right; the question is whether we chose the right theory."

One of the most interesting and challenging aspects of BMW's hiring prac-tices is a commitment to diverse subcultures in its multinational operations. BMW North America is a German firm operating in the U.S. South. Its team lead-ers and skilled workers are largely drawn from competing Japanese, American, German, Swedish, British, French, Italian, and Korean automobile manufactur-ers. This is an experiment in diversity—of different subcultures, languages, definitions of quality, and experiences in organizations—that most other companies have not been willing to undertake. In addition, BMW North Amer-ica competes in the global market with its parent company in Germany. At the Spartanburg plant, Americans build what are generally thought of as German automobiles.

FROM SIGNS TO PRACTICES

A sign is posted at the employee entrance to BMW's Spartanburg plant:

> Welcome to BMW. We are an information-processing and communications company that, as a happy by-product, shares in the building of fine automobiles for world markets.

What does this sign mean? Is it usual for an automaker to say that making automobiles is a "by-product" of its corporate identity as an "information-processing and communications company"? Why does BMW North America think of itself as a communications company? Postmodern theory helps to answer these questions.

One important tenet of postmodern organizational communication is that signs do not represent the territories they purport to describe; rather, they evoke meanings for those who read them. Therefore, the issue is not so much what BMW's sign means, but the kinds of reactions it elicits in employees who read it. The message of the sign is purposefully ambiguous and open to multiple interpretations (Eisenberg, 1984).

This leads us to another principle of postmodern or organizational communication: What gets read into the sign shapes action. That is, communication processes and multiple interpretations of meanings define and shape organizational outcomes. Unlike classical management and human relations theories, which focus on clear communication and interpretation of a single meaning, the postmodern approach is both more open-ended and concerned with the connection between multiple interpretations and overt behavior.

One interpretation of the BMW sign is that it represents the company's focus on complex information processing, a common feature of postmodern organizing. When BMW says it is an "information-processing and communications company," it recognizes that "organization" and "communication" are synonymous. Hence, in the postmodern view, all companies are communication companies because they rely on communication to organize processes and outcomes. In addition, the systems approach emphasizes the need for redundancy and information feedback to reduce information loss and interruption, to correct potential misinterpretations and errors, and generally to keep the company aware of how well it is functioning. BMW recognizes that doing business in a global market requires an interface between people and advanced information-processing and communications technologies. How people communicate through those advanced technologies is vital to the manufacturing process at BMW.

The BMW sign also suggests that the company views communication as the primary vehicle for organizing and managing work. In addition, managing communication and accomplishing work involves coordinating the construction of meaning; it must attain primacy over all other processes if the products of the company are to succeed. In this regard, BMW acknowledges that it is a global business made up of diverse subcultures of workers and managers who use communication to accomplish their jobs. The company thus has a flattened hierarchy and encourages its employees to share quality information. At BMW no employee makes a living observing, monitoring, or evaluating the work of others. Instead, all employees are communicators and members of a team of car manufacturers, marketeers, and salespersons.

DEMOCRACY IN THE WORKPLACE

As we tour the BMW plant, other postmodern principles can be observed. The plant floor is designed to encourage communication. Also inherent in its design are important organizing practices and strategic goals. For example, there is an emphasis on shared responsibility and accountability. BMW believes that every worker shares equally in the communication and information processing that leads to the manufacture of its products. Workers are paid to think and to communicate their thoughts to others. All employees, from the company president to the custodial staff, wear the same clothing: a white uniform with BMW's logo and the employee's first name stitched over the heart, thus emphasizing the equality of communication opportunities regardless of position.

This concept of equality and shared responsibility is also central to the company's team-based organizing in shipping and receiving, customer service, the assembly process, and the sales and marketing office. In this sense, BMW is a company with an empowered view of information sharing and decision making that is characteristic of the workplace democracies envisioned by Deetz (1995).

FACILITATING MULTICULTURAL COMMUNICATION

The plant floor at BMW North America is arranged in large, open circles so that all workers can see the entire operation at a glance. Workers may communicate at any time with other workers and, because power is shared equally, any worker can take responsibility for the quality of the product. Each employee must sign off on each car before it moves to the next station, thereby reinforcing the need to be accountable for all work performed.

Also apparent at the company is the belief that a message may have multiple meanings. Postmodern communication assumes that signs are ambiguous and that meanings are fluid and changing. Therefore, communication is viewed as a vehicle for interpretation, rather than for eliciting fixed or "correct" meanings. Unlike earlier models of communication as self-based and linear, the postmodern approach at BMW is other-oriented; that is, a message is adapted to the audience for which it is intended. Given the presence of *fourteen* different subcultures working to produce the same automobiles, it is likely that misinterpretations will occur among workers who speak different languages, in translations and cultural nuances, and as a result of other sources of ambiguity. However, BMW respects these sources of communication problems as natural and provides employees with ways of working them out.

In addition, suppliers and customers are primary concerns at BMW. For example, each work station along the assembly line is connected by computer to a network of dealers, who report on any problems encountered with the plant's automobiles. Referred to as "Continuous Quality Improvement," this reporting system allows workers to take time out from production, meet as a team at the point in the line where the problem occurs, and work to solve it. This concern for linking communication between the company and its customers and suppliers is typical of the learning organization we discussed in Chapter 4. Continuous quality improvements are multiculturally dependent on improved information processing, which, in turn, is dependent on learning from the multicultural information the company processes. BMW has thus fashioned itself as a networked company, opening channels for communicating information across all subcultures.

BMW's emphasis on customer service is based on the postmodern view that customers are important participants in the company's dialogue. As partners in the manufacturing and sales processes, customers must be "designed into" the system of communication. Their opinions, beliefs, and values are regarded as important sources of information for improving the quality and delivery of products and services.

As a multinational firm that manufactures automobiles for various countries located throughout the world, BMW must ensure that each car is built according to the exact specifications of the country it will be shipped to. Those specifications can differ significantly among countries, affecting, for example, how the electrical system is wired, where the steering wheel is positioned, and the type of tires the car receives. As a result, BMW's assembly line must be flexible. Workers are cross-trained in the various national standards of automobile manufacture, and quality control is continuously monitored to ensure that changes in those standards are incorporated into the specifications. The cost of resources is also monitored given the fluctuating exchange rates of global markets.

The company's emphasis on global marketing is part of a general postmodern challenge shaped by global competition and global economics. Not only must BMW's cars be built to the specifications of various markets, they must also be constantly upgraded to meet the demands of those markets. BMW thus hires employees from competing firms who represent the various markets and understand their unique needs.

BMW is committed to ecological awareness. The most toxic product used in manufacturing automobiles is a painting by-product called "slag." BMW designed its painting facility in a way that reduces slag production by 80 percent. It is also working toward a goal of recycling at least 90 percent of automobile parts.

CORPORATE IMAGE

BMW is a communications company represented by its logo or emblem. Marketed worldwide, that logo is itself a product. It creates an image in the minds of customers of a company culture characterized by "pastiche economics" (Jameson, 1984). (A *pastiche* is a kind of collage of information from various sources.) Contributing to BMW's image are various sources of rhetorical appeal: a distinguished automobile with a racing heritage, a highly sophisticated use of technology (ironically, BMW is actually among the lowest-tech firms in the business), European charm, and exclusive class appeal (in that most people cannot afford the expensive automobile). In addition, postmodernism is evident in BMW's aesthetic playfulness with real and imagined images of itself, as well as in its promotion of its ecological, community, and global awareness.

In its emphasis on creating and maintaining a responsible corporate image, BMW understands that customers do not simply purchase products; they also purchase what the products stand for, according to the image promoted by the company. Unlike earlier theories of organizational communication that separate "images" from "realities," postmodern approaches reflect a union of the two concepts (as revealed in the commonly heard postmodern slogan, "Trust the surfaces").

TEAMS AND GLOBAL NETWORKS

While classical theories of organizing and communicating value the rational individual, and systems and cultural theories move toward teams and communities, postmodern theories embrace teams and global networks. Thus, as we leave the BMW plant floor and move through the sales and marketing offices, we see that the company is dedicated to team-based organizing at all levels of production, marketing, and sales. We also see that it is attempting to be a valuable partner in the local as well as the global community.

BMW emphasizes a union of team productivity and communication effectiveness. The value of any theory is in its application, which in BMW's case is the ability to maximize plant efficiency through improved communication. Its focus on interconnected teams helps keep costs down while also serving as a reminder to employees of their need to communicate with each other in order to improve manufacturing and sales and the company's role in local and global communities. Unlike the rational employee who makes disinterested decisions based on principles of scientific management, the BMW worker is a knowledgeable employee who learns by making use of his or her experience of work.

Finally, postmodern organizations often demonstrate a commitment to being responsible members of the local community. Part of the BMW plant in Spartanburg houses a community center called the Zentrum. It serves as a meeting place for community groups and as an educational center for local schools. An obvious example of good corporate public relations, BMW's community center also serves civic groups and political leaders likely to have influence over the company's future. In addition, the center symbolizes the postmodern importance of the company's image in the community as a commodity. This multinational corporation's community center reminds us of Barnet and Cavanaugh's (1994) question about the future of organizing: "Can we build a global consciousness rooted in authentic local communities?" (p. 430).

The Postmodern Turn: Where Did It Come From?

Although the term *postmodern* is gaining widespread use in business and industry, it is still the subject of much debate. Various academic disciplines use the term to refer to different historical beginnings, material themes, and theoretical issues (Best & Kellner, 1991; Connor, 1989; Gergen, 1991). Partly because each discipline's interests are articulated differently, and partly because the term itself expresses different perspectives on knowledge and meaning in society, it may best be defined as a sign that resists a common signifier. Nonetheless, our focus here is on postmodern concepts as they relate to the academic study of organizational communication.

POSTMODERNITY AND POSTMODERNISM

Stephen Best and Douglas Kellner's (1991) distinction between *postmodernity* and *postmodernism* provides a useful starting point: "The term 'postmodernity' describe[s] the supposed epoch that follows modernity, and 'postmodernism' describe[s] movements and artifacts in the cultural field that can be distinguished from modernist movements, texts, and practices" (p. 5). Three important points arise in the distinction between postmodernity and postmodernism: (1) the idea of a historical break that brought (2) important political and aesthetic movements that led to (3) new cultural understandings and practices.

A Historical Break

Postmodernity refers generally to the period in history that followed modernity (Habermas, 1981; Harvey, 1990). But scholars in various disciplines disagree on when that period in history actually began. Historians D. C. Somervell and Arnold Toynbee (1947), for example, describe it as the fourth era in Western civilization: (1) the Dark Ages (675–1075), (2) the Middle Ages (1075–1475), (3) the modern age (1475–1875), and (4) the postmodern age (1875–present). In architecture, Charles Jencks's *The Language of Post-Modern Architecture* (1977) describes the 1972 demise of an urban housing project in St. Louis as the beginning of the postmodern age. In Western literature, postmodern fiction appears eclectically in the work of various avant-garde writers of the 1960s (Hassan, 1971, 1987) and, later, in Thomas Pynchon's *Gravity's Rainbow* (1973). In psychology, Kenneth Gergen (1991) argues that postmodernity marks a radical break from modern romantic conceptions of the self by removing that concept from the body's interior (e.g., the head and chest) and placing it in outward appearances and speech. Finally, in business, the term *postmodern* was first used by economist and management theorist Peter Drucker in *The Landmarks of Tomorrow* (1957) to describe a utopian vision of an automated, egalitarian workplace in which Western capitalism would thrive.

Despite the various interpretations of postmodernity provided by scholars in different disciplines, together they summarize the social, political, and aesthetic movements that are captured by the term *postmodernism.* From historians we gain an appreciation for postmodernism as representing a dramatic break from "the previous modern period as a middle-class bourgeois era marked by social stability, rationalism, and progress . . . to a 'Time of Troubles' marked by the collapse of rationalism and the ethos of the Enlightenment" (Best & Kellner, 1991, p. 6). Wars, revolutions, economic and social crises, and new ambiguities in cultural values thus led to a postmodern era in Western civilization.

In organizational theory, the distinction between the modern and postmodern periods is largely drawn from classical management (particularly Frederick Taylor's [1947] principles of scientific management) as well as from cultural and critical theories of human inquiry. As Jean François Lyotard (1984) puts it, "the postmodern condition" for organizations is one that challenges the domination of science as a vehicle for humane progress. In other words, in the postmodern period of organizations and communication, we recognize that science can answer some but not all of the questions of greatest interest and importance to us.

New Political and Aesthetic Movements

Again, note that postmodern*ism* refers to the social, political, and aesthetic movements that have arisen since the advent of postmodern*ity* (Foster, 1983). Cultural historians Rosenberg and White (1957) describe the postmodern world in this way:

> As Toynbee's Great West Wind blows all over the world, which quickly gets urbanized and industrialized . . . a certain sameness develops everywhere. Clement Greenberg can meaningfully speak of a universal mass culture . . . which unites a resident of Johannesburg with his neighbors in San Juan, Hong Kong, Moscow, Paris, Bogotá, Sydney and New York. African aborigines, such

as those . . . described by Richard Wright, leap out of their primitive past—straight into the movie house where, it is feared, they may be mesmerized like the rest of us. First besieged with commodities, postmodern [people themselves] become an interchangeable part in the whole cultural process. When [they are] momentarily freed from [their] own kitsch, . . . Soviet citizen[s] seem to be as titillated as [their] American counterpart[s] by Tin Pan Alley's products. In our time, the basis for an international solidarity of [men and women at their] lowest level, as some would say, appears to have been formed. (p. 4)

In short, according to Best and Kellner (1991), "the ambiguity of the new postmodern world, [and] its promising and threatening features . . . [offer us] everything and nothing" (p. 7). One outcome of this massive cultural process involving high-speed change and sameness is the idea "that reality is unordered and ultimately unknowable" (p. 9). Postmodern movements thus view social, cultural, and professional life as marked by three factors—(1) *relativism* (because there is no one truth by which to judge the value of competing ideas), (2) *populism* (because multicultural diversity challenges the domination of cultural elites), and (3) the *presence of multiple meanings and images*—all of which coexist and vie for expression. As pop artist Andy Warhol once commented, "In the future everyone will be famous for fifteen minutes."

In a defining account of postmodern communication theory, Jean Baudrillard (1983) argues that images and simulations of reality—or what he calls the "nonreflexive" surfaces of persons and things—have become the new currency of commodity capitalism. That is, "screen" (e.g., television and film) has replaced "scene" (staged dramas performed before live audiences) and "networks" (simulated channels and surfaces) have replaced "mirrors" (representations) as "the smooth operational surface of communication." In Baudrillard's view, then, theme parks such as Disney World and Epcot Center are the epitome of the postmodern appeal to images as commodities for purchase. Within this perspective is a growing body of literature about the displacement of national politics to what occurs (i.e., what gets bought and sold) on television (Goodall, 1989). As a result, political candidates compete to establish a smooth political surface and attempt to give the television audience the best show for its money.

However, not all observers see postmodern society as negative or nihilistic. Writing in 1957, Peter Drucker foresaw the themes of "pattern, purpose, and process" as ultimately emerging in postindustrial society. Arguing that new technologies would redefine our power over nature and bring new responsibilities and hazards, Drucker also held that a greater distribution of education and knowledge might mark the end of ignorance and poverty and further worldwide modernization. Similarly, Huston Smith (1982) suggests that the transformation of society from rational modernism to skeptical postmodernism "is only a transition to yet another intellectual perspective, one that hopefully will be characterized by a more holistic and spiritual outlook" (qtd. in Best & Kellner, 1991, p. 9).

Most contemporary observers agree that postmodern society is fluid, fast, and global (Aronowitz & DiFazio, 1994; Barnet & Cavanaugh, 1994; Rifkin, 1995). Although warnings of postmodern nihilism are warranted to a degree, Drucker's 1957 vision of the postmodern world has since emerged in most respects. New technologies have redefined how and how quickly we process information. As a result, economic markets have become global markets, decision making has moved from nation-states to multinational corporations, and the ideological battle that pitted communists against capitalists throughout most of the twentieth century has ended. Although technology has not brought us power over nature or an end to hunger, disease, and poverty, Drucker's vision of the postmodern future—particularly from the modern perspective of the mid-1950s—has been remarkably prescient.

Postmodern movements are characterized by what we call a *political aesthetic.* By "political," we mean that the rebellions against all forms of authority (e.g., governmental, artistic, scientific, and institutional) were regarded as attacks against the interests of the Enlightenment and Industrial Revolution and Western standards of rationality and domination (Featherstone, 1988). By "aesthetics," we mean that the rebellions were found in various discourses (e.g., graffiti, television, street theater, rock and rap music, avant-garde novels, new journalism, "retro" fashions, and everyday conversation) that emphasized *pleasure* over rationality, *novelty* over reason (often for its own sake), *difference* over consensus, and *rapid change* over static, middle-class sameness. It is, therefore, not surprising that the organizing site of postmodernism would be located in various cultural understandings and practices.

New Cultural Understandings and Practices

When we combine postmodern*ity* (as a period in time) with postmodern*ism* (as movements located within that period), we describe the territories claimed by the term *postmodern.* These postmodern territories are found in both the complex and often contradictory experiences of everyday work life and the culturally diverse and globally oriented world of work.

One major dimension of that work life is challenge to all forms of authority. As organizations have downsized and restructured, for example, the traditional model of organizing has been challenged by a political and economic aesthetic: team-based organizing made possible by advanced information technologies. Hierarchies have collapsed into matrix and other nonlinear systems of decision making, information processing, and communication. The traditional distinction between managers and workers has been blurred as team facilitators and coaches have entered team-based organizations dedicated to learning. At the same time, companies have demanded more of their employees' "free time" by providing them with day-care services and home computers and fax machines. Here we see challenges to the authority of international date lines and even the routine separation between day and night.

But these changes have not emerged without some resistance. Consider the challenge to committing one's life to work posed by Generation Xers (Coupland, 1991, 1995). They challenge the authority of the assumption that people should work to acquire more commodities and toys, arguing that it is the root cause of broken families, unhealthy practices, worldwide economic upheaval, and the poisoning of the Earth. Generation Xers believe in a different work ethic: do more with less, value families over workplaces, and promote ecological awareness.

Generation Xers are also well aware of what some observers describe as "the jobless future" (Aronowitz & DiFazio, 1994). It has been estimated that by the year 2025, the world's eight billion people will compete for only two billion available jobs. Rifkin (1995) suggests that the major changes in the nature of work will include a four-day workweek, which would serve to employ more people and increase leisure time. Unfortunately, as today's classified ads suggest, most of the work that is available is in lower-paying jobs (Aronowitz & DiFazio, 1994). One viable solution may be to create meaningful activities outside of traditional organizations. Clearly, the postmodern world is one in which even fundamental assumptions about work will continue to be challenged.

Postmodern rebellion in cultural understandings and practices is also found in everyday organizational life (Browning & Hawes, 1991; Goodall, 1989, 1991a). Business in the 1990s is characterized by global economic and cultural competition, and remaining competitive seems to require flattening traditional hierarchies as well as using new technologies to distribute information. Furthermore, employees are increasingly required to perform flexible roles and carry out multiple responsibilities. Cross-functional training enables workers to define and protect themselves in this environment.

The postmodern era brings new challenges to individuals in organizations as well as to organizations seeking to remain competitive in a global economy. Earlier in the chapter we saw how BMW questioned all aspects of its systems of organizing, managing, and communicating to become a nearly "flat" organization in which employees share responsibility and accountability. Every aspect of work is assigned to a team, and technologies are regarded as among the team's tools, rather than as replacements for team members. In addition, the company's borders include customers, suppliers, and local and global communities; these relationships result in improved quality processes. In giving up bureaucracy, reward systems based on individuality, and traditional forms of managerial control, BMW has created a new model for the intelligent, communication-based manufacturing of automobiles.

The postmodern turn also poses challenges to many of the assumed ideals of effective communication and its relationship to organizational survival. As the BMW example demonstrates, team-based organizing presupposes an inter-dependent network of open communicators within a larger organizational framework that values the thinking worker, the ongoing search for quality im-provements, and a spirit of "unified diversity" in accomplishing tasks (Eisenberg, 1984). In this postmodern system of communication, adapting messages to one's listeners takes precedence over individual eloquence, and ambiguity re-places certainty as the routine state of sense-making. It requires negotiation for shared activities to occur and ways for persons of good will to halt the work processes when better information can be applied to the problems they are hired to solve.

In the postmodern call for a new team-based order and revision of how power can be productively shared, we can see that the historical era (post-modernity) and the political aesthetics of shared authority (postmodernism) have significantly reformulated the ways in which organizing and communicat-ing are accomplished.

Objections to Postmodern Theory

Two major objections have been lodged against the postmodern approach to or-ganizations and communication: (1) that embracing postmodern concepts means giving up rationality, and (2) that adopting postmodern concepts requires replacing capitalism with Marxism.

Critics of the postmodern approach commonly question its lack of respect for Western rationality (Habermas, 1981). They ask how business can be ac-complished without hierarchies, divisions of labor, highly specialized tasks, quantitative assessments of performance, and centralized authority. If the post-modern approach embraces the counter-rational, then isn't it also counterbusi-ness? In addition, critics point to the radical political ideas that characterize the various postmodern movements. Because some of these ideas are historically derived from Marxism, they see a fundamental problem in applying the prac-tices of a competing ideology to contemporary capitalism and business.

However, the postmodern approach neither embraces antibusiness nor gives up rationality. Rather, it may even provide a new energy to business prac-tices. By using organizational cultures to provide fluid contexts for deconstruct-ing and acting on the strategic ambiguities of signs, it thereby redistributes information control and redefines power relations among employees. Let's examine why this is true.

POSTMODERN DECONSTRUCTION

Postmodernism relies heavily on *deconstruction,* the critical practice of "taking apart" meanings that have been socially constructed (Derrida, 1976). It involves asking social, professional, and political questions about what is taken for granted (or constructed) and how it got that way. As we saw in Chapter 6, critical theory exposes the interests represented and marginalized by the vision and tenets of that construction. Let's consider how deconstruction can be used to "take apart" the meanings of an organizational document.

An Example: The *Nordstrom Employee Handbook*

The *Nordstrom Employee Handbook* is an example of a postmodern document (see Figure 7.1). Notice first that it is very brief, only one page in length. Unlike the typical employee handbook, it does not contain multiple sections, precise language, or discussions of hierarchy or formal channels of organizational control. Instead, the Nordstrom document uses strategically ambiguous language to empower employees at all levels within the organization. Notice too that "personal and professional goals" are linked to emphasize their interdependence in the valuable employee.

This postmodern document states: "Rule 1: Use your good judgment in all situations." Then: "There will be no additional rules." Rules are considered the unnecessary baggage of a bureaucratic mentality that serves only to constrain creativity and discourage employees from learning on their own how to accomplish tasks within the contexts in which they occur. Nordstrom's one rule empowers employees to make responsible decisions.

Finally, the *Nordstrom Employee Handbook* informs employees that they may ask "any question at any time" when assistance is needed. While this statement embodies precisely what anyone using good judgment would do to manifest their personal and professional goals within the Nordstrom culture, it also emphasizes the interdependence of employees in ensuring the overall well-being of the organization. The postmodern logic seems to be: We are all in this together, and we are all responsible to each other for making sure the business prospers and we all do well. To be a Nordstrom employee thus means accepting responsibility for one's actions and decisions and valuing individual creativity and initiative. It also requires a willingness to accept ambiguity as a natural condition of work.

As our example demonstrates, the postmodern approach can contribute to a highly successful business operation. It does not act as a nihilistic or antirational influence. Rather, it seeks to empower employees to accept responsibility and make good decisions, to engage work contexts creatively, and to recognize the interdependent and ambiguous nature of the business culture. In addition, our deconstruction of the Nordstrom document reveals that the company values

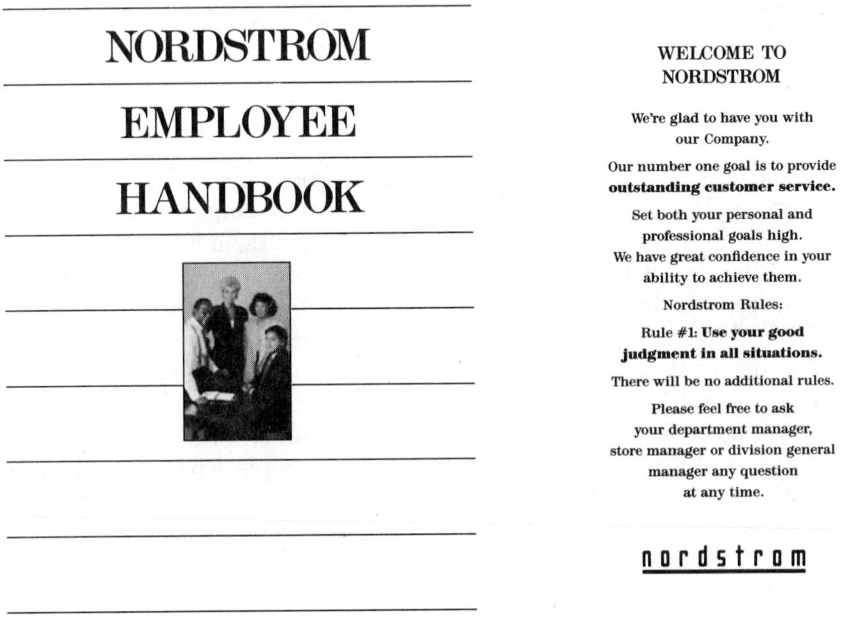

NORDSTROM

EMPLOYEE

HANDBOOK

**WELCOME TO
NORDSTROM**

We're glad to have you with
our Company.

Our number one goal is to provide
outstanding customer service.

Set both your personal and
professional goals high.
We have great confidence in your
ability to achieve them.

Nordstrom Rules:

Rule #1: **Use your good
judgment in all situations.**

There will be no additional rules.

Please feel free to ask
your department manager,
store manager or division general
manager any question
at any time.

nordstrom

FIGURE 7.1
Nordstrom Employee Handbook

Source: Courtesy of Nordstrom.

not only the commodities it sells but also the customer service it provides. Postmodern business cultures value organizational communication as a commodity, whose image is part of what customers consume. Communication no longer functions as the giving of orders in a hierarchy, nor is it something that merely bonds managers and employees, or a manifestation of information, feedback, or noise, or the deep structures of meanings that constitute everyday life through routines, rituals, rites, and communities. Unlike these earlier definitions of organizational communication, the postmodern approach holds that communication involves sharing power, accepting responsibility, and recognizing interdependence. It also encompasses global ways of generating capital and consuming commodities.

Of course, postmodern organizational logic is by no means perfect. After all, trusting the "surfaces" and seeing ourselves as "consumable commodities" can produce a superficial account of what it means to be a human being at work. (See Focus on Ethics 7.1.) It also requires us to accept more responsibility and power. The resulting loss of potential work stability can be confusing as well as

The Dilemma of Postmodern Ethics

The postmodern movement is generally associated with situational ethics: There are no absolute standards for determining right and wrong. We must interpret ethical choices based on our definition and analysis of the context that produces the need for the choice and on our understanding of the potential outcomes of those choices.

While this view of ethics is consistent with our interpretive approach to organizational communication, it suffers from a lack of ethical consistency. That is, without absolute standards of right and wrong, critics argue, we are too often left adrift on a sea of relativity. Furthermore, if we agree that contexts shape our interpretations of right and wrong, then it may also be argued that a lack of information about a context can lead to alternative ethical conclusions. Put simply, if we lack important information at the time we make the ethical choice, how can we be held accountable for our decision and actions?

Furthermore, some radical postmodernists, drawing strength from the extreme left of critical theory, ask: Isn't the whole concept of "ethics" critically suspect? In their view, *ethics* refers to and is informed by a narrative of right and wrong. That narrative, created and used by the powerful, is meant to suppress the powerless by limiting how right and wrong can be analyzed and understood. Thus, for example, an

(continued)

frustrating. As we have shown, one of the by-products of a global postmodern perspective is that it encourages businesses to rely more on part-time and temporary labor in order to reduce costs, thereby reducing the available pool of middle-income and high-paying jobs as well. With more part-time employees, companies can forgo health insurance, retirement, and corporate benefits packages. Still more intrusions into private life are afforded by providing employees with a flexible work schedule, company-sponsored day care, and home computers and fax machines. These moves to give employees more choice in how and when to accomplish tasks also demonstrate the postmodern blurring of traditional distinctions between work and home as well as work and leisure (Carlsson & Leger, 1990; May, 1988). Whatever its potential for abuse, the postmodern approach both encourages us to appreciate the fundamental differences

---

(continued)

employee who responds to a manager's act of sexual harassment with verbal outrage would be justified in doing so even though it is otherwise professionally unethical to scream at a manager.

Finally, how can we resolve the ethical dilemma posed, on the one hand, by the postmodern advice to "trust the surfaces" when, on the other hand, it is viable to examine a situation for evidence of deep structures of power? Do ethics reside in surfaces, in structures, in both, or in some other formulation? Consider the complexity of this dilemma in the following scenarios:

1. You are called to an emergency meeting by your supervisor, who informs you that the company needs a press release to "justify" a recent toxic waste accident that it claims was not its fault. "This is damage control," you are told, "and even though we don't have all the facts yet, we cannot afford to be made to look negligent by the media." How will you handle this situation? What are the ethical dimensions of your decision?

2. You discover that a co-worker has been reading your personal E-mail as well as others' E-mail in the company. But from your E-mail the co-worker found out about your secret romance with another company employee. The organization has a strict policy forbidding romantic relationships between its employees. Your co-worker has threatened to tell your boss about the romance if you report his reading of others' E-mail. How will you handle this situation? What ethical issues does it present?

---

in contemporary organizations and communication and helps prepare us for a new set of challenges in the twenty-first-century world of work.

A DEFINITIONAL DEBATE?

Objections to using postmodern concepts to describe contemporary organizations may be mostly a definitional debate. Some critics charge that what we are now experiencing is more "high modern" than "postmodern." Their argument is plausible in that many of the evolutionary changes made by organizations are designed to serve strategic, capitalistic goals well within the mainstream boundaries of modern organizing. Scientific rationality is still widely practiced, even though it has been modified by concerns about cultural diversity and abuses of power. Bureaucracies are still very much in charge, though they have become more customer-oriented and prone to initiate quality-control improvements. But by and large, they are still bureaucracies. What we are seeing, from this perspective, may be a full expression of modernism.

Although this argument has some merit, it fails to recognize the extent of change that has occurred in recent years. Thus, when we tour the plant at BMW or Saturn, read the *Nordstrom Employee Handbook,* or use on-line consumer services, we begin to see these changes. Every other age in history has been defined in hindsight, and the current one is not likely to be an exception. Therefore, whether we call the current trends in organizations "late modernism" or "postmodernism" is less important than what these trends may bring in the future. From our moment in time, that future seems likely to be marked by the end of the organizational age in which traditional jobs are replaced by many new types of work.

Implications of the Postmodern Approach for Creativity and Constraint

Our discussion of the postmodern approach has emphasized the complex relationships among contemporary organizations, people, languages, capitalism, and societies. Although postmodern concepts of organizing are productive and "rational" (though admittedly more global than Western), they also reframe our long-held conceptions of work and of who we are at work and in society. In this sense, postmodern theory contributes to the balancing of individual creativity and organizational constraint.

POSTMODERN DIALOGUE

Postmodern theories of everyday organizational life draw attention to the relationship between interpretation and communication. How we interpret signs and surfaces is both a momentary attempt at sense-making and an act of creating the conditions of our cultural understandings. The results of our interpretive efforts and communicative practices are themselves commodities. They are "bought" or "not bought" as reasonable accounts of what goes on in organizations. They also function to create audiences for their appeals.

This postmodern view of organizational communication is indeed revolutionary. When combined with an understanding of commodity capitalism (inherent in postmodern culture) and decentralized power (inherent in postmodern organizations), the postmodern view of communication suggests that meanings have value only insofar as they relate to current market conditions. Hence, in everyday work life, authority rests in the *postmodern dialogue* that empowers employees/teams and managers/facilitators (see Chapter 2). The basis for this new dialogue is straightforward: There is no authority outside of or beyond what we agree to.

NARRATIVES: THE SITES OF THE POSTMODERN CONSCIOUSNESS

Narratives contribute significantly to our understanding of postmodern organizations and are a powerful force in the balancing of creativity and constraint. Unlike the cultural approach, which views narratives as something people do to construct realities, the postmodern approach endorses a more radical notion: Narratives are the simulated realities of an organization's *consciousness*. Therefore, in the postmodern view, it is important to ask how the stories exchanged by managers and employees, members and coaches, suppliers and customers, and companies and communities act as commodities within markets. What balance of attitudes, styles, and images in dialogue contributes to conflicting accounts of creativity and constraint at work? Can a common ground be found among the differing accounts? Can it be used to construct a more unified sense of community?

For managers and employees, however, postmodern views of the role of narratives in organizations are problematic. Although we have long known that good managers tend also to be good storytellers (i.e., their credibility often depends on their ability to provide reasonable explanations of organizational situations), organizations are far more than mere storytelling systems (Boje, 1991). Similarly, although we applaud employee empowerment and cross-functional training, we are less willing to see these postmodern innovations succeed because they threaten to open the workplace to new, more interesting stories. Or, perhaps, by improving organizational storytelling we teach employees and managers how to work under conditions of shared authority, teamwork, deconstruction of dominant power structures, and respect for differences.

THE POSTMODERN VIEW OF WORK AS INTERPRETATION

The postmodern approach requires us to reformulate our conception of work as *interpretation*. Thus, work under conditions of postmodernity functions as a commodity whose value is determined by "signs" of doing one's job. Doing one's job, then, involves "telling the story" of what one does within and for the interpretive community. Hence, *what* one accomplishes is just as important as *how* it is accomplished. In an odd way, then, you are the story you tell about the work as much as the work itself, because the story is a commodity people may or may not buy and whose elements will shape interpretations of what you actually do.

In terms of balancing creativity and constraint, the postmodern view of work as interpretation is especially relevant. To work is to interpret signs within a continuum of possibilities. At one end of the continuum, the possibilities are represented by individual creativity; at the other end, the possibilities are represented by organizational constraint. Somewhere between these two extremes lies the everyday negotiation of meanings with others through dialogue.

Let's consider an example. We have a mutual friend who has long misunderstood why he lost his former academic job. According to his narrative of the event, his teaching and publication record exceeded the department's average and, therefore, he deserved tenure. But according to the narrative provided by the tenure evaluation committee, his teaching was uninspired and his writings seemed more aimed at publishing to keep his job than at contributing to research in the field. Even though the professor obviously did his job, his representation of himself as a college faculty member did not function as a meaningful sign for his colleagues. Therefore, he did not fail to do his job, but he did fail to create an appreciative audience for it. From the modernist's view of work as empirical performance, the tenure committee's decision was subjective and prejudiced; after all, the professor was doing his job of teaching classes and publishing research. But from the postmodernist's view of work as the interpretation of signs and the creation of a commodity value for those signs within a particular discourse community, the committee's decision is understandable. The professor did not live up to desirable commodity expectations; the stories he told were not highly valued; and he failed to engage in dialogue because he believed he was right. In postmodern logic, he acted effectively but failed to communicate effectively.

SUMMARY

This chapter began with a tour of an automobile manufacturing plant, many of whose practices, policies, and characteristics reflect postmodern theory. We also discussed various definitions and approaches to the postmodern, including those from art, architecture, and history. Central to these approaches is the idea that singular, integrated, rational stories about organizations, individuals, or cultures are no longer credible. Instead, postmodernism embraces a diverse, fragmented world in which both organizations and individuals must actively construct their sense of identity out of the various ideas, signs, and practices that litter the global landscape. Postmodernism leads companies to form global alliances and networks that require communication across diverse cultures. Out of all of this material corporations strive to construct a workable image that represents them as a whole.

In addition, the postmodern movement is characterized by a sense of rebellion, of resistance to any individual or group that wishes to assert the truth of its experience over others. As such, it has significant implications for the traditional management structure of most companies, which are arranged hierarchically and assume that greater expertise and authority lie with the people at the top of the pyramid. Postmodern theory suggests flattening traditional hierarchies and distributing power to match the more equal distribution of expertise throughout any social system. Effective communication in such a system has much more to do with the skillful coordination of multiple perspectives through dialogue than it does with the smooth transmission of orders or the cultivation of employee morale. The postmodern approach holds that effective communication involves sharing power, accepting responsibility, and recognizing interdependence. The approach is revolutionary in its challenge to traditional patterns of rationality, coordination, and control. In contrast to prior organizational theories, the aesthetic of postmodern thought is open-ended, unfinished, and fragmented. But it is precisely into this chaos that radical possibilities for the future may be born.

DESIGNING A POSTMODERN UNIVERSITY

In response to changing demographics, the state university system in Florida plans to open a new university on the Gulf Coast near Fort Myers. There has been much public debate about the nature and purpose of the project. The state sees it as an opportunity to address some long-standing problems in college education.

ASSIGNMENT

Using your knowledge of colleges and universities (and of education in general), and taking what you have learned about postmodern organizations in this chapter, write or discuss your plans for the design of this new university. Consider the following issues:

1. Given the changing nature of work and of organizations today, how can you design the university to prepare students for the future?
2. How will the university be structured, both in terms of administration and reporting relationships and in terms of delivery of services?
3. What communication systems will you suggest for students, faculty, administrators, staff, and other stakeholders?
4. How will you structure the compensation and reward systems for university employees?
5. How can you use architectural design to symbolize the new university's commitment to postmodern principles? What other aspects of the physical environment should you consider? Why?
6. How will globalization affect your plans for the university?
7. What type of information-processing systems will you develop (e.g., for registration and advising)? How will these systems differ from those in the traditional university?
8. How will you ensure that power and accountability are shared throughout the university?
9. What can be done to emphasize customer service in the university? Who are the "customers" in education?

The Experience of Work

The most important [factor] in emancipating oneself from social controls is the ability to find rewards in the events of each moment. If a person learns to enjoy and find meaning in the ongoing stream of experience, in the process of living itself, the burden of social controls automatically falls from one's shoulders.

• Mihaly Csikszentmihalyi, *Flow* (1990)

The future belongs to those knowledge workers who can make themselves understood to others who don't share their knowledge base.

• Peter Drucker, *Managing for the Future* (1992a)

QUESTIONS FOR DISCUSSION

- In what ways are you prepared to work in a highly competitive global market? How can you better prepare yourself?

- How are the stages of organizational entry and assimilation similar to your own experiences of work?

- What are the indicators of job satisfaction? How closely related is job satisfaction to communication ability?

- What are the indicators of job stress and burnout? What can be done to reverse or avoid them?

- What are the implications of a "jobless future" for the creation of wealth? What other options exist?

193

W hat is the *experience* of work? Is it about finding meaning in the work day or about learning to understand others? In our view, work encompasses these and many other experiences. It is about discovering the types of work we like to do as well as about making a living doing whatever work is available to us. It is about what we are asked to do on the job as well as what the job demands from us—physically, psychologically, socially, and spiritually. It is about how we feel about our jobs, our careers, and ourselves. And most important to us in this chapter, the experience of work is about coping with the inevitable changes that mark and define our passage through life.

Peter Drucker (1994) views today's revolutionary changes in the world of work and technology as signaling the dawn of a new age. Mirroring the work of anthropologist Jennifer James (1996), Drucker argues that just as humans evolved from hunters and gatherers to agriculturalists to urban industrialists, the current era involves another evolution—from the industrialist to the *"new knowledge worker."* According to Drucker, the new knowledge worker possesses four key characteristics:

1. A college education
2. The ability to apply analytical and theoretical learning
3. A commitment to lifelong learning
4. Good communication skills

The new knowledge workers of today will move through various job orientations, some of which will involve working for others in organizations and some of which will include globally networked or team-based entrepreneurial activities. Moreover, the single most important characteristic of the new knowledge workers is *their ability to communicate with others who do not share their worldview.*

Today, many students assume that their experience of work will be similar to that of their parents: a steady job within an organization and the option of changing jobs in order to advance a career or work for a better-paying company. But very few people have those options today and fewer still will have them in the future. Because the *future of work is unstable and uncertain,* those most likely to achieve success will be flexible in their orientation to work and able to manage the stress associated with a lifetime of change.

Therefore, many of today's students will enter a world of work that will involve both working for organizations as well as investigating entrepreneurial options (Kotter, 1995). The first section of this chapter discusses the experience of work within organizations; the second section examines the experience of independent work outside of organizations. As you will see, although the future world of work will be challenging, those prepared to deal with the challenges will find them exciting and fulfilling.

The Experience of Work within Organizations

The experience of work within organizations is marked in part by each company's set of rules and expectations for employee attitudes and behaviors. While the organization may seek to control us, it also provides us with resources that help us make sense of life experiences. Since the Industrial Revolution, most people in the United States and Europe have survived financially by working for organizations. In exchange for wages, they have allowed at least part of their lives to be controlled by the company. The organization, in turn, has sought to elicit employee *cooperation* in working toward its goals. From the employee's point of view, the challenge has been twofold: a quest for *individuality* (significance and legitimacy at work) and *identification* (participation in a common dialogue and commitment to a larger community that further defines the self) (Burke, 1969; Cheney, 1983). Communication plays an important role in achieving cooperation, individuality, and identification; it is used symbolically to induce cooperation among people who by their nature respond strongly to symbols (Burke 1969; Tompkins, 1987).

Even a cursory look at the corporate landscape reveals the enormous power that organizations have over the lives of individuals. Although some of this power is overt, most of it is more subtle or hidden (see Chapter 6). Competitive pressures increase the power of organizations. Even among the gainfully employed today, job stress is high and job security is low. Many of them cope with the stress and pressure at work by finding new ways of responding to difficult situations. As economic challenges have created the opportunity for rethinking the nature of work, new approaches to organization seek to improve both corporate survival and the individual's experience of work (Milbrath, 1989).

Our examination of the individual's experience of work within an organization begins with a discussion of *organizational assimilation;* that is, how people come to organizations initially and how they learn to make sense of and incorporate the organization's values and goals with their own belief systems. From a communication perspective, our concern here is how the new employee enters the organizational dialogue and finds (or fails to find) a legitimate voice within it. In addition, the experience of work within organizations is marked by indicators of cooperation and resistance or stress. The indicators of cooperation include job satisfaction, job involvement, organizational identification, organizational commitment, employee empowerment, and worker productivity. Conversely, the indicators of resistance include stress, burnout, absenteeism, and turnover. Finally, new directions for the organization of work are explored.

ASSIMILATION: ENTERING THE ORGANIZATIONAL DIALOGUE

Assimilation is a process by which people learn the rules, norms, and expectations of a culture over time and thereby become members of that culture. We are all to some extent assimilated into a national and local culture. As children, parents and others taught us how to become members of a family, community, religion, or country. Thus, assimilation involves learning the rules that guide what members of a culture think, do, and say. Studies reveal a close relationship between learning a culture and learning a language. For example, in the United States, children learn a lot about American culture during dinnertime conversations with family members (Ochs, Smith, & Taylor, 1989).

Similarly, in organizations, the assimilation process helps us understand how the new employee learns about and makes sense of the organization's culture (Jablin, 1987; Weick, 1996). While the employee's first week on the job is filled with surprises, over time the employee learns the formal and informal rules that govern behavior in the organization. This learning process has three broad stages: (1) anticipatory socialization, (2) organizational assimilation, and (3) organizational turning points or exits.

Anticipatory Socialization

In the *anticipatory socialization* stage, people learn about work through communication. There are two forms of anticipatory socialization—*vocational* and *organizational.* The vocational type, which begins in childhood, involves learning about work and careers in general from family members, teachers, part-time employers, friends, and the media. Children and adolescents acquire a general knowledge of accepted attitudes toward work, of the importance of power and status in organizations (Jablin, 1985), and of work as a source of meaningful personal relationships (Atwood, 1990).

Later in life, the organizational type of anticipatory socialization involves learning about a specific job and organization. It takes place *before* the first day of work and is typically conveyed through company literature (e.g., brochures and personnel manuals) as well as through interactions with others (e.g., job applicants, interviewers, and employees) (Jablin, 1987). Individuals develop expectations about the prospective job and organization. However, their expectations are often inflated and unrealistic due to interviewers' tendency to focus on positive aspects of the job and company (Wanous, 1980). In addition, because job interviews typically result in more information for the prospective employer than for the prospective employee, some researchers (Wilson and Goodall, 1991) advocate changing the nature of the interview to more closely reflect a model of dialogue (see Chapter 2).

Organizational Assimilation

According to Meryl Reis Louis (1980), the experience of *organizational assimilation* involves both surprise and sense-making. As new employees' initial expectations are violated, they attempt to make sense of their job and the organization. "The newcomer learns the requirements of his or her role and what the organization and its members consider to be 'normal' patterns of behavior and thought" (Jablin, 1987, p. 695).

Vernon Miller and Fred Jablin (1991) describe the ways in which newcomers learn about the organization. Their search for information carries a sense of urgency. Typically, new employees have some difficulty performing their jobs and getting along with others until they reach a level of familiarity. Potential sources of useful information for newcomers include (1) official company messages (e.g., from management, orientation programs, and manuals), (2) coworkers and peers, (3) supervisors, (4) other organizational members (e.g., secretaries, security guards, and employees in other departments), (5) customers and others outside of the organization, and (6) the task itself. Newcomers thus attempt to "situate" themselves in an unfamiliar organizational context, but to do so they must first learn a great deal about how existing members define the organization's culture. To solicit the information they need, new employees tend not to rely on direct questioning because substantial risks may be associated with asking irrelevant questions. Instead, they use other tactics to solicit information about the organizational culture (see Table 8.1).

Over time, new employees evolve from their initial newcomer status into full-fledged members of the organization (Jablin, 1987). This period of transition may or may not be lengthy depending on the organization and industry involved. In hotels and restaurants, for example, employees may feel like old-timers after only six months on the job, whereas in universities, hospitals, and professional associations the transitional period may last nearly a decade.

During the transitional period of organizational assimilation, employees begin to differentiate between rules and norms that must be followed and those that can be ignored. Feeling more comfortable with the rules of the organization, employees begin to individualize their job, develop their own voice, and behave in ways that both conform with and transform the existing rules. For example, a new supervisor who makes minor changes in how work is delegated distinguishes his or her department from others in the organization. Whereas

8.1 Newcomers' Information-Seeking Tactics

TACTIC	EXAMPLE
Overt question	"Who has the authority to cancel purchase orders?"
Indirect question	"I guess I won't plan to take a vacation this year." (Implied: "Do we work through the holidays if we don't finish the project?")
Third parties	To a co-worker: "I'm making a presentation to the president. Does she like it if you open with a joke?"
Testing limits	Arriving late to work or wearing casual clothes. (Observe others' reactions.)
Disguising conversations	"That safety memo was sure a riot. Can you believe the gall of those guys?" (Wait for reaction to see whether others also think it was funny.)
Observing	Watch which employees get praised in meetings and emulate those who do. (Pay attention to specific individuals.)
Surveillance	Eavesdropping on peer conversations; paying careful attention at office parties. (Monitor the environment for cues.)

Source: V. Miller and F. Jablin, "Information Seeking during Organizational Entry," *Academy of Management Review* 16 (1991): 92–120.

---

newcomer behavior focuses on discovering constraints, the transition toward assimilation is marked by a greater degree of creativity. The degree of balance between the two—and of the employee's satisfaction with his or her role in the organization—largely determines patterns of cooperation, resistance, and exit.

It is useful to apply to organizational assimilation the idea that all organizational communication is comprised of *lists* and *stories.* According to Larry Browning (1992):

> Lists are technical communication, progressive, public; and once shared they extend a power base. Stories are communications about personal experience told in everyday discourse. They reflect local knowledge, give coherence to group subcultures, change over time, and contain multiple voices. (p. 281)

Competent members of organizations are able to understand and work with itemized lists (e.g., of rules, procedures, and standard performance metrics) and relate to stories that highlight informal understandings (e.g., politics and traditions). Lists and stories can be used by organizational members as resources to either support the existing scheme of things or to initiate change.

Organizational Turning Points or Exits

Research by Connie Bullis and Betsy Bach (1989) extends the idea of organizational metamorphosis and socialization by focusing on *organizational turning points.* These are major changes in the employee's relationship with the organization that are inspired by key events that take place at work.

Consider as an example your experience as a student. The "turning points" in your experience have probably included identifying with your college or university and its organizations or teams as well as choosing your major area of study. Together with other episodes in your experience (some more positive than others, no doubt), these turning points in your experience as a student have permanently altered your understanding and interpretation of the school and your membership in it. In the same sense, employees come to understand their role in their place of work through organizational turning points. Examples might include receiving a favorable performance review, participating in genuine dialogue, or being unfairly criticized by a supervisor.

In addition to altering employees' perceptions of identification with the company, turning points can structure how they perceive career choices, job transfers, and even purpose in life. More powerful than memorable moments, turning points in the experience of work are capable of changing a person's life, determining in part how a person sets goals, determines career paths, and makes the important connection between work life and one's life course more generally (Fox, 1994).

As a result of the ongoing transformation of work and organizational instability in today's business world, turning points tend to occur between organizations more often than within organizations as workers transfer from one company to another. The job transfer process involves a unique form of sense-making, as Michael Kramer (1993, 1995) has demonstrated in job transfer studies of various companies. In the three-stage transfer process—(1) *loosening* from the current employer, (2) *transitioning* between jobs, and (3) *tightening* in the new position—Kramer found that communication is critical to an effective transfer. People need to make sense of the new job as well as the job transfer process and its implications for their sense of self and well-being.

INDICATORS OF COOPERATION

The *indicators of cooperation,* when present in the employee's experience of work, can have positive outcomes for both the individual and the organization.

The indicators include job satisfaction and involvement, identification with and commitment to the organization, and employee empowerment and productivity. The benefits of these indicators to the employee and organization far outweigh the risks associated with them (e.g., excessive employee commitment can lead to blind loyalty).

Job Satisfaction

The most common indicator of cooperation, *job satisfaction* is measured by researchers and managers alike in their attempt to understand organizational climates. Not surprisingly, this relatively new focus on employee satisfaction originated in the human relations and human resources approaches to organizations and communication (see Chapter 3). Douglas McGregor, Frederick Herzberg, and Abraham Maslow have argued, in different but related ways, that a satisfied employee is one whose needs are being met. Employees have three general levels of needs that correlate with degrees of job satisfaction:

- *Level 1 needs* include safe working conditions and sufficient pay, rewards, and equipment. In the United States, the 1970 Occupational Safety and Health Act (OSHA) was designed to regulate safe working conditions.
- *Level 2 needs,* which include supportive interpersonal relationships with co-workers and supervisors, contribute to employee morale and motivation (Richmond & McCroskey, 1979). (See Chapter 9 for more on interpersonal relationships at work.)
- *Level 3 needs* include opportunities for personal growth, such as those provided by challenging work tasks, greater responsibility, greater independence, and a clear career path for the future.

When the three levels of employee needs are satisfied, high levels of job satisfaction are likely to be reported by employees.

In some companies, basic job safety has the single greatest impact on employee satisfaction. Pressures to increase productivity and efficiency have been tied to the growing number of injuries sustained by workers in U.S. companies. In 1991, for example, twenty-five people died in a fire at a North Carolina poultry processing plant as a result of locked emergency exit doors and a history of negligent safety inspections (Baker, 1991).

A satisfied worker, then, is paid fairly, is provided with safe and pleasant working conditions, has supportive relationships with others at work, is challenged by his or her work, and has a significant degree of control over how tasks are performed. Although meeting the needs of employees can be costly for businesses, it is generally agreed among theorists that doing so leads to high levels of job satisfaction. However, there is less agreement on the importance of challenging work and on the consequences of a satisfied workforce. For example, critics argue that employees' perceptions of challenges differ. According to Loher et al. (1985), an individual's *expectations* for meeting this need affect the resulting level of job satisfaction. Hence, challenging work increases job satisfaction *only* when the employee desires it. For employees with different expectations, it plays a less important role in their satisfaction.

Considerable disagreement also exists regarding the direct results of a satisfied workforce. Although researchers and managers have long hoped to prove that a correlation exists between job satisfaction and productivity, research studies do not support this contention (Loher et al., 1985). Instead, most research in this area suggests that performers who are acknowledged by the company tend to be happier when their good work is rewarded. Therefore, an organization with high employee morale is as likely to have low productivity as it is to have high productivity because job satisfaction is not by itself a key factor in determining levels of productivity. However, research has shown an *indirect* relationship between employee absenteeism and turnover (which reflect a low level of job satisfaction) and worker productivity (Downs, Clampitt, & Pfeiffer, 1988; Futrell & Parasuramann, 1984). In other words, although happy workers may not necessarily be productive ones, unhappy workers are likely to increase a company's absentee and turnover rates.

Job Involvement

Job involvement, the degree to which employees personally involve themselves in their work and thereby satisfy personal goals, has been shown to have a direct effect on worker performance and productivity. The Industrial Revolution was in part a struggle to achieve appropriate levels of job involvement. At one extreme, the Protestant work ethic and workaholism suggest that work plays a central role in people's physical, emotional, and spiritual life. Thus, at this extreme level of job involvement, people consciously or unconsciously "live to work." At the other extreme are those who "work to live"—to pay the bills and support their life outside of work. For this group, work is merely a means to an end; it is not expected to fulfill any personal needs.

Surprisingly, these two extreme levels of job involvement are commonly found among workers today, even among high-ranking managers. As one engineering executive explains, "I come to work, put in my eight hours, get my paycheck, and go home to the things that really matter." For people who view work as a means to an end, there is an ongoing tension between making a living and making a life. At the other extreme are workaholics who would probably agree with Mihalyi Csikszentmihalyi's (1990) contention that people's experience tends to be more enervated, challenging, involved, and "functional" at work than it is at home.

Organizational Identification

George Cheney (1983) and Philip Tompkins (Tompkins & Cheney, 1985) have applied Kenneth Burke's (1969) notion of "identification" to organizations. They define *organizational identification* as the natural overlap that develops between an employee's values and those of the organization. "As members identify more strongly with the organization and its values, the organization becomes as much a part of the member as the member is a part of the organization" (Bullis & Tompkins, 1989, p. 289).

Organizational identification, the internalization of company values and assumptions by employees, can foster a sense of community (Bullis & Tompkins, 1989). However, it can also operate to control employee decision making. Specifically, it guides people toward "certain problems and alternatives" and thereby biases their choices "toward alternatives tied to the most salient identifications . . . [thereby] narrowing the decision makers' span of attention" (Tompkins & Cheney, 1985, p. 194). Identification can strongly shape interpretation in that the degree of employees' identification affects their definitions of what is real or taken for granted in any given situation. From a critical perspective, organizational identification operates as an *unobtrusive control* over decision premises (see Chapter 6).

Many organizations have recently restructured their operations, replacing isolated departments with teams of people that are expected to be more flexible and creative in accomplishing work tasks (see Chapter 10). As a result of restructuring, identification shifts from the organization as a whole to the individual team or work group (Barker & Tompkins, 1993). Interestingly, the power of team identification in regulating individual behavior has been shown to be as strong as that of organizational identification. Regardless of its source, then, identification is an effective way to shape behavior through concertive control.

Organizational Commitment

Organizational commitment refers to the degree of employee dedication to and support of the organization's goals and values. It encompasses explicit attitudes and behaviors, such as speaking positively or negatively about the company in public and stating one's intentions to remain with or leave the organization (Kiesler, 1971; Steers, 1977). Although organizational identification and commitment often go hand in hand, employees may be highly committed to the company but only minimally involved in their jobs.

Many factors contribute to a high level of organizational commitment, such as generous compensation packages and well-timed promotions. Other more strategic factors are geared explicitly toward creating loyalty to the corporation (e.g., Disney's intensive orientation and training programs). Still other factors operate from outside of the formal organizational structure; for instance, employees who dislike their work and managers may be committed to an organization within which they have many friends (Eisenberg, Monge, & Miller, 1983).

Employee Empowerment

In recent years, the tradition of company loyalty has eroded along with the dominating companies themselves. In their place, more competitively oriented firms have emerged that encourage commitment by emphasizing the employee's contributions to company success. This trend toward *employee empowerment* is sometimes referred to as "high-involvement management" (Lawler, 1986).

The basic idea underlying high-involvement management is that *people work best when they feel ownership over their work processes and decision making.* Empowerment is what gives employees control over significant aspects of their work. There are many levels of employee empowerment, from one-time involvement in a specific project to self-directed work teams. Osburn et al. (1990) identify six levels of employee involvement:

1. Managers make decisions on their own, announce those decisions, and then respond to employees' questions.
2. Managers make decisions, but only after seeking employees' views.
3. Managers create temporary employee groups to recommend solutions to particular problems.
4. Managers meet with groups of employees on a regular basis to identify problems and recommend solutions.
5. Managers establish and participate in cross-functional problem-solving teams.
6. Ongoing work groups assume expanded responsibility for a particular issue (e.g., cost reduction).

In some cases, empowerment may be achieved through compensation schemes that afford employees ownership in the company. The Scanlon Plan, for instance, encourages innovation and gives all employees a share in company profits (Monge, Cozzens, & Contractor, 1992). This trend toward employee involvement suggests a modification of capitalist thinking in that it provides workers with greater control over the means of production (which Karl Marx felt was essential).

When high-involvement management is successful, the workforce is highly committed and involved and individual employees feel responsible for the company's success or failure. It also redefines the traditional "us versus them" division between managers and employees as "we're all in this together." However, high-involvement management is not easy to implement. The supervisory behaviors associated with generating employee empowerment are unlike those of traditional management (see Chapter 9). Moreover, employees may resist em-

"Support Us or Else"

In the following 1994 E-mail memo, a senior vice president of the second largest retail chain business in the U.S. sought to increase employee support for a team-oriented project called MORE. At the time the memo was written, the company was under pressure to reverse a slump in sales and profitability.

TO: Project Managers

FROM: ▮▮▮▮

SUBJECT: MORE

I have just read several negative comments about the 15-minute video which introduced the MORE project. The comments ranged from "How can something that takes only 15 minutes be that important?" to "It really wasn't all that entertaining, so I didn't encourage my people to see it." I am [extremely angry] with the attitudes expressed in most of this feedback.

    I don't feel that I need to remind you that we have finished five quarters of very poor results. Nor should I have to remind you that we need to change. Nor should I have to remind you that the MORE project is the only major change initiative that

(continued)

powerment because they lack trust in management or are apprehensive about their new role and the greater accountability it would bring to them. Empowerment requires the cooperation of both managers and employees. Organizations and supervisors can help create the conditions for empowerment (e.g., by providing reward systems and opportunities for cooperation and personal growth), but employees must be willing to accept empowerment in order for it to succeed. As Peter Senge (1994) points out, management cannot "impose" loyalty to any company vision on employees; rather, each member of the organization decides whether and when to "enroll" in that vision. Focus on Ethics 8.1 gives an example of how an executive's enthusiasm for a new program led him to believe that managers and employees could be forced to accept it.

(continued)

> really attacks the underlying core problems (sales/square foot; in-stock position; customer service; etc.). Consider this a very serious alert and wake up call—If I trace any negativism to any of you I will personally write you up and conduct a constructive action interview and put you on probation.
>
> I have worked too hard and this is too important to all of our careers, jobs, and families to have my own group diluting or otherwise eroding these efforts. If the videos are still running, I suggest that you work very hard to make sure that ALL of your people see them and you personally encourage every one of your people to view it. You have my personal assurances that we will give them much more information as specific programs are outlined.
>
> By all means support the program and if you can't, then please have the guts to quit and get the hell out of the way of the rest of us who are committed to turn this company around.

Discussion Questions

1. If you were a project manager at this company, how would you react to this memo?
2. Why did the senior vice-president write this memo?
3. What assumptions does he make about communication and organizational change in the memo?
4. If you were in the executive's position, how would you address the lack of support for the MORE program?

There are many benefits of a committed workforce in today's competitive business environment. Committed employees not only work harder; they are also more likely to generate creative ideas about costs, quality, profitability, and schedules that benefit the company. Under the conditions of high involvement, employees feel that their opinions are valued by the organization and, therefore, that their role at work is significant.

Worker Productivity

From the organization's viewpoint, the most important indicator of cooperation is *worker productivity*. It is generally defined as the relationship between the outputs generated by a system and the inputs required to create those outputs (Campbell et al., 1988). Worker productivity has long been linked to *efficiency* (i.e., to the individual's ability to convert input into output within a specific time frame) (Sink, 1983). More recently, however, our understanding of productivity has been broadened to include *effectiveness* as well, which is usually measured in terms of product or service quality. For example, the productivity of insurance adjusters may be measured by the total number of claims processed per day as well as by the accuracy of those claims; telephone operators by the number of calls taken per hour as well as by how well those calls are handled; and manufacturing assemblers by the amount of time it takes to make a product as well as the amount of rework required to make the product acceptable to customers.

Many organizations do a poor job of measuring the individual worker's productivity, except in the simplest of jobs. Moreover, productivity measures in terms of products and services can be ambiguous, especially when the product or service is not clearly defined (as is often the case for teachers and judges, for example) (Jacobson, 1992). Although recent efforts toward achieving "total quality," "continuous measurable improvement," and "statistical process control" encourage employees at all levels to develop and track quantitative measures of their productivity, such measures are rare for most white-collar jobs, where evaluation of productivity remains highly subjective.

Research on the relationship between productivity and communication has been disappointing. Some studies show a positive correlation, while others show a negative correlation or none at all (Papa, 1989). As Annalee Luhmann and Terrance Albrecht (1990) conclude, "the nature of the communication–performance relationship has yet to be demonstrated unequivocally" (p. 2). Part of the problem may be that a wide range of factors are inconsistently defined by researchers as "communication" or "productivity." Certain types of communication, such as clear direction from supervisors and improved teamwork across related functions, have a positive impact on productivity, but other kinds of interaction that we would expect to improve productivity, such as supportive leadership, have been shown to have little impact on it (Scott, 1981). And still other kinds of communication, such as the boss who yells in anger, can raise productivity in the short term but have a negative effect over time.

Based on the available research, however, we can point to two general associations between communication and productivity. The first, which is based on a *monologic* approach, ties communication to productivity by promoting a work environment in which simple tasks and clear performance measures permit continuous and measurable improvement. In this view, all communication comes from the supervisor. Although reminiscent of scientific management, this approach is commonly used today, especially in manufacturing firms struggling to remain competitive.

The other general association between communication and productivity is based on a *dialogic* approach. It emphasizes mutual, two-way communication

Feedback about Results

Empowering Management
- Shares business information at all levels
- Eliminates status consciousness
- Solicits and uses employee input
- Supports teamwork
- Provides clear vision and direction
- Provides clear standards of accountability
- Makes decisions based on data
- Trusts employees

FIGURE 8.1
A Dialogic Model of Communication and Productivity

Source: E. Eisenberg and P. Riley, "A Closed-Loop Model of Communication, Empowerment, Urgency, and Performance," unpublished paper, University of Southern California, 1992.

between managers and employees working to accomplish complex tasks (see Figure 8.1). Here the relationship between communication and productivity is mediated by a sense of urgency. Sharing business information, encouraging employee participation in decision making, and providing employees with feedback about the successes and failures of their efforts lead to increased levels of identification, commitment, and involvement, which, in turn, increase worker productivity.

INDICATORS OF RESISTANCE

The indicators of resistance, when present in the employee's experience of work, can have a profoundly negative impact on both the individual and the organization. These indicators include stress and burnout, the causes of which are manifold. In this section, we group sources of stress into four areas—*environmental, organizational, job/role,* and *individual*—and identify in each case the most likely causes of negative feelings. We begin with a brief definition of stress at work.

Stress and Burnout

Employee stress is on the rise. Its symptoms can include chest pain, peptic ulcers, anxiety and depression, back pain, stomach problems, headaches, high blood pressure, and fatigue (Ray, 1987). Employee stress can cause serious problems in organizations, such as absenteeism, tardiness, sabotage, poor quality, turnover, and dysfunctional conflict (Cooper, 1984; Hall & Savery, 1987; Quick & Quick, 1984). Depression alone affects an estimated 17.6 million Americans annually and twice as many women as men. In organizations it can lead to low productivity and morale, absenteeism, substance or alcohol abuse, poor work quality, high turnover rates, and even accidents (NMHA, 1995). Lost working days due to heart disease alone cost companies $15 billion annually (Ivancevich & Matteson, 1980). In the early 1990s, the number of murders in the workplace doubled (Goodall, 1995b).

While stress is marked generally by heightened feelings of anxiety, tension, or pressure, *job stress* may be defined further as a psychologically disturbed response to work demands. Over time, a chronically stressed employee may become susceptible to *burnout,* which has three dimensions: emotional exhaustion, de-personalization (or a negative attitude toward others, especially clients), and a weak sense of accomplishment as a result of work pressures (Maslach, 1982).

Environmental Stressors

Individuals in organizations have the least amount of control over *environmental stressors,* which are generated by the national culture, intercultural difficulties, customers and the marketplace, and the physical characteristics of the workplace.

National Culture A nation's prevailing beliefs about the nature and importance of work in people's lives have a significant effect on job stress. While countries with insufficient safety laws promote sweatshops, low wages, and intolerable working conditions, a nation's attitudes about work play an equally important role in job stress. In Japanese society, for example, overworked employees use the term *Karoshi* to refer to "death by overwork." The United States and Japan rank lowest in the world in the average number of vacation days per year. After one year of service, the typical U.S. or Japanese worker receives only ten vacation days, whereas in Austria, Brazil, Denmark, and Sweden the average is thirty vacation days (Staimer, 1992). In Europe, a six-week vacation is the norm, and often it is granted by law (Rider, 1992). In addition, several industrialized nations have a four-day workweek (1995).

A country's values about the nature of work, expressed in policy statements and informal norms for behavior, can contribute to job stress. However, employees often have little or no control over this form of environmental stress.

Intercultural Difficulties The stress associated with business travel is a fact of organizational life. A global economy requires people in organizations to travel abroad more often. But it takes time for even the most seasoned business traveler to understand the cultures, customs, and nuances of doing business in other countries. According to Iris Varner and Linda Beamer (1995), the business traveler encounters six sources of stress in unfamiliar cultures:

1. *Culture shock:* The four stages of adapting to a new culture are *euphoria* (the new adventure is stimulating), *disillusionment and frustration* (the culture is too much unlike one's expectations or home culture), *adjustment* (the frustration begins to dissolve), and *integration* (one feels comfortable living and working in the culture). In reverse culture shock, a similar adjustment period often accompanies the return home.

2. *The challenge of diversity:* Many companies today prepare business travelers for dealing with people in other cultures. Still, it can be a challenging diversity task, particularly when unanticipated difficulties arise from subtle differences in cultural understanding. For example, when a Japanese businessman nods his head, he does so not to signal his agreement but to show only that he has heard what was said.

3. *Bias, discrimination, and prejudice:* American travelers abroad may encounter religious intolerance, sexual discrimination, deep racial barriers, and other forms of prejudice that cause stress in their dealings and communication with others. Even routine activities may be affected, as one of our colleagues discovered when she attempted to have dinner alone in a restaurant during a visit to Turkey. After two police officers approached her, she learned that because only prostitutes dine alone in Turkey, her safety was in jeopardy.

4. *Language barriers:* It can be extremely difficult for business travelers to interpret information conveyed in a foreign language. Even if they are fluent in the other language, colloquial expressions and subtle meanings within the language can cause barriers to effective communication between people of different cultures.

5. *Customs and taboos:* Various books outlining the customs and taboos of doing business in other countries can help alleviate the stress of the business traveler. However, as the following brief list of cultural taboos indicates, doing business abroad can be challenging: Never refuse a cup of coffee from a businessperson in Kuwait; in Bangkok, when crossing your legs, make sure the sole of your foot does not point toward someone; do not remove your jacket in Japan unless your Japanese colleagues do so first; never help yourself to food at a banquet in China when you are the guest of honor; expect to wait patiently a half-hour or more for an appointment with a Venezuelan businessperson; never discuss politics in Nigeria; do not offer your Saudi Arabian host gifts for his wife and children; plan on a two-hour business lunch in France.

6. *Physical stress:* Jet lag, feelings of dislocation, fatigue, and the difficulties of dealing with important problems at home or at the home office while abroad can take a toll on the health and well-being of business travelers.

Physical Characteristics of the Workplace Among the most common environmental causes of employee stress in the workplace are improper lighting, excessive noise, uncomfortable room temperatures, overcrowding, lack of privacy, and improperly designed tools and equipment (Altman, Valenzi, & Hodgetts, 1985). In the case of employees with disabilities, organizations that have neglected to modify their facilities to conform to the requirements of the American Disabilities Act present unnecessary obstacles to job performance.

In a study of female clerical workers at a university, Greg Oldham and Nancy Rotchford (1983) point out that dark, nonprivate work spaces have several negative effects on employees:

1. Employees have poor interpersonal experiences due to excessive contact with other employees.
2. Employees feel that they have little control over their work and that their jobs lack significance.
3. Employees' lack of privacy causes difficulties in concentration.
4. Employees are less satisfied with their work and more prone to experience job stress.

The physical design of a company's offices can influence opportunities for interpersonal communication. In particular, work spaces that inhibit informal interaction, privacy, and control over a work area are most likely to cause employee stress.

Organizational Stressors

Organizational stressors are found within an organization's culture. More specifically, the organization's norms and expectations about social support, participation in decision making, diversity, and expression of emotion can be sources of job stress. Different types of organizational cultures affect individuals in varying ways. Altman, Valenzi, and Hodgetts (1985) apply Deal and Kennedy's (1982) typology of organizational cultures to their analysis of stress at work:

> A high-feedback, high risk-taking environment is one in which we are likely to find macho-type people who walk fast, talk fast, dress in modern-style clothing, compete with each other for promotion and salary, and live what can be thought of as a very fast life. Conversely, in a low-feedback, low risk-taking environment, we are likely to find people who follow the rules, do not make

waves, write lots of memos to cover and explain their actions, and tend to live a very structured type of existence. Stress is an organizational culture problem for two reasons: (a) an individual who is mild-mannered may find him- or herself in a very stress-creating environment, and (b) regardless of the characteristics of the environment, even the most successful individuals may find the pressures of the situation to be extremely difficult. (p. 433)

Social Support Although organizations and occupations differ in terms of their expectations about social support, providing employees with access to a network of support is critical to controlling job stress. According to Eileen Berlin Ray (1987), "supportive interactions are those in which co-workers are able to vent feelings, clarify perceptions, and mutually define the work environment" (p. 188). Most evident in stable social relationships at work, this type of communication with others at work can help alleviate stress as well as establish a sense of control. In contrast, an organization that isolates employees from one another (through incompatible schedules, poor physical layout, or strict limitations on informal interaction) restricts their access to social support and increases the likelihood of job stress (Ray, 1987).

In Terence Albrecht and Mara Adelman's (1987) theoretical model of social support and job stress, employees with poor social support at work are less able to make sense of an uncertain work environment because they lack access to interpretive resources. As a result, they come to feel as if they have no control over the work situation, which, in turn, leads to stress. According to Albrecht and Adelman (1987), "supportive communication . . . reduces one's perceptions of uncertainty [and thereby] helps . . . develop a sense of perceived control over stressful circumstances" (p. 24).

Unlike the earlier human relations focus on supportive communication and leadership, current research on social support emphasizes the informational functions of supportive communication and the role that co-workers play in assisting each other in defining and making sense of their work environment.

Participation in Decision Making Participation in decision making can help reduce stress and improve quality of work life by giving employees a sense of meaningful control over their work (Miller et al., 1990). It also enhances employees' understanding of what the organization expects from its workers and how their efforts will be rewarded, thereby decreasing uncertainty and stress (Schuler & Jackson, 1986). However, organizations differ widely in terms of the amount of trust they have in employees' ability to make important decisions. At one extreme are organizations that take a scientific management approach, viewing employees as mere performers of managerial commands. At the other extreme are organizations that recognize the employee's expert knowledge of the job and the value of that knowledge in decision making.

Consider, for example, how the relationship between decision-making participation and job stress did not play a role in the decision of an automobile parts manufacturer to institute a new corporate strategy. Seeking to become the lowest-cost parts supplier in the industry, the company's senior management made the decision without consulting lower-level managers or workers and without considering how their lack of participation in the decision making would negatively affect the outcome of the new strategy. As a result, employees were not committed to the goal of becoming the lowest-cost parts supplier; instead, employee apathy, stress, and burnout contributed to placing the company on the verge of bankruptcy.

Organizations that do not value employee input tend to have high levels of job stress. They also tend to show their mistrust of employees' decision-making ability through surveillance systems, time clocks, strict supervision, compensation policies, working conditions, parking lot arrangements, and even the layout and condition of the building. The indirect messages sent by these elements within an organization reflect the more explicit message of nonparticipation in decision making. An organization thus can affect the quality of its employees' work life by how much it values their input in important decisions. Competitive companies seek to create an organizational culture that encourages honest dialogue and eliminates fear of reprisals.

Diversity How an organization deals with a diverse workforce can contribute to employee stress, particularly for minority employees. As Ann Morrison and Mary Ann Von Glinow (1990) point out, "the number of women, [African Americans], and Hispanics in management [positions] has quadrupled since 1970, and the number of Asians has increased eightfold" (p. 200). Nonetheless, racism and sexism exist in corporations.

A physically challenged, African American woman working as a middle manager in a high-tech electronics firm would likely encounter discrimination in the workplace and, as a result, would have to work harder to establish a voice of authority in the company. The suppression of the minority voice is sometimes referred to as a "glass ceiling." According to a 1991 report by the U.S. Labor Department, women and minorities face numerous barriers to career development:

1. *Recruiting and hiring:* Companies may fail to inform recruiters of equal opportunity requirements or of their desire to promote a diverse workforce.
2. *Succession and promotion:* Managers usually choose successors who are similar to themselves, and since most managers are white men, they tend not to promote women and minorities.
3. *Affirmative action:* Although the legal guidelines and restrictions of affirmative action are usually well known by human resources department personnel, the managers who hire, fire, and promote employees are less aware of the guidelines. At the executive level, where job offers are made within a

close informal network and records of hiring patterns are rarely maintained, affirmative action may be most often ignored.

4. *Performance standards:* Managers may apply different criteria in evaluating men, women, and minorities. While minorities tend to be subjected to tokenism (i.e., excessive scrutiny leads to collapse under pressure), women tend to be evaluated on the basis of emotional standards (e.g., their friendliness may be viewed to be as important as their job performance).

5. *Line management exclusion:* Most women and minority managers work in departments that support staff functions (such as human resources and facilities) rather than in line management (e.g., production and engineering) (Hawkins, 1991).

For women especially, taking time off "from work to raise children or to pursue other noncareer interests does permanent damage to [their] earning power" and increases job stress. (Silverstein, 1992, p. 1). In many corporate cultures, they are regarded as less dedicated than men to their careers, and they may be given less responsible jobs as a result.

An organization's lack of tolerance for diversity can be either overt or subtle. It was overt, for instance, when one of the authors of this text arranged for a training session to be conducted by a woman (with a Ph.D.) at a public utility and the general manager balked, "Our guys don't like being told things by women." Usually, however, discrimination is more subtle. Edward Jones, Jr. (1973), an African American manager, describes his encounters with white colleagues whose intolerance of diversity makes him tense and ill at ease.

More recently, researchers attempting to identify the specific challenges faced by African Americans in the workplace have found that despite significant economic strides over the last twenty-five years, African American professionals face "more frustration and anxiety—even rage—than their less affluent counterparts" (Tribune, 1995, p. 122). This may be due in part to a general inability to relax in a predominantly white workplace as well as to poor communication between blacks and whites. Whites may tend to be distrustful of blacks who advance in the workplace, and those who advance into management may tend to be held to a different interpretive standard of job performance. For example, a blunt white manager may be seen as being "decisive," while an African American counterpart may be seen as having "an attitude."

Significant communication problems can ensue between members of cultures that on the surface may not appear all that different. For example, one of us (Eisenberg) recently conducted a week-long communication training program for a Finnish paper manufacturer in which key communication differences were found in Americans and Finns. To most Finns, Americans seemed superficial because they often restated the obvious in small talk (e.g., "Have a nice day" or using the other person's name in conversation). To Americans, Finns appeared introverted and overly serious because they did not engage in small talk and seemed unwilling to use superlatives in conversation. Once these differences in cultural interpretation were exposed, however, communication between the two groups improved (Carbaugh, 1995).

An organization's tolerance of diversity is also expressed in its policy statements and general practices. For example, although gay and lesbian couples are usually denied health benefits for their dependent "spouse," the Disney Corporation recognizes gay and lesbian "spousal equivalents" in its benefit packages.

Expression of Emotion Certain industries and organizations tend to expect employees to hide their true feelings and to display only those emotions considered appropriate at work (Rafaeli & Sutton, 1987). For example, flight attendants are expected to be cheery, bill collectors hostile, and funeral directors comforting. An organization may reinforce these emotional expectations through its recruitment practices, socialization efforts, and systems of reward and punishment (Hochschild, 1979). As the pressure for improved customer service increases (see Chapter 1), more companies are following the lead of Disney and Nordstrom in training their employees to communicate positively with customers. While the organization benefits from these canned emotional displays through greater customer satisfaction and increased sales, their effect on individuals is less clear. Arlie Hochschild (1979) argues that emotional labor can be detrimental to mental health. She uses flight attendants as an example:

> A young businessman said to a flight attendant, "Why aren't you smiling?" She put her tray back on the food cart, looked him in the eye, and said, "I'll tell you what. You smile first, then I'll smile." The businessman smiled at her. "Good," she replied. "Now freeze and hold that smile for fifteen hours." (Hochschild, 1983, p. 127)

Others argue that disguising one's real emotions at work is at times necessary and advantageous. A friendly food server, for example, is likely to receive more in the way of tips than one who does not disguise negative emotions. For physicians, some emotional detachment is necessary to their personal well-being and professional success (Rafaeli & Sutton, 1987).

In a sophisticated analysis of the relationship between the expression of emotion and stress among human services workers, Katherine Miller, Jim Stiff, and Beth Ellis (1988) point to the lopsided nature of the caregiver–patient relationship. Caregivers (e.g., nurses, physicians, and social workers) must be careful to distinguish between the two forms of emotional communication: *emotional contagion* and *empathic concern.* When caregivers communicate empathic concern, they show concern for the other person but they do not experience the same feelings as the patient. Emotional contagion—the experience of the patient's emotional turmoil—is more likely to lead to stress and burnout

(Maslach, 1982). According to Miller, Stiff, and Ellis (1988), effective caregivers develop "a stance in which concern for another can be held independent of emotional involvement" (p. 262).

In a thorough critique of the strategic approach to handling emotions at work, Mumby and Putnam (1993) offer an alternative to Simon's (1957) concept of "bounded rationality" which they call "bounded emotionality." Unlike Simon and others, who recognize the limitations of rational decision making but view emotion as a "weak appendage to reason," Mumby and Putnam see emotion as central to organizational life (p. 471). They support a work life that is tolerant of ambiguity, is committed to diverse goals and values, seeks a sense of community, and views emotion as a spontaneous way to develop the work relationships through which goals are accomplished.

Job Stressors

In one respect, *job stressors* are created by organizations and their environments. For example, a restaurant chain that focuses on meeting customers' needs at the expense of employee participation in decision making is likely to create job stress. But there are other dimensions of jobs that also affect stress, such as workload, role uncertainty, and job design.

Workload Quantitatively, *workload* refers to the number of projects or processes an employee is responsible for completing within a given period of time. But qualitatively, *workload,* or *work overload,* can refer to either too much work or work that is too difficult. A new employee, for example, may have difficulty with the complexity of a task due to his or her lack of training or experience. This latter type of workload has been linked to a number of symptoms of stress (Miller et al., 1990). It is also highly dependent on an employee's ability (Farace, Monge, & Russell, 1977). Waiting tables in a busy restaurant requires physical coordination, a good memory, and interpersonal skills. A person lacking these skills would be unable to perform the job. However, an individual's level of ability does not necessarily remain constant. A college education, for instance, is intended in part to enhance skills and abilities in preparation for a career.

Work overload can be addressed in various ways. One method involves workload analysis. The number of hours required to complete a specific task is determined, and then the number of employees is modified to make the workload manageable. In addition, a work-flow analysis can be conducted to identify redundant operations within the overall work process and thereby balance the workload of all employees. For example, in a busy restaurant where it takes longer to prepare food than it does to seat customers and take their orders, it may be decided to seat customers at a slower rate in order to even out the workload in the kitchen, or to hire support staff to take on some of the work of food preparation.

Role Uncertainty Employees who understand their role and responsibilities in the organization are better able to cope with work overload than employees whose role is marked by uncertainty and a lack of direction. Even simple jobs can be subject to role stress when the employee is given unclear or conflicting information about job duties. Supervisors may neglect to explain the employee's responsibilities clearly, or managers may receive only vague information about jobs from higher-level management. In addition, an employee may receive conflicting directions from different supervisors (e.g., two managers in a matrix organization). Research has conclusively linked these types of role uncertainty to job stress (Miller et al., 1990).

Job Design The quality of the work experience can range from extreme boredom in an unchallenging job to extreme anxiety caused by overly challenging work and a fear of failure. According to psychologist Mihaly Csikszentmihalyi (1990), the best jobs fall midway between these two extremes: They are various and challenging enough to require close attention, but they do not demand more than the employee is able to perform. When such a balance is achieved, the individual may experience "flow" or "jamming"—a temporary loss of self-consciousness in the enjoyment of work performance (Eisenberg, 1990).

Research on the employee work life has found that job design is an important factor (Altman, Valenzi, & Hodgetts, 1985). A specific set of job characteristics has been linked to an enriched work life: variety, task identity, task significance, autonomy, and feedback (Hackman & Suttle, 1977). As illustrated in Figure 8.2, *job variety* encourages employees to use multiple talents and skills, while *task identity* allows employees to complete a whole piece of work, such as a major auto subassembly or a financial transaction from beginning to end, rather than isolated parts or components. *Task significance* refers to the impact the job has on other people's lives. *Autonomy* is the degree of freedom or control employees have in scheduling and performing their work. Finally, *feedback* is the communication that employees receive about their work from others. This set of job characteristics values the employee's need for meaningful and responsible involvement in organizational dialogue. Jobs designed with these factors in mind are also likely to create among employees greater work satisfaction, motivation, and performance (Hackman & Oldham, 1975). However, when jobs lack these important characteristics, employee stress, burnout, absenteeism, and turnover can be expected to increase.

Altman, Valenzi, and Hodgetts (1985) offer several other suggestions for enriching the work experience:

1. *Combine tasks.* Employees' perception of task identity and variety improves when tasks are combined. For example, rather than the car salesperson making the sale and someone else following up on customer satisfaction,

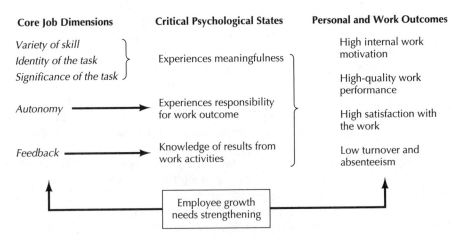

FIGURE 8.2
The Job Characteristics Model of Work Motivation

Source: Adapted from J. Richard Hackman and J. Lloyd Suttle, eds., *Improving Life at Work: Behavioral Science Approaches to Organizational Change* (Santa Monica, Calif.: Goodyear Publishing Co., 1977), p. 129.

   the two tasks could be combined to allow the salesperson to handle the entire transaction.

2. *Form natural work groups.* Greater task identity and task significance occur when people work in teams. For instance, rather than having a pool of typists, each one is assigned to a department's team of workers.

3. *Establish customer contact.* Autonomy and feedback occur when employees have direct contact with customers.

4. *Delegate decision making.* Employees at all levels of an organization should be involved in decision making and given greater discretion in determining schedules, methods, training, and the like. In addition, they should be provided with detailed financial and other information about the overall effects of their decisions. One food manufacturer, for example, gives its employees free access to their own productivity levels via computer terminals.

5. *Open feedback channels.* All types of feedback—between work groups, from customers, and between managers and employees—should be allowed to flow unimpeded. In addition, employee performance feedback should be provided regularly, rather than just once or twice annually in performance appraisals.

Notice that most of the preceding suggestions emphasize changes in communication that increase the individual's control over work processes.

   Autonomy is perhaps the most important factor in reducing job stress and improving quality of work life because it encourages employees to feel effective, resourceful, responsible, and trusted by others in the organization (Jackson, 1983; Karasek, 1979; Luhmann & Albrecht, 1990). From a managerial perspective, autonomy may be fostered through *RAA delegation;* that is, by encouraging employees to accept more *responsibility, authority,* and *accountability.* Thus, when a supervisor asks a junior engineer to design a new product, the supervisor gives the engineer the responsibility and authority to accomplish that task. The junior engineer does not have to compete with others for resources or information and does not need to seek the supervisor's approval of each step in the design of the product. At the same time, the junior engineer is accountable for designing the new product in a way that meets the company's objectives and needs, and the supervisor is responsible for providing this information. Therefore, the junior engineer is responsible not only for the product's design, but also for meeting certain standards (e.g., of delivery and cost).

RAA delegation gives employees the authority to accomplish tasks as they see fit and holds them accountable for specific performance goals. In contemporary management, it is similar to what Peters and Waterman (1982) call *managing the loose-tight paradox* of achieving a certain degree of autonomy within a capitalist system. In order to balance creativity and constraint, organizations should avoid giving employees too much or too little autonomy; instead, they should strive to provide enough autonomy to promote among employees a positive work experience, high involvement, and productivity.

However, it should be recognized that competitive pressures often work against empowerment and job enrichment in organizations. Some manufacturing companies, for example, use principles of scientific management to cope with the pressure to deliver high-quality products at low cost. Many organizations have responded to global competition by simplifying jobs and hiring less-skilled workers at lower wages. One manufacturing manager boasts that because it takes only three days to train unskilled workers to perform the assembly jobs, the company can hire people at the lowest possible wage. Nationally, manufacturing jobs have both declined in number and changed in nature—from an average of $14-an-hour for complex assembly work to $7-an-hour for repetitive work (U.S. Dept. of Labor, 1991). Although organizations may view these moves as short-term business strategies, jobs that lack the key characteristics of variety, task identity, task significance, autonomy, and feedback can be expected in the long term to increase stress and decrease motivation and productivity in the workforce.

Individual Stressors

Some causes of stress at work are unrelated to organizational factors or job design. *Individual stressors* may be caused by an employee's personality traits, personal life, or communication style.

Personality Traits A workaholic typically regards the importance of the work experience as above all else, including family, friends, leisure time, and so on. Although workaholism sometimes emerges as a way of dealing with stressful events in an individual's personal life, it is more often associated with people who exhibit what are called *type A personality traits.* "In addition to competing with others, they constantly compete with themselves, setting high standards of productivity that they seem driven to maintain. They tend to feel frustrated in the work situation, irritable with the work efforts of subordinates, and misunderstood by superiors" (Burke, Weir, & Duwors, 1979, p. 57). *Type B personalities* are less driven than type A. In the long term, type A behavior is dangerous because it causes people to sacrifice all other life pursuits to their goals.

Other research has focused on identifying those personality traits that help people cope with stress in more productive ways. Using the concept of "hardiness," Kobasa, Maddi, and Kahn (1982) argue that hardy individuals are likely to view negative news and events as opportunities or challenges. They feel in control of their lives, welcome change, and, as a result, are better able to handle stress than their less hardy counterparts.

Most dysfunctional personality traits are related to low self-esteem. The quality of a person's work experience is highly dependent on his or her self-image and self-knowledge (e.g., of strengths and weaknesses and likes and dislikes). As Warren Bennis (1985) reports in his study of great leaders, they know themselves well and feel confident in the face of others' criticism and advice.

Another aspect of personality that affects a person's work experience has to do with patterns of attention (Larkey, 1984; March & Olsen, 1976). Most people tend to pay more attention to the past and future rather than to the present. At work, this may mean holding a grudge, regretting a business decision, hoping for a certain level of sales, or anticipating changes in the marketplace. However, in today's turbulent business world, it has become more important than ever before to attend to and cope with present-day issues and changes. This requires a more functional attitude toward work as well as a focus on the need for ongoing feedback on progress and operations.

Personal Life Stressful events in an employee's personal life also affect the work experience. Family problems, such as marital difficulties or a sick child, can significantly increase an employee's level of stress. In addition, the stress of relocation commonly affects managers moving up the organizational ladder. Finally, financial problems, especially during difficult economic times, contribute to stress. Examples include overextended credit, unpaid bills, the cost of a child's education, and a laid-off spouse.

These sources of stress emphasize that the boundary between the work life and the personal life is highly permeable. As a result, people are only "partially included" in an organization (Weick, 1979).

Communication Style Communication style also affects the employee's level of stress and quality of life at work. For example, people who are shy or afraid to communicate with others tend to experience more stress at work and are less likely to do well in many organizational settings than people who communicate more openly (Phillips, 1991). Moreover, competent communicators tend to be evaluated more positively and to achieve greater success at work (Monge et al., 1982).

Certain communication skills help employees cope with job stress. In a study of assertive versus argumentative communicators, it was found that assertiveness—the ability to state a position without attacking the other person—is associated with creating positive impressions in others and with improving the work experience (Infante et al., 1984). Argumentative communicators, in contrast, tend to be more aggressive and insecure, and they are less likely to be well regarded by others or to enjoy their experience at work.

The results of another study indicate that the ability to exhibit empathic concern inhibits stress at work (Miller et al., 1990). As noted earlier in the chapter, many jobs in the health-care field require empathic concern for the client's problems but a detachment from the client's emotional state of mind. This is a learned skill that is essential in jobs that make high emotional demands on employees.

NEW DIRECTIONS FOR WORK ORGANIZATION

The challenge of improving the work experience has been made more difficult by globalization. Nonetheless, various approaches to meeting that challenge have been offered. One approach defines the problem as resulting from a general lack of coping skills among today's workers. In this view, employees' resistance to cooperation and increased job stress stem from their lack of knowledge of how to cooperate or their lack of desire to do so. By learning the strategies for coping with stress (see Table 8.2), employees can improve the quality of their work experience (Sailer, Schlachter, & Edwards, 1982).

Another approach focuses on redesigning jobs and organizations in ways that enrich the experience of work, empower employees, and value teamwork. In addition, the so-called *career planning* approach holds that individuals and organizations both benefit when they work together to place people in appropriate and satisfying jobs and provide them with educational and training opportunities. Employees can thereby acquire new skills and pursue a career, and companies can expect to retain valuable workers.

Yet another approach to improving the employee's work experience calls for a review of some of the underlying assumptions of capitalism. For example, the effects of changes in the marketplace and of shareholder influence on employees' work life are often overlooked.

TABLE 8.2 Strategies for Coping with Stress

Physical maintenance strategies
  Attention to diet and nutrition
  Required amounts of sleep
  Exercise
  Participation in leisure and recreational activities

Internal assistance strategies
  Relaxation response
  Biofeedback
  Meditation

Personal organization strategies
  Stress planning
  Delegate responsibility
  Choose or alter the work environment
  Engage in creative problem solving and decision
    making
  Set goals
  Manage time
  Manage conflict
  Restructure jobs
  Use self-assessment measures

Outside assistance strategies
  Psychoanalysis
  Stress counseling
  Employee development programs .
  Behavior-modification techniques

Situational and support group strategies
  Assertiveness training and role playing
  Development of supportive relationships
  Avoidance of substance abuse

Source: H. Sailer, J. Schlachter, and M. Edwards, "Stress,"
Personnel (July–August 1982) 59: 35–48.

However, work can be more than a source of stress. Extensive research by
Mihaly Csikszentmihalyi (1990) and Charles Garfield (1992) links peak employee performance with certain social and psychological conditions—e.g.,

clear goals, regular feedback, and a sense of confidence. Furthermore, these conditions may not necessarily be met at the expense of profits, such that peak employee performance can be consistent with peak organizational performance.

In a similar line of research, self-directed work teams are reported to encounter fewer obstacles to effective decision making and productivity (Willens et al., 1991). The concept of self-directed work teams, however, has gained slow acceptance due to manager's concerns about the types of decisions these teams can and cannot be expected to make. At New United Motors Manufacturing, Inc. (NUMMI), a joint venture involving Toyota and General Motors, self-directed work teams function successfully despite certain rules governing accountability, safety, and human resources.

Finally, Eisenberg (1990) discusses the preconditions and characteristics of what he calls "jamming" experiences—that is, moments of behavioral coordination that result in both peak experiences for individual participants and peak performance levels for the group. In practice, jamming requires proper staffing and risk-taking. All members of a team should possess comparable skills because the individual's work life is directly affected by the abilities of co-workers. In addition, jamming requires a commitment to taking risks, or a willingness to both perform and release control to fate and the group process.

The Experience of Work Outside of Organizations

As we witness the end of the organizational age in which companies and corporations played a major role in people's public and private lives (Deetz, 1992), the postmodern turn of the past decade is transforming the world of work. The erosion of the old social contract underscores the importance of the call for a new contract emphasizing partnerships (Chilton & Weidenbaum, 1994). Widespread dissatisfaction with downsizing, restructuring, team-based organizing, and job loss exists among American middle-class workers. We can expect continued loss of middle-class jobs in the United States as advanced technologies encourage multinational firms to move their operations abroad in search of lower labor costs. Moreover, many people are questioning the value of a system that requires them to dedicate much of their life to work in exchange for a corporate paycheck.

Several recent studies report a general trend toward a workforce that is independent of organizations. Susan Dentzer, writing in *U.S. News & World Report* (1995) about "the death of the middleman," attributes the 34,000 job losses in the airline ticket industry to advanced technologies that permit travelers to review flight schedules and reserve and purchase airline tickets via computers. Similarly, automatic teller machines (ATMs) have taken over some of the functions of bank tellers, and securing loans will soon involve contact with a computer network rather than a loan officer. *Fortune* magazine (Kiechel, 1994) attributes still other permanent job losses to technological advances: 250,000 jobs in four Fortune 100 companies during January 1994 alone, and 231,000 farmers by the year 2000. In addition, between 1991 and 1995, about 44 percent of middle managers and professional workers and 56 percent of hourly workers became temporary workers—permanently! Although 11 million Americans graduated from college in 1995, there were only about 5 million jobs waiting for them; moreover, about half of those jobs are expected to be lost to technological advancement and global competition by the end of the century. For college students, choosing a major in a "hot field" no longer guarantees organizational entry or success, as all industries are experiencing major change and all organizations are struggling to survive in the new global markets. Consider, for example, that in 1980 the "hottest" field to enter was banking.

Despite these frightening predictions, we remain optimistic about the future of work and the role of communication in work. Indeed, the availability of work outside of organizations has never been more lucrative than it is now. You might, for example, provide *outsource services*—such as technical writing, computer support, or management consulting—to downsized firms. You might become an *entrepreneur,* establishing your own business and using the Internet to advertise your skills. Or you might become an *independent contractor* for businesses unable to manage the costs associated with providing employee benefits or maintaining office space.

Another source of optimism about the future world of work is related to the emerging *third-sector organizations* for providing social services throughout the world. According to Jeremy Rifkin (1995), the largest growth in meaningful work is not in the public or private sector, but in the emerging third sector, which encourages forming or joining "soft money-supported" *volunteer* organizations and agencies. In France, for example, third-sector organizations are the fastest-growing sector of that nation's economy; in Japan, most urban neighborhoods are governed by volunteers who manage everything from implementing safety and ecology standards to improving the quality of lives for the homeless and poor. In the United States, where a massive volunteer organization already exists, the Clinton administration implemented a program in 1994 that provides money for a college education to persons who dedicate two years of their lives to public service.

In most cases, working in the third sector does not mean working for free. It means that you are responsible for seeking out alternative funding to support your organization from private and public grant organizations, and that you must demonstrate to those agencies annual needs and accomplishments. In such jobs you receive a salary and/or other forms of compensation for your work. But you accept the responsibility for finding meaningful work and, in most cases, for supporting yourself while you do it. A major benefit is that you can choose work that is socially and personally meaningful. To a large extent, this type of work is communication-intensive.

Yet another reason for our optimism is that many people, particularly in affluent nations such as the United States, are questioning the value of work in relation to their personal and spiritual life (Fox, 1994; Goodall, 1996). After two hundred years of industrial growth, technological improvements, and capitalism, there are new concerns about the deterioration of our planet and the meaning of work in relation to a paycheck. New ideas about "stewardship" (Block, 1993) and an "ecology of commerce" (Hawken, 1994) may chart a new direction for human labor and for how we define meaningful work (Handy, 1994).

Working outside of organizations as an outsourcer, entrepreneur, or independent contractor within the new global economy will require both self-reliance and capital. As a college student, you can prepare for the future by supplementing your education with the development of a specific set of skills. Others who have lost a managerial job can redefine themselves as independent workers.

OUTSOURCERS: THE NEW ECONOMY

While advancing information technology has contributed to a significant loss of jobs in nearly every industry, it has also created a new source of self-employment: the outsource service provider. *Outsourcers* are people who conduct work, often from home, and often via the information highway. In a widespread effort to reduce their operating budgets, many businesses now use outsource service providers. They save money by avoiding the costs of employee benefits (such as health insurance and pensions) and of maintaining office space, thereby making better use of available resources. In addition, competition among outsource service providers has meant that they usually charge less for improved services.

Outsourcers, as specialists who work for themselves, tend to bear the financial burden of skill upgrading, cross-training, and purchasing equipment. Although they pass along these costs to the businesses they serve, most companies still save money. The typical outsourcer earns more than if he or she had a similar job with salary and benefits in an organization. Many outsourcers also enjoy the flexibility of working at home, especially working parents, who can reduce their child-care expenses while also spending more time with their children. In 1993, more than 40 million Americans worked at home: 13 million as full-time outsourcers, 11 million as part-time outsourcers, 10 million as employees of corporations, and 8 million in telecommunications (Kiechel, 1994).

Outsourcers tend to provide what Peter Drucker (1992a) calls "knowledge work." Their services include a variety of managerial, secretarial, and technical tasks, computer documentation and training, and office equipment repair and maintenance. One outsourcer we know specializes in repairing and servicing laser printers; another develops on-line "help" systems for large-scale manufacturing firms.

A number of risks are associated with outsourcing. Businesses risk a loss of control over the services they no longer provide to themselves, though stiff competition among outsourcers tends to maintain high-quality services. In addition, some U.S. businesses have turned to outsource providers in less-developed countries, thereby increasing competition among local outsourcers and lowering the fees that they can charge. This risk will continue to become more threatening to Americans who work at home as communication technologies advance. Finally, outsourcing presents a number of societal risks. Increasing numbers of U.S. workers lack health insurance and retirement benefits. The cost of health care alone has been identified by the Clinton administration as a potential threat to the financial health of the nation. Uninsured outsourcers may thus contribute to these risks to national security.

SELF-RELIANCE: DEVELOPING A NEW SKILL SET

To be *self-reliant* in the new world of work means being open to change and willing to work in fields you may not have considered before. According to Walter Kiechel (1994), becoming a self-reliant worker is important for three reasons:

1. The new economy will be a service economy, and the majority of its workers will be service providers in a wide variety of specialties (from auto repair and physical therapy to systems engineering and investment banking). By the year 2000, factory workers will constitute less than 16 percent of the total U.S. workforce.
2. The core of the new economy will consist of converging telecommunications and computer technologies. As a result, strong computer skills will be required by all workers.
3. More work will involve single projects completed by teams. Although competitive companies have always used task forces to solve difficult problems, this trend is now evident in all industries. However, the task forces in the new economy will be made up of independent specialists, rather than employees of organizations, who have experience in particular projects and proven records of success.

Furthermore, the new economy will require the college-educated adult to prepare for a lifetime of learning by developing a set of skills, including individual and team-based specialties. A *skill set* includes the abilities and experiences that a person brings to a potential employer, such as skills in project management, partnering, innovation in using new technologies, mentoring, documentation and training, editing, publishing, change management, telecommunications marketing, and even developing a new client base. Skill sets are marketable as jobs in industry, but they also offer people the opportunity to go into business for themselves. Kiechel (1994) suggests that working with information from a variety of sources is helpful in understanding the importance of developing a skill set. He echoes the views of Michael J. Driver:

> The old industrial model primarily called for people [to be] focused, structured, analytical, and action-oriented. . . . As we move into the Information Age, we will have to develop adaptive, multifocused thinking . . . using lots of information, seeing it going in multiple directions. An integrative style. (cited in Kiechel, 1994, p. 68)

The basic key to self-reliance is an understanding of the market relationship between one's knowledge and skills and the services one can provide to others. While traditional jobs within organizations will continue to decline in number, both the work itself and the skills needed to accomplish it will continue to exist. Those who develop a set of skills geared at providing services will be most likely to succeed in the future.

Unfortunately, in most cases, a college education does not focus on developing a marketable skill set for the new global economy. As a college student, you will acquire knowledge, but you are not likely to gain the experience needed to define a skill set. Some colleges and universities are making some progress in this area by involving students in internships, co-ops, and team-based projects, but most students will need to supplement their education with work experiences and public seminars on skill set development.

Kiechel (1994) identifies what he calls the four "compass points" of a career in the new economy: (1) Be *self-reliant* (think of yourself as a business), (2) be a *generalist* (know enough about the various disciplines to be able to mediate among them), (3) be *connected* (a team player), and (4) be a *specialist* (an expert in some area). Similarly, Vicky Farrow, director of executive and workforce development at Sun Microsystems, gives employees the following advice on assuming responsibility for their careers:

1. The overarching principle [is]: Think of yourself as a business.
2. Define your product or service: What is your area of expertise?
3. Know your target market: To whom are you going to sell this [product or service]?
4. Be clear on why your customer buys from you: What is your "value proposition" . . . ?
5. As in any business, drive for quality and customer satisfaction, even if your customer is just someone else in your organization—like your boss.

6. Know your profession or field and what's going on there: What does success look like in your area? Is your profession . . . becoming obsolete?
7. Invest in your own growth and development, the way a company invests in R&D [research and development]: What new products or services will you be able to provide?
8. Be willing to consider changing your business or starting a new one . . . . I don't think it's possible anymore to have one career for your whole life. (cited in Kiechel, 1994, p. 71)

Although communication students develop valuable *process skills* (e.g., skills in team participation, leadership, written and oral communication, negotiation, and interpersonal relations), they typically lack *technical expertise* and *project experience.* Some technical expertise may be gained through coursework in other fields of study and off-campus seminars, while project experience may be found in internship and co-op opportunities that focus on completing real projects for actual customers. These supplements to a college education will help you think of yourself as a business and develop a marketable skill set.

REDEFINING WORK IDENTITY AT MIDLIFE

Let's consider the experiences of the typical middle-aged executive whose successful career comes to an end as a result of corporate downsizing. According to G. J. Meyer (1995), the executive goes through several stages. Initially, the executive seeks to find comparable employment in another organization. But after a year of working unsuccessfully with headhunters, the executive's self-image declines, and coping with that diminished identity becomes a daily challenge. Other avenues may then be investigated, such as the possibility of starting a new business with the skill set developed as an executive. However, the risks involved in a such a venture are significant. Indeed, the executive has a number of friends and colleagues—also victims of corporate downsizing—who have lost their life's savings in unsuccessful ventures. But like others whose lives have been dedicated to highly specialized work in large corporations or government agencies, the executive has accumulated a significant amount of debt (a home mortgage, car payments, and the cost of his or her children's college education) and is generally ill-equipped for dealing with change. Having achieved success under the old social contract, the executive lacks the generalist orientation and team-based organizing skills needed to succeed in the new economy.

Perhaps you are among other students in your class who have returned to school to acquire the knowledge and skills needed to find work in the new economy. Redefining your work identity is a challenging but worthwhile endeavor. By learning to live with the ambiguities of economic and social change, developing a marketable skill set, and gaining project- and team-based experience, you will increase your chances of finding satisfying work in the new economy.

THE SECRET FISHERMAN

Tom Douglas drives a delivery van for Sunshine Snacks. He had pursued a college education in business administration, but he did not receive his degree because he lacked the credits for one uncompleted course in the program. At work, Tom has turned down several promotions that would have made him a supervisor—with an office, a secretary, an expense account, a nine-to-five workday, and a higher salary. The regional manager, Renee Brown, does not understand why Tom has refused the opportunity to advance within the company. When she asks him about it, he responds, "I like my job. I do it well. Please don't ask me to give up what I like for something I know I won't like." Still, in Renee's opinion, Tom's talents could be put to better use in the office, and his family of four, including two small children, would benefit from the higher salary.

You work as a corporate consultant at Sunshine Snacks. You are also a friend of both Renee's and of a close friend of Tom's. You know the secret behind why Tom never completed college and why he has refused promotions at work: his interest in bass fishing. More than just a hobby, the sport has made Tom a trophy-winning bass fisherman. He frequently enters tournaments throughout the South and has won numerous prizes, including one worth $25,000 in cash last year. As a Sunshine Snacks deliveryperson, Tom can map his own routes and schedule

(continued)

SUMMARY

The experience of work within organizations is marked by a process of organizational assimilation, by indicators of cooperation and resistance, and by new directions in improving the employee's work life. Communication plays an important role in organizational environments that value the employee's input and that reduce employee stress through designing jobs with the key characteristics of variety, significance, freedom, and control. A trend toward giving the employee a greater voice in decision making is evident; it is likely to improve the employee's work life and make organizations more productive.

The experience of work outside of organizations includes entrepreneurial ventures and outsourcing. In the new service-oriented economy, the majority of

(continued)

deliveries at his own pace. His customers know that he will keep them well stocked with deliveries made early in the morning or late at night. This allows Tom to compete in tournaments that take place during daylight hours. Eventually, Tom hopes to win enough tournaments to gain a corporate sponsorship, which would allow him to quit his job and fish full-time. In addition, you know Tom never completed that one course for his college degree for two reasons: because it met on the same days as bass tournament registration, and because a college degree would probably result in more pressure from Renee to accept a promotion to supervisor.

Although at first you regarded Tom's situation as somewhat odd, you have come to realize that it is unfair for you to judge the meaning of fishing in Tom's life. Furthermore, you have come up with an idea that you think would benefit both Tom and the company: corporate sponsorship. Tom could enter the big tournaments, and Sunshine Snacks would benefit from the publicity linking their product to the fishing public, who are a natural customer base for Sunshine Snacks.

ASSIGNMENT

Your task is to convince Renee that the company's sponsorship of Tom's bass fishing talents is a worthwhile endeavor. Given what you have learned about the experience of work and the conditions under which people are most likely to feel successful, how can you structure your argument in a way that makes it as persuasive as possible?

workers will be outsource providers of specialized services. This will require the development of a marketable skill set and a commitment to a lifetime of learning. For people who have dedicated much of their life to working within organizations and who at midlife find themselves unemployed as a result of downsizing, redefining their work identity is necessary to meet the challenges of the new economy.

C A S E S T U D Y 2

DEVELOPING A SKILL SET

Develop your own skill set. Review the skills you have acquired as a college student and through your work experiences, and consider how you might use those skills in the new service-based economy. Complete the following tasks:

ASSIGNMENTS

1. Prepare a resumé that emphasizes your skill set.
2. Evaluate your skill set. Identify the gaps in your experience, knowledge, and abilities. Create a strategic plan for improving your skill set through experience and training seminars.
3. Compare your skill set with those of your classmates. Work together to create a plan for addressing the gaps or deficiencies within the skill sets.
4. Investigate the possibility of working as an outsource service provider for a local company. Use your skill set to determine how you can best prepare yourself to become an outsourcer for the company.

Relational Contexts for Organizational Communication

The importance of establishing good interpersonal relationships is illustrated by the Japanese preoccupation with preserving wa, which means, quite literally, harmony. For a typical American manager, preserving company harmony is not a major preoccupation. For the Japanese, it is Job One.
• John Rehfield, cited in Dean C. Barnlund (1994)

QUESTIONS

FOR DISCUSSION

- What is the relationship between interpersonal communication and the ability to work successfully under the new social contract?

- How can people better communicate with superiors, subordinates, and peers in organizations?

- How does the new idea of customers and suppliers as organizational partners affect communication issues?

- What communicative strategies can be used to deal with sexual harassment?

W e begin our account of interpersonal relationships and communication at work with an examination of the communicative implications of the new social contract. Within this framework, we discuss communication strategies designed to maintain economic viability in the changing job market as well as strategies for coping with organizational change. In addition, we explore the specific types of communication that are most effective with superiors, subordinates, peers, customers, and suppliers as well as the special communication challenges of a multicultural work environment. The new global economy demands intercultural communicative competence among employees, customers, and suppliers. Finally, we discuss some of the new directions taken by organizational theory and research.

The Role of Work Relationships under the New Social Contract

In 1996, in an industry that was pioneered and for many years dominated by American firms, Zenith, the last U.S. television manufacturer, was purchased by LG, a Korean conglomerate. On the same day the Zenith buyout was announced, Chrysler Corporation decided it would no longer make its "New Yorker" model, which had been associated with the company since 1939. A few hours later, Vice-President Al Gore announced that his three-year-long quest to reinvent government had resulted in the permanent loss of over 300,000 jobs. In 1996, it appeared that the Republican party's congressional efforts to downsize the federal bureaucracy by eliminating entire departments had a good chance of succeeding, which in the Department of Education alone would mean a permanent reduction of 976,000 jobs.

Imagine, for a moment, the effects these changes and proposals for change have on people's relationships at work, as well as on communities, the nation, and the world. Victims of so-called *organizational downsizing*—persons who lose their jobs—must deal with the trauma, while those who keep their jobs must deal with the shock and psychological effects of these changes going on around them (Brockner, 1985, 1986; Lifton, 1967; Merry & Brown, 1987; Noer, 1994). Clearly, such events put significant pressure on relationships at work. At the same time, experts observe that effective interpersonal communication helps people cope with change. In particular, the way in which the change is communicated largely determines how quickly the organization rebounds or, in some cases, is revitalized (Noer, 1993).

The key aspects of the new social contract expected to affect interpersonal communication are outlined by Noer (1994) in Table 9.1 as a "new employee contract." That contract specifies an empowered and flexible workforce, short-

9.1   The New Employment Contract

IMPLICIT ASSUMPTIONS	STRATEGIES	OUTCOMES
Employment relationship is situational.	Flexible and portable benefit plans Tenure-free recognition systems Blurred distinction between full-time, part-time, and temporary employees	Flexible workforce
Reward for performance is acknowledgment of contribution and relevance.	Job enrichment and participation The philosophy of quality Self-directed work teams Nonhierarchical performance and reward systems	Motivated workforce Task-invested workforce
Management is empowering.	Employee autonomy No "taking care" of employees No detailed long-term career planning Tough love	Empowered workforce
Loyalty means responsibility and good work.	Nontraditional career paths In/out process Employee choice Accelerated diversity recruiting	Responsible workforce
Explicit job contracting is offered.	Short-term job planning Not signing up for life No assumption of lifetime care-taking	Employee and organization bonded around good work

Source: Noer (1993), p. 158.

---

term contracts, and a reward system based not on tenure, position, or company loyalty but on responsible work. A similar employment contract has been adopted by IBM (see Table 9.2). Although the company has cut approximately 40 percent of its workforce, IBM has managed to regain its former leadership role in the computer industry.

As Tables 9.1 and 9.2 indicate, *interpersonal relationships are crucial to the survival of individuals, teams, and organizations today.* In order to remain com-

TABLE 9.2 IBM's Efforts to Redefine Its Workplace Compact

OLD SOCIAL COMPACT

	Employer	Employees
Expect to Receive	Ethics and honesty Satisfactory performance Retraining as required Compliance/support Loyalty to company	Respect/fair treatment Caring management Good pay Broad-based benefits Opportunity to advance Assistance to succeed Safe and healthy workplace Job security
Willing to Give	Defined expectations Assistive management Merit/good pay Promotion from within Leading company paid benefits Training/retraining "Job related" information Job security Family relationship	Diligence Flexibility/move, retrain Satisfactory performance plus/overtime Lifetime employment Loyalty/trust

EVOLVING SOCIAL COMPACT

	Employer	Employees
Expect to Receive	Ethics and honesty Superior performance Continuous improvement Ideas/participation Commitment to business success Personal investment	Respect/participation Principled leadership Success-based pay Cafeteria benefits Opportunity for growth/resumé Learning climate Safe and healthy workplace Work/life flexibility Secure transitions Trust . . .
Willing to Give	Trust/empowerment Facilitative management Variable pay earning opportunity Opportunity for growth Leading contributory/cafeteria benefits Learning support Information access Transition assistance Diversity/work-life programs	Participation/involvement Willingness to challenge Superior performance/sacrifice Life-long learning Commitment to vision . . . Business success

Source: Ross J. Williams, director of leadership and HR development, presentation to the 21st Issues Management Conference, Human Resources Institute, St. Petersburg, Fla., February 18, 1993.

petitive, organizations must be flexible and open to new information. Strict rules and procedures that limit the acquisition and processing of new information are a hindrance to organizations. Instead, flexibility requires the development of responsive informal systems for sharing information and getting work done, as well as social interaction that supports authentic dialogue, risk-taking, and an alertness to competition. Organizational success depends on the trust and honesty that develop through shared communicative experiences among people who are willing to take risks and learn.

Therefore, good interpersonal relationships at work are no longer a luxury but a prerequisite for effective job performance by both individuals and teams. Organizations know that without positive work relationships, work gets done slowly or poorly or not at all. For employees, positive work relationships provide social support and a sense of identification with and participation in the organizational dialogue. This enables them to anticipate change and remain flexible in response to it, such as by learning new skills or seeking cross-training. In contrast, people who are socially isolated at work often feel insignificant, which can have negative effects on both the employees and the organization. They tend also to be viewed by others as expendable because they fail to communicate effectively and thereby build honest relationships with others.

Management theorists generally agree about the importance of positive interpersonal relationships in organizations. According to Rosabeth Moss Kanter (1989), the focus of managerial work changed fundamentally in the 1980s, from planning, organizing, and coordinating to *communicating*. Management consultant Jack Hawley (1994) suggests that in the 1990s, transformative communication practices are required for organizational, team, and personal success. As a result, successful managers and employees have learned to put less emphasis on formal power and more emphasis on establishing informal influence through networks of relationships both inside and outside of the company.

Taking a similar approach, Bernard Keys and Thomas Case (1990) argue that "influence must replace the use of formal authority in relationships with subordinates, peers, outside contacts, and others on whom the job makes one dependent" (p. 38). Since "positional authority" is no longer sufficient to get the job done, a "web of influence" or a "balanced web of relationships" must be developed:

> Recently managers have begun to view leadership as the orchestration of relationships between several different interest groups—superiors, peers, and outsiders, as well as subordinates. Effectiveness at leadership requires balance in terms of efforts spent in building relationships in these four directions. (Keys & Case, 1990, p. 39)

According to Patricia Riley and Eric Eisenberg's (1991) ACE model of managerial work, effective managers excel in these three communicative areas:

1. *Advocacy,* or making winning arguments to those in power
2. *Cross-functional communication,* or forging connections across departmental and professional boundaries
3. *Empowerment* of subordinates

The role of relationships in organizations has changed. No longer viewed as a conduit for information or as unnecessary socializing, *relationships are now regarded as an important strategic resource for achieving influence, goals, and social support.* Furthermore, a variety of different types of relationships (e.g., with subordinates, co-workers, customers, and suppliers) is believed to contribute to employee and organizational effectiveness.

Communicating with Superiors

Views regarding effective communication with superiors have changed dramatically over time. The inherent differences in perception between superiors and subordinates in an organizational hierarchy and the communication problems associated with upward communication characterize the superior–subordinate relationship. However, subordinates can communicate strategically with supervisors. Through a process involving both mystery and transgression, individuals can help to define their role in the organizational hierarchy.

SEMANTIC INFORMATION DISTANCE

The superior–subordinate relationship has long been studied by researchers interested in organizational communication. Most research suggests that supervisors spend about one-third to two-thirds of their time communicating with subordinates, and that most of this communication is verbal in nature (Dansereau & Markham, 1987). Although this might also appear to suggest that supervisors and subordinates think about issues in similar ways, researchers have found instead that supervisors and subordinates hold dramatically different perceptions of organizational issues (Jablin, 1979). This gap in understanding, referred to as *semantic information distance,* is especially noted in issues related to participation in decision making (Harrison, 1985) and basic job duties (Jablin, 1979). In addition, as Fred Jablin (1979) points out, superiors and subordinates tend to perceive communication differently. While superiors tend to believe that they communicate with subordinates more frequently and effectively than they actually do, subordinates tend to believe that superiors are more open to communication than they actually are. Subordinates also tend to believe that they have more persuasive ability than superiors believe they possess.

Some degree of semantic information distance between superiors and subordinates is the inevitable result of the hierarchy in organizations. More important is the lack of awareness of these gaps in understanding. In other words, supervisors and subordinates not only have different perceptions of key issues but are also likely to be unaware of these differences. This situation leads to miscommunication between supervisors and subordinates.

Further research in this area has revealed the importance of meta-perception and co-orientation. *Meta-perception* refers to a supervisor's perception of a subordinate's perception. *Co-orientation* refers generally to the degree of alignment of perceptions in a dyad. It includes (1) *agreement* (e.g., "How similar are our perceptions of this product?"), (2) *accuracy* ("How well do I understand how you perceive the product?"), and (3) *perceived agreement* ("How similarly do I think we perceive the product?") (Farace, Monge, & Russell, 1977). Of these three types of co-orientation, perceived agreement is regarded as most important to superior–subordinate relationships. While a superior and a subordinate may agree or disagree on an issue and be relatively accurate in judging the other's opinion, the internal perception of agreement by both employee and supervisor leads to a more positive evaluation of the relationship between them (Eisenberg, Monge, & Farace, 1984). Shared understanding is crucial in some situations, such as in the high-risk operations of air-traffic control. In most other situations, however, it is more important that the individuals in the relationship perceive themselves as being in relative agreement. From the organization's perspective, low levels of agreement and accuracy lead to misunderstandings and organizational inefficiency.

Under the terms of the new employment contract, the issues related to semantic information distance have become more complex. New problems associated with attributing meanings to instructions, perceptions, team assignments, and the like demand that managers and team leaders work harder to ensure that messages are received and interpreted as intended.

UPWARD DISTORTION

While semantic information distance is viewed as a natural outgrowth of the organizational hierarchy, researchers identify *upward distortion* as a more purposeful attempt to create gaps in understanding (Roberts & O'Reilly, 1974). That is, subordinates may distort the information they send upward to superiors, particularly when that information reflects negatively on themselves (Dansereau & Markham, 1987). There are four common types of upward distortion (Fulk & Mani, 1986):

1. *Gatekeeping* (some but not all information is passed on from subordinates to superiors)
2. *Summarization* (emphasis is given to certain parts of a message)
3. *Withholding* (information is selectively withheld from superiors)

4. *General distortion* (entire messages are altered to suit the subordinate's motives or agenda)

Some types of upward distortion are an inherent part of the superior–subordinate relationship in a traditional hierarchy. For example, managers can expect subordinates to communicate selectively when issues deserving of attention are raised. However, other types of upward distortion, such as withholding and general distortion, can be problematic. Examples include the selective reporting of negative financial information to superiors and the failure to report safety hazards (which in the case of the space shuttle *Challenger* had disastrous consequences).

Subordinates who are ambitious and have high security needs are most likely to distort the information they send upward to superiors. In addition, messages that reflect negatively on subordinates are most likely to be distorted. However, the motivation to distort information derives largely from the subordinate's perception of his or her relationship with superiors. Subordinates tend to withhold information from supervisors they do not trust (Jablin, 1985) as well as from supervisors known to actively withhold information from subordinates (Fulk & Mani, 1986). According to Paul Krivonos (1982), subordinates also tend to distort information in ways that will please their superiors, to tell their superiors both what they want them to know and what they think superiors want to hear, and to convey information that reflects favorably on themselves.

As information is distorted on its way up the organizational ladder, the message received by senior management may be quite different from the original message. The ability of managers to do their jobs largely depends on the quality of the information they receive from others, particularly from subordinates. Reducing the amount of upward distortion is thus important. But it requires managers to be open to interpretations and opinions about issues that may differ markedly from their own. The *MBWA*—management by wandering around—technique, for instance, aims to reduce upward distortion by getting managers more involved with employees and rewarding their questions, suggestions, and innovations (Peters & Waterman, 1982). But like other programs, it cannot succeed unless employees trust management and feel comfortable with conveying negative information. Once that trust is established, reliable upward communication can occur. Authoritative management, in contrast, encourages both employee distrust and the filtering of information shared with superiors. Fearing repercussions for sharing negative information with superiors, employees distort that information.

MANAGING THE BOSS

Subordinates can use a variety of tactics to secure resources for maintaining positive relationships with superiors. A recent study of public-sector supervisors reveals that positive superior–subordinate relationships are characterized by a high degree of upward influence (Waldera, 1988). In their *Profile of Organizational Influence Strategies* (1982), David Kipnis and Stuart Schmidt identify six areas of upward influence: reasoning, friendliness, assertiveness, coalition-building, appealing to higher authorities, and bargaining. In addition, friendly ingratiation (making the superior feel important) and developing rational plans (reasoning) are commonly used to influence superiors (Kipnis, Schmidt, & Wilkinson, 1980). In a more recent study, Kipnis, Schmidt, and Braxton-Brown (1990) argue that employees use four very different approaches to influence superiors:

1. *Shotgun* (the employee uses all available approaches)
2. *Ingratiation* (the employee is friendly and warm)
3. *Tactician* (the employee uses reason)
4. *Bystander* (the employee avoids all approaches in general)

Research by Keys and Case (1990) also suggests that *rational explanation* is the most frequently used type of upward influence. As a rule, a rational explanation includes a formal presentation, analysis, or proposal. A host of other tactics of influence, such as arguing without support, using persistence and repetition, threatening, and manipulating, have been deemed ineffective (Keys & Case, 1990).

Positive upward influence may also be achieved through *personal communication*. As Vincent Waldron (1991) explains:

> by encouraging discussion of non-work issues, subordinates solidify friendship ties with supervisors while presumably adding stability and predictability to the formal authority relationship. . . . A history of such contacts may work to the advantage of the subordinate, by reducing the perceived "riskiness" of upward influence attempts and other potentially threatening messages (e.g., complaints, protests). (p. 300)

However, some supervisors may not respond positively to these informal advances. Subordinates must learn to tailor their approach to the supervisor accordingly (Keys & Case, 1990).

Some observers envision the process of relating to superiors as one of *"managing up."* In this view, the subordinate role is perceived as a performance. James Thompson (1967), for example, refers to subordinate "dramaturgy," which is geared at making the boss look good. More specifically, John Gabarro and John Kotter (1980) note that in order for subordinates to be successful at "managing up," they need to know the superior's main professional goals, personal goals, strengths and weaknesses, preferred working style, and attitudes toward conflict. This information is useful in fostering relationships with superiors that accommodate their needs and leadership style.

According to Riley and Eisenberg (1992), the primary skill involved in managing the boss is *advocacy*. It involves learning how to read a superior's needs and preferences and designing persuasive arguments to accomplish goals. Unlike traditional views of superior–subordinate communication that emphasize subordinate compliance, advocacy emphasizes the following principles:

1. *Plan a strategy.* Impromptu appeals for resources or decisions are often ineffective. Think through a strategy that will work.
2. *Determine why the supervisor should listen.* Connect your argument to something important to your boss, such as a key company objective or a personal goal.
3. *Tailor the argument to the supervisor's style and characteristics.* Will your boss respond more favorably to statistics or a poignant story? To details or generalities? Adapt your evidence and appeal accordingly.
4. *Assess the supervisor's technical knowledge.* Do not assume that your supervisor has technical knowledge of the issue.
5. *Build coalitions.* Support your argument with the views of others in the organization.
6. *Hone your communication skills.* Even the best ideas may sound unconvincing if they are not articulated well.

Underlying these six principles is the fundamental idea that effective communication is always tailored to an audience. Therefore, employees should focus on their audience's needs when communicating with superiors.

In the team-based postmodern organization, the new role of team facilitator or team member requires a willingness to act as a responsible and equitable partner. Occasionally asking for coaching from an experienced manager may open up the dialogue about getting work accomplished.

MYSTERY AND TRANSGRESSION

The superior–subordinate relationship is symbolic of the hierarchical distribution of power and status in most organizations as well as in society as a whole. Inevitable in social relations, hierarchy may be constructed on the basis of age, gender, fashion, family background, race, ethnicity, education, and so on (Goodall, 1989). In a workplace hierarchy, subordinates seek to satisfy superiors in the hopes of eventually taking their place. Many of the strategies described earlier in the chapter are aimed at that goal. For superiors, keeping some emotional distance from subordinates is needed to maintain authority and legitimacy. (See Focus on Ethics 9.1.)

Kenneth Burke (1969) describes these differences between superiors and subordinates as a kind of "mystery":

Managing the Superior–Subordinate Relationship

Major Ramone Martinez recently completed a management workshop on empowerment and has a new perspective on his role as an active listener at work. Ramone, who works for the U.S. Army, believes he has always been a good listener, but that the workshop has sharpened his skills. He is eager to put those skills to good use.

Captain Eileen Davis works for Ramone in the procurement department of the U.S. Army. She and Ramone have long shared a close professional relationship. Recently, however, Ramone has more actively sought to engage Eileen in conversations that are characterized by his attentive listening to her comments. This has made Eileen feel even closer to Ramone and more willing to share information.

As a result, Eileen decided to share some personal information with Ramone that she had kept secret in fear of losing her job: that she is a lesbian. Homosexuals are still not allowed in the military, but Eileen felt she could share her secret with her friend and confidant, Ramone.

However, Ramone now finds himself in the middle of an ethical dilemma. On the one hand, as a supervisor he is obligated by the military's code of conduct to report the information about Eileen to his supervisors. On the other hand, Ramone feels responsible for encouraging her to share the information with him. If he had maintained some emotional distance in the superior–subordinate relationship, Eileen would not have confided in him as she did.

In your opinion, how can Ramone best respond to this dilemma?

> Mystery arises at that point where different kinds of beings are in communication. In mystery there must be strangeness; but the estranged must also be thought of as in some way capable of communion. . . . The conditions of mystery are set up by any pronounced social distinctions, as between nobility and commoners, courtiers and kings, leader and people, rich and poor. . . . Thus even the story between the petty clerk and the office manager, however realistically told, draws upon the wells of mystery for its appeal. (p. 115)

The traditional hierarchy functions best when subordinates accept and pursue the "mystery" of the organizational ladder. But as corporate executive and critical theorist Earl Shorris (1981) points out, despite the widespread belief that satisfaction and happiness may be found at higher levels of the hierarchy, considerable evidence exists to suggest the contrary.

Transgression occurs when subordinates refuse to acknowledge their traditional role in the organization (hence the term *insubordinate* is used to describe their behavior). In most cases, controlled transgression is encouraged by organizations, such as in comic skits or at office parties (Goodall, 1989). At a major hotel in California, for example, employees meet annually to put on a humorous play in which they act out managerial roles. This type of transgression is viewed as nonthreatening to the organization, and it may even serve to reinforce the existing power structure through a kind of catharsis.

However, other types of transgression are more serious. In the current movement toward employee empowerment, for instance, a senior manager may charge a high-powered work team with the task of developing important strategies for the future. But as the team strives at the same time to forge a more equal partnership with management, the manager may react negatively to what is perceived as a loss of authority, status, and identity.

Communicating with Subordinates

Various theories propose different approaches to communicating with subordinates effectively. In classical management theory, downward communication is emphasized; it is formal, precise, and work related. Human relations theory stresses supportive communication, while human resources theory emphasizes the need for superiors to involve subordinates in innovative decision making. The systems and cultural approaches make no specific prescriptions about communicating with subordinates, whereas critical and postmodern theorists call for a radical leveling of power and authority among superiors and subordinates in which both are regarded as equally important to the organization.

However, most observers agree that effective communication with subordinates has at least four characteristics: It is open, supportive, motivating, and empowering.

OPENNESS

Openness in superior–subordinate communication should at a minimum be present in the sending and receiving of messages (Redding, 1972). According to Fred Jablin (1979), both parties in an open communication relationship "perceive the other interactant as a willing and receptive listener and refrain from responses that might be perceived as providing negative relational or disconfirming feedback" (p. 1204). Openness has both verbal and nonverbal dimensions. Nonverbally, facial expression, eye gaze, tone, and the like contribute to degrees of open communication (Tjosvold, 1984).

Studies conducted by W. Charles Redding (1972) and his students at Purdue University reveal a positive correlation between a supervisor's open communication and subordinates' satisfaction with the relationship:

1. The most effective supervisors tend to emphasize the importance of communication in their relationships with subordinates. For example, they enjoy talking at meetings and conversing with subordinates, and they are skilled at explaining instructions and policies.
2. Effective supervisors are empathic listeners. They respond positively to employees' questions, listen to suggestions and complaints, and express a willingness to take fair and appropriate action when necessary.
3. Effective supervisors ask or persuade, rather than tell or demand.
4. Effective supervisors are sensitive to others' feelings (e.g., reprimands are made in private rather than in public work settings).
5. Effective supervisors openly pass along information to subordinates, including advance notices of impending changes and explanations of why the changes will be made.

Other researchers suggest that openness plays a more complex role in the superior–subordinate relationship and that its effects are not always easy to predict. Eric Eisenberg and Marsha Witten (1987) identify three distinct types of openness: *supportive listening, personal and nonpersonal disclosure,* and *ambiguous communication.* Depending on the communicative context, they argue, openness can have dramatically different outcomes. For example, a supervisor may use openness in indiscreet or insincere ways or even as a way to intimidate subordinates. Eisenberg and Witten thus stress that the role of openness in organizational communication needs to be considered in light of its multiple potential uses, and that its effectiveness depends largely on the communicative situation. Although supervisors should strive for open communication with subordinates in appropriate contexts, openness should not override other concerns, such as confidentiality and ethics. Problems can arise when open communication is viewed ideologically as full and honest disclosure, rather than as a sensitivity to the communicative context of any given situation (Bochner, 1982; Eisenberg, 1984).

SUPPORTIVENESS

Research suggests that *supportive* communication with subordinates is more useful to supervisors than openness. According to George Graen's (1976) theory of *leader–member exchange* (*LMX*), supervisors tend to discriminate in their behavior toward subordinates, resulting in the communicative negotiation of leader–member roles. Two types of superior–subordinate relationships are formed in the process: *in-group relationships,* which are "characterized by high trust, mutual influence, support, and formal/informal rewards," and *out-group relationships,* which are "characterized by . . . formal authority [and] low trust, support, and rewards" (Fairhurst & Chandler, 1989, pp. 215–16). In general, in-group relationships are associated with greater employee satisfaction, performance, agreement, and decision-making involvement as well as lower turnover rates than out-group relationships (Graen, Liden, & Hoel, 1982; Liden & Graen, 1980; Scandura, Graen, & Novak, 1986).

In a recent study, Sias and Jablin (1995) apply the LMX model to an analysis of co-worker communication to show how an employee's privileged relationship with a supervisor affects the employee's relationship with peers. In most cases, the employee's co-workers engaged in communication aimed at making sense of the preferential treatment, made judgments about the unfairness of the in-group relationship, and experienced a general erosion of trust in management.

While Graen's (1976) LMX distinction focuses on broad issues of trust and support, it does not prescribe open communication as the sole means for attaining supportive relationships. Instead, supervisory communication is viewed as an ongoing attempt to balance the multiple and competing relational, identity, and task goals (Dillard and Segrin,1987; Eisenberg, 1984). Moreover, certain types of communication may ensure subordinates' compliance but may also demoralize employees, thereby affecting their commitment to and stress at work. Effective supervisors, in contrast, strive to communicate in ways that simultaneously show concern for the relationship, demonstrate respect for the individual, and promote task accomplishment.

However, limited data exist on specific ways of achieving this complex balance in actual superior–subordinate communication. Gail Fairhurst and Theresa Chandler (1989) extend LMX theory in an examination of actual in-group and out-group conversations involving a warehouse supervisor and three subordinates. Their analysis reveals some consistency in the communication resources deployed by those in each type of relationship. The in-group relationship is characterized by influence by mutual persuasion (in which both parties challenge and disagree with each other frequently) and greater freedom of choice for subordinates. In contrast, the out-group relationship is marked by the supervisor's authority, a traditional chain of command, little freedom of choice for subordinates, and a general disregard for their suggestions.

MOTIVATION

Kreps (1991) defines *motivation* as "the degree to which an individual is personally committed to expending effort in the accomplishment of a specified activity or goal" (p. 154). While various other factors contribute to employee motivation (see Chapter 8), our focus here is on how supervisors encourage or discourage employee motivation through their communication with subordinates. Their communication can function in two ways to motivate employees: managers can (1) provide information and feedback about employees' tasks, goals, performance, and future directions, and (2) communicate encouragement, empathy, and concern. In both cases, however, the motivating effect comes from the manager's ability to endorse particular interpretations of organizational issues through communication (Sullivan, 1988).

The four traditional theories of employee motivation are the goal-setting, expectancy, equity theory, and compliance-gaining.

Goal-setting Theory

Goal-setting theory, championed by Edwin Locke and Gary Latham (1984), maintains that because employees' conscious objectives influence their performance, supervisors should assist subordinates in developing goals that are motivating. Some of the most important findings of this research are as follows:

1. Set clear and specific goals, which have a greater positive impact on performance than do general goals.
2. Set goals that are difficult but attainable; they will lead to higher performance than will easy goals.
3. Focus on participative rather than assigned goals.
4. Give frequent feedback about the goal-setting and work processes.

Note that most of these findings deal with issues of communication. To be motivating, goals must be clear and specific, be set through a dialogue with employees, and be the subject of performance feedback. Derived from systems theory, feedback is especially important to employee motivation because it shows employees how their efforts contribute to the success or failure of the company. Subordinates who receive such feedback from superiors tend to be more satisfied, to perform better, and to be less likely to leave the company than subordinates who do not receive feedback on their work (Jablin, 1979; Parsons, Herold, & Leatherwood, 1985).

A field experiment conducted by Pritchard et al. (1988) supports the importance of goal setting and feedback in shaping employee performance. Eighty air force employees who repaired electronic equipment or distributed materials and supplies took part in the study. Productivity measures for the nine months prior to the study were compiled. For five months, employees were given monthly feedback on their productivity. For the next five months, employees working in groups set difficult but attainable goals for themselves. During this five-month feedback period, productivity improved by an average of 50 percent over the initial nine-month baseline. Improvements in morale were also recorded.

Feedback on goals can take many forms, but to be effective it must be frequent and specific. Annual performance reviews have been shown to be ineffective in influencing employee behavior (Ilgin & Knowlton, 1980). They also encourage managers to focus on negative behavior that was noticed but not discussed throughout the year. The best time to give suggestions for improved performance is as soon as possible.

Not all feedback, however, should be negative. Peters and Waterman (1982) argue that successful managers give formal or informal recognition for a job well done. Positive feedback encourages job satisfaction, identification, and commitment among employees (Larson, 1989).

Recently, some companies have made feedback part of certain jobs through the management of information systems. At Frito-Lay's factory in California, for example, computer terminals are located in the packaging areas so that machine operators can access feedback on their daily performance (e.g., on the amount of raw material used, the number of hours an assembly line was nonworking due to repairs, and the number of person hours employed). According to one operator:

> People have more pride in their work now. We go to the computer at the end of the day and see how much we made or lost. If the numbers are good, we feel proud because we know we did it. If the numbers aren't good, we get with our team members and figure out what went wrong. Before, we seldom even saw the numbers. It's no wonder we weren't very interested in the business. (Grant, 1992, p. D7)

As this example shows, clear goals and immediate feedback are important in the increasingly popular shift from feedback from interpersonal communication to feedback from computer-accessed data.

However, because many supervisors do not provide enough feedback, subordinates may actively seek it out (Ashford & Cummings, 1983). Similar to the newcomer stage of organizational assimilation (see Chapter 8), in the feedback-seeking process the employee is "faced with a conflict between the need to obtain useful information and the need to present a favorable image. . . . [M]anagement plays a key role in [this] process" (Morrison & Bies, 1991, p. 523). Perhaps when both parties face the risk of presenting an unfavorable or embarrassing image, supervisors are reluctant to give negative feedback and subordinates avoid seeking it out (Larson, 1989).

Expectancy Theory

Initially developed by Victor Vroom (1964), *expectancy theory* makes three assumptions about employee behavior:

1. Employees perceive a relationship between a specific work behavior and some form of payoff or reward; that is, the behavior is viewed as instrumental to obtaining the reward.
2. Each reward or positive outcome is associated with a valence that determines how much the individual wants the reward.
3. Employees develop expectations about their ability to perform the desired behavior successfully.

Analysis of these factors indicates that employee motivation increases when both outcome valences are positive, expectancies are high, and when outcomes are clear. Under these circumstances, then, the employee desires the reward or outcome, feels capable of performing the desired behavior, and has a clear understanding of what will be rewarded as a result of that performance.

In practice, the expectancy model has been shown to benefit individuals and organizations by increasing employee motivation and improving the quality of the work life (Steers, 1981). In addition, because expectancy theory demands clear communication of performance outcomes, communication plays a key role in its successful implementation.

In a variation of expectancy theory, Robert House's (1971) *path–goal theory* focuses not so much on the performance–reward relationship but on the role that managers play in identifying both rewards and specific ways of attaining them. One popular technique associated with path–goal theory is *management by objectives (MBO),* in which supervisors and subordinates negotiate goals and rewards (Kreps, 1991).

Equity Theory

In a different approach to employee motivation, *equity theory* examines the role of perceived inequities in the reward-to-work ratio (Altman, Valenzi, & Hodgetts, 1985). Employees who feel that they receive fewer rewards than their co-workers for performing the same work are not likely to be motivated to perform their jobs well. Judgments of equity and perceptions of fairness are largely shaped by communication. In particular, the communication of superiors can affect subordinates' perceptions of equity. For example, a supervisor who takes the time to explain long-range plans for an employee's development helps the employee put present differences in position and salary into context.

Equity theory highlights the highly subjective nature of employee performance and cooperation. While supervisors may strive to establish supportive relationships with subordinates and organizations may be structured in ways that make identification and cooperation likely, employees may still lack motivation if they perceive themselves as underrewarded for their efforts. Like in Elton Mayo's (1945) and Herbert Simon's (1957) conceptualization of employee decision making, the judgments and decisions that lead to variations in employee attitude and performance are subjectively determined by factors in the social environment.

Compliance-Gaining

Informal compliance-gaining tactics may help to motivate employees to perform. Supervisors who encourage subordinates with positive feedback are most likely to achieve task compliance and subordinate satisfaction (Daniels & Spiker, 1991). In a recent investigation of the informal strategies used by superiors to influence subordinate behavior, Keys and Case (1990) note that managers more often explain tasks or delegate assignments than give orders. They also tend to convey confidence, encouragement, or support in their attempts to influence subordinates and to use reasoning and facts to suggest the merits of a new procedure or desired behavior. In addition, managers often attempt to gain compliance by soliciting subordinates' ideas regularly (Keys & Case, 1990).

However, these informal tactics of influence may be ineffective when dealing with chronically poor performers. In a study of the compliance-gaining strategies used by bank managers, the researchers note a discrepancy between how administrators claim to deal with problem employees and how they actually do so:

> Branch and personnel administrators in the banks we studied advocated the use of the punitive approach only after the problem-solving approach repeatedly failed. Yet, in the field, we find that the punitive approach predominates from the start for many, [while] the problem-solving approach is used by some but is quickly abandoned. (Fairhurst, Green, & Snavely, 1984, p. 289)

Most current research on compliance-gaining tactics suggests that supervisors who rely on traditional lines of authority and punitive approaches are less effective motivators than supervisors who use a *variety of influence tactics* tailored to the needs and personalities of individual employees as well as to the specific goals involved. Indeed, setting clear goals, articulating ways of achieving them, and providing immediate feedback are an important part of the supervisor's job. From a communication perspective, conveying the right combination of these messages will help to motivate employees.

EMPOWERMENT

Definitions of *empowerment* vary considerably, from the sharing of power with subordinates through delegation and decision making to enabling and motivating employees by building feelings of self-efficacy. According to Conger and Kanungo (1988), the empowerment process "enhanc[es] feelings of self-efficacy among organizational members through [identifying and removing] conditions that foster powerlessness" (p. 474). Furthermore, to feel empowered, an employee must also feel capable of performing the job and possess the authority to decide how to do the job well (Chiles & Zorn, 1995).

Empowerment requires the manager to act more like a coach than a traditional supervisor by listening to employees' concerns, avoiding close supervision, trusting employees to work within a framework of clear direction, and being responsive to employee feedback. An organization committed to empowerment encourages employees to take on ever-increasing responsibilities that utilize their knowledge and skills. In a study of W. L. Gore and Associates, Michael Pacanowsky (1988) identifies six rules of the empowering organization:

1. Distribute power and opportunity widely.
2. Maintain an open and decentralized communication system.
3. Use integrative problem solving to involve diverse groups and individuals.
4. Practice meeting challenges in an environment of trust.
5. Reward and recognize employees to encourage a high-performance ethic and self-responsibility.
6. Learn from organizational ambiguity, inconsistency, contradiction, and paradox.

Notice that these rules focus on providing the resources and opportunities for creating an environment in which subordinates become empowered by taking greater responsibility for their work.

According to Conger and Kanungo (1988), the empowerment process is marked by the five stages illustrated in Figure 9.1. For example, the process begins by eliminating feelings of powerlessness and continues with building self-efficacy through communication. However, others argue that empowerment does not occur as a result of a supervisor's skill in removing obstacles. Instead, numerous potential predictors of empowerment exist, the most important of which is the company's culture. According to Chiles and Zorn (1995), an organizational culture that encourages managers to share information, recognize good work, and promote positive morale is most likely to foster empowerment.

Organizations also vary in terms of degrees of empowerment. According to Ford and Fottler (1995), the degree of empowerment within an organization is related to how decision-making authority is defined. As illustrated in Figure 9.2, a distinction exists between the employee's control of job *content* (how the job gets done) versus job *context* (the conditions under which the job gets done, including goals, strategies, and standards). It is of particular importance that managers and employees maintain a clear understanding of the expected degree of empowerment in order to avoid misunderstandings that can foster resentment and mistrust in organizations.

Promoting empowerment is at once a pragmatic and paradoxical endeavor. Pragmatically, organizations and employees are made more productive when

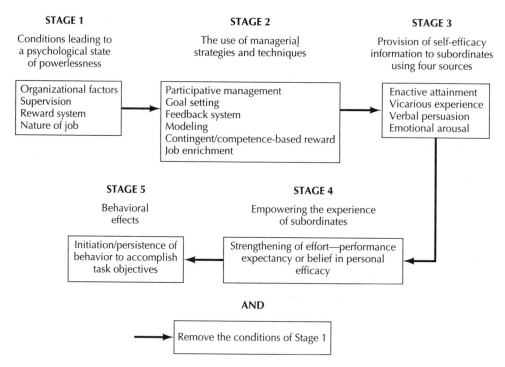

STAGE 1

Conditions leading to
a psychological state
of powerlessness

STAGE 2

The use of managerial
strategies and techniques

STAGE 3

Provision of self-efficacy
information to subordinates
using four sources

Organizational factors
Supervision
Reward system
Nature of job

Participative management
Goal setting
Feedback system
Modeling
Contingent/competence-based reward
Job enrichment

Enactive attainment
Vicarious experience
Verbal persuasion
Emotional arousal

STAGE 5

Behavioral
effects

STAGE 4

Empowering the experience
of subordinates

Initiation/persistence of
behavior to accomplish
task objectives

Strengthening of effort—performance
expectancy or belief in personal
efficacy

AND

Remove the conditions of Stage 1

FIGURE 9.1
The Five Stages of the Empowerment Process

Source: Adapted from J. Conger and R. Kanungo, "The Empowerment Process: Integrating Theory and Practice," *Academy of Management Review 13* (1988): 411–82.

an empowered workforce has some authority and control over work processes. But empowerment also implies a paradox in that while it encourages employee autonomy and initiative, it is often initiated by management. Although organizations and managers can provide a context that encourages empowerment, employees must be willing to accept greater responsibility for their work.

Communicating with Peers

Communication with peers at work provides social support. However, because informal work group norms can enhance or inhibit employee morale and commitment, managerial success increasingly depends on maintaining a web of influence not just up and down the hierarchy but also with co-workers and peers.

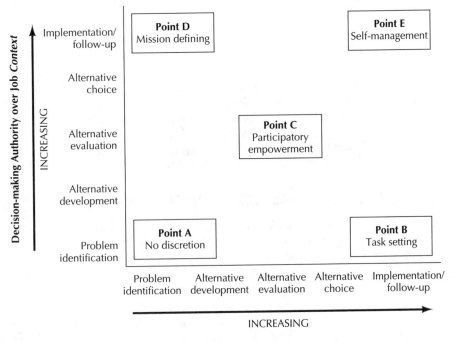

FIGURE 9.2
Employee Empowerment Grid

Source: R. Ford and M. Fottler (1995)

Three types of peer communication are common in organizations: within-group communication, cross-functional communication, and unstructured communication.

WITHIN-GROUP COMMUNICATION

Although Chapter 10 is devoted to a detailed discussion of work teams, it should be noted here that most research on peer communication focuses on *within-group communication.* For example, various studies have shown that the use of humor among manufacturing workers helps boost morale (Boland & Hoffman, 1983; Roy, 1960). In addition, human relations theorists emphasize the importance of informal group norms in shaping organizational effectiveness and the experience of work.

Interpersonal communication in groups or teams warrants special attention because these groups are increasingly becoming the basic building block of contemporary organizations. This is happening because tall hierarchies with extensive chains of command are too slow and not sufficiently creative to remain competitive, while individuals working in isolation do not benefit from the multiple perspectives needed to solve complex problems. Work teams, then, are a kind of compromise between too big and too small.

Working in teams is not a simple matter. Like attitudes toward communication more generally, too often management assumes team communication is both straightforward and unproblematic. Nothing could be further from the truth. Communicating effectively in teams requires a specific set of skills that are not commonly held in the general working population.

CROSS-FUNCTIONAL COMMUNICATION

Cross-functional communication is communication that takes place *across* departmental and/or professional boundaries. An example will help explain why organizations have become more concerned about promoting cross-functional communication. In the traditional bureaucracy of most U.S. automobile manufacturers, clear roles and divisions of labor mean that little cross-functional communication occurs among the isolated departments of engineering, manufacturing, sales, and administration. Instead, internal communication within departments is emphasized. Engineering designs the automobile, manufacturing makes it, and sales tries to sell it. However, because each function or specialty is isolated, problems can occur when a design is impossible to manufacture or when a product is impossible to sell. Recent attempts by Ford (with the Taurus) and General Motors (with Saturn) have shown some success in breaking down the boundaries that obstruct cross-functional communication. Concurrent engineering, for instance, which involves assembly workers in the design process, cuts down on the time and cost of assembly.

Cross-functional communication among peers in organizations is important because it enhances the flow of work within and among departments and, therefore, is essential to the success of companies in all industries. An increasingly competitive marketplace and rising customer expectations have encouraged organizations to see the need for effective communication across departments and functions. As a result, cross-functional work teams have become more common, wherein people who design, manufacture, and sell products or systems work together rather than in relative isolation from each other.

However, most organizations find it difficult, at least initially, to cultivate cross-functional communication among co-workers who are not accustomed to such interaction. They may prefer to continue with their assigned tasks or fail to see the importance of communicating and working with peers in other departments. In some cases, their attempts to cooperate may be hindered by conflicts or disagreements among different professions. Conflicts between engineering and manufacturing, for example, are common. Despite these difficulties, contemporary organizations must work to promote cross-functional relationships in order to succeed in a global market.

Various informal and formal strategies help organizations meet the challenges associated with promoting effective cross-functional relationships among employees. At informal gatherings, such as company picnics and sports leagues, accountants, engineers, assemblers, maintenance workers, and others have the opportunity to get to know each other. In addition, orientation programs and company tours help employees understand their contributions to the overall work process. Two other effective methods for promoting cross-functional communication are referred to as "managing the white space" and "cultivating internal customers and suppliers."

Managing the White Space

Cross-functional communication encourages employees to identify with the overall organization as a processing system or workflow process. Each employee's function is viewed as a subprocess that contributes to the overall work process of the organization. While an organizational chart outlines functions and reporting relationships, *most of the actual work takes place between functions,* or in what is called the "white spaces." *Managing the white space* in an organizational chart thus means charting, analyzing, and ultimately managing horizontal workflow processes (Rummler & Brache, 1991). An outgrowth of the systems approach, informal relationships are viewed as a key to improving workflow processes in organizations.

Cultivating Internal Customers and Suppliers

In addition to external customers and suppliers, organizations are increasingly recognizing the importance of their *internal customers and suppliers*—the people within an organization who depend on others' output as input to their jobs. In the traditional bureaucracy, employees function not as internal customers and suppliers but as independent entities who at times may even compete for resources. Because they are generally unaware of their role in the overall work process, there is little incentive for performing high-quality work in a bureaucracy. The new concept of employees as internal customers and suppliers is intended to address this problem. Workers are encouraged to think of each other as "customers" and "suppliers" of work tasks. For example, a human resources worker supplies data on workers' compensation claims to a manager who is viewed as a customer of the worker's (supplier's) output. As a result, employees become more concerned with passing on high-quality work to their customers at the next stage in the work process.

Hewlett-Packard is one of many companies that have cultivated the idea of internal customers and suppliers to promote cross-functional relationships among employees in various departments. The positive results have included more frequent and effective communication among employees and greater commitment to the common goal of satisfying external customers.

UNSTRUCTURED COMMUNICATION

Another form of peer interaction important to organizations is the *unstructured communication* that takes place in informal work settings, such as in the mail-room, in a car pool, or during lunch. Typically a valuable source of social support and identification, unstructured communication can also be a source of innovative ideas. Thus, for example, some progressive companies, such as 3M, now require employees to spend up to 30 percent of their time in work outside of their primary job in order to promote new ideas.

The greatest limitation of unstructured communication is people's tendency to communicate with similar others. As a result, unstructured peer communication may tend to be marked by gender and racial lines. Effectively managing diversity in organizations can help overcome this limitation of unstructured communication.

Communicating with Customers and Suppliers

Product quality and customer satisfaction are primarily the results of effective work relationships, including an organization's relationships with its external customers and suppliers. The overall work process thus extends beyond the doors of most companies to include an outside network of customers and suppliers.

THE CUSTOMER SERVICE REVOLUTION

Despite the growing demand for quality customer service, only limited research has been conducted on communicating with customers. Among the few researchers in this area are Karl Albrecht (1992) and Tom Peters (1987), who advocate a *customer service revolution* in dealing with consumers. They emphasize the importance of listening to and understanding customers' feedback and needs.

According to Albrecht (1992), successful companies approach the customer service challenge by managing the customer's experience, rather than by just "doing things":

> Th[e] "doing things" mindset seems to express an unconscious view of the customer as a nuisance. There is a powerful, unconscious tendency in most organizations to depersonalize and dehumanize the conception, discussion, and operation of the service delivery. Things are easier to deal with than humans, so we prefer to think of the people—both customers and employees—as just interchangeable elements of a big impersonal blueprint. (p. 35)

Peters's (1987) detailed approach gives more emphasis to communication issues. He argues that the following guidelines can help organizations achieve customer satisfaction:

1. *Specialize, create niches, and differentiate.* From a communication perspective, specialization involves tailoring a product or service (and messages about it) to a clearly defined consumer audience. Products and services that appeal to a broad customer base are being replaced by those that target the needs of a more narrowly defined market.
2. *Provide quality as it is perceived by the customer.* Organizations must be responsive to customer feedback about quality and take action that is based on the customer's perception of the product or service.
3. *Provide superior service and emphasize intangibles.* Customers form positive or negative impressions of organizations based on their encounters with service providers. Research suggests that intangibles—such as the accuracy, dependability, and interpersonal skills of service providers—outweigh other factors in determining customer satisfaction (Zeithmal, Parasuraman, & Berry, 1990). At Nordstrom, for example, gift wrapping is provided, all merchandise may be returned for any reason, and salespeople are encouraged to use their good judgment in achieving their primary goal of outstanding customer service. Another example is a software company that sponsors an annual "user's convention" to obtain customer feedback on its products and thereby make the needed improvements in product design.
4. *Achieve speedy responsiveness.* Because time is often a customer's most precious commodity, an increasing number of organizations are utilizing communication technologies to reduce the amount of time it takes to respond to consumers. At Federal Express, for instance, trucks are equipped with computers, and at Motorola communication technology has reduced the time it takes to ship a pager from forty-five days to just under two hours after the customer orders it.
5. *Be an internationalist.* Cultivating relationships with domestic as well as global customers requires patience, empathy, and the ability to communicate with people from other cultures. In addition, global competition requires organizations to adapt their products or services to meet the needs of different cultures.

6. *Create uniqueness.* In a competitive market, an organization's product or service must stand out as unique in some way, and employees must be able to articulate why it is unique.

7. *Be obsessed with listening.* Listening to customers means respecting their opinions, recognizing their needs, avoiding distractions, paying close attention to their main points or concerns, and taking action on their complaints or suggestions.

8. *Turn manufacturing into a marketing tool.* Most customer feedback is related to needed improvements in manufacturing. Employee empowerment and effective cross-functional communication help ensure that the workforce attends to issues in ways that promote customer satisfaction.

9. *Make sales and service people into heroes.* Reverse the current trend toward undervaluing those employees who have regular contact with consumers. To the customer, the employee answering the telephone *is* the company. An organization that values these employees also places top priority on customer responsiveness.

10. *Launch a customer service revolution.* From a communication perspective, this involves focusing discussions on customer service. For example, the manager at one organization gathers employees together at the end of each workday to ask them what they did for customers and gives an award for the best deed.

While Peters's (1987) guidelines on servicing customers are intended to meet the challenges of the current economic climate, other observers are more concerned with the emotional effects on employees of intense customer service work. In an investigation of the behavior of service providers, for example, Anat Rafaeli and Robert Sutton (1991) note that certain types of jobs are emotionally demanding because they require employees to display emotions that differ from their true feelings in order to satisfy customers. Organizations recruit, reward, and punish these employees for appropriate or inappropriate displays of emotion (see Chapter 8). Waiters, flight attendants, and retail salespeople, for instance, are required by their employers to smile, give friendly greetings, and convey only positive emotions in their dealings with customers throughout the workday. However, Sutton and Rafaeli (1988) also note that employees do not as a rule submit to the control of their emotions; instead, they develop coping strategies for various situations. Thus, for example, a cashier may smile and make eye contact with customers during slow times, but during busy times the cashier avoids making eye contact so as not to prolong interactions with customers.

Rafaeli and Sutton (1991) also point out that some jobs require employees to use negative displays of emotion in their dealings with customers. Bill collectors, for example, tend to adopt what Rafaeli and Sutton call "emotional contrast strategies" to gain customers' compliance. Alternating between positive and negative displays of emotion, the bill collector seeks to induce fear, relief, and compliance in the customer.

Today's progressive companies train their employees to deal with both customers and the emotional demands of customer service work effectively. Communication skills are essential to making a good impression as well as to developing coping strategies. Achieving a balance between employee well-being and customer satisfaction gives companies a strong competitive advantage. Even in the realm of high-tech products, services, and technology, the quality of interpersonal relationships (with internal and external customers) can mean the success or failure of a company.

SUPPLIERS AS ORGANIZATIONAL PARTNERS

In most organizations, the responsibility for communicating with customers and suppliers is limited to certain employees known as *boundary role occupants* or *boundary spanners* (Adams, 1980). Examples include tellers and account representatives in banks and hosts and waiters in restaurants. In large manufacturing firms, entire departments may function as boundary spanners in the procurement and management of suppliers. Their work depends on establishing good relationships with those who supply the company with needed parts or services.

Generally speaking, close relationships with suppliers are the most productive type. In an increasingly popular trend toward *partnership arrangements,* companies work with their suppliers to identify areas needing improvement. In some cases, an organization may even insist that its standards of cost, service, or efficiency be used by suppliers. Generally, companies are redefining suppliers as members of the organizational team. As such, suppliers are also held accountable for their role as team members. Partnership arrangements with suppliers help organizations to become more flexible and responsive, and, therefore, to remain competitive.

Intercultural Communication

Although most research on work relationships assumes that people share similar cultural understandings, Varner and Beamer (1995) point out an important distinction between *results-oriented cultures* and *relationship-oriented cultures* that can affect communication. In a results-oriented culture such as the United States, it is assumed that work and communication at work are governed by the management of objectives: Identify a goal, then work systematically to achieve it. Anything that gets in the way of achieving that goal is perceived as a problem, and measurements of success are based on the results of goal achievement.

In contrast, a more relationship-oriented culture exists in many other countries of the world (Varner & Beamer, 1995; Victor, 1994). In Japan, for example, maintaining *wa* or "harmony" in relationships with others is a primary concern, and in Spain businesspeople do not conduct business until they have had the opportunity to get to know each other. While Asians tend to value the means to an end more than the end itself, the French find the American preoccupation with measurements (of everything from job satisfaction to performance) peculiar and humorous.

Effective intercultural communication depends on an awareness of and sensitivity to the many differences between results- and relationship-oriented cultures. According to Varner and Beamer (1995), the following three areas of cultural understanding are especially important:

1. *Ways of thinking and acquiring knowledge:* Unlike American culture, which views knowledge as rooted in concepts, other cultures place greater value on knowledge that is gained from firsthand experience (e.g., many Latin American countries) or from intuition (e.g., followers of Daoism, Hinduism, and Buddhism). Cultural differences can influence not only *what* one knows but also *how* one comes to know it. Thus, in Asian, Latin American, and southern European cultures, learning comes less from asking questions than from receiving information from teachers and significant others. Moreover, while Western cultures view scientific knowledge as separate from religious faith, many non-Western cultures do not make that distinction (e.g., Hindus view all life as sacred, including science). In addition, ways of thinking in most Western cultures are based on the cause-and-effect reasoning that derives from scientific inquiry, whereas in China and many other non-Western cultures logical thought is based on an appreciation of the *yin* and the *yang* (parallelism, in which opposites are not necessarily mutually exclusive).

2. *Ways of doing and achieving:* The American's preoccupation with doing and achieving things in life can seem odd to people from cultures that value silence, serenity, peace, and stillness in life. Similarly, the ways in which tasks are done can vary by culture. Tasks tend to be completed sequentially in results-oriented cultures and simultaneously in relationship-oriented cultures. In America, uncertainty and shyness are viewed as obstacles to achieving success. But to most non-Westerners, our communication model of uncertainty reduction would seem inappropriate or rude, and throughout most of Asia, where quietude is prized, frequent talkers are mistrusted. In addition, whereas Westerners believe that planning is a key to achieving success, in many Buddhist, Taoist, and Hindu cultures, people are born with *karma,* or destiny, that they learn from and deal with to achieve success. Similarly, some Asians believe in *feng shui* or geomancy, wherein the arrangement of buildings, earth and rocks, offices, doorways, windows, and the like is determined by *chi,* the spiritual forces that govern the universe. At

Hitachi's Greenville, South Carolina, plant for example, about $150,000 was spent on installing large rocks in front of the plant to attract the spirits that reward harmonious business practices. Cultures throughout the world have their own ways of expressing their belief in fate: In India, astrologers routinely function as business consultants; in Taiwan, during "ghost" month, people avoid making business decisions that will ultimately fail; and in the United States, most hotels and office buildings do not have a thirteenth floor.

3. *Ways of thinking about universal issues:* Cultures also differ in their understanding of universal issues, such as life and death, divine powers, nature, and change. Such differences in understanding can also affect business dealings, relationships, and communication.

In the United States, immigrant and guest workers may possess different cultural understandings, values, and beliefs in addition to speaking a different language. Furthermore, guest workers may be the target of racism and discrimination in nations where political sects still hold hostile attitudes based on old animosities. Managers and team leaders must be well informed about world politics and religions in order to deal effectively with these issues.

NONVERBAL DIMENSIONS

Most American businesspeople know that the *nonverbal* communication of English-speaking people is as important as the spoken word. Similarly, the nonverbal dimensions of intercultural communication are both important and culturally determined. Although some international firms provide intercultural training programs for business travelers who will deal with the verbal and nonverbal dimensions of communication, most companies do not invest enough of their resources in such training. This is surprising, since the subtleties of nonverbal intercultural communication can often mark the difference between what is considered appropriate (respectful) and inappropriate (rude or insulting) behavior.

Americans, for example, use various nonverbal behaviors—eye contact, head nodding, body posture, and movement, and other gestures—to show respect for people with power and wealth (Scott, 1990). Americans tend also to be relatively abrupt and to accept abruptness from superiors. But respect for authority in Japan is expressed nonverbally by the depth of a bow, for example (Barnlund, 1994).

American businesspeople who fail to respect the nonverbal customs of other cultures create the impression that they are disrespectful or arrogant. Among the many nonverbal dimensions of intercultural communication, *tone of voice* and *eye contact* are perhaps the most important. Speaking softly among

Asians shows respect for the value they attribute to harmony in relationships. Accepting the brash communicative style of Germans shows respect for the value they attribute to assertiveness. Finally, looking directly into a Japanese person's eyes for lengthy periods will be seen as inappropriate and aggressive.

NEGOTIATING A MIDDLE GROUND

While generalizing about another culture is helpful, individual differences must also be taken into account. New intercultural thinking suggests that an appreciation for the *middle ground* of negotiated meanings can improve the interpersonal relations among persons of good will in business dealings. Appreciating the need to adapt to another's culture is balanced with a recognition of the person's individuality. When people from different cultures have only cultural expectations for each other, miscommunication is likely to occur.

Here again, we confront the enormous challenges of intercultural communication in business relationships. Dealing effectively with these challenges involves finding productive ways to communicate with others whose understandings and values may differ considerably from your own.

New Directions in Leadership

Leadership is among the most studied phenomena in organizational behavior. Contemporary researchers define *leadership* as a system of relationships through which individuals motivate followers toward performing desired behaviors (Hollander & Offerman, 1990). However, the history of theories on leadership reveals a developing awareness of the importance of interpersonal relationships and communication.

The earliest theories of *leadership* held that certain people were born with leadership skills or traits. By the late 1940s, however, *situational leadership* theory had emerged; it held that "situations varied in the qualities demanded of leaders, so those qualities were appropriate to a particular task and interpersonal context" (Hollander & Offerman, 1990, p. 180). Thus, for example, different types of leaders were believed to be suited to the start-up phase of a high-tech company or the management of a mature government agency. Many *contingency theories of leadership* followed, most notably Fred Fiedler's (1967) least preferred co-worker (LPC) model. Although highly controversial, the LPC model distinguished between two types of leadership styles: the *task-oriented* and *relationship-oriented* styles. According to Fiedler, a leader's effectiveness depended on certain aspects of the situation, including the nature of the task and the relationship with followers.

During the past twenty years, researchers have gradually shifted their focus from leaders to followers to the *leader–follower relationship.* In this view, followers' perceptions of a leader determine the leader's success or failure (Calder, 1977). Sometimes called the *transactional approach* (because of the role of leader–follower communicative transactions in forming perceptions), Graen's (1976) leader–member exchange (LMX) model is an example. Individuals are leaders only because they are perceived as such by followers, with whom they share an in-group relationship and with whom they exchange resources (e.g., support for employee performance). Although the transactional approach considers the importance of communication in leadership, it assumes that the needs and desires of followers are fixed.

In contrast, the *transformational leader* seeks to transcend the bounds of routine follower behavior to offer the possibility of a new vision for the organization. Transformational leadership theory suggests that communication recasts leadership as the management of meaning (Bennis & Nanus, 1985). In addition to setting goals and focusing on tasks, then, leaders help followers interpret organizational events and make sense of the world of work in general. Karl Weick (1980) thus argues that contemporary leaders must be experts in the symbolic framing of situations for employees.

Among the new metaphors guiding organizational studies is spirituality (Fox, 1994; Goodall, 1996; Spretnak, 1993). Transformational leaders often draw inspiration and techniques from spiritual leaders, movements, and events. According to Jack Hawley (1994), "real leadership" has always been spiritual leadership. Since the Industrial Revolution, however, managers have replaced leaders, and their concerns differ (see Table 9.3). Many of the communication-based themes discussed in this book (e.g., sense-making, stewardship, and community-based cultural organizing) are represented in Hawley's account. But Hawley argues that "leaders work at the more abstract level of people's energy, heart, and spirit" (p. 166). While managers and leaders are similarly engaged in spiritual work, their tasks and approaches to work often differ. For example, leaders tend to define organizational realities and visions, whereas managers implement those visions. In addition, managers specialize in getting the most from workers, but leaders specialize in giving of themselves to others. Managers divide tasks that have been envisioned by leaders, whose actions are driven by a sense of deep purpose and conviction.

In Japan, leadership skills are referred to as a "warrior spirit" and associated with the idea of a life of service to work. In the West, and particularly in the United States, the new spiritual dimension of work—and especially of leadership—is in part a response to the troubling questions posed by the end of the organizational age (Campbell & Campbell, 1988; Fox, 1994; Goodall, 1996; Rushing, 1993). As contemporary organizations deal with increasing competition, decreasing market shares, and the need to downsize their operations, the most successful companies survive because their leaders are effective communicators. They know how to inspire employees with honesty and optimism. Effective leaders treat the business problems of today as problems that affect each worker's whole being—their minds, bodies, hearts, and spirits.

LEARNING LEADERSHIP SKILLS

Russ Moxley et al. (1994) at the Center for Creative Leadership (CCL) in Greensboro, North Carolina, surveyed 45,665 leaders in business, industry, and government to discover how people acquire leadership skills. Their study reveals that a *variety of experiences* and the ability to *accept and meet challenges* are most important in developing the skills of effective leadership. More specifically, experiences that provide the following are noted:

1. A change in the scope and scale of a job
2. The opportunity to introduce a new product or to start a new project or business
3. A "fix it" opportunity, such as being called upon to solve problems
4. Task force opportunities that are important, yield positive results, and encourage communication with senior managers
5. Line-to-staff moves that involve negotiating with, influencing, and motivating others.

Challenging assignments, according to Moxley et al. (1994), also involve learning new skills, but they are marked by a need to deal with difficulties or obstacles. Examples include working with effective and ineffective supervisors and with difficult employees, business failures, career stalls (e.g., not receiving a promotion or losing a job), and personal traumas that indirectly affect the work life. Through experiences such as these, people learn how to confront and overcome challenges to their work and work identities.

Interestingly, leadership training programs are most effective when they focus on both challenging assignments and varied experiences. In contrast, a program that neglects one or the other component does not train people well for a leadership role.

LEADERSHIP AND ORGANIZATIONAL EFFECTIVENESS

Researchers at the Center for Creative Leadership (CCL) have studied the relationship between leadership and organizational effectiveness since the 1970s. Three basic attributes of leaders have been linked to overall organizational effectiveness: (1) certain innate skills, (2) the ability to lead others, and (3) good communication skills (Moxley, 1994).

TABLE
9.3 **The Management/Spiritual Leadership Model:
The Functions, Interests, and Concerns of Management and
Leadership—and Their Spiritual Basis**

MANAGEMENT	LEADERSHIP	SPIRITUAL BASIS	LEADER AS:
is mostly concerned with:	*is mostly concerned with:*		
Goals and objectives	Vision	Covenant	Sense-maker
Honesty	Integrity	Dharma (Truth)	Moral architect
Priorities	Values	Virtue	Values steward
Plans and strategies	State (of mind)	Equanimity (Inner peace)	Yogi
Getting	Giving	Service	Servant
Management of people	People's Energy and Heart	Spiritual Awareness	Guide
Organization structure/ Sense of team	Organization culture/ Sense of community	Unity/(Cosmic) oneness	Whole-maker
Error correction	Acknowledgment	Gratitude (Basic belief)	Optimist
Problem solving/ Decision making	Presence	Inner/Higher power	Warrior

Source: Jack C. Hawley (1994), p. 168.

The *innate skills* of leadership include resourcefulness, decisiveness, and determination. A person who possesses these innate skills is able to adapt well to change, take appropriate action in response to change, and learn from these experiences how to make good decisions. The *ability to lead others* encompasses various skills aimed at balancing sources of creativity and constraint in organizations. Examples include delegating work tasks effectively among employees, establishing appropriate developmental or learning climates, dealing with difficult employees fairly, fostering a team-based orientation toward work, and hiring talented staff members. Finally, the *communication skills* of leaders include the ability to be straightforward but flexible, to build and mend relationships with followers, to maintain a balance between one's work and personal lives, to possess self-awareness, and to express compassion and sensitivity in order to make others feel comfortable in their relationship with the leader (Moxley, 1994).

The three sets of leadership skills related to organizational effectiveness rely heavily on communication. Although mastering all of these skills while also remaining open to new situations and learning may not always be possible, organizations should strive to provide the opportunities for developing those leadership skills as often as possible.

More specifically, CCL researchers suggest that an organization can "grow" leaders by satisfying their needs for varied and challenging experiences as well as by allowing enough time for people to develop leadership skills (Moxley, 1994). Jobs thereby become developmental experiences, and career paths are marked by challenging opportunities that stimulate the growth of leadership skills. In addition, movement up the organizational ladder (e.g., promotions and new assignments) must bring new experiences and new challenges. Organizations need to resist the temptation to make specialists out of people, focusing instead on providing employees with a variety of experiences and challenges. When employees are expected to specialize in a certain type of work, they do not have the opportunity to develop leadership skills through new and challenging experiences.

Furthermore, organizations need to recognize that leadership skills take time to develop, and that moving employees from one job to another too quickly is counterproductive. According to CCL researchers, an average of three to four years is needed to learn most new jobs (Moxley, 1994). Leadership training is time-consuming because the ability to confront and meet new challenges develops gradually over time. The CCL research suggests that promotions and training programs, for example, cannot substitute for nor reduce the amount of time it takes to develop leadership skills through varied and challenging work experiences (Moxley, 1994). Instead, training programs are effective only when employees can bring to them the knowledge and skills they have gained over time and an ongoing desire to learn.

Intimacy in Work Relationships

Most organizations seek to foster close interpersonal relationships at work and to discourage romantic and sexual relationships. However, as Jones (1972) points out, "sex is like paperclips in the office: Commonplace, useful, underestimated, ubiquitous, [and hardly] appreciated until it goes wrong" (p. 12). Intimacy in work relationships can range from flirtation to romance or harassment. Classical management theorists view any type of fraternizing among workers as a source of inefficiency. However, most contemporary organizations are more tolerant of such relationships and have no formal policy pertaining to them (Dillard & Miller, 1988).

However, in an attempt to deal with the problem of sexual harassment, some organizations have developed policies that prohibit personal relationships between superiors and subordinates. In addition, workshops, films, and literature may be used to make employees more aware of the types of behavior that constitute sexual harassment in the workplace. Firms that operate with public monies are especially concerned with this issue. The University of North Carolina, for example, recently accepted the resignation of a tenured faculty member who was engaged to be married to a student because, the board argued, the university must serve as a moral leader in the community.

ROMANTIC RELATIONSHIPS AT WORK

Robert Quinn (1977), the first to study why employees establish romantic relationships with others at work, identifies three underlying motives: *love, ego,* and *job.* Employees motivated by love have a sincere desire to find a long-term companion or spouse, whereas those motivated by ego are looking for sexual excitement and adventure. Employees with job-related motives may pursue a romance with the hope of gaining more job security or power.

More recent research suggests that social stereotypes about why people form romantic relationships at work may be overly simplistic (Dillard & Miller, 1988). For example, in a study conducted by Dillard and Segrin (1987), only 14 percent of the romantic relationships surveyed included a woman with job-related motives and a man with more power in the organization. In contrast, 59 percent of the relationships studied were marked by partners motivated by love or by a combination of love and ego. (Pairings of powerful women with less powerful subordinate men have received little attention in the research literature.) Dillard and Miller (1988) thus conclude that the motivation underlying organizational romance is often more complex than is typically assumed. They also point out that the consequences of such relationships are not always what we might expect. Rather than negatively affecting productivity, careers, and workplace environments, Dillard and Miller argue that romantic relationships may lead to improved performance when employees attempt to overcompensate for others' negative expectations.

Negative perceptions and interpretations by others, however, can create problems for romantic partners at work. Even after a romance has ended, co-workers may cling to negative perceptions about the motives, character, or performance of the involved parties. Whether or not the relationship has affected their work performance, co-workers may assume that it has.

SEXUAL HARASSMENT IN THE WORKPLACE

Romance and sexuality in organizations are predictable sites for the use and abuse of power. *Sexual harassment* is behavior that humiliates people. Women are usually the targets of sexual harassment by men because "as a group [women] have less formal and informal power than men in organizations, confront more obstacles on their path to developing organizational power, and have fewer opportunities to acquire organizational power through activities and alliances" (Bingham, 1991, p. 92). Commonplace in organizations, sexual harassment is the unacceptable behavior of men who cling to outdated notions of a male-dominated society and organizational status quo.

In a special issue of the *Journal of Applied Communication Research* (1994) edited by Julia T. Wood, a rich and complex assortment of firsthand accounts of sexual harassment on the job reveal a disturbing trend: Most often experienced initially by teenagers and students working a first job, sexual harassment may thereafter be accepted as normal or ordinary behavior. This may explain why many women tend to avoid reporting instances of sexual harassment to superiors, to underestimate their importance, or to be uncertain about identifying such behaviors (Clair, 1993). As a result, Robin Clair (1993) argues, sexual harassment remains outside of mainstream communication in organizations, and women participate in both their own subjugation and the perpetuation of the male ideology.

In order to deal with the problem of sexual harassment, some observers focus on the need to define its characteristic behaviors more precisely. Once defined, this information can be used to raise men's awareness and potentially change their abusive behavior. Julie Tamaki (1991), for example, identifies the following behaviors as characteristic of sexual harassment:

Inappropriate verbal comments, even those defended as compliments (e.g., "I wish my wife was as pretty as you")
Inappropriate nonverbal gestures, such as outlining body parts or eyeing someone up and down
Inappropriate visual displays or objects (e.g., posters or calendars depicting nude women or men)
Terms of endearment (e.g., "sweetie," "dear," "honey")
Inappropriate physical acts, such as patting, fondling, stroking, or standing in a doorway to obstruct someone's passage through it
Submission to sexual advances as a basis for continued employment or advancement in the company
Fear of retaliation for reporting instances of sexual harassment

In addition, Tamaki (1991) outlines a series of strategies for dealing with sexual harassment: (1) confront the harasser, (2) report the behavior to a supervisor or to the human resources department, (3) keep a written record of the offenses, and (4) confide in supportive colleagues, family members, and friends. If the harassment continues, a formal investigation by the Department of Fair Employment and Housing or the Federal Equal Employment Opportunity Commission (EEOC) may be requested or a lawsuit may be filed. Although the 1991 Anita Hill–Clarence Thomas hearings made the public aware of the difficulties of proving sexual harassment, legal awards for victims of sexual harassment at work are becoming increasingly common, especially when written records and support from others in the organization are provided as evidence.

Shereen Bingham (1991) offers a communicative approach to managing sexual harassment in the workplace. She argues that direct confrontation with a harasser is complicated by multiple risks, including losing a job, receiving an unfavorable recommendation, being demoted, losing interest in the job, and so on. Bingham suggests that various responses—assertive, nonassertive, and even aggressive—may be appropriate in certain circumstances. Most observers agree that assertiveness helps to confront the harasser in a direct but nonthreatening way. However, assertiveness may also be interpreted as a rejection of the other person. It may be more appropriate, as Bingham suggests, to temper assertiveness with empathy when responding to a sexual advance. Consider this example:

Assertive: "No, I will not have sex with you, and I think your behavior is completely inappropriate. This is a workplace and I expect to be treated accordingly."

Assertive and empathic: "I don't mean to hurt your feelings, but no, I won't sleep with you. I enjoy working with you and I want to keep our relationship strictly professional."

Organizations can design educational programs for employees to assist them in analyzing sexual harassment and strategies for dealing with it in particular situations. Responding effectively to sexual harassment requires paying close attention to ways of communicating appropriately at work.

Creativity and Constraint in Work Relationships

Good interpersonal relationships among employees benefit organizations in numerous ways. But supportive work relationships also improve the overall quality of people's lives. Effective communication skills are a key to establishing positive relationships at work.

C A S E   S T U D Y

THE TOTAL EMPOWERMENT PROGRAM

Lovitt International is a medium-sized electronics manufacturer. Although it is located in the Midwest, it is owned by the French-English conglomerate Sagem-Lucas. Lovitt uses multinational work teams to design world-market parts for electronic ignition systems (i.e., high-quality parts that are interchangeable and meet ISO 9000 standards). The parts are marketed to various automobile manufacturers, including Geo, Nissan, Volkswagen, Peugot, and Ford.

The company has been relatively successful. Recently, however, it has experienced some problems attributed to communication issues, such as difficulty in coordinating its team-based operations and meeting customers' deadlines. Lovitt has also introduced a new program, called "total empowerment" (TE), which is aimed at creating self-directed work teams, giving employees the power to make decisions about their work, and making employees more accountable for the results of their work. The TE program also includes an incentive plan: a 60/40 split in bonuses that is divided between team and individual members according to their performance ratings. However, team members have received little or no training in how to accomplish the objectives of the new TE program, other than an initial meeting with the senior managers who initiated it and a company party to celebrate the new endeavor.

The TE program, though designed to empower Lovitt employees, has instead led to a number of unexpected problems. Difficulties between employees from different cultures, for example, have emerged. American workers believe that their non-native counterparts neglect to share negative information with teams and facilitators, while Latino,

(continued)

In terms of managing sources of creativity and constraint in organizations, the formation of interpersonal relationships is relevant. For example, while a cross-functional team may be convened by a manager, some of its members likely shared close relationships previously. Similarly, groups of employees who band together informally over time may form meaningful relationships at work.

(continued)

Cambodian, and South African employees feel that their American co-workers neglect to convey information clearly and tend to express a "superior attitude" in general. In addition, team leaders are dissatisfied with the way the program has been implemented as well as with its lack of recognition of their complex role in the distribution of incentive bonuses.

Many Lovitt employees view the company's move toward empowerment as a short-term "management fad." Others believe that it is merely a way for the company to demand more from them for less. Still other employees, particularly those with strong cultural ties to England or France, argue that genuine participative decision making is not possible in a top–down bureaucracy. Moreover, they argue, a number of competitors failed in their attempts to introduce similar innovative programs involving self-directed work teams.

ASSIGNMENT

You are the communication training specialist retained by Lovitt International to design workshops aimed at improving employee communication and ensuring the success of the TE program. Using what you have learned in this chapter about the role of communication in establishing good interpersonal relationships at work, design the Lovitt workshops. Also consider the following issues:

1. In your analysis of the situation at Lovitt, what are the key problems?
2. How can you best address those problems in a series of workshops? What solutions will you propose?
3. How can you design the workshops to encourage team members' commitment to the TE program? What kinds of experiences will team members need to have in order to understand and learn from the empowerment process?

However, work relationships, like dialogue, are hard to manage or control, especially when the members of a team do not share a common culture or language. While changes in members' power or status may alter existing relationships and create new ones, the constraints of a hierarchical organization ensure that the variations in these relationships will be limited.

SUMMARY

Effective interpersonal relationships at work depend in large part on how people communicate with one another. Listening to others and respecting their opinions, being assertive, possessing a clear sense of direction and control, receiving valuable performance feedback, responding to the need to adapt to others' cultures, and feeling valued as an employee all contribute to relationships that benefit both employees and organizations.

Communicating in
Teams and Networks

The word team *can be traced back to the Indo-European word* deuk *(to pull),
[but the] modern sense of a team, "a group of people acting together,"
emerged in the sixteenth century. . . .*

We define team *as any group of people who need each other to accomplish a
result. This definition is derived from a statement made by former Royal
Dutch/Shell Group planning coordinator Arie de Geus: "The only relevant
learning in a company is the learning done by those people who have the
power to take action."*

● Peter Senge, *The Fifth Discipline Handbook* (1994)

*The sudden burgeoning of teams and team solutions is in part a product of the
complexity of our world, which demands radically more effective means of
integrating what bureaucracy has split apart.*

● Gifford and Elizabeth Pinchot,
The End of Bureaucracy and the Rise of the Intelligent Organization (1993)

FOR DISCUSSION

● What are the advantages and disadvantages of using a team-based approach in organizations?

● Why is conflict an inherent part of effective team communication?

● What are communication networks?

● Why do electronic networks complicate our understanding of communication?

● Why are networks especially important during times of economic and social change?

I n this chapter, we address teams and networks. The future of work within organizations will emphasize a team-based approach, while the future of work outside of organizations (e.g., entrepreneurship and independent contracting or consulting) will also rely on networks of relationships.

Teams play various roles in contemporary organizations that are essential to organizational success. But a team-based approach also poses new problems and challenges to organizations. In addition to utilizing different types of teams, organizations seek to understand the processes of team communication and team learning.

Networks of specialists command a growing segment of the business world, and network communication plays a special role in marketing products, services, and information worldwide. Together, teams and networks pose special challenges to balancing creativity and constraint in organizations at the turn of the century.

Teams

WHAT IS A TEAM-BASED ORGANIZATION?

As many as half of all American employees are expected to be working in team-based organizations by the year 2000. The importance of teamwork has long been appreciated; the Boston department store Filene's introduced the concept in 1898. But today's emphasis on teams goes beyond teamwork or working together. A *team-based organization* has restructured itself in order to include all levels of employees in teams and to improve work processes and outcomes. A radical departure from the formal organizational groups used to make decisions or solve problems, the contemporary team-based approach is used to deal with the highly competitive global market (Goodall, 1990c).

However, in many cases a company's past successes with a traditional hierarchy make it difficult to incorporate a team-based approach. Pinchot and Pinchot, in *The End of Bureaucracy and the Rise of the Intelligent Organization* (1993), identify a number of organizational changes that need to accompany the move to a team-based approach. Team-based organizing differs sharply from the bureaucratic form of organizing. In the latter, a hierarchical chain of command distinguishes between managers (as "thinkers") and workers (as "nonthinkers") and emphasizes the need for close supervision. Team-based organizations, in contrast, view all employees as capable of making decisions about how to manage work tasks. In the ideal team-based organization, most supervisory work is replaced by self-managed work teams.

In addition, the task specialization and functional management inherent in a bureaucracy are replaced by cross-functional training, internal learning or "intrapreneuring," and market-mediated networking in a team-based organization. Similarly, employee rights, a sense of culture and community, self-directed management, and a commitment to market ethics replace the bureaucracy's formal rules and standard operating procedures. Careers are viewed less as providing upward mobility and more as offering competence in multiple specialties as well as a network of contacts. Employees thus become "knowledge workers" dedicated to self-improvement, positive results, and productive collaboration.

As Pinchot and Pinchot (1993) conclude:

> In the conversion to postbureaucratic organizations, teams form the basic unit of empowerment, small enough for efficient high involvement and large enough for the collective strength and the synergy generated by diverse talents. Within teams people can take wide responsibility for one another, for the organization, and for the quality of their products and services. Behind the success of such innovations as total quality, project management, high performance work teams, time-based competition, reengineering, intrapreneurship, and a host of others is a shift in the location of power and decision-making from individuals in bureaucratic management functions to more independent teams, both formal and informal. (p. 194)

MANAGING THE TRANSITION TO TEAMS

Although the move toward teams is highly appealing, the transition to post-modern forms of team-based organizing has not been without problems. For example, in many cases, people whose jobs give them control over others tend to resist a team-based approach. For managers and supervisors, team-based organizing requires a fundamental change in their role—from operational expert or overseer to coach or facilitator.

In addition, for teams to succeed, the reward system has to recognize the contributions of both the team and its individual members. Organizations continue to struggle with the challenges posed by evaluating and rewarding teams whose members contribute unequally to the whole team. Similarly, differences in the knowledge and skills of team members can cause some members to work harder than others and, therefore, to be more deserving of rewards for their efforts.

Furthermore, many organizations provide insufficient transition and management training to employees who are redefined as team members and reassigned to new team-based jobs. For example, one of the authors of this book was asked by the director of quality at a major aerospace company to assist in reorganizing the company's 40,000-member workforce into teams within a 12-month period. Managing the transition to teams is a time-consuming endeavor that involves the following:

1. *Preparation:* Employees must be prepared for the change, including those who will lose their jobs as well as those who will be reassigned to new team-based jobs.
2. *Training:* Employees must receive training in teamwork, team communication, and team-based learning.
3. *Learning:* Employees must be given the time to learn their new roles (productivity is likely to decrease during this time).
4. *Rewards:* A fair reward system must be established.
5. *Consultation services:* Teams will need expert support as they struggle to learn their new jobs, roles, and cross-functional responsibilities.

TYPES OF TEAMS

Despite widespread enthusiasm for team-based organizing, definitions of what constitutes a team remain ambiguous (particularly in the United States, where hierarchical forms of organizing have a long history). The current interest in work teams is rooted in both the Hawthorne studies (which attest to the importance of informal groups; see Chapter 3) and European experiments with autonomous work groups (Kelly, 1992). Eric Trist's (1981) study of teams of British coal miners in the 1950s, for example, emphasizes how communication processes optimize social and technical systems:

> In the mines, employees worked together, helping each other and often trading jobs. Trist discovered clear indications of higher productivity and job satisfaction among those workers who were given more control of their jobs. Trist's studies also indicated that organizations with workers who were more involved in the operation were better equipped to respond to changing markets and political conditions—something that large and rigid organizations found difficult. (Wellins, Byham, & Wilson, 1991, p. 8)

Together, Trist's work and other European experiments in self-management have become known as the *sociotechnical* school of thought, in which participative and open-ended jobs with minimal critical specifications and constraints are regarded as superior to jobs in a hierarchy (Herbst, 1976).

However, all groups in an organization are not necessarily teams. A collection of working people may be a committee, a task force, or an ad hoc group. Teams, in contrast, generally fall into these three categories or types: project teams, work teams, and quality improvement teams.

Project Teams

Project teams, which help coordinate the successful completion of a particular project, have long been used by organizations in the design and development of new products or services. For example, a project team might include "engineers, programmers, and other specialists who design, program, and test prototype computers" (Sundstrom, DeMeuse, & Futrell, 1990, p. 121). A project team might instead be assigned to address a specific issue or problem. For example, a savings and loan recently charged a project team with the task of developing ways to bring in new business.

A special type of project team exists within matrix organizations, as Scott (1981) explains:

> The hallmark of the matrix [organization] is the simultaneous operation of vertical and lateral channels of information and of authority. The vertical lines are typically those of functional departments that operate as "home base" for all participants; the lateral lines represent project groups that combine and coordinate the services of selected functional specialists around particular projects. All participants are responsible to their functional superior and one or more project leaders. . . . Matrix organizations are . . . found in . . . highly innovative industries such as contract research, electronics, and aerospace. (p. 220).

Despite the difficulties posed by a matrix form of organizing (such as having to report to two supervisors and the redundancy that occurs across project teams), cross-functional project teams help to prevent people from becoming isolated in particular functions and from losing sight of customers' requirements.

Work Teams

A *work team* is defined as "an intact group of employees who are responsible for a 'whole' work process or segment that delivers a product or service to an internal or external customer" (Wellins, Byham, & Wilson, 1991, p. 3). For example, one such work team at a California aerospace company is responsible for all metallizing of components in the company. The team resides together, outlines its own workflow (e.g., the steps for applying metal coatings to parts), and is engaged in making ongoing improvements in the work process (in this case, making the metal coating as thin as possible). In addition, Federal Express, General Electric, Corning, General Mills, and AT&T have recorded significant productivity improvements after incorporating work teams (Wellins, Byham, & Wilson, 1991). Kodak reportedly reduced its turnover rate (by one-half of the industry's average) and improved its handling of customer call-ins by 100 percent after reorganizing into work teams. Similarly, Texas Instruments Malaysia managed to boost employee output by 100 percent and cut cycle time by 50 percent after moving to a team-based approach.

The most successful work teams are supported by a commitment to empowerment. Because they are given the discretion and autonomy to make decisions and solve problems, they are not frustrated by a lack of authority to implement their ideas and solutions. Lyle Sussman (1976) explains why managers

FIGURE 10.1
The empowerment continuum of work teams

Source: R. Wellins, W. Byham, and J. Wilson, *Empowered Teams* (San Francisco: Jossey-Bass, 1991), p. 26.

should seek to empower work teams with as much decision-making authority as possible: "a group can more effectively allocate its resources when and where it is required to deal with its total variance in work conditions" (p. 183).

In practice, however, work teams differ in terms of degrees of empowerment. As indicated in Figure 10.1, four levels of empowerment are delegated to work teams. Low levels of empowerment are indicated by "housekeeping" responsibilities (such as conducting meetings) and cross-training responsibilities. As empowerment increases, the team assumes responsibility for the continuous improvement of work processes, the selection of new members, the election of a team leader, and capital expenditures. At the highest level of empowerment, the self-directed work team is also responsible for performance appraisals, disciplinary measures, and compensation (Wellins, Byham, & Wilson, 1991). This type of self-directed work team is rare even today.

Another barrier to the effectiveness of work teams, union agreements often prohibit cross-training or specify rules that conflict with self-management goals. In addition, managers may resist the move to empower self-directed work teams (Tjosvold & Tjosvold, 1991). The ability to oversee an empowered work team will become an increasingly important management skill. It requires the supervisor overseeing a team to:

1. act as a facilitator, keeping the group on track while respecting a free exchange of ideas;
2. be hard on rules, agenda, goals, and accountability, but soft on the means by which the team chooses to organize itself and do its work;
3. communicate extensively with others in order to keep the team informed of the work of other teams and of the organization as a whole.

Effective managers of work teams create a climate for honest and supportive dialogue and possess the necessary communication skills to do so. The considerable challenges involved in such an undertaking are well reflected in Focus on Ethics 10.1.

Finally, the empowerment process may involve an employee stock ownership program (ESOP) to encourage team members' motivation and dedication to the team approach: "I will be motivated to do my best because the fruits of my labor are now visibly mine." However, according to Harrison (1994), there are two general types of ESOPs. One is financially motivating, giving employees some ownership in the company but providing no incentive for a psychological change to take place because the command and control structure remains intact. The other type of ESOP is ideologically motivating, in that the structure and philosophy of the company reflect a commitment to employee participation and involvement.

Quality Improvement Teams

Popular in organizations in the 1980s, informal problem-solving groups called "quality circles" met voluntarily to address work-related issues on a weekly basis (Kreps, 1991). Quality circles have since been replaced by *quality improvement teams* whose goals are to improve customer satisfaction, evaluate and improve team performance, and reduce costs. Such teams are typically cross-functional, drawing their members from a variety of areas in order to bring different perspectives to the problem or issue under study. In theory, a quality improvement team uses its diverse talents to generate innovative ideas.

Some organizations have taken a novel approach in creating quality improvement teams. For example, in a program called "Work-Outs at General Electric," which was initiated by CEO Jack Welch in 1989, forty to one hundred

The Dilemmas of Midlevel Management in Fostering Empowerment

Fred Myerson is a midlevel manager trained in the traditional approaches to management. His company has shifted to self-directed work teams, including an intensive employee empowerment program. Fred is now a "coach" responsible for facilitating work teams. He is also dedicated to making the program work.

However, Fred recently encountered a problem that the empowerment training seminars did not address: how to diplomatically handle unusable ideas from work teams without discouraging them from contributing new ideas in the future. In addition, Fred does not want to create the impression that he is resisting change, but he also cannot isolate himself entirely from the decision-making process. He has been an effective manager in the past, but he feels less effective in his role as team facilitator.

In Fred's opinion, he has three bad choices: (1) pass along what he perceives as nonworkable ideas (thereby supporting the empowerment program but violating his ethical responsibility to the company), (2) ignore the proposals he considers unsound (thus behaving unethically toward the work teams by undermining their empowerment), or (3) argue against the unsound proposals (thereby creating the impression of himself as a control-oriented manager, disempowering the work teams, and discouraging them from contributing innovative ideas in the future).

Given what you have learned thus far about teams in organizations, what other options might Fred consider? How can he deal with both the problem and the ethical dilemmas it poses most effectively?

employees are selected by management to attend a three-day conference (Stewart, 1991). A facilitator divides the employees into five or six smaller groups, and each group works independently for two days to identify problems with the company and to prepare a presentation to its supervisor regarding recommended changes. On the third day, the supervisor is confronted by each group and its proposals, and he or she must agree or disagree with each proposal or ask for more information (in which case, the group agrees to supply it by an agreed-upon date). One manager describes the experience in this way: "I was wringing wet within half an hour. . . . They had 108 proposals, and I had about a minute to say yes or no to each one" (Kiechel, 1994, p. 70). This is one example of how organizations are using teams to encourage creativity and to open the dialogue between managers and employees.

COMMUNICATIVE DIMENSIONS OF TEAMWORK

Roles

Inherent in teamwork is the need to achieve a balance between the diverse goals of individual members and those of the entire team. While individual member behavior can vary significantly, members tend to play typical *communication roles* that reveal patterns in task behavior or socioemotional concerns. (Goodall, 1990c). According to the classic typology of group member roles developed by Kenneth Benne and Paul Sheats (1948), the three broad types of communication roles are the task, maintenance, and self-centered roles. In the *task role,* the team member summarizes and evaluates the team's ideas and progress or initiates the idea-generating process by offering new ideas or suggestions. In the *maintenance role* the team member's communication seeks to relieve group tension or pressure (e.g., by telling jokes or changing the subject of a conversation) or to create harmony in the group (e.g., by helping to reconcile conflict or disagreements) (Shockley-Zalabak, 1991, pp. 189–90). In the *self-centered role,* the team member seeks to dominate the group's discussions and work or to divert the group's attention from serious issues by making them seem unimportant. Unlike the positive effects of task and maintenance roles, the self-centered role is considered inappropriate and unproductive.

Two other roles have been identified by Goodall (1990c). The so-called *prince role* is exhibited by group members who view themselves as brilliant political strategists and the world as a political entity. In the *facilitator role,* a team member focuses on group processes (e.g., following an agenda and maintaining consensus in decision making) to the exclusion of other important issues.

People who both serve on teams and facilitate team communication often need to play different roles in various group situations. A training manager, for example, may act as a facilitator if during a team meeting the conversation sways off-topic and suggestions for refocusing on target issues are needed. At the same time, the manager may suspend the facilitator role by offering information or opinions relevant to the discussion. Two other roles played by team facilitators—as sponsors and coaches—help organizations ease the transition to a team-based approach. A *sponsor,* who is not a member of the team and who has significant power in the organization, is responsible for keeping the team informed of organizational developments, removing obstacles to effective teamwork, and advocating on the behalf of teams to ensure their access to necessary resources. A *coach,* typically a former supervisor and a respected team member, is responsible for helping the other team members acquire the cross-functional skills needed to accomplish team-based tasks. Coaching is especially important to team success because it addresses the specific problems associated with transitioning from a classical management approach to a team-based one. In addition, a coach teaches team members how to ask for coaching and thereby to deal with errors, weaknesses, or deficiencies in ways that promote the team's performance.

Norms

Norms are the informal rules that "designate the boundaries of acceptable behavior in the group" (Kreps, 1991, p. 170). For example, team members may be expected to attend meetings on time, to prepare for meetings in advance, and to distribute the meeting's agenda by an agreed-upon deadline. Norms about conflict may express an intolerance or acceptance of disagreement. Some observers attribute Motorola's recent success to its norm about conflict that encourages team members to engage in loud debates at meetings (Browning, 1992). Similarly, 3M's success has been linked to a norm that says, in effect, "when in doubt, take action."

Team norms, which are shaped by the national and organizational culture as well as by personal agendas, influence member roles. At a U.S. aerospace company, for instance, where the organizational culture is generally intolerant of conflict, work teams tend also to avoid conflict by focusing on maintaining group harmony and relieving tension and by de-emphasizing summary, evaluation, and the motivation to take action. These team norms are enforced informally through members' approval of them as well as by the organizational culture.

Decision Making

Decision making by teams is generally more productive than decision making by individuals for various reasons. Teams get more people involved in the decision-making process and usually generate more information and ideas. In addition, the act of participating in decision making makes team members more aware of important issues, more likely to reach a consensus, and better able to communicate about issues with co-workers. Team members are also encouraged to think, to solve problems, and thereby to become more responsible and productive.

Unlike the classical management approach, which separates the tasks of making decisions and implementing them, the team-based approach gives employees control over decisions that affect their work and has been shown to decrease job stress (see Chapter 8). According to Kreps (1991), "the more complex and challenging the issues under evaluation, the more powerful the outcomes of decisions, and the greater the number of people affected, the better groups are for making the decisions" (173–74).

However, group decision making also poses a number of problems. In what is called the *risky shift phenomenon,* a team may tend to make decisions that involve more risks than decisions made by individuals because of the perceived safety in numbers (Cartwright, 1977). In addition, strong-willed or verbose team members may dominate conversations, intimidate others, or manipulate team decisions to benefit themselves (e.g. to gain power or improve their image). A well-known problem associated with team decision making initially identified by Irving Janis (1971), *groupthink* occurs when team members go along with rather than evaluate the group's proposals or ideas. According to Janis (1972):

> In a cohesive group, the danger [of groupthink] is not so much that each individual will fail to reveal his [or her] objections to what the others propose but that he [or she] will think the proposal is a good one, without attempting to carry out a careful . . . scrutiny of the pros and cons of the alternatives. When groupthink becomes dominant, there is also considerable suppression of deviant thoughts, but it takes the form of each person deciding that his [or her] misgivings are not relevant and should be set aside, that the benefit of the doubt regarding any lingering uncertainties should be given to the group consensus. (p. 44)

Jane Gibson and Robert Hodgetts (1986) suggest the following strategies for dealing with teams that exhibit symptoms of groupthink which are consistent with our ideal of organizational dialogue:

1. Encourage team members to voice their objections and to evaluate others' ideas.
2. Encourage team members to remain impartial and, therefore, to maintain objectivity in decision making.
3. Use more than one group to work on a problem to generate a variety of proposed solutions.
4. Encourage team members to discuss the team's deliberations with people outside of the group in order to obtain objective feedback.
5. Invite outside experts into the group to obtain their input and feedback.
6. Make one team member responsible for ensuring that all sides of an issue are explored by the team.
7. Divide the team into subunits that work independently on a problem and then report back to the team.
8. Arrange a special meeting after a consensus has been reached to give team members the opportunity to discuss any doubts or concerns that have since emerged.

Decision making by teams also requires team members to face the challenge of sorting through multiple interpretations of a problem or issue to find the single best recommendation or course of action. Members who are intolerant of others' different perspectives may find this task especially challenging. For this reason, extensive research has been conducted on identifying effective decision-making strategies.

Most early research on team decision making divides the process into discrete phases. For example, Robert Bales and Fred Strodtbeck (1960) identify *orientation, evaluation,* and *control* as the three phases of problem-solving interaction in a group. Thomas Scheidel and Laura Crowell (1964) propose a *spiral reach-testing model* of the group decision-making process. It holds that as groups attain agreement in one area, they reach out to test their ideas in new areas. While through agreement, they spiral forward, disagreement causes them to spiral back to their last position and begin the cycle anew. Because group decisions emerge only slowly, progress occurs through this back-and-forth building on prior commitments.

Aubrey Fisher's (1980) well-known model of group decision making sees decisions as the product of four stages:

1. Orientation
2. Conflict
3. Emergence
4. Reinforcement

In the *orientation stage,* the members of a newly formed team get to know and trust each other before beginning their work. Their communication tends to focus on clarifying the team's purpose and function and on reducing tension and uncertainty. After the orientation stage, communication about tasks inevitably initiates the *conflict stage,* as team members express and debate different ideas, perspectives, positions, styles, and worldviews, forming alliances and coalitions in the process. A team that manages the conflict stage well will emerge with a diverse assortment of perspectives and valuable information that is used to move toward a single position. However, the conflict stage is not well managed by teams that neglect to spend enough time on defining the problem and generating proposed solutions, resulting in a premature decision made in haste. In contrast, from well-managed conflict emerges the team's position on the problem or issue. Thus, in the *emergence stage,* coalitions give way to a working consensus as a delicate balance of compromise and negotiation is worked out. If trust is lacking in the group or if members' differences are significant, the team will be unable to function. Some members may withdraw, while others may assert their power over the rest of the group. In addition to making a decision, this stage involves determining how to implement the decision. Finally, the *reinforcement stage* is marked by a strong spirit of cooperation and accomplishment among team members (Fisher, 1980).

Other studies of team decision making challenge the stage models proposed by Fisher (1980) and others by suggesting that most teams follow a less linear path toward decision making. Marshall Scott Poole (1981, 1983) maintains that group decision making is more varied and complicated than these models suggest. According to Poole and Roth (1989), teams experience periods of disorganization that are unpredictable, tend to go through cycles and to repeat stages multiple times, and may engage in activities (e.g., managing tasks and establishing work relationships) in a haphazard rather than a coordinated fashion. In many cases, Poole and Roth thus argue, neither patterns nor stages are discernible.

Similarly, Connie Gersick's (1991) *punctuated equilibrium model* suggests a new way of viewing the group decision-making process. Drawing on similarities across various fields and subject areas (e.g., individuals, groups, organizations, academic disciplines, and species), Gersick offers these three concepts related to group development: (1) *deep structure,* which is the team's set of assumptions and performance strategies used to approach the problem; (2) *the equilibrium period,* during which the team works within the established framework without questioning its fundamental approach to the task; and (3) *the revolutionary period,* when the team examines its operating framework and reframes its approach as a basis for moving forward. Gersick (1988) notes further that work groups experience revolutionary periods at a point halfway between their inception and a predetermined deadline. Successful teams approach this transitional period as an opportunity to examine their basic assumptions, whereas unsuccessful teams ignore that opportunity for self-examination and proceed on the basis of their initial assumptions.

Other important contributions to our understanding of effective group decision making have been made by Randy Hirokawa and Kathryn Rost (1992), who argue that effective teams give more attention to the group process (i.e., the procedures used to solve problems) than do ineffective teams. Referred to as *vigilant interaction theory,* Hirokawa and Rost (1992) note that successful teams focus on four areas of assessment: (1) of the nature of the task, (2) of the standards for evaluating various decision options, (3) of the positive aspects of the various options, and (4) of the negative qualities of the various options. The authors conclude that "group decision performance is directly related to a group's efforts to analyze its task, assess evaluation criteria, and identify the positive and negative qualities of alternative choices" (p. 284).

Finally, in a sustained effort to apply communication technology to group decision making, so-called *group-decision support systems* (GDSS) are used to give teams access to various decision-making tools (Poole & DeSanctis, 1990). For example, software that creates an electronic display for and accepts input from all group members, and software for problem solving, decision analysis, and expert systems can help teams make better decisions (Contractor & Seibold, 1992). Although only in its infancy, GDSS will increasingly assist teams in the retrieval and communication of information relevant to decision making.

Conflict and Consensus

Conflict occurs among members of organizations and teams largely because people in different positions of power pursue different interests (see Chapter 6). But here we are concerned with *teams as sites of conflict* and with *team-based strategies for achieving consensus.* Team conflict may occur among members who come from different fields or professions, such as in a cross-functional team, or between line and staff teams. It may also occur as a result of perceived inequities in group member status or productivity, personality differences, and work-related problems, among many other reasons.

Conflict is a form of communication that is defined as "the interaction of interdependent people who perceive opposition of goals, aims, and values, and who see the other part[ies] as potentially interfering with the realization of these goals," which in organizations most often refers to the acquisition and use of resources (Putnam & Poole, 1987, p. 552). Like other types of communication, conflict changes or evolves over time and is unpredictable. It also takes place in the interdependent relationships among people who depend on each other for resources. Some degree of team conflict is essential to achieving high levels of productivity and effective communication (Franz & Jin, 1995). An absence of conflict over an extended period of time is more likely a sign of group stagnation than of effective communication.

Attitudes toward conflict in organizations have changed significantly since the 1950s, when overt conflict was viewed as counterproductive and was avoided in most contexts. By the 1970s, however, some recognition of the benefits of conflict had emerged, such as its role in generating different ideas and perspectives (and thereby in avoiding groupthink) as well as in facilitating the sharing of information. The constructive role of conflict is mostly accepted today, although it remains difficult to realize in practice.

Research on conflict in organizations includes classical management studies that view conflict as a breakdown of communication (Hunger & Stern, 1976) and cultural studies that define it as a dispute over different perspectives of organizational realities (Smith & Eisenberg, 1987). Most research on the cycles and escalation of conflict has been approached from a systems perspective (Putnam & Poole, 1987), whereas critical theorists view conflict as reflecting deep imbalances of power in the organization (Mumby, 1993).

Therefore, because team conflict is inevitable and unavoidable, we are most concerned with how team members handle it. As illustrated in Figure 10.2, *conflict style* is an indicator of how a person manages conflict. Broadly distinguished as emphasizing a "concern for self" or a "concern for others," conflict style is also marked by degrees of assertiveness and cooperation (Kilmann & Thomas, 1975). The most effective conflict styles emphasize high assertiveness combined with competition and collaboration. In contrast, compromise is considered less effective in resolving conflicts because neither party's solution is adopted. Collaboration is more likely to lead to a novel solution that satisfies

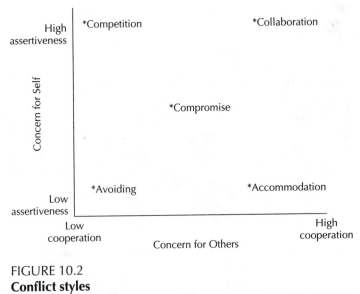

FIGURE 10.2
Conflict styles

Source: From R. Kilmann and K. Thomas, "Interpersonal Conflict-handling Behavior as a Reflection of Jungian Personality Dimensions," *Psychological Reports* 37 (1975): 971–980.

both parties. In addition, accommodation may at times be effective, but in most conflict situations it is counterproductive, causing stress for the team member who accommodates others and undermining the team's ability to generate creative ideas.

However, research has not demonstrated a clear relationship between conflict style and actual communication in a conflict situation. For example, while the conflict styles of supervisors seem to reflect their strategies for dealing with conflict when it first emerges, more coercive strategies usually follow regardless of the conflict style (Fairhurst, Green, & Snavely, 1984). The supervisor's tendency to use increasingly coercive compliance-oriented strategies generally takes less time for men than for women (Conrad, 1991). Therefore, because multiple situational factors and goals affect conflict strategy selection, conflict style is not a predictor of communication behavior (Conrad, 1991).

A team's commitment to collaboration and consensus, however, involves ongoing communication and results in good decisions with long-term impact. *Consensus* does not mean that all team members agree with a decision but that they feel that their views have been considered by the team. According to Ed Schein (1969), "If there is a clear alternative which most members subscribe to, and if those who oppose it feel they have had their chance to influence, then a consensus exists" (p. 56). Effective conflict management thus means accepting the inevitability of differences and being committed to an ongoing dialogue that is open to alternative perspectives and that encourages creative decision making.

Cultural Diversity

As corporations continue to make greater use of intercultural teams in response to global competition, researchers are increasingly concerned with the effects of cultural differences on team member communication. In one such study, Charles Bantz (1993) reports on his experiences as a member of a ten-person intercultural research team. Using Hofstede's (1983) dimensions of cultural diversity—power distance, uncertainty avoidance, individualism, and instrumentalism or expressivity—and difference factors—language, norms, status, and politics—Bantz (1993) offers the following conclusions:

> The range of difficulties generated by the diversity in a cross-cultural research team [leads] to a variety of tactics to manage those differences. The tactics include . . . alternating leadership styles across time and tasks; agreeing on long-term goals, while continuing to negotiate shorter-term goals; building social cohesion; [ensuring that] longer-term goals [meet] individual needs; alternating task and social emphases; maintaining social support by engaging in confirming communication even when disagreeing; adapting to language difference[s] by slowing down, checking out, restating, and using more than one language; discussing work schedules; using varying conflict modes across different issues; discussing group procedures; initiating social discussion of work life to ascertain perspectives; and responding to political differences. While . . . tactics vary, [the] four [most] common [ones are] (1) gather information, (2) adapt to differing situations, issues, and needs, (3) build social as well as task cohesion, and (4) identify clear, mutual long-term goals. (p. 19)

In addition, Bantz (1993) points out that "awareness of cultural differences is necessary, but [it is] not sufficient for the accomplishment of cross-cultural team research" (p. 19).

According to Varner and Beamer (1995), *negotiation* is a key to managing intercultural team differences. They argue that the following four phases in the negotiation process occur in all cultures, but that the amount of time devoted to each phase and its relative importance can differ:

1. *Developing relationships with others:* In order for the members of a newly formed intercultural team to develop productive work relationships, they need to be given sufficient time to explore long-term team goals, build trust, and adapt to cultural differences. In most cultures, candid answers to questions mark the beginning of a productive relationship, even when the required answers may be perceived as self-disclosing. However, face-saving

is just as important to members of Asian and African cultures. Therefore, it is wise to avoid insensitive remarks, to express tolerance of others' goals and values, and to respect the status that others enjoy in their native culture.

2. *Exchanging information about topics under negotiation:* Honest or "frank" disclosures help to generate trust among members of an intercultural team. But information exchange may also be enhanced by responding to questions with other questions that open up the team dialogue. Questions can be used not only to access information and clarify ideas, but also to call bluffs, to show interest in another's ideas, to control the direction of a conversation, and to address controversial issues in nonthreatening ways. The types of exchanges generated by such questions help team members adapt to their cultural differences while also communicating with trust and openness. Team members also become more aware of how culture plays a role in the answers generated by questions; for example, *why* questions are answered with explanations of cause and effect in Western cultures, but they are answered more generally through stories, personal narratives, and cultural myths in non-Western cultures.

3. *Recognizing multicultural techniques of persuasion:* Rational arguments are considered persuasive by members of many cultures, but different perspectives on what is considered rational and different ways of communicating rational arguments can pose difficulties in intercultural teams. It is thus recommended that teams focus more on gaining information than on persuading, and that team members respect their cultural differences when persuasion is necessary. For example, using *I* is less persuasive than the more inclusive *we,* and using such words as *must, should,* and *ought* may be viewed as arrogant by members of non-Western cultures. In addition, many non-Western cultures do not recognize the relationship between facts and conclusions that is commonly accepted in Western cultures; instead, historical and cultural inferences may form the basis of persuasive arguments.

4. *Emphasizing the role of concession in achieving agreement:* Most cultures appreciate the value of fair exchange, including the value of concession in gaining agreement. In general, concessions are best expressed as *if* comments (e.g., "We can deliver those services if your suppliers can meet this schedule"), rather than as directives (e.g., "We can deliver those services but your suppliers must meet this schedule"). However, while Americans tend to emphasize the importance of concessions in the form of a well-executed plan, such as a business contract, Asians tend to emphasize the same principles in a different form—in their informal relationships with others. Thus, for example, an American businessperson may be surprised when an Asian businessperson does not observe the stipulations of a signed contract. A contract is considered binding in American culture, but in most Asian cultures a contract may be superseded by informal relationships. Similarly, an American conducting business in Finland may be surprised to learn that for-

mal written agreements are often considered unnecessary because verbal agreements are executed with trust.

TEAM LEARNING

Successful team-based organizations foster an environment that values and rewards team learning (Pinchot & Pinchot, 1993; Senge, 1994). Peter Senge (1994) defines *team learning* as "alignment" or the "functioning of the whole":

> Building alignment is about enhancing a team's capacity to think and act in new, synergistic ways, with full coordination and a sense of unity [among] team members. . . . As alignment develops, [members do not] have to overlook or hide their disagreements to make their collective understanding richer. (p. 352)

Senge (1994) goes on to suggest that team learning transforms the following skills of "reflection and inquiry" into "vehicles for building shared understanding" (p. 352):

1. *Balancing inquiry and advocacy:* Teams need to balance inquiry (i.e., asking questions that challenge the existing assumptions and beliefs about work) with advocacy (i.e., stating opinions and taking action). Neither inquiry nor advocacy should control the team's learning process. Figure 10.3 identifies various types of inquiry and advocacy commonly used by teams.
2. *Bringing tacit assumptions to the surface of team dialogue:* Senge (1994) suggests that because "we live in a world of self-generating beliefs which remain largely untested," (a) our beliefs are the truth; (b) the truth is obvious; (c) our beliefs are based on real data; and (d) the data we select are the real data (p. 242). A team that learns to question these assumptions moves down the "ladder of inference" (see Figure 10.4). As the team brings tacit assumptions to the surface of its dialogue, it discovers the role of those assumptions in the development of beliefs and conclusions.
3. *Becoming aware of the assumptions that inform conclusions:* Once assumptions have surfaced, it is beneficial for teams to reflect on how these particular beliefs give rise to interpretations of events that support specific conclusions about work processes, employees, or customers. Making these connections explicit makes them easier to change. Conclusions, then, are filtered through members' assumptions and beliefs, which are unobservable and highly personalized. This is what makes the generation of new ideas challenging. However, by counteracting these abstract influences on the thought process, teams can promote creative thinking.

Dialogue is also important to team learning. According to Senge's (1994) model of the "evolution of dialogue," shown in Figure 10.5, team dialogue

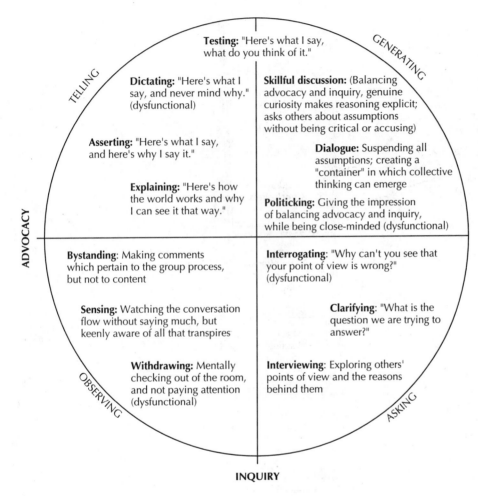

Testing: "Here's what I say, what do you think of it."

GENERATING

TELLING

Dictating: "Here's what I say, and never mind why." (dysfunctional)

Skillful discussion: (Balancing advocacy and inquiry, genuine curiosity makes reasoning explicit; asks others about assumptions without being critical or accusing)

Asserting: "Here's what I say, and here's why I say it."

Dialogue: Suspending all assumptions; creating a "container" in which collective thinking can emerge

Explaining: "Here's how the world works and why I can see it that way."

Politicking: Giving the impression of balancing advocacy and inquiry, while being close-minded (dysfunctional)

ADVOCACY

Bystanding: Making comments which pertain to the group process, but not to content

Interrogating: "Why can't you see that your point of view is wrong?" (dysfunctional)

Sensing: Watching the conversation flow without saying much, but keenly aware of all that transpires

Clarifying: "What is the question we are trying to answer?"

Withdrawing: Mentally checking out of the room, and not paying attention (dysfunctional)

Interviewing: Exploring others' points of view and the reasons behind them

OBSERVING

ASKING

INQUIRY

FIGURE 10.3
Balancing Inquiry and Advocacy

Source: Peter Senge et al., *The Fifth Discipline Fieldbook* (1994), p. 254.

moves initially from invitation to conversation to deliberation. From deliberation, the dialogue may follow a path to *discussion* (debate or skillful discussion) or to *suspension* (dialogue and metalogue). Team learning thus encourages members to think about dialogue as allowing the "free flow of meaning," unencumbered by logical analysis (e.g., skillful discussion) or debate. People from Western cultures may find it difficult to learn the speech and listening skills associated with this type of dialogue because of the value they attribute to rational

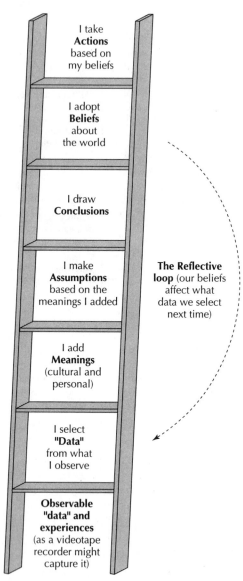

FIGURE 10.4
The Ladder of Inference

Source: Peter Senge et al., *The Fifth Discipline Fieldbook* (1994), p. 243.

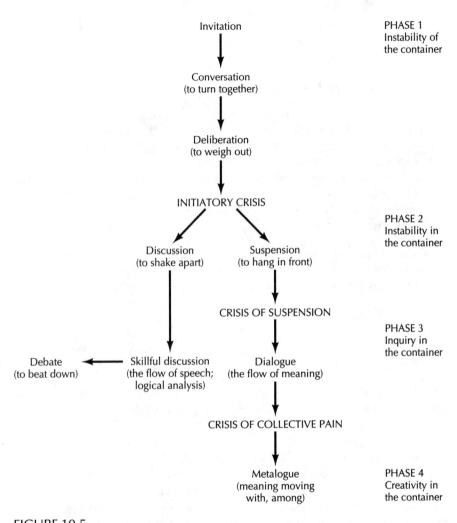

Invitation

PHASE 1
Instability of
the container

Conversation
(to turn together)

Deliberation
(to weigh out)

INITIATORY CRISIS

PHASE 2
Instability in
the container

Discussion
(to shake apart)

Suspension
(to hang in front)

CRISIS OF SUSPENSION

PHASE 3
Inquiry in
the container

Debate
(to beat down)

Skillful discussion
(the flow of speech;
logical analysis)

Dialogue
(the flow of meaning)

CRISIS OF COLLECTIVE PAIN

Metalogue
(meaning moving
with, among)

PHASE 4
Creativity in
the container

FIGURE 10.5
The Evolution of Dialogue

Source: Peter Senge et al., *The Fifth Discipline Fieldbook* (1994), p. 361.

argument. In addition, such dialogue challenges many of the assumptions of traditional communication in organizations. The objective is not to argue a point effectively but to balance inquiry with advocacy in ways that contribute to the knowledge of the team as a whole.

In the transition to a team-based approach, therefore, the organization must not only help employees cope with change but also help them learn new ways of communicating. This is a formidable challenge that requires a commitment to training and team learning.

A RETREAT FROM TEAMS?

Ideally, self-directed work teams help contemporary organizations deal with the pressures of global competition and help promote autonomy, responsibility, and empowerment in the workforce. In practice, however, the ideals of the team-based approach are often not realized by organizations.

In one recent example, Kiwi Air attempted to implement self-directed work teams but found that decision making was hindered by disagreements among team members. Kiwi's experience reveals the importance of the following factors in successful team formation:

1. Teams are only as good as their members; the careful selection of members is thus essential.
2. Teams must be sufficiently trained in group decision making and communication.
3. Only some decisions can be assigned to teams; others are best assigned to individuals.
4. Some members of a team have more expertise and experience than do other members; therefore, all members do not contribute equally.

Similarly, Ford, Procter & Gamble, and Honda have found that teams require too much time to make decisions and tend to shield their members from taking responsibility (Chandler & Ingrassia, 1991). Similarly, GM's renowned Saturn plants have been "steadily moving back to the Detroit-style assembly line" (Drucker, 1992b, p. 16). Why are teams failing? One reason may be related to the move to downsize organizations and lay off employees, which can strain the partnership between labor and management that is essential to teaming. In addition, teams may fail because they suggest a radical reframing of traditional power relationships in organizations that managers, in particular, may resist. But employees also tend to view the move to teams with skepticism, at least initially. If employees are empowered by the team approach, they become its strongest advocate. More often, however, management does not follow through on its promise of empowerment and teams inevitably fail.

Furthermore, Peter Drucker (1992b) argues that teams fail when management neglects to define the types and functions of teams it seeks to establish. As a result, teams do not have a clear understanding of their function in the organization. A highly empowered, cross-functional team that does not receive strong leadership support is likely to fail. When a team's expectations about empowerment or responsibilities are not met by the organization, the team cannot function effectively.

Networks

Networks, initially thought of as mere extensions of organizational groups, are now regarded as important resources for doing business. The future of work is expected to rely on personal, technical, and entrepreneurial *networks* of people serving as information resources.

The concept of a "network" has emerged as a result of researchers' long-term interest in the structure of organizational groups. Human relations theorists recognized that small groups do much of the important work in organizations. The pattern of communication among group members, called the group's *communication structure,* is affected by many factors. For example, management may design a group in a way that limits its communication, or employees with low status in a group (e.g., newcomers) may be less willing to communicate freely than those with high status. Formal lines of authority and rules about communication may also restrict the flow of information in a group. These investigations into communication structures have led to the idea of *communication networks.*

TYPES OF NETWORKS

Small-group Communication Networks

Early research on communication structure focused on examining *small-group communication networks* (groups of five people) to determine the effects of centralized versus decentralized networks on decision making. As Richard Scott (1981) explains:

> In a technique developed by Bavelas (1951), a small number of individuals are placed in cubicles and allowed to communicate only by means of written messages passed through slots in the cubicle walls. The slots connecting each cubicle can be opened or closed by the experimenter, so that different communication patterns can be imposed on the interacting subjects. . . . A typical task presented to groups of individuals placed in these networks is to provide each individual with a card containing several symbols, only one of which is present on the cards of all subjects. The task is . . . completed when all participants are able to . . . identify the common symbol. (pp. 148–49)

Four types of small-group communication networks were typically studied—the *circle, wheel, chain,* and *all-channel* networks (see Figure 10.6). The circle and all-channel networks are highly decentralized, whereas the chain and wheel are centralized. It was found that centralized networks are more efficient than decentralized networks, as reflected in the speed with which they can complete a

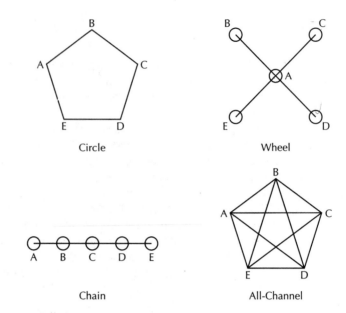

FIGURE 10.6
Small-group communication networks

Source: W. R. Scott, *Organizations: Rational, Natural, and Open Systems* (Englewood Cliffs, N.J.: Prentice-Hall, 1981), p. 8.

task (Leavitt, 1951). Further investigations, however, reveal that centralized networks are not necessarily superior to decentralized networks:

> [A]s tasks become more complex or ambiguous, decentralized net[works] are usually superior to centralized structures . . . formal hierarchies aid the performance of tasks requiring the efficient coordination of information and routine decision making whereas they interfere with tasks presenting very complex or ambiguous problems. . . . Specifically, hierarchies impede work on the latter by stifling free interactions that can result in error-correction, by undermining the social support necessary to encourage all participants to propose solutions, and by reducing incentives for participants to search for solutions. (Scott, 1981, pp. 149–50)

This early research also yielded some interesting findings about small-group decision making. For example, when a group faces a routine task or a tight deadline, participation by and input from all members is not expected. In contrast, when a group faces more complex issues or problems, a more open dialogue promotes member satisfaction and better solutions.

However, many critics argued that the experimental small-group networks studied had little in common with actual groups in organizations (Farace,

Monge, & Russell, 1977). Therefore, the focus of communication network research was broadened to include not only patterns of interaction in decision-making groups, but also informal patterns of organizational communication.

Emergent Communication Networks

The most powerful groups in organizations are those that emerge from the formal and informal communication among people who work together. These groups are referred to as *emergent communication networks.*

The current focus on communication networks in organizations is attributed to a general acceptance of systems theories, which emphasize the connections between people and the relationships that constitute an organization (see Chapter 4). In terms of communication networks, researchers examine those relationships that emerge naturally within organizations as well as the groups and member roles associated with them (Rogers & Kincaid, 1981). Formal networks and emergent networks coexist in organizations, and each is best understood in the context of the other (Monge & Eisenberg, 1987). For example, although new employees may rely on a copy of the formal organizational chart to understand reporting relationships and the structure of departments, over time they realize that the actual communication relationships among employees do not precisely mirror the organizational chart. Departments with no formal connections may nonetheless communicate in order to manage the workflow, and salespeople working on different product lines may share common experiences at lunchtime. A great deal can be learned about an organization's culture by identifying the discrepancies between informal emergent networks and the formal organizational chart.

Early research on emergent communication networks investigated the so-called organizational "grapevine." (During the Civil War, telegraph wires were strung through trees and resembled grapevines [Daniels & Spiker, 1991]). Building on the work of Chester Barnard (1938), Keith Davis (1953) noted the importance of informal communication to the health of an organization. Subsequent research has shown that informal communication on the "grapevine" is more efficient and accurate than the formal dissemination of information (Hellweg, 1987).

Researchers and managers alike seek to identify the paths of informal communication and the structure of informal networks in order to understand the distribution of information and informal power in organizations. Complex network analysis techniques have been used to "map" the emergent communication networks of an organization (Monge & Eisenberg, 1987). For example, in one such effort employees are asked to participate in a survey to determine how often they engage in informal communication with co-workers and to identify the topics of their conversations.

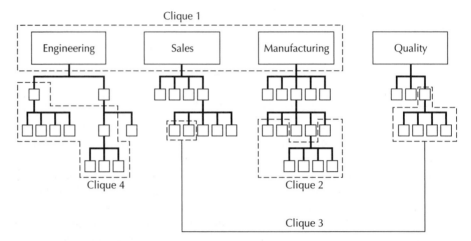

FIGURE 10.7
A sample organizational communication network

COMMUNICATION NETWORKS

Analyses of communication networks are useful to any examination of the structure of informal, emergent communication in organizations, particularly because they sensitize us to the creative tendency of individuals to forge new linkages, regardless of formal rules or boundaries. Informal communication in organizations is fluid and in a constant state of change. While formal reorganizations may occur only infrequently, informal reorganizations occur frequently or continuously (Monge & Eisenberg, 1987). In studying emergent communication networks, we are concerned mainly with overall patterns of interaction, communication roles, and areas of communication content.

Patterns of Interaction

As illustrated in the sample communication network shown in Figure 10.7, a number of informal groups or cliques emerge as a result of communication among people in organizations, both within and across departments or functions. Communication networks also vary in density, which is determined by dividing the number of connections among all organizational members by the number of possible connections. For example, a professional association is a low-density network because communication among its members is infrequent, but the kitchen crew of a restaurant is a high-density network in which most or all members communicate regularly with one another. Similarly, formal hierarchies are less dense than more progressive organizations that encourage employee participation and communication.

In a study of a community church, McPhee and Corman (1995) report that "joint involvement in focused activities" is crucial to the development of networks of relationships (p. 133). In addition, people who are frequently involved in joint activities are also likely to be well connected in the communication network.

Research conducted by Albrecht and Hall (1991) suggests that dense organizational networks have considerable influence over whether other employees adopt a new idea or technology. In their study of elementary schools and administrations, Albrecht and Hall report that personal relationships play a key role in the development and acceptance of new ideas when cliques form to focus on those ideas. These close connections help people overcome feelings of uncertainty and make them more likely to accept and adapt to change.

The density of an organizational communication network can have some less obvious implications for organizational effectiveness. Mark Granovetter (1973) notes the importance of "weak ties" in networks as sources of new information. When all members are closely connected, the risk of groupthink increases. Michael Papa (1990) makes a similar point about network density in his study of an insurance company: "the more diverse an employee's network [is], the more coworkers he or she talk[s] to about [a] new technology, and the more frequently he or she talk[s] about [it], the more productive that employee [is] likely to be using the new system" (p. 361). In addition, Karl Weick (1976) notes the benefits of loosely coupled systems (in which decisions and actions can occur independently) as sources of organizational flexibility, adaptation, creativity, and competitiveness.

Finally, Marshall and Stohl (1993) use what they call a "network approach to participation" to redefine the notion of empowerment as a "process of developing key relationships in the organization in order to gain greater control over one's organizational life" (p. 141). In this view, the employee's personal communication network affects the experience of empowerment, involvement, and participation at work.

Communication Roles

A *communication role* in a network is determined by a person's influence on the flow of information. Well-connected individuals in an organization tend also to be the most influential (Brass, 1984). Four types of communication roles occur in networks: the isolate, group member, bridge, and liaison roles. *Isolates* have little contact with others in the organization; they work alone either by choice or because their jobs require them to be structurally or geographically isolated from other employees. *Group members* communicate mainly within an informal clique, which may at times involve communication with a departmental, professional, or demographic grouping. *Bridges* (who are also group members) have significant communication contact with at least one member of another informal group, while *liaisons* have connections with two or more cliques but are not exclusive members of any one group.

Recent developments in information technology have eliminated the jobs of many isolates (e.g., toll-booth operators) or have connected them to computers and other forms of mediated communication (e.g., travel agents). Research has not yet been conducted on whether these types of connections sufficiently substitute for face-to-face contact. Under the new social contract, however, a person's network of connections outside the organization may be more important than organizational communication networks.

Within organizations, liaisons are the dominant interpreters of the organizational culture (see Chapter 5). As key communicators with tremendous influence on the direction of the company, they are able to transform any message into an interpretation that is consistent with their beliefs and to pass that interpretation quickly throughout the company (and at times to customers and the community). When organizational improvement efforts fail, it is most often a result of the improper mobilization of liaisons.

Any attempt to analyze network communication roles in an organization may be a sensitive issue for employees, who do not always perceive their degree of communication contact with others in the same way (e.g., a subordinate might report having daily contact with a superior, whereas the superior may claim to have no communication with the subordinate). Differences in status or perception may also cause employees to respond in ways that reflect not actual but expected communication roles, reporting contact only with people they "ought" to communicate with at work. In addition, employees may be reluctant to participate in a network analysis because the results may reflect negatively on themselves (e.g., in our analysis of network roles in a professional association, a department head who was identified by subordinates as an isolate was dismissed from the organization).

Content Areas of Communication

Emergent communication networks develop around specific topics or *content areas* of communication (Farace, Monge, & Russell, 1977). Each content area is regarded as defining a separate network; for example, a bank may have a social network for communication about personal matters and a task network for discussion of work duties. Distinctions in network content often mark differences in the structure of emergent communication networks, such that the roles of bridges, isolates, group members, and liaisons in a task network may differ significantly from those in a social network within the same organization. Furthermore, the identification of multiple types of communication content contributes to our understanding of the relationships between people in networks. Thus, for example, two people who communicate about only one topic—say, task issues—are said to have a *uniplex relationship,* whereas people who communicate about two or more topics—say, personal issues, task issues, and new ideas—are said to have a *multiplex relationship.* Multiplex linkages have been identified as sources of social support and organizational innovation (Albrecht & Hall, 1991; Ray, 1987).

The content of communication networks takes on added significance when we consider it in terms of the sense-making process. In their attempt to extend the cultural approach to organizations, Peter Monge and Eric Eisenberg (1987) suggest that analysis of so-called *semantic networks* (in which people hold similar interpretations of key organizational symbols or events) may be useful. The same network measures may be applied (e.g., bridge, group member, isolate, and liaison), but in this case they would refer to groups that share similar interpretations, that are isolated from mainstream values and beliefs, or that connect disparate subcultures. For example, in a dense semantic network there is shared meaning about major organizational issues. This approach has been successfully applied to the analysis of perceptions of organizational missions and value statements (Contractor, Eisenberg, & Monge, 1992; Peterson, 1995).

INTERORGANIZATIONAL COMMUNICATION NETWORKS

Employees communicate with co-workers within the organization as well as with customers, suppliers, and others in different organizations or institutions. In an advertising agency, for example, account managers interact with people from various newspapers and television stations, and in a university, the gifts and development staff communicates with alumni, accountants, attorneys, and local officials. Communication networks thus cross organizational boundaries.

Interorganizational communication networks are the "relatively enduring transactions, flows, and linkages that occur among or between . . . organizations" (Oliver, 1990, p. 241). Such networks can vary in terms of their openness, density, and interdependence. Tightly coupled or highly interdependent interorganizational networks are sensitive to environmental jolts that threaten entire industries (e.g., in the deregulated airline industry, a minor change introduced by one carrier, such as reduced fares, significantly affects other carriers).

Open systems theory affords great significance to an organization's environment (see Chapter 4). Some researchers regard organizational environments "as consisting mainly of networks of other organizations. The complexity of this network of interorganizational relations is a variable, and higher levels of causal texturing present increasing challenges to organizational adaptation" (Metcalfe, 1981, p. 505). According to Charles Perrow (1986), an organization's environment is a kind of "nested box problem," wherein each network exists within a larger network, ranging from one's division, to one's industry, nation, and the world.

Organizations participate in interorganizational communication networks in various ways. Two organizations are said to be *vertically integrated* when one builds parts or provides services that the other needs for its delivery of a product or service (e.g., Pratt-Whitney manufactures aircraft engines for sale to Boeing). In contrast, two or more companies are *horizontally integrated* when their customers are passed from one to the other in the service cycle (e.g., from a cancer screening clinic to a hospital to outpatient counseling). In addition, a company may form *strategic alliances,* or joint ventures, with competitors.

According to Eisenberg et al.'s (1985) typology of interorganizational communication, three types of network linkages exist for the exchange of materials and information: institutional, representative, and personal. An *institutional linkage* occurs without human communication, as in the automatic transfer of data between companies. A *representative linkage* exists when people from various organizations meet to negotiate a contract, plan a joint venture, and the like. A *personal linkage* occurs when members of two organizations communicate privately. However, it may be difficult to distinguish between personal and representative linkages when people meet informally and without any intentions of discussing business, but business does get discussed and the results are significant. The various types of linkages may also change over time; for example, two companies planning to engage in a joint venture may initially host luncheons or dinners intended to make people more comfortable with each other personally. Later, representatives may be identified to work out the details of the plan, part of which may include the automatic transfer of data between the organizations.

Interestingly, the most efficient way of sharing information across organizational lines may not be through overt communication but by hiring employees from other companies. Ideas about management, marketing, structure, communication, and employee treatment are "imported" through personnel changes. In some cases, new employees who bring both their technical ability and interpretive framework to organizations can help promote needed change (e.g., when Hughes Aircraft Company hired a former IBM executive to serve as its CEO, the company's emphasis shifted from engineering to business and financial management). In other cases, however, new employees' previous experience may become an obstacle to initiating change.

In the contemporary economic environment, organizations are most likely to turn to strategic alliances—such as mergers, acquisitions, and joint ventures—in order to enhance their financial status and political power. Most companies recognize that they need to narrow the scope of their services by coordinating their activities with other organizations. Especially common among highly specialized health-care providers (e.g., transplantation centers), strategic alliances are increasingly seen in higher education, where universities can no longer afford to offer a wide array of programs, as well as among companies engaged in international business. Similarly, high-technology organizations are investing in joint research and development ventures in order to cut costs and improve the collective work of scientists.

However, interorganizational communication networks can at times be difficult to manage. For example, scientists from one organization may be reluctant to share their best ideas with scientists from the other organization. Formal interorganizational alliances are risky because they require a good deal of trust, a willingness to give up autonomy, and the juxtaposition of potentially incompatible organizational cultures. Many mergers and acquisitions in recent years have been problematic because the organizational partners brought different levels of formality and different attitudes toward employees to the alliance.

Like multidisciplinary groups, interorganizational communication networks are potential sites of dialogue. As interorganizational cooperation across organizational, industrial, and national boundaries increases, the challenges of communication will become greater in turn. In particular, ways of promoting productive dialogue among diverse networks will become increasingly important.

THE NETWORKED SOCIETY

Within only a few years, our understanding of what constitutes a network has changed considerably, from the connections among people within a single organization, such as a hospital, manufacturing plant, or school, to the connections among people in a global society. During this short period of time, we have seen tremendous growth in both network marketing and in computer networks on the Internet and World Wide Web.

Companies that specialize in *network marketing* are redefining work and discovering the power of networking. One highly successful network marketing company, AMWAY, is a multibillion-dollar worldwide organization that has grown as a result of the unique relationships it has with its distributors. Each network marketing distributor is expected not only to distribute products but also to recruit others to become distributors (who, in turn, recruit others still). AMWAY's distribution networks thus expand exponentially, and those nearest to the top receive increasingly high revenues from the distributors they recruit. However, in network marketing there is a tendency to regard all relationships as business relationships, such that people find it difficult to establish friendships with others who are thought of as potential distributors. Only limited research has been conducted on the personal and social impacts of this new form of organizing (Church & Eisenberg, 1996).

Communication networks are also being transformed by the *Internet* and the *World Wide Web,* whereby people engage in on-line communication with others around the world. Significant changes in communication behaviors have been noted in this trend, especially in information seeking and relational development. For example, computer users post their questions about issues on Internet bulletin boards and receive responses within hours from people around the world. Moreover, in search of meaningful relationships, millions of computer users participate in thousands of virtual gathering places, sharing real or apparent disclosures in pursuit of intimacy.

Network marketing and computer networks have significantly contributed to the emergence of a global *networked society*. The implications of such a society on our relationships and communication with others are yet to be seen. Some critics mourn the demise of local communities, whereas others envision an electronic global village that provides people with instantaneous access to information and other people worldwide. (Some of the potential effects of technology on communication are discussed in Chapter 11.)

Creativity and Constraint in Networks and Teams

Team-based organizations face the challenges of balancing creativity and constraint in group relationships and of productively dealing with diverse interpretations. The members of a newly formed team are typically anxious about their role in the group and struggle to find a voice for themselves in the context of the group. This can be a formidable challenge during the orientation phase of a team's development.

During the conflict and emergence stages, members attempt to articulate their perceptions creatively, but their efforts are heavily weighted with constraints (e.g., "We tried that and it didn't work" or "Management will never take our proposal seriously"). Other constraints can be useful in promoting team effectiveness, such as meeting times and places, agendas, and problem-solving procedures. In general, however, team members' ability to function as a group depends on their skill in balancing the creative contributions of individual members with the constraints imposed by the group as a whole.

ⓈUMMARY

Teams and networks within and among organizations create and respond to norms, decision-making processes, cultural differences, and conflict and consensus. In team and network communication, different cultures, languages, and interpretations of meaning make communication complex and miscommunication likely. Communication across networks is also affected by electronic communication channels.

C A S E   S T U D Y

THE NETWORKED COMMUNITY

BACKGROUND

Founded in 1913, Fleeberville is an average American city of 1.5 million people with typical urban American problems. Although the city is located on a large, spring-fed lake in a mountain setting, industrial pollution has over the years become a serious problem there. Traffic on the two major highways gets worse each year, as does the rate of violent crime. The software companies that dominate the local economy are downsizing, and the remaining jobs require extensive technical experience. The result has been a growing underclass, much of which has been forced to seek public assistance. Those with resources have increasingly acted to isolate themselves from the town as a whole, and gated communities and private schools grow more numerous each year. Meanwhile basic city services and public schools are in decline.

ASSIGNMENT

Imagine that you are an activist, community organizer, and communication expert who has recently decided to make Fleeberville your permanent home. You intend to put down roots, start a career, get married, and raise children there. So for many reasons you are concerned that the city embark on a path of self-renewal.

You observe that many citizens seem to care about the city, but isolated efforts to improve things (e.g., clean up the lake, clothe the homeless, sponsor a school) don't appear to be very effective.

1. Knowing what you do about systems, teams, networks, and organizing, how would you approach the problem of making Fleeberville a better place to live?
2. What actions would you take to begin with, and whom would you contact for help?
3. What patterns of communication would you encourage, and how ought they change over time?
4. How would you deal with existing groups who felt uniquely responsible for determining the future direction of the city?
5. What teams and networks would you build to promote such a massive effort, and how would you prepare these groups for their challenge?
6. How would you evaluate the success or failure of your efforts?

Project teams, work teams, and quality improvement teams play critical roles in the high-involvement organization. Team member communication roles and cultural communication processes characterize team contexts within and among organizations, and team learning occurs through dialogue.

The role of communication networks in our global society continues to expand. In organizations, small-group networks include the circle, wheel, chain, and all-channel networks. The more powerful emergent networks (grapevines, cliques, and loosely coupled systems) emerge from the formal and informal communication among people in organizations. Interorganizational networks include institutional, representative, and personal linkages. Network communication is affected by patterns of interaction, communication roles, and content areas. Network marketing and computer networks (e.g., the Internet and World Wide Web) have contributed to the creation of a networked society.

Managing the Total Organization: Strategy, Image, and Communication Technology

Corporations are [among] the most . . . important institutions of modern society. . . . As . . . repositories of resources and knowledge, companies shoulder a huge responsibility for generating wealth by continually improving their productivity and competitiveness. Furthermore, their responsibility for defining, creating, and distributing value makes [them a] principal agent of social change. At the micro level, companies are important forums for social interaction and personal fulfillment.

Purpose is the embodiment of an organization's recognition that its relationships with its diverse stakeholders are interdependent. In short, purpose is the statement of a company's moral response to its broadly defined responsibilities, not an amoral plan for exploiting commercial opportunity.

● Christopher Bartlett and Sumantra Ghoshal,
"Changing the Role of Top Management: Beyond Strategy to Purpose" (1994)

QUESTIONS

FOR DISCUSSION

- Why do contemporary organizations need to develop a clear strategy?

- What is organizational image, and how does it affect employees' work life and performance?

- How does communication influence the strategic alignment process?

- How does communication technology affect contemporary organizations and employee productivity?

- What is meant by the term *virtual office?*

Contemporary organizations must *position* themselves effectively in the social and economic landscape, and *align* their operations and practices in ways that are consistent with that position. Positioning involves selecting a strategy or purpose that distinguishes the organization from its competitors. In addition, the strategy must be effectively communicated to employees who use it as a guide to work decisions, as well as to customers, who use it to judge the company's image or reputation.

While the positioning of a company is accomplished in part by developing both a strategy and an image, strategic alignment is also involved. Central to strategic alignment are communication technologies, which ensure effective positioning. Effective positioning and alignment are critical to contemporary organizational success.

Positioning the Organization through Strategy and Image

COMPETITIVE STRATEGY

Strategy is of critical importance to the long-term success of a business. But unlike a company's mission, vision, objectives, goals, or methods of implementation, a *competitive strategy* is a clear statement of why customers should choose a company's products or services over those of competing companies. Simple descriptors such as *cheapest, fastest, most reliable, friendliest,* and *best quality* are typically used in the expression of a company strategy. In addition to communicating a strategy, however, a company must ensure that all aspects of its business reflect the strategy.

Despite the importance of a strategy, few organizations actually have one, relying instead on their success with a particular product or service (typically introduced before the competition's). However, contemporary organizations that lack a strategy are at risk in today's highly competitive global market.

As an example of how a competitive strategy works in practice, let's suppose that you own a new fast-food eatery that serves, among other foods, hamburgers stuffed with mashed potatoes. After your initial six months in business, your customers are only beginning to warm up to the idea of stuffed burgers. However, as a local business owner, you have been invited to attend tonight's reception hosted by the city's chamber of commerce, providing you with a special opportunity to promote your fast-food business. You will dress appropriately for the event and bring your business cards with you. More important, you need to prepare what you will say about your business to others at the reception. Keep in mind that it should take only about fifteen seconds to explain to others what you do and why your business is worthy of their attention. They, in turn, should be able to convey the same brief message to others later on, and they should want to do so. If you succeed in both respects, and if your message is memorable and distinct, your company has a competitive strategy.

As competition continues to increase in today's business world and the markets for products and services become more specialized, competitive strategies must adapt to these changes by targeting market niches and a more narrow consumer audience. In publishing and broadcasting, for example, companies now provide magazines and news programs that cover specific rather than broad topics in order to target specific market segments. Similarly, in this trend called *narrowcasting,* cable television companies typically offer a number of channels that focus exclusively on sports, comedy, news, or home shopping programs. Large companies may pursue two or more strategies to target multiple market niches; for example, to appeal to an older audience, MTV created its VH1 channel, Honda created its Acura model, and Toyota introduced the Lexus.

For communication specialists, crafting a competitive strategy involves close attention to message design. Thus, for instance, an effective strategy for your hypothetical potato-stuffed burger restaurant would likely focus on uniqueness: "The only place in town with potato-stuffed burgers!" However, your strategy would be successful only if a niche market existed for your product. A company that does not narrow its focus and attempts instead to target broad markets (e.g., "We are open twenty-four hours, and offer home delivery, service with a smile, and the lowest prices") is not likely to be able to serve the demands of all consumer markets or to distinguish itself as unique in any one market.

Developing a strategy for a new company often begins with the founder's intuition about the potential demand for a product or service. Thereafter, careful analyses of the target market, of the business environment (which includes potential customers, stakeholders, and community and government agencies), and of the existing competition are performed. Competitor analysis is especially important in identifying whether a similar product or service is offered by other companies in nearby or remote locations or if any past attempts to offer the product or service had failed. In formulating a competitive strategy, then, the prospective business owner must consider not only the potential demand for a product or service but also how the company's strategy will be received by various publics. A serious objection by any one group can threaten the survival of the business.

Types of Business Strategies

There are two basic types of business strategies: those that emphasize *lowest cost* and those that focus on *differentiation* (Porter, 1980).

Adopting a *lowest-cost strategy* involves a commitment to offering a product or service at the lowest possible price. Examples include discount appliance stores, no-frills airlines, and manufacturers of generic products. These companies emphasize their lowest-cost products or services in order to target consumers motivated by that strategy. In order to reach that consumer market, however, the strategy must be communicated effectively. Among the disadvantages of a lowest-cost strategy is the need to reduce operating costs in order to maintain a cost advantage. In a competitive global market, it may be difficult for such companies to manage the high costs of labor and materials. At the same time, these companies' survival depends on their ability to offer the lowest prices in the business in order to attract cost-conscious customers (Porter, 1980).

A more popular business strategy is *differentiation*, which involves highlighting the unique or special qualities of a company's product or service. For example, a company may be the most reliable, have the quickest delivery time, or offer the most comprehensive warranty service in the business. In the automobile industry, Volvo highlights safety whereas BMW highlights performance. Differentiation is a highly communication-based strategy, in that its success depends less on actual differences among competing products and more on the company's ability to create the *perception* of its product as unique in some way.

Developing a successful strategy may be as simple as noticing an unfilled niche in a particular market. For example, a physician might notice that a community's residents do not have access to medical care on weekends and may develop a strategy that addresses that need. Or the owner of a car rental company may respond to consumer demands for hourly rentals with a strategy that incorporates both daily and hourly rates. In most cases, however, developing a successful strategy is more difficult and complex because multiple businesses often compete within the same market (e.g., three Los Angeles supermarkets seeking to become the lowest-cost leader conduct ongoing comparison studies to assert their superiority). Similarly, in the battle among leaders in the overnight package delivery business, various strategies are used to compete within the same market. Federal Express differentiates its service as being the most reliable, whereas the U.S. Postal Service emphasizes lowest cost. Although the major long-distance phone carriers—AT&T, Sprint, and MCI—claim to offer the highest quality service or the lowest possible cost and tend often to dispute each other's claims, their prices are actually quite similar.

Strategy is especially important in highly cost-sensitive industries with low brand loyalty, such as in the deregulated airline industry. Following deregulation, relatively small airlines entered the marketplace and offered fares on major routes that were significantly less than the fares charged by major carriers. A fare war ensued; airfares continued to drop, but so did profits. Many of the small lowest-cost airlines failed, taking a few major carriers with them. The survivors, scrambling for a way to encourage brand loyalty, settled on frequent-flyer programs. Airfares increased, and the carriers developed differentiation strategies to entice consumers (e.g., "the most on-time departures" and "the best food").

In developing a differentiation strategy, a company chooses the most competitive aspect of its operation. This does not mean that the company is without other positive attributes, but that the company does not communicate them to the public as competitive advantages. At Nordstrom, for instance, customer service is highlighted even though the company is also concerned with cost, quality, and other factors. More than any other attribute, Nordstrom believes its customer service is what most differentiates it from competitors.

In a comprehensive discussion of business strategy, Robert (1993) identifies some popular strategies as well as areas in which a company should strive for excellence:

1. *Product- or service-driven companies,* such as IBM, Volvo, and Boeing, strive to provide the highest quality products or services in the business. They continuously focus on how to improve their products or services as well as their work processes.
2. *Market-driven companies* offer a wide range of products to a specific group of consumers (e.g., Johnson & Johnson sells its products to doctors, nurses, patients, and parents). Such companies engage in ongoing market research and strive to cultivate consumer loyalty.
3. *Production-capacity driven companies,* such as hotels and airlines, make substantial investments in facilities and equipment and aim to have them running at full capacity at all times. They engage in market research in order to meet customers' needs and demands; they also offer special incentives (e.g., reduced fares or discounted vacation packages) to increase business during slack periods.
4. *Technology-driven companies,* such as 3M, Hughes Aircraft, Sony, Gore, and DuPont, own or specialize in a unique technology (e.g., DuPont invented nylon). Such companies invest a considerable amount of money in research and development.
5. *Sales- and marketing-driven companies,* such as AMWAY, Mary Kay, and Tupperware, provide a wide range of products or services to customers in unconventional ways, including door-to-door selling, home shopping club sales, and network marketing. These companies strive to recruit top-quality sales and marketing personnel.
6. *Distribution-driven companies,* such as Wal-Mart, Federal Express, food wholesalers, and some Internet providers, have unique ways of getting their products or services to the customer. Some may also push a variety of products through their distribution channels. Such companies strive to maintain a highly effective distribution system.

The overriding factor in strategy development is *a keen awareness of the related industry as a whole as well as its potential for change or improvement.* Before air travel was made possible, people crossed the oceans in boats owned by the transportation companies that provided this service. With the advent of passenger air travel, however, these companies were threatened with obsolescence. But some of them survived by redefining their strategy—from providing transportation to providing entertainment on cruise lines. Similarly, McDonald's, a leader in competitive strategy, knows well what business it is in—and it isn't food! McDonald's sells comfort, security, predictability, and safety, which are reflected in the location and cleanliness of its restaurants and its rigid standards for food worldwide. Recently, McDonald's has formalized this strategy by dubbing itself "the world's community restaurant" and by licensing its name to selected children's toys. If it had instead thought of itself only as a burger restaurant, McDonald's could not have envisioned these opportunities. There are many advantages to be gained from understanding why people buy products or services.

Strategy and the Business Life Cycle

Strategy changes as an organization progresses through the stages of the business life cycle (Kimberly & Miles, 1980). Strategic and communicative challenges also differ at each stage.

At "birth," a new company is concerned mainly with developing a strategy and finding a niche, securing financial investments, and making an initial foray into the marketplace. In "childhood," the company's major challenge is managing its growth and development. In its pursuit of multiple opportunities, the growing organization may be distracted from its basic strategy or lack the discipline needed to maintain a focus on its competitive advantage. Effective leadership can help counteract these problems.

When the company reaches "adolescence," it typically encounters stiff competition. As a result, the original strategy no longer functions as a competitive advantage and the company must work to change or fine-tune it accordingly. This may require paying special attention to both internal communication (in order to streamline processes, cut costs, and develop new competencies) and external communication (to remind customers of why the company's product or service is superior to those of competitors).

In the final phase of the business life cycle, "maturity," the company faces the difficult challenge of renewal—of letting go of the old business in favor of a new one, while also maintaining a position in the marketplace. J. C. Penney's recent attempt to upgrade its entire inventory and appeal to a different market niche is an example. Mature companies must come to terms with the legacy of their past success. In the face of a declining military budget and a mature product line, one engineering firm that had been successful in satisfying military customers with high-technology products finds itself unable to compete in the current business environment.

In contrast, Honda, which entered the world market in the 1970s with the tiny Honda Civic, is known for its strategic excellence. Since the 1970s, Honda has focused not on a particular product but on the customers who purchased the early Civics—baby boomers buying their first car. Transforming and upgrading its products to match those customers' needs, Honda introduced the Prelude and Accord as these young adults moved into their thirties and the upscale Acura line as they moved into their forties and became more affluent. Honda's strategy is thus tied to satisfying a well-defined market niche.

IMAGE

Today's sophisticated customer does not make financial decisions based solely on competitive advantage but is increasingly sensitive to a company's *image* and *reputation*—where it invests its money and how it fits into society as a whole. Employees, too, are affected by the positive or negative reputation of their employer.

Reputation

Reputation is the perception by outsiders of an organization's overall quality. It is based on information from various sources, such as personal contacts, financial performance records, and the media. As such, reputation is shaped largely by communication. Charles Fombrun and Mark Shanley (1990) identify the types of information people use to develop impressions about reputation: profitability, media visibility, and contributions to society, policy decisions, and social networks. Moreover, a competitive strategy is not sufficient to create a superior reputation. Social performance and environmental responsibility are also important. For example, some people refused to purchase gasoline from Exxon after the *Valdez* oil spill.

For many companies, reputation is communicated through a corporate logo. Many consumer products manufacturers have redesigned their logos to appeal to contemporary tastes (e.g., Campbell's Soup) or to create a worldwide image (e.g., Pepsi, Coca-Cola, Procter & Gamble) (Horovitz, 1991).

John Meyer and Richard Scott (1983) use the term *institutional organization* to refer to companies that are more concerned with social issues than profitability. Focusing on hospitals and schools, they note that public support of such institutions is more critical to their survival than financial success. An increasing number of contemporary businesses are holding themselves accountable to standards of social legitimacy. For example, many corporations and universities have divested their financial holdings in South Africa in protest of apartheid, and other companies have begun using recycled materials in their products and packaging. Although controversial, these moves indicate a clear need for companies to build their reputations.

An example of the importance of reputation is the early demise of Uptown cigarettes, a product developed for a niche market—upwardly mobile African Americans. Although the company's strategy had a good chance of success, the product was never brought to market because government and public interest groups objected to targeting segments of the population for the purpose of selling a health-hazardous product to them. These pressures caused the manufacturer to withdraw the product.

Public Relations

The profession of *public relations* is designed to manage the reputation of organizations. Public relations professionals scan the business environment, monitor the public's interest, and find ways to develop public appreciation for an organization's position and performance (Heath & Nelson, 1986). According to George Cheney and Steven Vibbert (1987), public relations originated in the attempts by U.S. railroads at the turn of the century to defend their actions. In the 1920s, the founder of modern public relations, Edward Bernays (1923), defined the task as one of two-way interpretation. By the 1960s and 1970s, public relations became more professional, proactive, and strategic, making greater use of brochures, booklets, and press releases as well as informal networking with interest groups. Public relations professionals are now recognized as agents who continuously monitor and shape the business environment (Cheney & Vibbert, 1987).

The public relations function is highly rhetorical in that it entails communicating multiple messages and goals to diverse audiences. It also requires a balance between (1) developing a distinct image while also being recognized as a cooperative member of society and the business community, and (2) shaping the public's perceptions and maintaining credibility with employees (Cheney & Vibbert, 1987). In both cases, communication issues are similar to those associated with balancing creativity and constraint.

Cheney and Vibbert (1987) point out that an unusual form of public relations—*corporate issue advocacy*—originated with the 1973 oil embargo. At this time, when oil companies had few good options for communicating with the public, Mobil began running full-page advertisements in major newspapers to offer opinions about the politics of regulation and the free marketplace (Crable & Vibbert, 1983). In a similar effort, Phillips 66 launched a campaign that celebrated its company values and successful employees. More recent examples of corporate issue advocacy include Esprit's political videos of customers answering the question "What would you do to make the world better?" and Nike's television spots featuring Spike Lee as a spokesperson for racial harmony. One result of corporate issue advocacy is a blurring of the traditional distinctions among corporate, political, and personal issues. Contemporary organizations know that an ideal market position makes them an integral part of the consumer's life and daily routine. Hence, they vie for control over communicative arenas that can help them foster associations with public values in ways that do not focus on their products or services. The economic power of some corporations gives them the opportunity to make positive contributions to society (e.g., McDonald's is a world leader in recycling). But within a capitalist system, all corporate communication is ultimately aimed at selling a product or service, even when the product or service is not prominently featured. Stanley Deetz (1991) calls this phenomenon *corporate colonization* (see Chapter 6).

Public relations work is likely to become more challenging as information technology makes organizations more open to scrutiny by consumers. Dissatisfied customers can now use the Internet to tell computer users around the world about their bad experiences with a company's product or service. For example, in Florida a scuba instructor has filed a lawsuit against a dissatisfied student diver who used a popular Internet discussion group to give information to others about the instructor (including the instructor's name and place of work) and about the student diver's experience. Although the Internet will continue to make public relations work more difficult for organizations, for consumers it will mean better service overall.

Identity versus Image

Unlike reputation, which is defined by outsiders' perceptions of an organization, identity and image are defined by insiders' (employees') perceptions. However, as Jane Dutton and Janet Dukerich (1991) point out, "an organization's *identity* describes what its members believe to be its character [whereas] an organization's *image* describes . . . insiders' assessments of what outsiders think" (p. 547; emphasis added). In the language of communication theory, image is a metaperception.

A fast-food chain employee, for example, may see the organization's identity as marked by convenience, inexpensive food, and friendly service, and at the same time believe the chain has a negative image (unjustifiably). In addition, the employee's perception of the restaurant's image may differ from the restaurant's reputation, which is based on the perceptions of customers and other outsiders. Moreover, an organization may have multiple identities and images when certain groups of employees and consumer segments perceive the company in different ways. If they are made public, differences in identity—that is, in how employees view the company—may lead to negative changes in an organization's image and reputation.

In a study of employees of the Port Authority of New York and New Jersey who routinely confronted the problem of homelessness at work, Dutton and Dukerich (1991) note that identity-threatening events can provide the impetus for organizations to take corrective action. The Port Authority did not effectively deal with the homeless problem until it saw it as a threat to its identity: "In particular, [employees'] sense of the Port Authority as a high-quality, first-class institution made the presence of homeless people problematic. . . . When the organization took actions that members saw as inconsistent with its identity, they judged the issue as more important" (Dutton & Dukerich, 1991, pp. 534, 545). Organizational members also monitor the company's image, and "deterioration of an organization's image is an important trigger to action as each individual's sense of self is tied in part to that image" (Dutton & Dukerich, 1991, p. 520). In an extension of Cheney's (1983) discussion of identification, Dutton and Dukerich (1991) argue that an employee's desire to identify with the organization can motivate action that will protect his or her preferred image of the company. In many respects, then, image, identity, and reputation are constructed through communication.

Although only limited research has been conducted on organizational image, an interesting study by Treadwell and Harrison (1994) suggests a relationship among shared image, frequent communication, and organizational commitment. In their study of a religiously affiliated liberal arts college, Treadwell and Harrison found considerable variation in students' and faculty members' definitions of the school's image. However, perceptions of image were somewhat more similar among individuals who communicated frequently and shared a commitment to the college (though this relationship was stronger for students than for faculty members). In addition, it was found that definitions of image tended to change over time in unpredictable ways. Clearly, more research is needed on the practical and ethical consequences of organizational image.

Corporate Crises

Corporate crises may include scandals, safety violations, or accidents. In recent years, corporate crises involving Union Carbide (Bhopal), Exxon (the *Valdez* oil spill), and Johnson & Johnson (the Tylenol scare) have sensitized both businesspeople and the general public to the difficulties of communicating effectively during a crisis. Some companies handle crises more effectively than others. Johnson & Johnson's exemplary performance following the Tylenol poisoning, for example, has improved its reputation in the long run and even made the company an expert in dealing with crisis situations (Cheney & Vibbert, 1987).

In a study of communication in crisis situations, Marcus and Goodman (1991) note that tension exists between messages aimed at comforting victims and those intended to comfort shareholders. Not surprisingly, in cases involving an accident, shareholders prefer the company to take a defensive stance, whereas victims prefer the company to be more accommodating. In cases involving a scandal, however, both shareholders and victims agree that accommodation is the appropriate company response.

In a related study of the crisis management strategies used by organizations to retain their legitimacy, Allen and Caillouet (1994) note that (1) ingratiation strategies are used most frequently, (2) influential stakeholders receive the most messages from the company, and (3) various stakeholders tend to receive different messages. Most research in this area supports a rhetorical view of crisis communication, which recognizes that multiple audiences require different types of messages in crisis situations.

STRATEGIC ALIGNMENT

A company may communicate a strategy such as "environmentally friendly" or "superior customer service," but if customers and employees do not see evidence of the company's claim, the strategy will be unconvincing and ineffective. Therefore, in addition to communicating the strategy to various internal and external publics (e.g., employees and customers), the strategy must be reflected in various other aspects of the organization. *Strategic alignment,* then, refers to the process of modifying organizational systems and structures to support the competitive strategy. This may affect such areas as job design, levels of authority, job training, reward systems, and staffing, among many others.

In the absence of strategic alignment, a business can neither accomplish its strategy nor create a desired image. For example, a printshop that claims to have the lowest prices in town but pays its employees above-average wages is not likely to achieve strategic success. Similarly, a company that claims to be responsive to customers would be unable to implement that strategy if its automated phone system does not give customers the option of speaking with a service representative directly.

Successful strategic alignment is difficult because it requires systems thinking, forcing the company to consider the relationship between its strategy and its internal systems. In addition, strategic alignment is complicated by employees' reluctance to see themselves as part of a system and by managers' tendency to make decisions in isolation rather than based on the company's strategy. Companies that overcome these obstacles to strategic alignment and that pursue a carefully chosen strategy invariably achieve success.

The Original 7-S Model of Strategic Alignment

The *original 7-S model* of strategic alignment, developed by members of the consulting firm McKinsey & Company is shown in Figure 11.1. According to this model, strategic alignment involves the following seven factors:

1. *Strategy:* Companies that lack a clear strategy or competitive advantage succeed only when competition is minimal or nonexistent.
2. *Superordinate goals:* More specific than a company's mission statement, superordinate goals (e.g., obtaining a return on an investment or winning a

specific contract) may also be stated ambiguously to allow for employee innovation and creativity (Eisenberg, 1984). However, they must flow logi-
cally from the company's strategy.

3. *Structure:* The formal reporting relationships as prescribed by the organizational chart should reflect the company's strategy and symbolically represent the company's values.

4. *Systems:* The flow of information through various media (e.g., telephones
and computer systems and meetings), the formal systems of operation (e.g.,
management information systems), the informal operating procedures (e.g.,
cultural practices), and the informal connections among people (e.g., emergent networks) should all be aligned with the company's strategy. Systems
are relevant to communication in that they deal with the distribution of information throughout a company. Certain strategies can be used only with
certain types of systems (e.g., a quality manufacturing strategy would require a control system to identify and correct defects immediately).

5. *Staffing:* Here the company's strategy is reflected in its hiring practices, job
assignments, and its workforce generally.

6. *Skills:* Employees' technical and interpersonal skills are used in ways that
promote the company's strategy (e.g., a company striving to differentiate itself as a leader in customer service would need employees with excellent
interpersonal skills).

7. *Style:* Both management style and organizational culture (how a company
perceives and treats its employees) can contribute to the success or failure
of a business strategy (e.g., a company that strives to be competitive but that
routinely permits its employees to miss deadlines is not likely to survive).

The strategic alignment process is best approached by thinking of the organization as a communication system. In this way, we see how the information in
each subsystem (or *S*) reflects and affects the whole organization. In an organization that is out of alignment, decisions in one system are made without considering their potential effects on other systems. Over time, an organization's
systems usually drift out of alignment as internal functions become outdated and
as external developments in technology and market demographics necessitate
internal change. In addition, employees are highly sensitive to alignment problems; that is, if the company claims to promote trust and empowerment,
employees are likely to voice their objections if their actual decision-making
participation is limited. At Disneyland, for example, employees objected to
what they perceived as inconsistencies between the company's strategy—"The
happiest place on Earth"—and its treatment and compensation of employees
(Smith & Eisenberg, 1987).

The strategic alignment process begins with the development of a strategy,
preferably one that focuses on reliable information about the future and that
aims to reinvigorate the company. Once a strategy is formed, it needs to be trans-

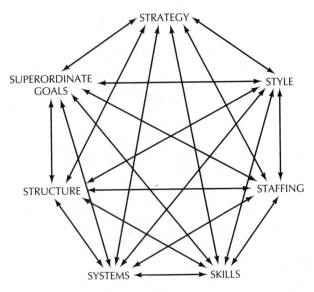

FIGURE 11.1
The Original 7-S Model of Strategic Alignment

Source: R. D'Aveni, *Coping with Hypercompetition: Utilizing the New 7-S Model* (1995), p. 48.

lated into superordinate goals so that it can be communicated to all employees. Structure is examined next, to determine whether it supports the strategy. For example, in the process of transitioning from a government business to a commercial supplier, a major electronics company sought to become a customer-driven firm (unlike its competitors). However, the company's existing structure, characterized by vertical lines of expertise and authority and minimal cross-functional communication, would not support its new focus on customer relations. The company thus decided to modify its structure by creating a centralized customer service office to act as an interface for customer communication, a repair center designed to meet customers' needs, and cross-functional teams to promote effective communication.

An analysis of systems typically occurs at this point in the strategic alignment process. In our example, the electronics firm found that its existing voice-mail system kept customers on hold for too long and changes were made to ensure that customers could reach a service representative within a reasonable amount of time. In addition, the company's past experience with military projects and lax schedules meant that group meetings would need to focus on addressing work issues more expediently. With the help of the human resources department, the company's chief decision-making groups worked together on creating a greater sense of urgency in its informal systems.

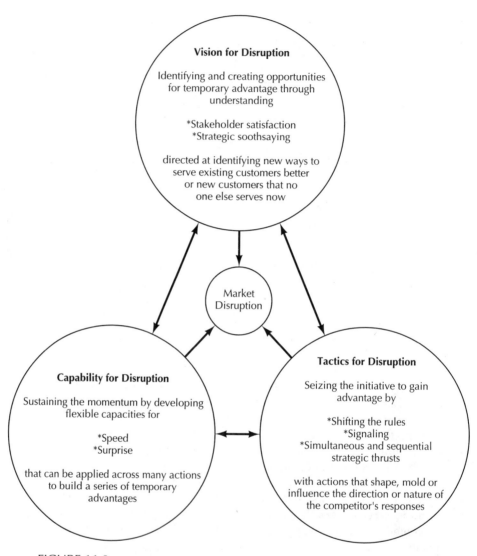

FIGURE 11.2
The New 7-S Model of Strategic Alignment

Source: R. D'Aveni, *Coping with Hypercompetition: Utilizing the New 7-S Model* (1995), p. 52.

Staffing, skills, and style are the final considerations in strategic alignment. The electronics firm recruited employees with the technical and communicative skills needed to enact the proposed strategy. Managers and employees in the customer service offices were trained in how to cultivate new customer-oriented styles of working and communicating with openness and empathy. Employees who were less open to this change were reassigned to positions that were less visible to customers.

In most cases, strategic alignment is accomplished gradually; a management team focuses on each stage of the process before proceeding to the next stage. Sometimes, however, large-scale strategic alignment may be attempted, as in the case of *total quality management (TQM)*. In pursuing the strategy of "total quality," a company may simultaneously redefine its objectives (superordinate goals), overhaul its organization (structure), fire managers from the "old school" (style), recruit new managers with skills better suited to the redefined structure (staffing), and train all employees in empowerment, teamwork, and other areas (skills). However, as a large-scale intervention, strategic alignment is only rarely successful. In addition to the difficulties associated with maintaining a focus amidst rapid change in multiple areas, employees tend to react negatively to change that is radical rather than gradual. They may become suspicious of the company's intentions, worry about losing their jobs, and be less willing to commit themselves to the program's success. Another problem associated with TQM occurs when a company focuses mainly on winning external recognition for its efforts. The Malcolm Baldrige Award, for example, is awarded by the U.S. government to companies for excellence in total quality management. Winning the award provides a company with excellent publicity and some powerful advertising copy. But in the case of a Florida utility company that pursued TQM to win the award, its misdirected efforts led to internal havoc and "a complaint record worse than [that of] several other Florida utilities" (Sashkin, 1991, p. 164).

The New 7-S Model of Strategic Alignment

Despite its many strengths, the original 7-S model of strategic alignment has one major weakness in today's highly competitive global economy: It assumes that organizations can succeed by *adapting* to environmental conditions. In an attempt to overcome this weakness, D'Aveni (1995) has developed his *new 7-S model* of strategic alignment (see Figure 11.2). According to this model, organizations build strategic advantage not by adapting to the marketplace but by taking speedy, flexible actions that disrupt the environment and create temporary competitive advantages. (This is similar to Weick's (1995) notion of organizational sense-making—that organizations must act first to disrupt the environment, and in so doing open up new possibilities and shape their environments.)

Communication Technology

Regardless of a company's position in the marketplace or society, it must utilize some form of *communication technology*. In the 1950s and 1960s, organizational researchers emphasized the importance of face-to-face communication between supervisors and employees and among co-workers (see Chapter 3). While face-to-face interaction is still important in today's organizations, advances in communication technology—from computer networks and facsimile transmissions to voice and electronic mail—have overcome some of the limits of interpersonal interaction, especially those associated with speed, geographical distance, and processing capacity. As a result, most organizations can no longer function effectively without using some type of communication technology. Furthermore, implementing a new technology usually affects work processes, employees' productivity and work life, and the character of interpersonal and power relationships (Aydin & Rice, 1992).

TYPES OF COMMUNICATION TECHNOLOGY

Two broad types of communication technology are currently available to organizations (Huber, 1990):

1. *Computer-assisted communication technologies* include the various methods of image transmission (e.g., facsimile, image modems, videoconference), electronic and voice mail, and computer networks.
2. *Computer-assisted decision-aiding technologies* include on-line management information systems, group decision support systems, information-retrieval database systems, and expert systems or programs that provide technical information.

Computer-assisted communication technologies are designed to enhance the speed of communication as well as the ability of people to communicate regardless of their geographical location. Electronic mail, or *E-mail,* for example, allows people to receive asynchronous messages via computers without telephone or personal interruptions (Turnage, 1990). (Despite the potential of video-conferencing, it has not yet been accepted as a substitute for face-to-face meetings [Long, 1987].) Other popular computer-assisted communication technologies include voice mail, voice messaging (radio paging), answering machines (increasingly connected to personal computers), audiographic conferencing, and cellular telephones. The recently introduced *personal communication unit (PCU),* which contains a pager, fax, and telephone, allows the user to send voice or text messages (typed or handwritten) from a small mobile unit.

Computer-assisted decision-aiding technologies are designed primarily to provide easy access to hard-to-find information needed to make decisions. For example, a company may use market data accessed via an external database to decide whether it should introduce a new product. Internally, a sales manager may access information about last quarter's sales to decide whether the company's salespeople would benefit from a proposed training program. Information on virtually any topic is available on-line. In practice, however, the systems that "support decision-making [but leave the] final decisions . . . to the user are [more] successful [than the] systems that substitute machine decisions for human decisions or [that] significantly curtail the user's freedom of action" (Turnage, 1990, p. 172).

An especially useful decision-aiding program is the *personal digital assistant* (*PDA*), which allows computer users to direct a search for information based on their personal input. For instance, the PDA user might input information about a desired vacation itinerary (e.g., location, price range, and other preferences) and have the computer shop for and book the trip. The PDA may eventually be able to search not only databases but also bulletin boards and listservs (on which other computer users chat about various topics of interest related to decision making).

EFFECTS OF COMMUNICATION TECHNOLOGY ON THE WORKPLACE

The potential effects of communication technology on the workplace are multiple and varied. Contemporary observers usually support one of four major views on the subject: the utopian, dystopian, neutral, or contingent view.

In the *utopian* view, information technology serves to equalize power relationships at work by bridging time and space, thereby improving both productivity and the work life. Proponents of this highly optimistic view "see the computer as freeing employees to work on more challenging tasks by taking over the routine aspects of jobs, thus increasing productivity and competition and creating more employment in the long run" (Turnage, 1990, p. 171).

In contrast, the more pessimistic *dystopian* view sees communication technology as benefiting an economic elite and—through the modification and loss of jobs—as causing such problems as downsizing (particularly among middle managers), the lowering of work skill requirements, and physical and mental disorders (Braverman, 1974; Cohen, 1985). Sometimes called *luddites,* proponents of the dystopian view range from extremists, who advocate a return to simpler times, to moderates, who suggest that a technology's consequences be considered carefully before it is adopted.

The *neutral* view of communication technology holds that it has no significant effects on human behavior, and that people can be expected to behave in predictable ways whether they use a traditional telephone or a computer to communicate. Proponents of this view believe that the potential effects of technology on communication and behavior are exaggerated by utopians, dystopians, and others.

However, the *contingent* view of communication technology is well sup-

TABLE
11.1 **Six Concerns in the Analysis of
Communication Technology**

1. *Humans are agents.* Accept the fact that "humans are reflexively monitoring what goes on in a particular social system, that they are motivated by wants and aspirations, and that they have the power not to perform the prescription laid down by systems designers" (p. 312).

2. *Tacit knowledge should be respected.* "People know more about their lives than they can put into words. People do know how to handle practical affairs without being able to explain fully what they are really doing" (p. 312).

3. *Understanding is partial.* "There are always unacknowledged conditions for and unintended consequences of people's behavior" (p. 313).

4. *Technology is politically ambiguous.* While a technology can be used to promote dialogue and improve individual quality of life, the same technology can also be used to constrain, limit, and control.

5. *Informal communication needs to be acknowledged.* "Informal informing is an organizational fact . . . it is necessary to understand how formal information is mediated through various more or less structured patterns of informing" (p. 313).

6. *Counter-rational decision making should be acknowledged.* "The rational model is not a viable way of understanding the intricacies of modern business management. On the one hand it is questionable that decision-makers cognitively are able to cope with the complexity and amount of information needed to make rational decisions, and on the other hand, it is probable that all sorts of political and social pressures are called upon in everyday management" (pp. 313–14).

Source: Jan Mouritsen and Niels Bjorn-Andersen, "Understanding Third-Wave Information Systems," in C. Dunlop and R. Kling (eds.), *Computerization and Controversy* (San Diego: Academic Press, 1991), pp. 308–20.

---

ported by research. In this view, the effect of a given innovation depends on the context or situation in which it is adopted. For example, the health hazards associated with video display terminals (VDTs) (e.g., radiation exposure, headaches, eyestrain, sleeplessness, anxiety, and repetitive motion disorders) may be more the result of how an organization uses the technology (e.g., long working hours and poor design of work stations) than the technology itself (Smith et al., 1981; Steelman & Klitzman, 1985).

Another example is the computerized monitoring of employee productivity, wherein the frequency and speed of work are measured and stored by the computer and reviewed by management. The productivity of approximately six million U.S. workers is now monitored electronically, and the telephone and airline reservation industries are leaders in the use of this technology (Turnage, 1990). Employees' reactions have been mixed; while some employees consider electronic surveillance an invasion of their privacy, others believe it is useful in giving good performers greater recognition for their efforts (Bell-Detienne, 1992).

Most communication technologies, though designed for specific uses, take on other functions related to the individual user's needs (Poole & DeSanctis, 1990). The telephone answering machine, for instance, was designed to receive and record incoming calls; however, some people also use it as a call-screening device. Similarly, medical information systems designed to help physicians keep track of patients' prescriptions, diagnostic testing, and treatments are now used by pharmacists as well (Aydin & Rice, 1992). In Table 11.1, Jan Mouritsen and Niels Bjorn-Andersen (1991) identify six important considerations in the analysis of a communication technology.

A significant amount of research has been conducted on computer systems designed to support group decisions. These so-called *GDSS* or *group decision support systems* allow teams to retrieve obscure facts or other hard-to-find information instantaneously via a computer database. In addition, GDSS allows team members to communicate via multiple channels, thereby improving the distribution of information in the organization and promoting team members' involvement. Some studies of GDSS show that it enhances team decision making only under certain conditions (Poole & Holmes, 1995).

The successful implementation of a communication technology takes into account the social and political aspects of the organizational environment in which it will be used. The "rational" use of communication technology is "subjective, retrospective, and influenced by information provided by others" (Fulk, Schmitz, & Steinfeld, 1990, p. 123). According to Noshir Contractor and Eric Eisenberg (1990):

> There is no such thing as pure technology. To understand technology, one must first understand social relationships. . . . Everything about the adoption and uses of media is social. . . . Logical expectations for the adoption and use of the new media are rarely met. The pragmatics of technological communication must always be understood in the context of motives, paradoxes, and contradictions of everyday life. (p. 143)

SYNCHRONICITY AND MEDIA RICHNESS

Two particular aspects of communication technology are of special interest to communication scholars: synchronicity and media richness. *Synchronicity* refers to the capacity of a technology to allow for two-way communication. For example, a telephone is synchronous, but an answering machine allows the telephone to become asynchronous. Similarly, while most E-mail is asynchronous, the recent proliferation of chat rooms on the World Wide Web has created more possibilities for synchronicity. Both synchronous and asynchronous communication have their particular advantages. For instance, certain requests and work tasks are best approached via two-way communication, whereas other tasks may be well communicated and performed through asynchronous channels (e.g., when busy people communicate across time zones). However, asynchronous communication can lead people to make more contacts than they can reasonably handle (Gergen, 1992). This is why many people in high-status or high-visibility jobs avoid using voice and electronic mail systems.

Media richness, a concept introduced by Daft and Lengel (1984), refers to the number of channels of contact afforded by a communication medium, such that a letter would fall at the low end of media richness and face-to-face interaction would be at the high end of media richness. From a communication perspective, people tend to choose one medium over another in certain circumstances.

SECRECY AND PRIVACY ISSUES

The primary benefit of communication technology—the radical expansion of connections between people and institutions—is also its main liability. Every connection leaves a trail, one that might be followed and exploited by others for personal gain. Issues of privacy, secrecy, and even copyright in computer-aided interaction are currently under investigation in courts around the world. In most companies, for example, managers have access to employees' E-mail messages. Major credit-card companies follow consumer spending patterns very closely, including where transactions are made by clients. The effects of electronic surveillance on people's right to privacy will likely become a major issue in the future.

MEDIATED INTERPERSONAL COMMUNICATION

With the widespread use of telephones, fax machines, computers, and overnight delivery services, many interpersonal work relationships are routinely conducted by persons who never actually meet one another face-to-face. In addition, mediated forms of written communication are popular, particularly in international companies. For example, at Ryobi Manufacturing Company, a Japanese firm with several U.S. subsidiaries, more money is spent on faxes than on any other form of communication. The same is true of many Asian-owned firms that operate in the United States, where culture demands strict adherence to procedures and an ongoing flow of information about work processes. However, at Sagem-Lucas, a French and British partnership with U.S. subsidiaries, appointed representatives are sent to the United States for several weeks to be-

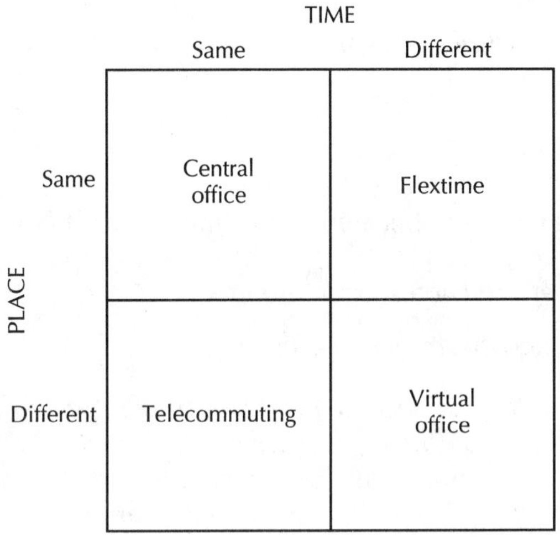

TIME

	Same	Different
Same	Central office	Flextime
Different	Telecommuting	Virtual office

PLACE

FIGURE 11.3
Varieties of Distributed Work

Source: C. Grantham, "The Virtual Office." *At Work* 4(5):1, 12–14.

come acquainted with business colleagues and the local culture. The representatives report back to the company's headquarters in Europe, where their on-site observations become the topic of internal memos, faxes, and computer-based communication.

Similar patterns of mediated communication are found in U.S. companies. According to Grantham (1995), the office of the future may be a *virtual office,* rather than a central office, if the current trend toward distributed work continues. While having all the usual functions of an office, a virtual office can be literally *anywhere* the user can gain access to a modem. Figure 11.3 shows four basic types of distributed work: central office work, flextime work, telecommunicating, and virtual office work. A 1994 study reported in Grantham of fourteen hundred distributed workers in the United States reveals that more than 50 percent are males earning in excess of $45,000 per year, only 34 percent have graduate degrees, and about half their work time is devoted to interacting with customers and co-workers. In addition, desktop computers, modems, and multiple phone lines serve their communication needs, while their productivity is up to 20 percent higher than that of nondistributed workers. Distributed workers also tend to experience less job-related stress.

The proliferation of computer networks on the Internet and World Wide Web may be analyzed in terms of our theory of creativity and constraint. On the one hand, computerized access to thousands of other people with similar interests may be an exhilarating, creative, and informative experience. On the other

Surfing Sickness

The following message appeared on the Internet in 1995.

To: Internet addiction support group

Subject: Literally got sick, surfing

I got on the Net . . . because I was convalescing from back surgery. Previously, being physically active, I had no time for the PC or the Internet. Initially, I spent only thirty to forty-five minutes on the PC, twice a day, exploring various bbs and doing infantile Net explorations. Then one night I woke up in the middle of the night and went on-line. I rationed myself to one hour for surfing. I needed reading glasses to focus on the screen. Sitting close enough to focus with my glasses caused me to strain my back (less than one week after surgery). After five and a half hours on the Net, my back ached from bending, my head ached from the eye strain, and I was nauseated from the distorted images I was processing visually. I remained disabled and sick in the stomach, pained in the neck and leg, and with a throbbing headache for at least twenty-four hours. . . .

My wife was disgusted with me. I couldn't believe I'd stayed on the Net so long. Since that time I have lost hundreds, maybe even thousands of dollars in unearned income due to

(continued)

hand, participation in a computer network may constrain the obsessive computer user (see Focus on Ethics 11.1).

SUMMARY

Strategy, image, strategic alignment, and communication technologies are all part of managing the total organization. Moreover, these factors work together, rather than separately, to influence both the employee's work life and the organization's fate. The meaning of any given strategy or the usefulness of any given communication technology depends on the situation or context in which it is

(continued)

> *unfinished proposals and projects. . . . I [have] lost rapport with friends and associates, missed deadlines on discount travel and airfares, [and been late] to appointments. . . . I've spent countless hours typing out messages like this to people I don't know and will probably never hear from. I've typed out more letters and messages since my back surgery . . . than in my entire life before then. My own kids since then have received no more than two or three notes from me in the snail mail. They won't get on the Net so I won't even write to them.*
>
> *My back surgery was so successful that after a few weeks I could do anything. . . . And yet I still gravitate to the PC several times a day. My wife is annoyed that my office here at the house is stacked with months of snail mail and other projects I used to do on a regular basis. I'm annoyed, too.*
>
> *But it's too much fun writing to you, whoever you are.*

Consider the following questions:

1. Do you know someone who is an overly involved Internet user? Why do you think this problem occurs? Is it a personal problem or one that affects society as a whole?
2. In what ways do face-to-face communication and on-line communication differ? How might these differences affect employees of organizations moving toward distributed types of work? What effect might they have on the organization's culture?
3. What advice would you give to the person who posted this message?

applied. Successful organizations, therefore, use strategic alignment to ensure that all aspects of a system reinforce the whole.

The potential effects of communication technology on the workplace are the subject of an ideological debate among theorists. However, communication technologies are recognized as powerful tools with the potential for positive or negative effects on organizations depending on how they are used in certain situations. Chief among these situational factors are organizational culture and management style. Although the many potential effects of computers, computer networks, and other forms of mediated communication are not yet known, it seems likely that Prasad's (1993) symbolic interactionist theory of computerization—which holds that the meaning of any technology is open to interpretation—is especially relevant in the organizational context.

C A S E   S T U D Y

A TALE OF TWO STRATEGIES:
ABC PROSPERED WHILE CBS BLINKED

NEW YORK—Back in the mid-1980s, they were a couple of bloated, unfocused TV networks, adrift in the rapidly changing media world. Then two rescuers rode in—one for each.

The end of the chapter in this tale of two networks came last week, and their fates could hardly be much more different. On Monday, Capital Cities-ABC Inc. announced a stunning deal to sell itself to Walt Disney Co. for $19 billion, combining superstars into a well-integrated production and distribution giant.

Tuesday CBS Inc.'s rescuer, New York tycoon Laurence Tisch, agreed to sell that network, too—for about $5 billion to Westinghouse Electric Corp. But that combination unites an odd couple of stragglers: a floundering industrial conglomerate and the weakest television network.

In 1986, no one would have bet on last week's twin earthquakes. ABC, for most of its life, had been broadcasting's also-ran, scrapping for every eyeball. CBS, for all its woes, was still known as the Tiffany Network.

Capital Cities and Tisch took divergent paths at almost every fork in the road.

From the start, the two rescuers were a study in contrasts—and expectations. Tisch was a celebrated investor with a record of spotting value in any industry he touched, from cigarettes to insurance to hotels. By 1986, Loews Corp., which he and his family controlled, owned nearly 25 percent of CBS's common stock. In the roaring 1980s, Wall Street believed gold-plated money men such as Tisch had the right remedy for any ailing company.

"He is doing everything every analyst and investor would love to do if they had the power: run CBS more like a business, find out what all these people do, and make more money in what is inherently a good business," an analyst at the now-defunct E. F. Hutton investment firm effused during Tisch's first months at the helm.

Meanwhile, Capital Cities was regarded as a drab team of penny-pinching station managers. Its top executives, Thomas Murphy and Daniel Burke, were little-known outsiders to New York's glitzy media world. They had started out running a tiny Albany, N.Y., UHF television station in a decrepit former home for aging nuns.

(continued)

(continued)

Both new owners promptly began cutting costs. Both shed employees by the hundreds, garaged limousines, canceled parties and slashed funds for news-division executives who used to make frequent jaunts to the London and Paris bureaus.

But right away, there were telling differences in management style and culture at CBS and ABC. Tisch brought in teams of management consultants, who roamed the halls of CBS's "Black Rock" headquarters tower on West 52nd Street, stirring anxiety and instability.

The CBS cutbacks came in several messy rounds. Many managers were kept in the dark about the timing and couldn't reassure subordinates that the cutbacks were finished. Soon the painful steps turned into a highly public soap opera, with daily installments funneled into the newspapers by a chorus of leakers within the network. A low point came in 1987, when Tisch and Howard Stringer, then CBS News president, wound up in an embarrassingly public bout of fingerpointing over which one had ordered cuts of more than 250 news-division positions.

At ABC, Murphy and Burke set out a new management structure just two weeks after taking over and carefully made their managers part of the cost-cutting effort. Within six months, they carried out a single, decisive round of personnel cutbacks and then vowed to employees that the worst of the pain was over—a promise they kept. There were virtually no leaks, no histrionics and no distracting publicity.

When it came to ABC's portfolio of businesses, the Capital Cities team eschewed harsh cuts. Even though they had to trim fat, they gambled that a TV network would operate best as one piece of a well-synchronized media machine, with a slew of other production and distribution properties. So they kept nearly all of ABC's stations and cable investments; the only sales were those required by regulatory restrictions.

Tisch, by contrast, cut assets to the bone and built up a mountain of cash. He sold CBS's magazine division for $650 million, its book-publishing operations for $500 million, a song-publishing division for $125 million and its records unit for $2.2 billion.

"With 100 percent hindsight, selling records was the first major thing that CBS did wrong, although it's understandable why Tisch did it, as a financial player," says John Reidy, an analyst at Smith Barney. "The assets sale didn't really need to be done, but they provided money to buy back stock."

Turning CBS into a pure-play broadcasting company wasn't a crack-

(continued)

(continued)

pot idea. The age of the great conglomerates was ending, and Wall Street was cheering such companies as Gulf & Western and International Telephone & Telegraph for simplifying their empires.

But in hindsight, CBS's play was too pure—and the company was, in effect, becoming a baseball team with no infield or outfield. In the late 1980s, when the U.S. economy took a downturn and CBS's prime-time fortunes went into a free fall, its broadcasting business became exposed.

Source: The Tampa Tribune-Times, Sunday, August 6, 1995.

ASSIGNMENTS

1. Describe the strategies pursued by ABC and CBS. How are they similar to or different from the types of strategies discussed in this chapter?
2. Why has ABC's strategy been the most successful? What might other organizations learn from the approach taken by ABC?
3. Describe the strategic alignment processes undertaken at ABC and CBS. Do you see any evidence of the original or new 7-S model of strategic alignment?

The Future of Organizational Communication

We look out into the future, trying our best to make wise decisions, only to find ourselves staring into . . . widespread uncertainties. How do we decide [on a] career path . . . when it's not clear what industries will exist in 10 or 15 years? How do we plan [for] our children's education . . . ? As we face each of these problems, we confront a deeper dilemma: How do we strike a balance between prediction—believing that we can see past these uncertainties when in fact we can't—and paralysis—letting the uncertainties freeze us into inactivity?

• Lawrence Wilkinson, "How to Build Scenarios" (1995)

In a world that is constantly changing, . . . the most important skill to acquire now is to learn how to learn.

• John Naisbett, *Megatrends 2000* (1990)

QUESTIONS

FOR DISCUSSION

- What global challenges will organizations face in the future?

- Which technological developments are most likely to influence organizations and communication in the future?

- How will our decisions about communication, organizations, and society affect the ecology of the planet?

- How can scenario planning help us plan for the future?

- How can a balance of creativity and constraint be achieved through communication?

In this final chapter of the book, we explore the future roles of communication in organizations. First, we identify the major issues that will likely dominate organizational life in the future. Next, we focus on the need for organizations and their members to commit themselves to a lifetime of learning new skills, new technologies, and new ways of organizing in order to survive. We also look at the moral dimensions of organizational communication, particularly in relation to ethics and ecology. In addition, we consider how scenario planning can help us think and make decisions about organizational communication in the future. Finally, in returning to our questions about creativity and constraint, we offer a communicative means of confronting the limitations of individualism and, therefore, of transcending this tension.

Our exploration of what the future may hold for organizational communication is intended to contribute to what Charles Garfield (1992) calls the "new story of business." In this story, organizations are characterized as dynamic, living ecosystems that promote sustainable human and environmental growth, that explore workable alternatives to hierarchy, and that support forms of organizing in which all employees are treated as full participants.

The Learning Organization

In our rapidly changing world, *learning organizations* have a distinct advantage. Comprised of people who not only learn from past mistakes but also question the assumptions that led to those mistakes, learning organizations are better equipped to deal with change (Argyris & Schon, 1978; Senge, 1991, 1994; Steier, 1989). Yet how does a company become a learning organization whose members question existing assumptions and devise new ways of doing business? The three basic requirements include learning (1) basic skills, (2) new technologies, and (3) new ways of organizing.

LEARNING BASIC SKILLS

Most organizational practitioners, educators, and politicians agree that the U.S. educational system does a poor job of providing students with even the most basic job skills. The U.S. Labor Secretary's Commission on Achieving Necessary Skills (1991) identifies three foundational abilities and five learning areas as most important to success in the workplace (see Table 12.1). Creativity and learning how to learn, sociability, and skills in teamwork, negotiation, feedback, and using new technologies are among other basic skills that many high school graduates do not possess. In addition to negatively affecting people's quality of life, widespread basic skills deficits pose a threat to the business world. Quality and customer service suffer in any industry that must depend on an inadequately skilled workforce. In an attempt to deal with this problem, many fast-food chains have resorted to equipping cash registers with pictures of food items rather than monetary figures. Similarly, a growing number of manufacturing firms are re-designing complex, good-paying positions into simple, low-paying, dead-end jobs. The result is a downward spiral of quality, service, job skills, wages, and employee self-esteem.

One proposed solution to these serious problems is to establish workplace literacy programs designed to teach basic skills to employees. These programs, which are offered by private companies, public agencies, or corporations them-selves, vary widely in their focus and intensity. For example, some programs fo-cus on job-related language skills, whereas others teach a broad array of basic skills that are useful in work and personal situations. In addition, the programs vary in terms of length (from forty to four hundred hours). While some training programs are sensitive to employees' different needs, others make no such dis-tinctions.

The most successful programs thus far are those initiated and taught by the companies themselves. At American Honda and General Motors, for instance, databases are used in some locations to match employees' level of education and skill with job opportunities. However, such programs are rare, and even when they do exist, they cannot adequately address the underlying problems in the U.S. educational system. As Laura Tyson points out (1991), "the share of the nation's economy invested . . . in education and training, children's programs, infrastructure, and civilian research and development has plummeted 40% since 1980. America ranks behind all its major competitors in each of these cat-egories" (p. D2). Although a tremendous amount of effort will be directed at teaching basic skills to employees of the twenty-first century, without changes in the educational system and in the nation's spending priorities, those efforts will do little to solve the problem.

LEARNING NEW TECHNOLOGIES

As we move from the industrial age into the new information age, we are wit-nessing an unprecedented increase in the rate at which information becomes obsolete. This is indeed a unique occurrence in history. Previously, when infor-mation aged no faster than people did, engineers, physicians, and others could as a rule depend on their education and training because the fundamental tech-nology underlying their work remained the same throughout their careers. But this is no longer the case. The life cycle of any given technology is limited. In the computer and aerospace industries, for example, where a skill set lasts only five to ten years, workers in their forties and fifties are discovering that their techni-cal knowledge and old set of skills are less important than their ability to learn a new set of skills. The recent demand for managers who can start and operate a

Necessary Workplace Skills

12.1

THE FOUNDATION

Basic: Reading, writing, mathematics, speaking, and listening

Thinking: Creativity, making decisions, solving problems, seeing things in the mind's eye, knowing how to learn, reasoning

Personal qualities: Responsibility, self-esteem, sociability, self-management, and integrity

JOB SKILLS

Resources: Allocating time, money, materials, space, and staff

Interpersonal: Working on teams, teaching, serving customers, leading, negotiating, and working well with people from culturally diverse backgrounds

Information: Acquiring and evaluating data, organizing and maintaining files, interpreting and communicating, and using computers to process information

Systems: Understanding social, organizational, and technological systems; monitoring and correcting performance; and designing improved systems

Technology: Selecting equipment and tools, applying technology to specific tasks, and maintaining and trouble-shooting technologies

Source: U.S. Labor Secretary's Commission on Achieving Necessary Skills, June 1991.

---

business on the Internet is an example of how some people manage to seize an opportunity afforded by a new technology and learn the new skills they need along the way to succeed. Learning, once primarily an activity of the young, is now a lifelong project, as well as the cornerstone of global competitiveness and economic success.

In the twenty-first century, recertification and reeducation will be common in all professions, which, in turn, will alter the fundamental role of primary, secondary, and college education. The education that people receive in the first twenty years of their lives will focus not so much on conveying information (which will become obsolete before long) but on helping people learn how to think and learn. Still, certain content areas will grow in importance. Two wideranging technologies will likely have the greatest impact on organizations: biotechnology and virtual reality.

Biotechnology

Over the past decade, enormous amounts of time and money have been invested in *biotechnology*—the purposeful creation or modification of genetic material (DNA) for commercial applications. For example, pharmaceutical companies have developed gene therapies to treat certain diseases, supermarkets sell genetically altered produce that has a longer shelf life, and the U.S. Army is implementing a gene bank to facilitate the positive identification of soldiers.

The potential uses of biotechnology are both amazing and frightening, as are the legal and ethical challenges to this line of work. But biotechnology also will have a major impact on organizations. In a recent contract between Merck Pharmaceuticals and the government of Costa Rica, for example, Costa Rica agrees to send small parcels of biological samples (bushels of twigs, packages of ground-up caterpillars) to Merck for possible use in research and development. For any product that Merck develops from a Costa Rican sample, the country receives a percentage of the pharmaceutical company's profits. The arrangement is interesting in other respects as well. It suggests, for instance, that a country "owns the rights" to its biological resources. But once Merck identifies a biological specimen that can be developed into a product, the company does not need any additional material from Costa Rica to manufacture the product. Based on the genetic code found in the original sample, scientists can re-create or synthesize the material, which suggests that Costa Rica is selling not biological resources but biological *information* that provides the clues for genetic engineering.

In their award-winning book, *2020 Vision,* Stan Davis and Bill Davidson (1991) discuss biotechnology in a historical framework. They argue that we are presently in the latter half of an information economy, and that by the year 2020 a major shift toward a bioeconomy will make genetics as important to business success as information is today. Noting that the most successful corporations of the past two decades are those that have taken advantage of the opportunities afforded by new information technologies, Davis and Davidson persuasively argue that business success in the twenty-first century will mean pursuing a strategy, product, or service that is based on some aspect of biotechnology.

Virtual Reality

The term *virtual reality* is used to describe a technology that allows a user to experience imaginary worlds in strikingly realistic sensory detail. For example, one type of virtual reality requires the participant to wear a device, such as wraparound goggles or a headset, which can simulate a realistic scene (such as a battlefield or crime scene) as well as adjust the sensory input based on the user's command (such as by movement of the hands or head).

Two familiar precursors to virtual reality are *computer-aided design* (*CAD*) and *holography.* CAD allows engineers, graphic artists, and others to work with their drawings in a three-dimensional computerized format. CAD also permits the movement or rotation of objects in the computer-generated diagrams, which eliminates the time-consuming task of drawing several versions of a building's floor plan or a graphic design by hand. Holography is also an advanced form of image projection whereby three-dimensional scenes appear on a flat surface or are suspended in the air in front of the viewer (such as in some video games and on some of the rides at Disneyland). Holograms will soon be used in engineering and design as well as in education, where, for example, holographic images of three-dimensional molecules spinning in space will appear in the engineer's drafting "box" or will be suspended in air in the chemistry classroom.

Other potential uses of virtual reality may include "driving" a virtual car as a student driver or "walking through" a virtual prehistoric scene during science class. Harold Rheinhold (1991) has chronicled many present-day uses of this growing technology; for example, some pilot training programs now use virtual reality to simulate flight conditions rather than the old-fashioned flight simulators. In entertainment, education, health care, and other areas, numerous applications of virtual reality will be forthcoming.

LEARNING NEW WAYS OF ORGANIZING

As contemporary organizations struggle to make empowerment a reality, finding workable alternatives to the traditional hierarchy has been difficult. While many companies are implementing some form of the self-directed or semiautonomous work team, others are redesigning themselves in more radical ways.

Some of the most exciting developments in alternative organizational forms have been seen in Scandinavia. Consider, for example, Skaltek AB, a Swedish company that designs and manufactures packaging machines for the wire industry. The company has ninety employees and an average annual revenue of $17 million. In 1972, Oystein Skallenberg founded the company in a small basement shop, with the assumption that human potential is unlimited when it is allowed to grow. Since that time, Skaltek AB has grown in innovative ways:

> No hierarchy or titles exist at Skaltek. Members of the staff are called "responsible persons," not "employees." Openness is total; everyone in the company has access to all information. Each morning the entire staff . . . exchanges information about the volume of orders, the cash situation, and similar matters.
>
> Control, as such, does not exist, not even quality control. Everyone is . . . personally responsible [for the quality of their work]. On each unit of the packaging machines that are manufactured there is a little aluminum label on which is written: "Quality-Security. I am responsible," along with the signature of the person who has done the work. If there are any questions about the work later

in the production chain, people don't turn to a . . . supervisor but go to the one "responsible." (Osterberg, 1992, p. 10)

Skaltek AB and other firms like it often have very low profit margins (by American standards) because they operate within a cultural environment that values full employment over profit maximization. But some of these companies thrive despite the absence of many traditional organizational characteristics. Their performance has led many observers to question the effectiveness of traditional ways of organizing.

Other avenues of change have been pursued by companies engaged in participative action research or proposed by advocates of ecofeminism.

Participative Action Research

Participative action research (PAR), developed in Scandinavia, is pursued by companies interested in promoting a more democratic, politically equal, and socially fair work environment. PAR professionals conduct organizational research projects that are specially designed to bring about social change. In Norway, for example, participative action researchers share the following four assumptions (Elden & Levin, 1991):

1. Democracy and economic improvement help to ensure people's right to good-quality jobs.
2. Good organizations maximize human potential, equalize power, and promote self-management.
3. Researchers are co-learners rather than experts in charge of change.
4. The political infrastructure supports workplace democracy through labor legislation, official agreements, and traditions.

For students of organizational communication, PAR embodies many of the values of employee empowerment associated with effective communication. In addition, the participative action research process relies heavily on the dialogue between researchers and organizational members in creating a new interpretive framework. According to Max Elden and Morten Levin (1991):

> Empowering participation occurs between insiders and outsiders in what we call cogenerative dialogue. Both insiders and outsiders operate out of their initial frames of reference but communicate at a level where frames can be changed and new frames generated. Exchange on a level that affects one's frame of reference is a much more demanding form of communication than mere information exchange. (p. 134)

In other words, PAR uses dialogue itself to turn traditional organizations toward employee empowerment and participation.

Ecofeminism

Ecofeminism is a theoretical reinterpretation of human history in which archaeological evidence is used to support the claim that "partnership" societies existed well before the "dominator" societies of today (Eisler, 1987; Milbrath, 1989; Spretnak, 1991). Characterized by equality in male–female relationships, partnership societies also viewed power as a source of nurturance rather than of domination (Eisler, 1987). Ecofeminists thus believe that we live in an interconnected global web rather than a hierarchy, and they advocate a "decentralized global movement . . . founded on common interests yet celebrat[ing] diversity and oppos[ing] all forms of domination and violence" (King, 1989, pp. 19–20). By emphasizing their opposition to all types of domination, ecofeminists view the domination of women and the exploitation of nature as part of the same problem—the problem of hierarchy.

Communication researchers Connie Bullis and Hollis Glaser (1992) champion ecofeminism as a framework for identifying alternative forms of organizing that are decentralized, small, and egalitarian, and that focus on local concerns. Further research is needed to determine how ecofeminist ideas might be applied in organizations.

The Moral Dimensions of Organizational Communication

The growing concerns about *communication ethics* and *ecological responsibility* will continue to hold importance in the future. In both cases, communication plays a role in facilitating moral judgment.

COMMUNICATION ETHICS

Ethical issues are not new to organizations, and many business schools and corporations require their students and employees to receive formal training in ethical decision making. Why? Because, since 1985, more than two-thirds of Fortune 500 firms have been convicted of serious crimes, ranging from fraud to the illegal dumping of hazardous wastes. In addition, employees who make poor business decisions also tend to take unethical actions aimed at covering up their mistakes.

Indeed, most business decisions involve ethical choices, and communication is at the heart of any ethical dispute (Redding, 1991). Moreover, as some scholars argue, theories of human communication tend to assume that people tell the truth, but in many cases, people do not (Bok, 1988; Goodall, 1996). In our culture, for instance, "telling white lies" and "stretching the truth" are more or less condoned. In pursuing a career or searching for a job, we are advised to

Who's Responsible?

Recently, a federal court ruled against a manufacturer of oil pipeline for showing a blatant disregard of environmental standards in the construction and installation of their product. The judge added that her decision was meant to "put the entire pipeline industry on notice" that there will be significant consequences for future abuses of this kind.

An interesting wrinkle in this and many similar cases is that the complainants in the lawsuit are not content to seek damages from the offending company—they are filing criminal charges against the owners of the company which, if won, could lead to significant financial penalties and even jail time.

What is your opinion on the ethics of prosecuting owners and senior managers for the wrongdoings of their companies? On the one hand, the idea behind the corporation is to protect individual owners in exchange for their willingness to take significant financial risk. On the other hand, too many people are injured or killed by supposedly "nameless" corporations which do, in fact, implement the decisions of actual human beings.

As a consumer and citizen, to what degree do you feel owners and managers should be liable for the actions of their company? If you were to start a business of your own, would your opinion be different? Does the global nature of the economy and of many companies affect your opinion on this issue?

---

paint only positive portraits of ourselves and our past employment experiences. (See Focus on Ethics 12.1.)

Terence Mitchell and William Scott (1990) argue that "the ethic of personal advantage" has led to a general lowering of the standards of business ethics. Associated with the ethic of personal advantage are "(1) a present versus a future orientation; (2) an instrumental as opposed to a substantive focus; and (3) an emphasis on individualism contrasted with community" (pp. 25–26). In addition, the capitalist system has created a culture of denial in which businesspeople remain generally unconcerned about the effects of their activities on others. Although ethics education can strive to build moral character, at some point our society will need to address the underlying problems of the business culture. As an alternative to the typical business ethics course, which through problem solving and case studies teaches the rules of ethical conduct, Mitchell and Scott (1990) suggest that moral discourse may be more effective:

> Moral discourse is a process of rhetorical engagement by students and professors in free and open forums of conversation and debate. One tries to persuade others of the truth of his or her point of view on moral issues. In the process, widely divergent opinions are expressed and each individual is exposed to alternative propositions about values. The whole point is to provide knowledge of moral options and the opportunity to choose among different value systems. . . . The function of ethics courses should be to instill an open, moral, loving, humane, and broadly informed mentality, so that students may come to see life's trials and business's ethical challenges as occasions to live through with integrity and courage. (p. 29)

ECOLOGICAL RESPONSIBILITY

The deterioration of our physical environment (red tides, deforestation, acid rain, toxic waste) and the rapid depletion of natural resources are the results of our inability or refusal to see the world as an interconnected system (Hawken, 1992; Mitchell & Scott, 1990). Cancer rates in areas known for industrial pollution are on the increase, and many by-products of human industrialization threaten the health of people and the planet. As Charlene Spretnak's (1991) dark postmodern vision intimates, business organizations *have the potential to be* among the most thoughtless enemies of nature:

> Within the value structure of the intensification of competition in production and consumption that will characterize the focus of life in the global market and mass culture that are presently being constructed, the felt connections between the person and the family, the community, the bioregion, the country, other peoples, other species, the Earthbody, and the cosmos merely get in the way. (p. 9)

We are only now beginning to understand that the exploitation of our natural resources will create an unsustainable world if limits are not imposed. According to James Robertson (1985), shifting from hyperexpansionism to a more sane, humane, and ecologically safe world in the future will mean reevaluating our most basic assumptions. Rose (1983) argues that this will require a return to forms of "caring labor"—nurturing and helping—that have been devalued by expansionist systems (Rose, 1983).

But promoting a stable and sustainable ecological future will also involve important socioeconomic and political changes. Consider, for example, the U.S. economy, which for about fifty years has been highly dependent on the military. Following World War II, the U.S. government allocated a substantial part of the federal budget to developing the military into a powerful industrial complex, thereby creating jobs and making the military a major customer of many of the nation's largest corporations. However, the trade-offs involved in a military-based economy have been enormous; for example, with the money allocated to developing and manufacturing one intercontinental ballistic missile (ICBM) the nation could instead feed 50 million children, build 160,000 schools, and open 340,000 health-care centers (Sivard, 1983). Still, a military-based economy supports the ideals of business ownership in the United States (even though only 2 percent of American families own businesses that control 54 percent of the nation's assets). The end of the Cold War has raised questions about the relevance of a military-based economy and has initiated a trend toward shifting resources away from the military. But dismantling such a vast military empire will be difficult, given the negative consequences of this effort on the many people employed by defense contractors or the military itself. Proposals to shrink military spending also raise important questions about our national security, which at times continues to seem at risk.

Most decisions about ecological issues also involve significant economic and personal trade-offs. The twenty-first century will be marked by increased concern about how our choices affect the well-being of the planet and ourselves. In one sense, the movement toward sustainability is rooted in systems theory, in that both recognize that survival depends on attending to the needs and requirements of the whole. According to Spretnak (1991):

> The ecologizing of consciousness is far more radical than ideologies and strategies of the existing political forms . . . seem to have realized. They often try to tack ecology onto programs born on instrumental rationality, scientific reductionism, and the modern belief that further advances in the manipulation of nature for human ends will deliver a future filled with peace, freedom, and goodwill. It seems quite unlikely that political versions of democracy that are steeped in these values of modernity [and] that have proven so deficient can serve as the vehicles for transformation . . . into our new relationship with the entire Earth community and our own potential. It is already clear that visionary, political developments lag behind the ecological and spiritual awakening. Increasingly, moral authority lies less in official position than in wisdom, in an experiential sense of the interrelated nature of our reality. (p. 229)

Scenario Planning: A Guide to the Future of Organizational Communication

Senior managers at large corporations use a technique called *scenario planning* to help them make decisions about the future. Scenario planning attempts to make predictions about the future based on current trends. Consulting firms that specialize in scenario planning are successful because their predictions are more often accurate than inaccurate. Scenario planners, rather than recommending a decision based on a single scenario, suggest solutions to current challenges that will play out well across various future scenarios. Known as articulating a *robust scenario,* this strategy involves constructing multiple, plausible narratives about the future that focus on large-scale cultural, political, environmental, technological, and economic engines of change. The point is to identify the major factors that are most likely to affect a company's future (Wilkinson, 1995).

Scenario planners begin with a single issue or question in order to narrow their focus. For example, let's consider this question: *What is the future of organizational communication?* The next step in scenario planning is to identify current trends or factors that are likely to shape the course of events in the future. The following list identifies major issues related to organizational communication:

Cultural factors: How will organizational communication be affected by changing consumer markets (e.g., aging baby boomers and Generation Xers)? Will the Internet be used primarily for entertainment or will it create a demand for new businesses? How will the increasingly diverse workforce affect people's decisions about careers and where to live? How will a retreat from public assistance, increases in the possession of firearms, and a rise in workplace violence influence corporate demands for security and worker surveillance?

Political factors: How will the policies of new world leaders influence the trend toward globalization? How will tax legislation affect the new generation of outsourcers? How will the regulation of information on the Internet affect society? How will the powers of multinational corporations be negotiated by the courts when individual or national rights are violated?

Environmental factors: Will nations conserve or exploit natural resources? How might the automobile industry recover from a potential oil crisis? How will future methods of waste management impact local economies?

Technological factors: How will the Internet influence corporate training and development? How might a computer virus be used by terrorists?

Economic factors: How will people deal with job losses caused by technological advancement and global competitiveness? How might the structure of industry change in response to direct-to-satellite communications systems? How will the educational system ensure that people have the new skills required for success?

Once the major issues are identified, scenario planners turn to the critical uncertainties associated with those issues (e.g., the uncertainty about whether or-

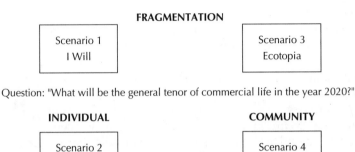

FIGURE 12.1
A Scenario-Planning Matrix

Source: Lawrence Wilkinson, "How to Build Scenarios," *Wired* (1995): 4–81.

ganizations will continue to be the model on which most other institutions are based). The idea at this stage is to limit the search to a few critical uncertainties and issues so that a matrix of four possible scenarios may be developed. Figure 12.1 shows four scenarios for this question posed by *Wired* magazine: "What will be the general tenor of commercial life in the year 2020?" (qtd. in Wilkinson, 1995, p. 78). The matrix has two axes: the *individual/community axis,* which allows us to speculate about the future based on individual versus communal values, and the *fragmentation/coherence axis,* which allows us to speculate about the future stability or instability of society. The four scenarios developed by this matrix are as follows:

1. *I Will:* the quadrant where individualism is increasingly free from the control of large organizations. In this scenario of the future, the Internet has become the medium through which people realize their desires and perform a few, relatively unimportant social duties. Through privatization, government has been replaced by a large electronic marketplace and centralized institutions have been replaced by individuals who act as both producers and consumers and whose loyalty is to a set of tools, knowledge, and skills.
2. *Consumerland:* the quadrant where individual desires are fulfilled by large social and corporate centers. In this scenario of the future, the Internet is the medium through which corporations deliver marketing messages and products tailored directly to individuals' unique preferences. Unlike I-will, however, in this scenario government plays an active role in regulating the activities of corporations, whereas social organizations serve the individual's needs. The citizen is thus primarily a consumer who is served by society.

3. *Ecotopia:* the quadrant marked by a sense of community and a strong social center. In this scenario of the future, widely shared ecological values have emerged among people who voluntarily embrace cohesion, cooperation, and reduced consumption, which have been backed by legislation and corporate policies. Government plays a significant role in supporting the commonwealth.

4. *The New Civics:* the quadrant where values are shared but in many small, competing groups. In this scenario of the future, a decentralized world of tribes, clans, and networks exists. Each group builds and enjoys the benefits of community but without the help of a central government. Thus, government's influence is eclipsed by that of these emergent groups. Small—often deadly—conflicts among tribes pop up continually around the globe. People's primary concern is to be good members of their group, promoting feelings of pride, heroism, and belonging.

The primary value of scenario planning is not in the potential accuracy of the predictions it generates but in the way it encourages us to think about the future and to plan our responses accordingly.

Creativity and Constraint: A New Interpretation

As we live our lives through institutions—schools, organizations, churches, marriages, and so on—we seek a balance between autonomy and dependence, freedom and conformity, creativity and constraint. However, the notion of balance in any context is also one of human interpretation or construction. Moreover, individualism plays a role in how people variously interpret the concept of balance.

According to Robert Bellah et al. in *Habits of the Heart* (1985) and *The Good Society* (1991), the language and ideology of individualism, particularly in the contexts of the family and organization, act as significant obstacles to what people desire most—a sense of belonging to a community. Moreover, they argue, extreme forms of individualism may lead to exploitation when people feel isolated from others and the world and have no sense of belonging. In this sense, then, Bellah et al. (1991) define a "good society" as one that is consistent with ecofeminist ideals:

> Americans have pushed the logic of exploitation about as far as it can go. It seems to lead not only to failure at the highest levels, where the pressure for short-term payoff in business and government destroys the capacity for thinking ahead, whether in the nation or in the metropolis, but also to personal and

familial breakdown in the lives of our citizens. . . . [We propose] a new paradigm, which we . . . call the pattern of cultivation . . . [which] attempt[s] to find, in today's circumstances, a social and environmental balance, a recovery of meaning and purpose in our lives together, giving attention to the natural and cultural endowment we want to hand down to our children and grandchildren, and avoiding the distractions that have confused us in the past. (p. 271)

In their vision of a good society, Bellah et al. (1991) assume that most problems in society today can be attributed to our general unwillingness or inability to face reality and our tendency to engage ourselves in denial. Similarly, Mitchell and Scott (1990) see the ethic of personal advantage as an obstacle to open dialogue and the acceptance of alternative worldviews. At a still deeper level, Bellah et al. (1991) hint at the potential rewards of living in a "good society":

We can indeed try genuinely to attend to the world around us and to the meanings we discover as we interact with that world, and hope to realize in our own experience that we are part of a universal community, making sense of our lives as deeply connected to each other. As we enlarge our attention to include the natural universe and the ultimate ground that it expresses and from which it comes, we are sometimes swept with a feeling of thankfulness, of grace, to be able to participate in a world that is both terrifying and exquisitely beautiful. At such moments we feel like celebrating the joy and mystery we participate in. (p. 285)

Communication helps us cope with feelings of alienation—whether in love, at work, or in society. Through communication, we construct stories about ourselves and our roles in society, organizations, families, and other social institutions that define, justify, and explain both who we are and what we do. We can get so emotionally attached to our identities that dialogue becomes difficult and it becomes increasingly hard to work together (Sennett, 1978). However, as postmodern theorists note, identity is a human construction, one made from the stories we tell about ourselves (Hyde, 1995). Moreover, identity limits human potential by defining who we are, rather than who we can become. By seeing ourselves as part of the large, interconnected web of life, we also see ourselves as capable of much more than identity permits. A rigid view of one's identity leads to an unwillingness to engage in open dialogue and the belief that one exists "in" and against the world, which, in turn, foster denial and exploitation (Bellah et al., 1991). Even in everyday communication we reinforce our belief in our identity, act in defensive and aggressive ways to protect our identity, and thereby turn difference into opposition and create the very conditions that we fear.

Nonetheless, communication plays a role in reenvisioning ourselves as parts of an interconnected web or whole. Quality dialogue, which is marked by a respect for and tolerance of others, is the key to building a true community in the future. It encourages us to position ourselves in the world and to take responsibility for what our world can become in the future.

Finally, if each of us is an expression of the whole, then creativity and constraint are inseparable parts of the same activity—of life itself.

Summary

Above all, successful organizing today is characterized by a commitment to learning. This learning takes many forms, from acquiring basic skills, to learning new technologies (such as biotechnology and virtual reality) and new ways of organizing (such as those suggested by Participative Action Research and ecofeminism). In each case, the principles of dialogue create an attitude of openness that permits people to let go of old patterns and explore new possibilities.

No method of organizing, however, is free of moral or ethical implications. In particular, the ethic of personal advantage and the inability to ecologize consciousness perpetuate a me-first attitude in communicating and organizing that is hard to overcome. Our best hope as a species is to learn how to think together and build future organizational structures that are broadly moral, ecologically sustainable, and wholly supportive of communication and community.

References

Ackoff, R. (1957). Towards a behavioral theory of communication. *Management Science* 4:218–234.

Adams, J. (1980). Interorganizational processes and organizational boundary activities. In L. L. Cummings & B. Staw, eds., *Research in organizational behavior.* Vol. 2 (pp. 321–355). Greenwich, Conn.: JAI Press.

Adorno, T. (1989). *Kierkegaard: The construction of the aesthetic.* Minneapolis: University of Minnesota Press.

Adorno, T., & Horkheimer, M. (1972). *Dialectic of enlightenment.* New York: Herder and Herder.

Ahrne, G. (1990). *Agency and organization.* London: Sage Publications.

Albrecht, K. (1992). *The only thing that matters: Bringing the power of the customer into the center of your business.* New York: HarperBusiness.

Albrecht, T., & Adelman, M. (1987). *Communicating social support.* Beverly Hills, Calif.: Sage Publications.

Albrecht, T., & Hall, B. (1991). Facilitating talk about new ideas: The role of personal relationships in organizational innovation. *Communication Monographs* 58: 273–288.

Aldrich, H., & Pfeffer, J. (1976). Environments of organizations. *Annual Review of Sociology* 2: 79–105.

Alexander, G., & Giesen, B. (1987). From reduction to linkage: The long view of the micro–macro debate. In J. Alexander, ed., *Action and its environments.* New York: Columbia University Press.

Allen, M., & Caillouet, R. (1994). Legitimation endeavors: Impression management strategies used by an organization in crisis. *Communication Monographs* 61: 44–62.

Altman, S., Valenzi, E., & Hodgetts, R. (1985). *Organizational behavior: Theory and practice.* New York: Academic Press.

Alvesson, M. (1993). *Cultural perspectives on organizations.* New York: Cambridge University Press.

Anderson, J. (1987). *Communication research: Issues and methods.* New York: McGraw-Hill.

Anderson, W. T. (1995). *The truth about the truth.* New York: Tarcher/Putnam.

Arendt, H. (1971). *The life of the mind.* San Diego: Harcourt Brace Jovanovich.

Argyris, C. (1957). *Personality and organization.* New York: Harper & Row.

Argyris, C. (1994). Good communication that blocks learning. *Harvard Business Review,* July–August, pp. 77–85.

Argyris, C., & Schon, D. (1978). *Organizational learning: A theory of action perspective.* Reading, Mass.: Addison-Wesley.

Aronowitz, S., & DiFazio, W. (1994). *The jobless future*. Minneapolis: University of Minnesota Press.

Ashford, S., & Cummings, L. (1983). Feedback as an individual resource: Personal strategies of creating information. *Organizational Behavior and Human Performance* 32: 370–398.

Atwood, M. (1990). Adolescent socialization into work environments. Unpublished Master's thesis, Department of Occupational Science, University of Southern California.

Atkouf, O. (1992). Management and theories of organizations in the 1990's: Toward a critical radical humanism? *Academy of Management Review* 17: 407–431.

Axley, S. (1984). Managerial and organizational communication in terms of the conduit metaphor. *Academy of Management Review* 9: 428–437.

Aydin, C. (1989). Occupational adaptation to computerized medical information systems. *Journal of Health and Social Behavior* 30: 163–179.

Aydin, C., & Rice, R. (1992). Bringing social worlds together: Computers as catalysts for new interactions in health care organizations. *Journal of Health and Social Behavior* 33: 168–185.

Bachrach, P., & Baratz, M. (1962). Two faces of power. *American Political Science Review* 56: 947–952.

Baird, J. (1977). *The dynamics of organizational communication*. New York: Harper & Row.

Baker, B. (1991). Safety risks: The price of productivity. *Los Angeles Times,* October 6, pp. 35–36.

Bakhtin, M. (1981). *The dialogic imagination*. Trans. C. Emerson and M. Holquist. Austin: University of Texas Press.

Bakhtin, M. (1984). *Problems of Dostoevsky's Poetics*. Trans. M. Holquist. Austin: University of Texas Press.

Bakhtin, M. (1986). *Speech genres and other late essays*. Trans. C. Emerson. Minneapolis: University of Minnesota Press.

Bales, R., & Strodtbeck, F. (1960). Phases in group problem solving. In D. Cartwright & A. Zander, eds., *Group dynamics: Research and theory* (pp. 624–638). New York: Harper & Row.

Banta, M. (1993). *Taylored lives: Narrative productions in the age of Taylor, Veblen, and Ford*. Chicago: University of Chicago Press.

Bantz, C. (1993). *Understanding organizations: Interpreting organizational communication cultures*. Columbia, S.C.: University of South Carolina Press.

Barker, J., & Tompkins, P. (1994). Identification in the self-managing organization: Characteristics of target and tenure. *Human Communication Research* 21: 223–240.

Barley, S. (1983). Semiotics and the study of occupational and organizational culture. *Administrative Science Quarterly* 23: 393–413.

Barley, S. (1986). Technology as an occasion for structuring: Evidence from observations of CT scanners and the social order of radiology departments. *Administrative Science Quarterly* 31: 78–108.

Barnard, C. (1938–1968). *The functions of the executive*. Cambridge, Mass.: Harvard University Press.

Barnet, R., & Cavanagh, J. (1994). *Global dreams*. New York: Simon & Schuster.

Barnlund, D. (1994). *Communicative styles of Japanese and Americans*. Belmont, Calif.: Wadsworth.

Bartlett, C., & Ghoshal, S. (1994). Changing the role of top management: Beyond strategy to purpose. *Harvard Business Review*, November–December, 79–88.

Bastien, D., & Hostager, T. (1988). Jazz as a process of organizational innovation. *Communication Research* 15: 582–602.

Bateson, G. (1972). *Steps to an ecology of mind.* New York: Ballantine.

Bateson, M. C., & Bateson, G. (1987). *Angels fear: Towards an epistemology of the sacred.* New York: Bantam Books.

Baudrillard, J. (1983). *Simulations.* New York: Semiotext(e).

Baudrillard, J. (1988). *America.* London: Verso.

Baudrillard, J. (1990). *Cool memories.* London: Verso.

Bavelas, A. (1951). Communication patterns in task oriented groups. In D. Lerner & H. Laswell, eds., *The policy sciences* (pp. 193–202). Stanford, Calif.: Stanford University Press.

Bell-Detienne, K. (1992). *The control factor: An empirical investigation of employees' reaction to control in an organizational work environment.* Unpublished doctoral dissertation, Communication Arts & Sciences, University of Southern California.

Bellah, R., Madsen, R., Sullivan, W., Swidler, A., & Tipton, S. (1985). *Habits of the heart.* Berkeley: University of California Press.

Bellah, R., Madsen, R., Sullivan, W., Swidler, A., & Tipton, S. (1991). *The good society.* New York: Alfred A. Knopf.

Bendix, R. (1956). *Work and authority in industry.* New York: John Wiley and Sons.

Benne, K., & Sheats, P. (1948). Functional roles of group members. *Journal of Social Issues* 4: 41–49.

Bennis, W., & Nanus, B. (1985). *Leaders: Strategies for taking charge.* New York: Harper & Row.

Benson, T. (1981). Another shootout in cowtown. *Quarterly Journal of Speech* 67: 347–406.

Berger, P., & Berger, B. (1983). *The war over the family.* Garden City, N.Y.: Anchor Doubleday.

Berger, P., & Luckmann, T. (1967). *The social construction of reality.* Garden City, N.Y.: Anchor.

Berlo, D. (1960). *The process of communication.* New York: Holt, Rinehart & Winston.

Bernays, E. (1923). *Crystallizing public opinion.* New York: Boni & Liveright.

Best, S., & Kellner, D. (1991). *Postmodern theory: Critical integrations.* New York: Guilford Press.

Beyer, J., & Trice, H. (1987). How an organization's rites reveal its culture. *Organizational Dynamics* 15: 4–35.

Bhabha, H. (1990). Dissemination: Time, narrative, and the modern nation. In H. Bhabha, ed., *Nation and narration* (pp. 291–322). London: Routledge.

Bingham, S. (1991). Communication strategies for managing sexual harassment in organizations: Understanding message options and their effects. *Journal of Applied Communication Research* 19: 88–115.

Blair, C., et al. (1995). Disciplining the feminine. *The Quarterly Journal of Speech* 81: 1–24.

Blake, R., & Mouton, J. (1964). *The managerial grid.* Houston, Tex.: Gulf.

Block, P. (1993). *Stewardship.* San Francisco, Calif.: Berrett-Koehler.

Blumer, H. (1969). *Symbolic interactionism: Perspective and method.* Englewood Cliffs, N.J.: Prentice-Hall.

Bochner, A. (1982). The functions of human communication in interpersonal bonding. In C. Arnold & J. Waite-Bowers, eds., *Handbook of rhetorical and communication theory* (pp. 544–621). Boston: Allyn-Bacon.

Bohm, D. (1980). *Wholeness and the implicate order.* London: Ark Paperbacks.

Boje, D. (1991). The storytelling organization: A study of story performance in an office-supply firm. *Administrative Science Quarterly* 36: 106–126.

Boje, D. (1995). Stories of the storytelling organization: A postmodern analysis of Disney in "Tamara-Land." *Academy of Management Journal* 38: 997–1035.

Bok, S. (1983). *Secrets.* New York: Pantheon.

Boland, R., & Hoffman, R. (1983). Humor in a machine shop. In L. Pondy, P. Frost, G. Morgan, & T. Dandridge, eds., *Organizational symbolism* (pp. 187–198). Greenwich, Conn.: JAI Press.

Brass, D. (1984). Being in the right place: A structural analysis of individual influence in an organization. *Administrative Science Quarterly* 29: 518–539.

Braverman, H. (1974). *Labor and monopoly capital: The degradation of work in the twentieth century.* New York: Monthly Review Press.

Brown, M., & McMillan, J. (1991). Culture as text: The development of an organizational narrative. *Southern Communication Journal* 57: 49–60.

Browning, L. (1992). Lists and stories as organizational communication. *Communication Theory* 2: 281–302.

Browning, L. (1992). Reasons for success at Motorola. Paper presented at the applied communication pre-conference of the International Communication Association, Miami, May.

Browning, L., & Hawes, L. (1991). Style, process, surface, context: Consulting as postmodern art. *Journal of Applied Communication Research* 19: 32–54.

Buber, M. (1985). *Between man and man.* 2nd ed. New York: Macmillan.

Buckley, W. (1967). *Sociology and modern systems theory.* Englewood Cliffs, N.J.: Prentice-Hall.

Bullis, C., & Bach, B. (1989). Socialization turning points: An examination of change in organizational identification. *Western Journal of Speech Communication* 53: 273–293.

Bullis, C. & Glaser, H. (1992). Bureaucratic discourse and the Goddess: Towards an ecofeminist critique and rearticulation. *Journal of Organizational Change Management* 5: 50–60.

Bullis, C., & Tompkins, P. (1989). The forest ranger revisited: A study of control practices and identification. *Communication Monographs* 56: 287–306.

Burke, K. (1966). *Language as symbolic action.* Berkeley: University of California Press.

Burke, K. (1969). *A rhetoric of motives.* Berkeley: University of California Press.

Burke, K. (1982). Personal communication.

Burke, K. (1989). *On symbols and society.* Chicago: University of Chicago Press.

Burke, R., Weir, T., & Duwors, R., Jr. (1979). Type A behavior of administrators and wives' reports of marital satisfaction and well-being. *Journal of Applied Psychology* 64: 57–65.

Burke, W. (1986). Leadership as empowering others. In S. Srivasta, ed., *Executive power* (pp. 51–77). San Francisco: Jossey-Bass.

Burrell, G. (1988). Modernism, postmodernism, and organizational analysis 2: The contribution of Michel Foucault. *Organization Studies* 9: 221–235.

Buzzanell, P. (1994). Gaining a voice: Feminist organizational communication theorizing. *Management Communication Quarterly* 7: 339–383.

Calas, M. & Smircich, L. (1993). Dangerous liaisons: The "feminine in management" meets "globalization." *Business Horizons* 36: 71–81.

Calder, B. (1977). An attribution theory of leadership. In B. Staw & G. Salancik, eds., *New directions in organizational behavior.* Chicago: St. Clair Press.

Calvert, L., & Ramsey, V. (1992). Bringing women's voices to research on women in management: A feminist perspective. *Journal of Management Inquiry* 1: 79–88.

Campbell, J., Campbell, R., & Associates. (1988). *Productivity in organizations.* San Francisco: Jossey-Bass.

Campbell, J., with Moyers, B. (1988). *The power of myth.* New York: Doubleday.

Carbaugh, D. (1995). "Are Americans really superficial?" Notes on Finnish and American cultures in linguistic action. Working paper, University of Massachusetts.

Carey, J. (1992). *Sexual harassment in the workplace.* New York: Practicing Law Institute.

Carlsson, C., & Leger, M. (1990). *Bad attitude: The processed world anthology.* London: Verso.

Cartwright, D. (1977). Risk taking by individuals and groups: An assessment of research employing choice dilemmas. *Journal of Personality and Social Psychology:* 361–378.

Cascio, W. (1986). *Managing human resources.* New York: McGraw–Hill.

Chandler, C., & Ingrassia, P. (1991). Shifting gears. *Wall Street Journal,* April 11, p. 1.

Cheney, G. (1983). The rhetoric of identification and the study of organizational communication. *Quarterly Journal of Speech* 69: 143–158.

Cheney, G., & Vibbert, S. (1987). Corporate discourse: Public relations and issues management. In F. Jablin, L. Putnam, K. Roberts, & L. Porter, eds., *Handbook of organizational communication* (pp. 165–194). Newbury Park, Calif.: Sage Publications.

Chiles, A. & Zorn, T. (1995). Empowerment in organizations: Employees' perceptions of the influences on empowerment. *Journal of Applied Communication Research* 23: 1–25.

Chilton, K., & Weidenbaum, M. (1994). *A new social contract for the American workplace.* Center for the Study of American Business Policy, No. 123, November, St. Louis, Mo.: Washington University.

Church, K., & Eisenberg, E. (1996). A communication perspective on network marketing. Unpublished working paper, University of South Florida, Tampa, Florida.

Clair, R. (1993). The use of framing devices to sequester organizational narratives: Hegemony and harassment. *Communication Monographs* 60: 113–136.

Clegg, S. (1989). *Frameworks of power.* Newbury Park, Calif.: Sage Publications.

Clegg, S. (1990). *Modern organizations.* Newbury Park, Calif.: Sage Publications.

Clifford, J. (1983). On ethnographic authority. *Representations* 1: 118–146.

Clifford, J. (1992). Traveling cultures. In L. Grossberg, C. Nelson, & P. Treichler, eds., *Cultural studies* (pp. 96–116). New York: Routledge.

Clifford, J., & Marcus, G. (1985). *Writing culture: The poetics and politics of ethnography.* Berkeley: University of California Press.

Cohen, H. (1985). The development of research in speech communication: An historical perspective. In T. Benson, ed., *Speech communication in the 20th century* (pp. 282–298). Carbondale: Southern Illinois University Press.

Compo, S. (1990). *Life after death.* Winchester, Mass.: Faber & Faber.

Conger, J., & Kanungo, R. (1988). The empowerment process: Integrating theory and practice. *Academy of Management Review* 13: 471–482.

Connor, S. (1989). *Postmodernist culture: Theories of the contemporary.* New York: Basil Blackwell.

Conquergood, D. (1991). Rethinking ethnography: Towards a critical cultural politics. *Communication Monographs* 58: 179–194.

Conquergood, D. (1992). Ethnography, rhetoric, and performance. *Quarterly Journal of Speech* 78: 80–97.

Conrad, C. (1983). Organizational power: Faces and symbolic forms. In L. Putnam & M. Pacanowsky, eds., *Communication and organizations* (pp. 173–194). Beverly Hills, Calif.: Sage Publications.

Conrad, C. (1985). Chrysanthemums and swords: A reading of contemporary organizational communication theory and research. *Southern Speech Communication Journal* 50: 189–200.

Conrad, C. (1988). Work songs, hegemony, and illusions of self. *Critical Studies in Mass Communication* 5: 179–201.

Conrad, C. (1990). Nostalgia and the nineties. Paper presented at the conference on Organizational Communication in the 1990s: A Research Agenda, Tempe, Arizona.

Conrad, C. (1991). Communication in conflict: Style-strategy relationships. *Communication Monographs* 58: 135–155.

Contractor, N. (1992). Self-organizing systems perspective in the study of organizational communication. In B. Kovacic, ed., *Organizational communication: New perspectives.* Albany, N.Y.: SUNY Press.

Contractor, N., & Eisenberg, E. (1990). Communication networks and the news media in organizations. In J. Fulk & C. Steinfeld, eds., *Organizations and communication technology* (pp. 143–172). Newbury Park, Calif.: Sage Publications.

Contractor, N., & Seibold, D. (1992). Theoretical frameworks for the study of structuring processes in group decision support systems. Unpublished manuscript, University of Illinois, Urbana, Ill.

Contractor, N., Eisenberg, E., & Monge, P. (1992). Antecedents and outcomes of interpretive diversity in organizations. Unpublished manuscript, Department of Communication, University of Illinois, Urbana, Ill.

Cooper, C. J. (1984). Executive stress: A ten country comparison. *Human Resource Management* 23: 395–407.

Cooper, R., & Burrell, G. (1988). Modernism, postmodernism, and organizational analysis: An introduction. *Organizational Studies* 9: 91–112.

Coupland, D. (1991). *Generation–X.* New York: HarperCollins.

Coupland, D. (1995). *Microserfs.* New York: Regan Books.

Crable, R., & Vibbert, S. (1983). Mobil's epideictic advocacy: "Observations" of Prometheus-bound. *Communication Monographs* 50: 380–394.

Csikszentmihalyi, M. (1990). *Flow: The psychology of optimal experience.* New York: Harper & Row.

Cummings, T. (1978). Self-regulating work groups: A socio-technical synthesis. *Academy of Management Review* 3: 625–634.

Cusella, L. (1987). Feedback, motivation, and performance. In F. Jablin et al., eds., *Handbook of organizational communication* (pp. 624–678). Beverly Hills, Calif.: Sage Publications.

Czarniawska-Joerges, B. (1988). Dynamics of organizational control: The case of Berol Kemi Ab. *Accounting, Organizations, and Society* 11: 471–482.

Daft, R., & Lengel, R. (1984). Information richness: A new approach to managerial information processing and organizational design. In B. Staw & L. Cummings, eds., *Research in organizational behaviors* (Vol. 6, pp. 191–233). Greenwich, Conn.: JAI Press.

Daniels, T., & Spiker, B. (1991). *Perspectives on organizational communication.* Dubuque, Iowa: Wm. C. Brown.

Dansereau, F., & Markham, S. (1987). Superior–subordinate communication: Multiple levels of analysis. In F. Jablin et al., eds., *Handbook of organizational communication* (pp. 343–388), Beverly Hills, Calif.: Sage Publications.

Dao, D.-M. (1992). *365 Tao.* San Francisco, Calif.: HarperCollins.

D'Aveni, R. (1995). Coping with hypercompetition: Utilizing the new 7s model. *Academy of Management Executive* 9 (3): 45–57.

Davis, K. (1953). Management communication and the grapevine. *Harvard Business Review* 31: 43–49.

Davis, K. (1972). *Human behavior at work.* New York: McGraw-Hill.

Davis, S., & Davidson, B. (1991). *2020 Vision.* New York: Simon and Schuster.

Deal, T., & Kennedy, A. (1982). *Corporate cultures.* Reading, Mass.: Addison-Wesley.

deCerteau, M. (1984). *The practice of everyday life.* Berkeley: University of California Press.

Deetz, S. (1991). *Democracy in an age of corporate colonization.* Albany, N.Y.: SUNY Press.

Deetz, S. (1995). *Transforming communication, transforming business.* Albany, N.Y.: SUNY Press.

Deetz, S., & Mumby, D. (1990). Power, discourse, and the workplace: Reclaiming the critical tradition. In J. Anderson, ed., *Communication Yearbook* 13 (pp. 18–47). Newbury Park, Calif.: Sage Publications.

Dentzer, S. (1995). The death of the middleman. *US News and World Report,* May 22.

Derrida, J. (1972). Structure, sign, and play in the discourse of the human sciences. In R. Macksay & E. Donato, eds., *The structuralist controversy: The language of criticism and the science of man.* Baltimore: Johns Hopkins University Press.

Derrida, J. (1976). *Speech and phenomenon.* Evanston, Ill.: Northwestern University Press.

Desmonde, W. (1962). *Magic, myth, and money: The origin of money in religious ritual.* New York: Free Press of Glencoe.

Dessler, G. (1982). *Organization and management.* Reston, Va.: Reston.

Dillard, J., & Miller, K. (1988). Intimate relationships in task environments. In S. Duck, ed., *Handbook of personal relationships* (pp. 449–465). New York: John Wiley and Sons.

Dillard, J., & Segrin, C. (1987). Intimate relationships in organizations: Relational types, illicitness, and power. Paper presented at the Annual Conference of the International Communication Association, Montreal, Canada.

Donnellon, A. (1992). Team work: Linguistic models of negotiating difference. In B. Shepard et al., eds., *Research and negotiations in organizations.* Vol. 4. Greenwich, Conn.: JAI Press.

Donnellon, A., Gray, B., & Bougon, M. (1986). Communication, meaning, and organized action. *Administrative Science Quarterly* 31: 43–55.

Downs, C., Clampitt, P., & Pfeiffer, A. (1988). Communication and organizational outcomes. In G. Goldhaber & G. Barnett, eds., *Handbook of organizational communication* (pp. 171–212). Norwood, N.J.: Ablex.

Drucker, P. (1957). *The landmarks of tomorrow.* New York: Harper & Row.

Drucker, P. (1973). *Management.* New York: Harper & Row.

Drucker, P. (1992a). *Managing for the future: The 1990's and beyond.* New York: Truman Talley Books/Dutton.

Drucker, P. (1992b). There's more than one kind of team. *The Wall Street Journal,* Feb. 11, p. 16.

Dutton, J., & Dukerich, J. (1991). Keeping an eye on the mirror: Image and identity in organizational adaptation. *Academy of Management Journal* 34: 517–554.

Edwards, L. (1991). Samurai hackers. *Rolling Stone,* September 19, pp. 67–69.

Eisenberg, E. (1984). Ambiguity as strategy in organizational communication. *Communication Monographs* 51: 227–242.

Eisenberg, E. (1986). Meaning and interpretation in organizations. *Quarterly Journal of Speech* 72: 88–98.

Eisenberg, E. (1990). Jamming: Transcendence through organizing. *Communication Research* 17: 139–164.

Eisenberg, E. (1995). A communication perspective on interorganizational cooperation and inner–city education. In L. Rigsby, M. Reynolds, & M. Wang, eds., *School-community connections* (pp. 101–120). San Francisco, Calif.: Jossey-Bass.

Eisenberg, E., Farace, R., Monge, P., Bettinghaus, E., Kurchner-Hawkins, R., Miller, K., & Rothman, L. (1985). Communication linkages in interorganizational systems: Review and synthesis. In B. Dervin & M. Voight, eds., *Progress in Communication Sciences* 6: 231–258. Norwood, N.J.: Ablex.

Eisenberg, E., Monge, P., & Farace, R. V. (1984). Co-orientation on communication rules in managerial dyads. *Human Communication Research* 11: 261–271.

Eisenberg, E., Monge, P., & Miller, K. (1983). Involvement in communication networks as a predictor of organizational commitment. *Human Communication Research* 10: 179–201.

Eisenberg, E., & Phillips, S. (1991). Miscommunication in organizations. In N. Coupland, H. Giles, & J. Weimann, eds., *"Miscommunication" and problematic talk* (pp. 244–258). Newbury Park, Calif.: Sage Publications.

Eisenberg, E., & Riley, P. (1988). Organizational symbols and sense-making. In G. Goldhaber & G. Barnett, eds., *Handbook of organizational communication* (pp. 131–150). Norwood, N.J.: Ablex.

Eisenberg, E., & Riley, P. (1991). A closed-loop model of communication, empowerment, urgency and performance. Unpublished working paper, University of Southern California.

Eisenberg, E. & Riley, P. (In press). A communication approach to organizational culture. In L. Putnam & F. Jablin, eds., *New handbook of organizational communication*. Newbury Park, Calif.: Sage Publications.

Eisenberg, E., & Witten, M. (1987). Reconsidering openness in organizational communication. *Academy of Management Review* 12: 418–426.

Eisler, R. (1987). *The chalice and the blade.* San Francisco: HarperCollins.

Elden, M., & Levin, M. (1991). Cogenerative learning: Bringing participation into action research. In W. F. Whyte, ed., *Participatory action research* (pp. 127–142). Newbury Park, Calif.: Sage Publications.

Eliot, T. S. (1949). *Notes toward the definition of culture.* New York: Harcourt, Brace.

Emerson, C. (1983). Bakhtin and Vygotsky on internalization of language. *Quarterly Newsletter of the Laboratory of Comparative Human Cognition* 5: 9–13.

Emery, F., & Trist, E. (1965). The causal texture of organizational environments. *Human Relations* 18: 21–32.

Erez, M. & Earley, P. (1993). *Culture, self-identity, and work.* New York: Oxford University Press.

Etzioni, A. (1961). *A comparative analysis of complex organizations.* New York: Free Press of Glencoe.

Etzioni, A. (1988). *The moral dimension: Toward a new economics.* New York: Free Press.

Evered, R., & Tannenbaum, R. (1992). A dialog on dialog. *Journal of Management Inquiry* 1: 43–55.

Fairhurst, G., & Chandler, T. (1989). Social structure in leader–member interaction. *Communication Monographs* 56: 215–239.

Fairhurst, G., Green, S., & Snavely, B. (1984). Face support in controlling poor performance. *Human Communication Research* 11: 272–295.

Fairhurst, G., Rogers, E., & Sarr, R. (1987). Manager–subordinate control patterns and judgments about the relationship. *Communication Yearbook* 10: 395–415.

Fairhurst, G., & Sarr, R. (1996). *The art of framing.* San Francisco, Calif.: Jossey-Bass.

Farace, R., Monge, P., & Russell, H. (1977). *Communicating and organizing.* Reading, Mass.: Addison-Wesley.

Farley, L. (1978). *Sexual shakedown: The sexual harassment of women on the job.* New York: McGraw-Hill.

Fayol, H. (1949). *General and industrial management.* London: Pitman.

Featherstone, M. (1988). In pursuit of the postmodern. *Theory, Culture, and Society* 5: 195–216.

Feldman, M., & March, J. (1981). Information in organizations as signal and symbol. *Administrative Science Quarterly* 26: 171–186.

Feldman, S. (1991). The meaning of ambiguity: Learning from stories and metaphors. In P. Frost et al., eds., *Reframing organizational culture* (pp. 145–156). Newbury Park, Calif.: Sage Publications.

Fenster, M. (1991). The problem of taste within the problematic of culture. *Communication Theory* 1: 87–105.

Ferguson, K. (1984). *The feminist case against bureaucracy.* Philadelphia: Temple University Press.

Ferguson, T., & Dunphy, J. (1992). *Answers to the mommy track: How wives and mothers in business reach the top and balance their lives.* Far Hills, N.J.: New Horizon Press.

Fiedler, F. (1967). *A theory of leadership effectiveness.* New York: McGraw-Hill.

Fineman, S. (1993). *Emotion in organizations.* London: Sage Publications.

Fisher, A. (1980). *Small group decision making.* 2nd ed. New York: McGraw-Hill.

Fisher, W. (1984). Narration as a human communication paradigm: The case of public moral argument. *Communication Monographs* 51: 1–22.

Fombrun, C., & Shanley, M. (1990). What's in a name: Reputation building and corporate strategy. *Academy of Management Journal* 33: 233–258.

Ford, R., & Fottler, M. (1995). Empowerment: A matter of degree. *Academy of Management Executive* 9: 21–31.

Foster, H. (1983). *The anti-aesthetic: Essays on postmodern culture.* Port Townshend, Wash.: Bay Press.

Foucault, M. (1972). *The archaeology of knowledge.* London: Tavistock.

Foucault, M. (1979). *The birth of the prison.* Hammondsworth, England: Penguin.

Fox, M. (1994). *The reinvention of work.* San Francisco: HarperCollins.

Franklin, B. (1970). *The complete Poor Richard almanacs published by Benjamin Franklin.* Barre, Mass.: Imprint Society.

Franz, C., & Jin, K. (1995). The structure of group conflict in a collaborative work group during information systems development. *Journal of Applied Communication Research* 23: 108–122.

Freeman, S. (1990). *Managing lives: Corporate women and social change.* Amherst: University of Massachusetts Press.

Freire, P. (1968). *Pedagogy of the oppressed.* Berkeley: University of California Press.

French, R., & Raven, B. (1968). The bases of social power. In D. Cartwright & A. Zander, eds., *Group dynamics* (pp. 601–623). New York: Harper & Row.

Friedman, M. (1992). *Dialogue and the human image.* Newbury Park, Calif.: Sage Publications.

Frost, P., Moore, L., Louis, M., Lundberg, C., & Martin, J. (1991). *Reframing organizational culture.* Newbury Park, Calif.: Sage Publications.

Fulk, J., & Mani, S. (1986). Distortion of communication in hierarchical relationships. *Communication Yearbook* 9 (pp. 483–510). Newbury Park, Calif.: Sage Publications.

Fulk, J., Schmitz, J., & Steinfeld, C. (1990). A social influence model of technology use. In J. Fulk & C. Steinfeld, eds., *Organizations and communication technology* (pp. 143–172). Newbury Park, Calif.: Sage Publications.

Futrell, C., & Parasuramann, A. (1984). The relationship of satisfaction and performance to salesforce turnover. *Journal of Marketing* 48: 33–40.

Gabarro, J., & Kotter, J. (1980). Managing your boss. *Harvard Business Review* 58: 92–100.

Galbraith, J. (1973). *Designing complex organizations.* Reading, Mass.: Addison-Wesley.

Garfield, C. (1992). *Business in the ecological age.* San Francisco: Berrett-Koehler. (Audiotape.)

Geertz, C. (1973). *The interpretation of cultures.* New York: Basic Books.

Geist, P., & Dreyer, J. (1992). A dialogical critique of the medical encounter: Understanding, marginalization, and the social context. Paper presented at the Annual Meeting of the Speech Communication Association, Chicago.

Geist, P., and Dreyer, J. (1993). The demise of dialogue: A critique of medical encounter ideology. *Western Journal of Communication* 57: 233–246.

Gergen, K. (1985). The social constructionist movement in modern psychology. *American Psychologist* 40: 266–275.

Gergen, K. (1991). *The saturated self.* New York: Basic Books.

Gersick, C. (1988). Time and transition in work teams: Toward a new model of group development. *Academy of Management Journal* 31: 9–41.

Gersick, C. (1991). Revolutionary change theories: A multi-level explanation of the punctuated equilibrium paradigm. *Academy of Management Review* 16: 10–36.

Gibson, D., & Rogers, E. (In press). *Synergy on trial: Texas high tech and the MCC.* Newbury Park, Calif.: Sage Publications.

Gibson, J., & Hodgetts, R. (1986). *Organizational communication: A managerial perspective.* New York: Academic Press.

Giddens, A. (1979). *Central problems in social theory.* London: Hutchinson.

Ginsberg, E. (1982). The mechanization of work. *Scientific American* 247: 66–75.

Gitlin, T. (1987). *The sixties: Years of hope, days of rage.* New York: Bantam.

Glaser, H., & Bullis, C. (1992). Ecofeminism and organizational communication. Paper presented at the Speech Communication Association Annual Meeting, Chicago.

Goldstein, I., & Gilliam, P. (1990). Training systems issues in the year 2000. *American Psychologist* 45: 134–140.

Goodall, H. L. (1989). *Casing a promised land.* Carbondale: Southern Illinois University Press.

Goodall, H. L. (1990a). Interpretive contexts for decision-making: Toward an understanding of the physical, economic, dramatic, and hierarchical interplays of language in groups. In G. M. Phillips, ed., *Teaching how to work in groups* (pp. 197–224). Norwood, N.J.: Ablex.

Goodall, H. L. (1990b). Theatre of motives. In J. Anderson, ed., *Communication Yearbook* 13 (pp. 69–97). Newbury Park, Calif.: Sage Publications.

Goodall, H. L. (1991a). *Living in the rock 'n' roll mystery.* Carbondale: Southern Illinois University Press.

Goodall, H. L. (1991b). Unchained melodies: Toward a poetics of organizing. Blair Hart lecture on communication, Department of Communication, University of Arkansas, Fayetteville, Arkansas.

Goodall, H. L. (1993). Empowerment, culture, and postmodern organizing: Deconstructing the Nordstrom's Employee Handbook. *Journal of Organizational Change Management* 5: 25–30.

Goodall, H. L., Jr. (1995). Work-hate narratives. In R. Whillock & D. Slayden, eds., *Hate speech.* Thousand Oaks, Calif.: Sage Publications.

Goodall, H. L., Jr. (1996). *Divine signs: Connecting spirit to community.* Carbondale, Ill.: Southern Illinois University Press.

Goodall, H. L., Wilson, G., & Waagen, C. (1986). The performance appraisal interview: An interpretive reassessment. *Quarterly Journal of Speech* 72: 74–87.

Gouldner, A. (1971). *The coming crisis of western sociology.* New York: Basic Books.

Graen, G. (1976). Role making processes within complex organizations. In M. Dunnette, ed., *Handbook of industrial and organizational psychology* (pp. 1201–1245). Chicago: Rand McNally.

Graen, G., & Ginsburgh, S. (1977). Job resignation as a function of role orientation and leader acceptance: A longitudinal investigation of organizational assimilation. *Organizational Behavior and Human Performance* 19: 1–17.

Graen, G., Liden, R., & Hoel, W. (1982). Role of leadership in the employee withdrawal process. *Journal of Applied Psychology* 67: 868–872.

Graen, G., & Schiemann, W. (1978). Leader member agreement: A vertical dyad linkage approach. *Journal of Applied Psychology* 63: 206–212.

Gramsci, A. (1971). *Selections from the prison notebooks.* London: Lawrence & Wishart.

Granovetter, M. (1973). The strength of weak ties. *American Journal of Sociology* 78: 1360–1380.

Grant, L. (1992). Breaking the mold: Companies struggle to reinvent themselves. *Los Angeles Times,* May 3, pp. D1, D16.

Grantham, C. (1995). The virtual office. *At Work: Stories of Tomorrow's Workplace.* September/October, Vol. 4 (5), pp. 1, 12–14.

Gray, B., Bougon, M., & Donnellon, A. (1985). Organizations as constructions and destructions of meaning. *Journal of Management* 11: 83–98.

Greenblatt, S. (1990). Culture. In F. Lentricchia & T. McLaughlin, eds., *Critical terms for literary study* (pp. 225–232). Chicago: University of Chicago Press.

Gronn, P. (1983). Talk as the work: The accomplishment of school administration. *Administrative Science Quarterly* 28: 1–21.

Grossberg, L. (1991). Review of theories of human communication. *Communication Theory* 1: 171–176.

Grossman, H., & Chester, N. (1990). *The experience and meaning of work in women's lives.* Hillsdale, N.J.: Lawrence Erlbaum.

Habermas, J. (1972). *Knowledge and human interests.* London: Heinemann Educational Books.

Habermas, J. (1981). Modernity versus postmodernity. *New German Critique* 22: 3–14.

Hackman, R., and associates. (1990). *Groups that work (and those that don't): Creating conditions for effective teamwork.* San Francisco: Jossey-Bass.

Hackman, R., & Oldham, G. (1975). Development of the Job Diagnostic Survey. *Journal of Applied Psychology* 60: 159–170.

Hackman, R., & Suttle, J. (1977). *Improving life at work: Behavioral science approaches to organizational change.* Santa Monica, Calif.: Goodyear Publishing.

Hage, J., & Aiken, M. (1970). *Social change in complex organizations.* New York: Random House.

Hall, D. (1986). *Career development in organizations.* San Francisco: Jossey-Bass.

Hall, E. T. (1973). *The silent language.* New York: Anchor Books.

Hall, K., & Savery, L. (1987). Stress management. *Management Decision* 25: 29–35.

Hammer, M., & Champy, J. (1993). *Reengineering the corporation.* New York: HarperCollins.

Hamper, B. (1991). *Rivethead.* New York: Warner Books.

Handy, C. (1994). *The age of paradox.* Cambridge, Mass.: Harvard University Press.

Hardin, G. (1968). The tragedy of the commons. *Science,* December 13.

Harrigan, B. (1977). *Games mother never taught you: Corporate gamesmanship for women.* New York: Warner Books.

Harrison, J. (1991). *Just before dark.* Livingston, Mont.: Clark City Press.

Harrison, T. (1985). Communication and participative decision-making: An exploratory study. *Personnel Psychology* 38: 93–116.

Harrison, T. (1994). Communication and interdependence in democratic organizations. In S. Deetz, ed., *Communication Yearbook* 17: 247–274.

Hart, R., & Burks, D. (1972). Rhetorical sensitivity and social interaction. *Speech Monographs* 39: 75–91.

Harvey, D. (1989). *The conditions of postmodernity.* London: Basil Blackwell.

Hassan, I. (1971). *The dismemberment of Orpheus: Toward a postmodern literature.* Madison: University of Wisconsin Press.

Hassan, I. (1987). *The postmodern turn: Essays in postmodern theory and culture.* Columbus: Ohio State University Press.

Hatch, M. (1993). The dynamics of organizational culture. *Academy of Management Review* 18: 657–693.

Hawes, L. (1974). Social collectivities as communication: Perspective on organizational behavior. *Quarterly Journal of Speech* 60: 497–502.

Hawken, P. (1992). *The ecology of commerce.* New York: HarperCollins.

Hawking, S. (1988). *A brief history of time.* New York: Bantam.

Hawley, J. (1994). *Reawakening the spirit in work: The power of Dharmic management.* San Francisco: Berrett-Koehler.

Hayes-Bautista, D. (1988). *The burden of support: Young Latinos in an aging society.* Stanford, Calif.: Stanford University Press.

Hearn, J., Sheppard, D., Tancred-Sheriff, P., & Burrell, G. *The sexuality of organization.* Newbury Park, Calif.: Sage Publications.

Heath, R. (1980). Corporate advocacy: An application of speech communication perspectives and skills—and more. *Communication Education* 29: 370–377.

Hebdige, D. (1979). *Subculture: The meaning of style.* London: Methuen.

Helgeson, S. (1990). *The female advantage: Women's ways of leadership.* New York: Doubleday.

Hellweg, S. (1987). Organizational grapevines: A state of the art review. In B. Dervin & M. Voight, eds., *Progress in the communication sciences* 8. Norwood, N.J.: Ablex.

Herbst, P. (1976). *Alternatives to hierarchies.* Leiden: M. Nijhoff Social Sciences Division.

Herzberg, F. (1966). *Work and the nature of man.* New York: Collins.

Hirokawa, R., & Rost, K. (1992). Effective group decision making in organizations. *Management Communication Quarterly* 5: 267–388.

Hirschman, A. (1970). *Exit, voice, and loyalty.* Cambridge, Mass.: Harvard University Press.

Hochschild, A. (1979). Emotion work, feeling rules and social structure. *American Journal of Sociology* 85: 551–575.

Hochschild, A. (1983). *The managed heart: Commercialization of human feeling.* Berkeley: University of California Press.

Hoffman, L. (1982). *Foundations of family therapy.* New York: Basic Books.

Hofstede, G. (1983). National cultures in four dimensions. *International Studies of Management and Organization* 13: 46–74.

Hofstede, G. (1991). *Culture and organizations: Software of the mind.* New York: McGraw-Hill.

Hollander, E., & Offerman, L. (1990). Power and leadership in organizations. *American Psychologist* 45: 179–189.

Holquist, M. (1990). *Dialogism: Bakhtin and his world.* London: Routledge.

Holt, G. (1989). Talk about acting and constraint in stories about organizations. *Western Journal of Speech Communication* 53: 374–397.

Homans, G. (1961). *Social behavior: Its elementary forms.* New York: Harcourt, Brace & World, Inc.

Horovitz, B. (1991). Firms focus on logos to project right image. *Los Angeles Times,* October 1, p. D6.

House, R. (1971). A path–goal theory of leader effectiveness. *Administrative Science Quarterly* 16: 321–338.

Huber, G. (1990). A theory of the effects of advanced information technologies on organizational design, intelligence, and decision-making. In J. Fulk & C. Steinfeld, eds., *Organizations and communication technology* (pp. 237–274). Newbury Park, Calif.: Sage Publications.

Hume Corporation (1987). *Improving your financial profile.* USA: Hume Corp.

Hunger, R., & Stern, L. (1976). Assessment of the functionality of superordinate goals in reducing conflict. *Academy of Management Journal* 16: 591–605.

Hyde, B. (1990). Personal communication.

Hyde, B. (1991). Speaking being: Ontological rhetoric as transformational technology. Paper presented at the Thirteenth Annual Conference of the Association for Integrative Studies, St. Paul, Minnesota.

Ilgin, D., & Knowlton, W., Jr. (1980). Performance attributional effects on feedback from supervisors. *Organizational Behavior and Human Performance* 25: 441–456.

Infante, D., & Gordon, W. (1985). Superior's argumentativeness and verbal aggressiveness as predictors of subordinate's satisfaction. *Human Comm. Research* 12: 117–125.

Infante, D., Trebing, J., Sheperd, P., & Seeds, D. (1984). The relationship of argumentativeness to verbal aggression. *Southern Speech Communication Journal* 50: 67–77.

Isaacs, W. (1993). Taking flight: Dialogue, collaborative thinking, and organizational learning. *Organizational Dynamics*, Fall.

Israel, et al. (1989). The relation of personal resources, participation, influence, interpersonal relationships and coping strategies to occupational stress, job stress, and health: A multivariate analysis. *Work and Stress* 3: 163–194.

Ivancevich, J., & Matteson, M. (1980). *Stress and work: A managerial perspective.* Glenview, Ill.: Scott, Foresman.

Jablin, F. (1979). Superior–subordinate communication: The state of the art. *Psychological Bulletin* 86: 1201–1222.

Jablin, F. (1985). Task/work relationships: A life-span perspective. In M. Knapp & G. Miller, eds., *Handbook of interpersonal communication* (pp. 615–654). Newbury Park, Calif.: Sage Publications.

Jablin, F. (1987). Organizational entry, assimilation, and exit. In F. Jablin, L. Putnam, K. Roberts, & L. Porter, eds., *Handbook of organizational communication* (pp. 679–740). Newbury Park, Calif.: Sage Publications.

Jackson, S. (1983). Participation in decision-making as a strategy for reducing job-related strain. *Journal of Applied Psychology* 68: 3–19.

Jackson, M. (1989). *Paths toward a clearing.* Bloomington: Indiana University Press.

Jacobson, R. (1992). Colleges face new pressure to increase faculty productivity. *Chronicle of Higher Education* 38 (32): 1, 16.

James, J. (1996). *Thinking in the future tense.* New York: Simon & Schuster.

Jameson, F. (1984). Postmodernism, or the cultural logic of late capitalism. *New Left Review* 146: 53–92.

Janis, I. (1971). *Victims of groupthink.* 2nd revised ed. Boston: Houghton Mifflin.

Jantsch, E. (1980). *The self organizing universe.* Oxford: Pergamon Press.

Jencks, C. (1977). *The language of postmodern architecture.* New York: Pantheon.

Johnson, B. (1977). *Communication: The process of organizing.* Boston: Allyn-Bacon.

Jones, B. (1972). Sex in the office. *National Times* 12 (June).

Jones, E., Jr. (1973). What it's like to be a Black manager. *Harvard Business Review* (July/August).

Kanter, R. M. (1977). *Men and women of the corporation.* New York: Basic Books.

Kanter, R. M. (1989). The new managerial work. *Harvard Business Review* (November–December): 85–92.

Karasek, R. (1979). Job demands, job decisions, latitude and mental strain: Implications for job redesign. *Administrative Science Quarterly* 24: 285–308.

Katz, D., & Kahn, R. (1966–1978). *The social psychology of organizations.* New York: John Wiley and Sons.

Katzell, R., & Thompson, D. (1990). Work motivation. *American Psychologist* 45: 144–153.

Keeley, M. (1980). Organizational analogy: A comparison or organismic and social contract models. *Administrative Science Quarterly* 25: 337–362.

Kelly, J. (1992). *Scientific management, job redesign, and work performance.* London: Academic Press.

Keys, B., & Case, T. (1990). How to become an influential manager. *Academy of Management Executive* 4: 38–50.

Kiechel, W. (1994). A manager's career in the new economy. *Fortune,* April 4, pp. 68–72.

Kiesler, C. (1971). *The psychology of commitment.* New York: Academic Press.

Kilmann, R., & Thomas, K. (1975). Interpersonal conflict handling behavior as a reflection of Jungian personality dimensions. *Psychological Reports* 37: 971–980.

Kimberly, J., & Miles, R. (1980). *The organizational life cycle.* San Francisco: Jossey-Bass.

King, Y. (1989). The ecology of feminism and the feminism of ecology. In J. Plant, ed., *Healing the wounds: The promise of ecofeminism.* Philadelphia: New Society Publishers.

Kipnis, D., & Schmidt, S. (1982). *Profile of organizational influence strategies.* San Diego, Calif.: University Associates.

Kipnis, D., & Schmidt, S. (1983). An influence perspective on bargaining. In M. Bazerman & R. Lewicki, eds., *Negotiating in organizations* (pp. 303–319). Beverly Hills, Calif.: Sage Publications.

Kipnis, D., Schmidt, S., & Braxton-Brown, G. (1990). The hidden costs of persistence. In M. Cody & M. McLaughlin, eds., *The psychology of tactical communication.* Philadelphia: Multilingual Matters.

Kipnis, D., Schmidt, S., & Wilkinson, I. (1980). Intraorganizational influence tactics: Explorations in getting one's way. *Journal of Applied Psychology* 65: 440–452.

Knorr-Cetina, K., & Cicourel, A. (1981). *Advances in social theory and methodology.* Boston: Routledge & Kegan Paul.

Kobasa, S., Maddi, S., & Kahn, S. (1982). Hardiness and health: A prospective study. *Journal of Personality and Social Psychology* 42: 168–177.

Kotter, J., & Heskett, J. (1992). *Corporate culture and performance.* New York: Free Press.

Kotter, J. (1995). *The new rules.* New York: Free Press.

Kramer, M. (1993). Communication and uncertainty reduction during job transfers: Leaving and joining processes. *Communication Monographs* 60: 178–198.

Kramer, M. (1995). A longitudinal study of superior–subordinate communication during job transfers. *Human Communication Research* 22: 39–64.

Kreps, G. (1991). *Organizational communication: Theory and practice.* 2nd ed. New York: Longman.

Krippendorff, K. (1985). On the ethics of constructing communication. ICA Presidential Address, Honolulu, Hawaii.

Krivonos, P. (1982). Distortion of subordinate to superior communication in organizational settings. *Central States Speech Journal* 33: 345–352.

Kuhn, T. (1972). *The structure of scientific revolutions.* Chicago: University of Chicago Press.

Kunda, G. (1993). *Engineering culture: Control and commitment in a high-tech corporation.* Philadelphia: Temple University Press.

Kavale, S. (1990). Themes of postmodernity. *The Humanistic Psychologist,* 18(1).

Laing, R. D. (1965). *The divided self.* Harmondsworth, England: Penguin.

Larkey, P. (1984). The management of attention. In P. Larkey & L. Sproull, eds., *Advances in information processing in organizations, Vol. I.* Greenwich, Conn.: JAI Press.

Larkey, P., & Sproull, L. (1984). *Advances in information processing in organizations.* Vol I. Greenwich, Conn.: JAI Press.

Larson, J., Jr. (1989). The dynamic interplay between employees: Feedback-seeking strategies and supervisors' delivery of performance feedback. *Academy of Management Review* 14: 408–422.

Lavie, S. (1990). *The poetics of military occupation: Mzeina allegories of identity under Israeli and Egyptian rule.* Berkeley: University of California Press.

Lawler, E., III. (1986). *High involvement management.* San Francisco: Jossey-Bass.

Lawrence, P., & Lorsch, J. (1967). *Organization and environment: Mapping differentiation and integration.* Boston: Graduate School of Business Administration, Harvard University.

Leavitt, H. (1951). Some effects of certain communication patterns on group performance. *Journal of Abnormal and Social Psychology* 46: 38–50.

Leeds-Hurwitz, W. (1992). Social approaches to interpersonal communication. *Communication Theory* 2: 131–138.

Lerner, M. (1992). Looters were living out the cynical American ethos. *Los Angeles Times,* May 14, p. B7.

Levering, R., Moskowitz, M., & Katz, M. (1984). *The 100 best companies to work for in America.* Reading, Mass.: Addison-Wesley.

Levine, S. (1984). *The flight from ambiguity.* Chicago: University of Chicago Press.

Liden, R., & Graen, G. (1980). Generalizability of the vertical dyad linkage model of leadership. *Academy of Management Journal* 23: 451–465.

Likert, R. (1961). *New patterns of management.* New York: McGraw-Hill.

Lipsitz, G. (1990). *Time passages: Collective memory and American popular culture.* Minneapolis: University of Minnesota Press.

Locke, E., & Latham, G. (1984). *Goal setting: A motivational technique that really works!* Englewood Cliffs, N.J.: Prentice-Hall.

Loher, B., Noe, R., Moeller, N., & Fitzgerald, M. (1985). A meta-analysis of the relation of job characteristics to job satisfaction. *Journal of Applied Psychology* 70: 280–289.

Long, R. (1987). *New office information technology.* London: Croom Helm.

Louis, M. (1980). Surprise and sense-making: What newcomers experience in entering unfamiliar organizational settings. *Administrative Science Quarterly* 23: 225–251.

Luhmann, A. D., & Albrecht, T. L. (1990). The impact of supportive communication and personal control on job stress and performance. Paper presented at the International Communication Association, Chicago.

Lukes, S. (1974). *Power: A radical view.* London: Macmillan.

Lukes, S. (1986). *Power.* New York: New York University Press.

Lunneborg, D. (1990). *Women changing work.* New York: Greenwood Press.

Lyotard, J. (1984). *The postmodern condition: A report on knowledge.* Trans. G. Bennington and B. Massumi. Minneapolis: University of Minnesota Press.

Manning, P. (1977). *Police work.* Cambridge, Mass.: MIT Press.

March, J. (1965). Introduction. In J. March, ed., *Handbook of organizations* (pp. ix-xvi). Chicago: Rand McNally.

March, J., & Olsen, J. (1976). *Ambiguity and choice in organizations.* Bergen, Norway: Universitetsforlaget.

March, J., & Simon, H. (1958). *Organizations.* New York: John Wiley and Sons.

Marcus, A., & Goodman, R. (1991). Victims and shareholders: The dilemmas of presenting corporate policy during a crisis. *Academy of Management Journal* 34: 281–305.

Marcus, G., & Fischer, M. (1986). *Anthropology as cultural critique.* Chicago: University of Chicago Press.

Marshall, J. (1984). *Women managers: Travelers in a male world.* New York: John Wiley and Sons.

Marshall, J. (1993). Viewing organizational communication from a feminist perspective: A critique and some offerings. In S. Deetz, ed., *Communication Yearbook* 16 (pp. 122–143). Newbury Park, Calif.: Sage Publications.

Marshall, A., & Stohl, C. (1993). Participating as participation: A network approach. *Communication Monographs* 60: 137–157.

Martin, J. (1992). *Cultures in organizations: Three perspectives.* New York: Oxford University Press.

Martin, J., & Myerson, D. (1988). Organizational culture and the denial, channeling, and acknowledgment of ambiguity. In L. Pondy, R. Boland, & H. Thomas, eds., *Managing ambiguity and change.* New York: John Wiley and Sons.

Martin, J., & Siehl, C. (1983). Organizational culture and counter-culture: An uneasy symbiosis. *Organizational Dynamics* 12: 52–64.

Maruyama, M. (1963). The second cybernetics: Deviation-amplifying mutual causal processes. *American Scientist* 51: 164–179.

Maslach, C. (1982). *Burnout: The cost of caring.* Englewood Cliffs, N.J.: Prentice-Hall.

Maslow, A. (1965). *Eupsychian management.* Homewood, Ill.: R.D. Irwin.

Maslow, A. (1970). *Motivation and personality,* 2d edition. New York: Harper & Row.

May, S. (1988). The modernist monologue in organizational communication research: The text, the subject, and the audience. Paper presented at the Annual Convention of the International Communication Association, San Francisco.

Mayo, E. (1945). *The social problems of industrial civilization.* Cambridge, Mass.: Graduate School of Business Administration, Harvard University.

McClenahan, J. (1991). It's no fun working here anymore. *Industry Week,* March 4, pp. 20–22.

McDonald, P. (1988). The Los Angeles Olympic Organizing Committee: Developing organizational culture in the short run. *Public Administration Quarterly* 10: 189–205.

McGregor, D. (1960). *The human side of enterprise.* New York: McGraw-Hill.

McLuhan, M. (1964). *Understanding media: The extensions of man.* New York: McGraw-Hill.

McPhee, R. (1985). Formal structures and organizational communication. In R. McPhee & P. Tompkins, eds., *Organizational communication: Traditional themes and new directions* (pp. 149–177). Beverly Hills, Calif.: Sage Publications.

McPhee, R., & Corman, S. (1995). An activity based theory of communication networks in organizations, applied to the case of a local church. *Communication Monographs* 62: 132–151.

Mead, G. (1934). *Mind, self, and society*. Chicago: University of Chicago Press.

Mead, G. (1991). The new old capitalism: Long hours, low wages. *Rolling Stone,* May 30, n605, p. 27(3).

Metcalfe, J. (1976). Organizational strategies and interorganizational networks. *Human Relations* 29: 327–343.

Meyer, G. J. (1995). *Executive blues*. San Francisco: Franklin Square Press.

Meyer, J., & Rowan, B. (1977). Institutionalized organizations: Formal structure as myth and ceremony. *American Journal of Sociology* 83: 340–363.

Meyer, J., & Scott, W. (1983). *Organizations and environments*. Newbury Park, Calif.: Sage Publications.

Milbrath, R. (1989). *Envisioning a sustainable society*. Albany, N.Y.: SUNY Press.

Miller, G. R. (1991). Applied communication in the 21st century. Paper presented at the SCA/University of South Florida Conference on applied communication in the 21st century, Tampa, Fla.

Miller, J. G. (1978). *Living systems*. New York: McGraw-Hill.

Miller, K. (1995). *Organizational communication: Approaches and processes*. Belmont, Calif.: Wadsworth.

Miller, K., & Monge, P. (1985). Social information and employee anxiety about organizational change. *Human Communication Research* 11: 365–386.

Miller, K., & Monge, P. (1986). Participation, satisfaction, and productivity: A meta-analytic review. *Academy of Management Journal* 29: 727–753.

Miller, K., Ellis, B., Zook, E., & Lyles, J. (1990). An integrated model of communication, stress, and burnout in the workplace. *Communication Research* 17: 300–326.

Miller, K., Stiff, J., & Ellis, B. (1988). Communication and empathy as precursors to burnout among human service workers. *Communication Monographs* 55: 250–265.

Miller, V., & Jablin, F. (1991). Information seeking during organizational entry: Influences, tactics, and a model of the process. *Academy of Management Review* 16: 92–120.

Minh-Ha, T. (1991). *When the moon waxes red: Representation, gender, and cultural politics*. New York: Routledge.

Mintzberg, H. (1973). *The nature of managerial work*. New York: Harper & Row.

Mitchell, T., & Scott, W. (1990). America's problems and needed reforms: Confronting the ethic of personal advantage. *The Executive* 4: 23–35.

Mitroff, I., & Kilmann, R. (1975). Stories managers tell: A new tool for organizational problem-solving. *Management Review* 64: 18–28.

Mohan, M. (1993). *Organizational communication and cultural vision*. Albany, N.Y.: SUNY Press.

Monge, P., Bachman, S., Dillard, J., & Eisenberg, E. (1982). Communicator competence in the workplace: Model testing and scale development. *Communication Yearbook* 5, (pp. 505–528). New Brunswick, N.J.: Transaction Books.

Monge, P., Cozzens, M., & Contractor, N. (1992). Communication and motivational predictors of the dynamics of organizational innovation. *Organizational Science* 3: 250–274.

Monge, P., & Eisenberg, E. (1987). Emergent communication networks. In F. Jablin et al., eds., *Handbook of organizational communication* (pp. 204–342). Beverly Hills, Calif.: Sage Publications.

Monge, P., Farace, R., Eisenberg, E., Miller, K., & Rothman, L. (1984). The process of studying process in organizational communication. *Journal of Communication* 34: 22–43.

Morgan, G. (1986). *Images of organization*. Newbury Park, Calif.: Sage Publications.

Morrill, C. (1991). Little conflicts: The dialectic of order and change in professional relations. In D. Kolb & J. Bartunek, eds., *Disputing in the crevices: New perspectives on organizational conflict.* Newbury Park, Calif.: Sage Publications.

Morrison, A., & Von Glinow, M. A. (1990). Women and minorities in management. *American Psychologist* 45: 200–208.

Morrison, E., & Bies, R. (1991). Impression management in the feedback-seeking process: A literature review and research agenda. *Academy of Management Review* 16: 522–541.

Moskowitz, M., & Townsend, C. (1991). The 85 best companies for working mothers. *Working Mother* (October): 29–64.

Mouritsen, J., & Bjorn-Andersen, N. (1991). Understanding third-wave information systems. In C. Dunlop & R. Kling, eds., *Computerization and controversy: Value conflicts and social choices* (pp. 308–320). San Diego, Calif.: Academic Press.

Moxley, R. (1994). *Foundations of leadership.* Center for Creative Leadership, Greensboro, N.C., September.

Moyers, B. (1989). *A world of ideas.* New York: Doubleday.

Mumby, D. (1987). The political function of narratives in organizations. *Communication Monographs* 54: 113–127.

Mumby, D. (1993). *Narrative and social control.* Newbury Park, Calif.: Sage.

Mumby, D., & Putnam, L. (1993). The politics of emotion: A feminist reading of bounded rationality. *Academy of Management Review* 17: 465–486.

Myerson, D. (1991). "Normal" ambiguity? A glimpse of an occupational culture. In P. Frost et al., eds., *Reframing organizational culture* (pp. 131–144). Newbury Park, Calif.: Sage Publications.

Naisbett, J. (1982). *Megatrends.* New York: Warner.

Naisbett, J., & Auberdene, P. (1990). *Megatrends 2000.* New York: Morrow.

Newton, I. (1803). *The mathematical principles of natural philosophy.* Trans. Andrew Motte. London: H. D. Symonds.

Newton, J. (1789) *Apologia.* New York: Hodge, Allen, & Campbell.

Noer, D. (1993). *Healing the wounds: Overcoming the trauma of layoffs and revitalizing downsized organizations.* San Francisco: Jossey-Bass.

Ochs, E., Smith, R., & Taylor, C. (1989). Detective stories at dinnertime: Problem solving through co-narration. *Cultural Dynamics* 2: 238–257.

Odiorne, G. (1986). The crystal ball of HR strategy. *Personnel Administrator* 31: 103–106.

Offerman, L., & Gowing, M. (1990). Organizations of the future: Changes and challenges. *American Psychologist* 45: 95–108.

Okabe, R. (1983). Cultural assumptions of east and west: Japan and the United States. In B. Gudykunst, ed., *Intercultural communication theory* (pp. 212–244). Newbury Park, Calif.: Sage Publications.

Oldham, G., & Rotchford, N. (1983). Relationships between office characteristics and employee reactions: A study of the physical environment. *Administrative Science Quarterly* 28: 542–556.

Oliver, C. (1990). Determinants of interorganizational relationships: Integration and future directions. *Academy of Management Review* 15: 241–265.

Ong, W. (1958). *Ramus, method, and the decay of dialogue.* Cambridge, Mass.: Harvard University Press.

Ortner, S. (1980). Theory in anthropology since the sixties. *Journal for the Comparative Study of Society and History:* 126–166.

O'Reilly, B. (1994). The new deal: What companies and employees owe each other. *Fortune,* June 13, p. 44.

Osborn, J., Moran, L., Musselwhite, E., & Zenger, J. (1990). *Self-directed work teams.* Homewood, Ill.: Business One Irwin.

Osterberg, R. (1992). A company without hierarchy. *At Work: Stories of Tomorrow's Workplace* 1: 9–10.

Ouchi, W. (1981). *Theory Z.* Reading, Mass.: Addison-Wesley.

Ouchi, W., & Wilkins, A. (1985). Organizational culture. *Annual Review of Sociology* 11: 457–483.

Pacanowsky, M. (1988). Communication in the empowering organization. In J. Anderson, ed., *Communication Yearbook* 11 (pp. 356–379). Newbury Park, Calif.: Sage Publications.

Pacanowsky, M., & O'Donnell-Trujillo, N. (1983). Organizational communication as cultural performance. *Communication Monographs* 50: 126–147.

Papa, M. (1989). Communicator competence and employee performance with new technology: A case study. *The Southern Communication Journal* 55: 87–101.

Papa, M. (1990). Communication network patterns and employee performance with new technology. *Communication Research* 17: 344–368.

Parks, M. (1982). Ideology in interpersonal communication: Off the couch and into the world. In M. Burgoon, ed., *Communication Yearbook* 5 (pp. 79–108). New Brunswick, N.J.: Transaction Books.

Parsons, C., Herold, D., & Leatherwood, M. (1985). Turnover during initial employment: A longitudinal study of the role of causal attributions. *Journal of Applied Psychology* 70: 337–341.

Parsons, T. (1951). *The social system.* New York: Free Press of Glencoe.

Patterson, J., & Kim, P. (1991). *The day America told the truth.* Englewood Cliffs, N.J.: Prentice-Hall.

Percy, W. (1991). *Sign posts in a strange land.* New York: Farrar, Straus, Giroux.

Perrow, C. (1986). *Complex organizations: A critical essay.* 3rd ed. New York: Random House.

Peters, T. (1987). *Thriving on chaos.* New York: Alfred A. Knopf.

Peters, T., & Waterman, R. (1982). *In search of excellence.* New York: Harper & Row.

Peterson, L. (1995). The influence of sharing a semantic link on social support in work relationships at a hospital. Paper presented at the annual meeting of the Speech Communication Association, San Antonio, Texas.

Pettigrew, A. (1979). On studying organizational cultures. *Administrative Science Quarterly* 24: 570–581.

Phillips, G. (1991). *Communication incompetencies: A theory of training oral performance behavior.* Carbondale: Southern Illinois University Press.

Phillips, G., & Goodall, H. L. (1983). *Loving and living.* Englewood Cliffs, N.J.: Prentice-Hall.

Phillips, G., & Wood, J. (1982). *Communication in human relationships.* New York: Macmillan.

Pinchot, G., & Pinchot, E. (1993). *The end of bureaucracy and the rise of the intelligent organization.* San Francisco: Berrett-Koehler.

Poole, M. S. (1981). Decision development in small groups I: A comparison of two models. *Communication Monographs* 48: 1–24.

Poole, M. S. (1983). Decision development in small groups II: A study of multiple sequences in decision making. *Communication Monographs* 50: 321–341.

Poole, M. S. (1992). Structuration and the group communication process. In L. Samovar & R. Cathcart, eds., *Small group communication: A reader.* 6th ed. Dubuque, Iowa: William C. Brown.

Poole, M. S. (1996). A turn of the wheel: The case for a renewal of systems inquiry in organizational communication research. Conference on Organizational Communication and Change, Austin, Texas, February 11–13, 1996.

Poole, M. S., & Desanctis, G. (1990). Understanding the use of group decision support systems: The theory of adaptive structuration. In J. Fulk & C. Steinfeld, eds., *Organizations and communication technology* (pp. 173–193). Newbury Park, Calif.: Sage Publications.

Poole, M. S., & Holmes, M. (1995). Decision development in computer-assisted group decision making. *Human Communication Research* 22: 90–127.

Poole, M. S., & Roth, J. (1989). Decision development in small groups V: Test of a contingency model. *Human Communication Research* 15: 549–589.

Porter, M. (1980). *Competitive strategy.* New York: Free Press.

Prasad, P. (1993). Symbolic processes in the implementation of technological change: A symbolic interactionist study of work computerization. *Academy of Management Journal* 36: 1400–1429.

Prigogine, I. (1980). *From being to becoming.* San Francisco, Calif.: W. H. Freeman.

Pritchard, R., Jones, S., Roth, P., Steubing, K. (1988). Effects of group feedback, goal setting, and incentives on organizational productivity. *Journal of Applied Psychology* 73: 337–358.

Putnam, L. (1982). Paradigms for organizational communication research: An overview and synthesis. *Western Journal of Speech Communication* 46: 192–206.

Putnam, L. (1985). Contradictions and paradoxes in organizations. In L. Thayer, ed., *Organization and communication: Emerging perspectives* (pp. 151–167). Norwood, N.J.: Ablex.

Putnam, L., & Pacanowsky, M. (1983). *Communication and organizations: An interpretive approach.* Beverly Hills, Calif.: Sage Publications.

Putnam, L., & Poole, M. S. (1987). Conflict and negotiation. In F. Jablin et al., eds., *Handbook of organizational communication* (pp. 549–599). Newbury Park, Calif.: Sage Publications.

Pynchon, T. (1973). *Gravity's rainbow.* New York: Viking Press.

Quick, J., & Quick, J. (1984). *Organizational stress and preventative management.* New York: McGraw-Hill.

Quinn, R. (1977). Coping with Cupid: The formation, impact, and management of romantic relationships in organizations. *Administrative Science Quarterly* 22: 30–45.

Raban, J. (1991). *Hunting mister heartbreak: A discovery of America.* San Francisco: HarperCollins.

Rabinow, P., & Sullivan, W. (1986). *Interpretive social science—a second look.* Berkeley: University of California Press.

Rafaeli, A., & Sutton, R. (1987). The expression of emotion as part of the work role. *Academy of Management Review* 12: 23–37.

Rafaeli, A., & Sutton, R. (1991). Emotional contrast strategies as means of social influence: Lessons from criminal interrogators and bill collectors. *Academy of Management Journal* 34: 749–775.

Ralston, S. & Kirkwood, W. (1995). Overcoming managerial bias in employment interviewing. *Journal of Applied Communication Research* 23: 75–92.

Ray, E. (1987). Supportive relationships and occupational stress in the workplace. In T. Albrecht & M. Adelman, eds., *Communicating social support* (pp. 172–191). Newbury Park, Calif.: Sage Publications.

Redding, W. C. (1972). *Communication within the organization.* New York: Industrial Communications Council.

Redding, W. C. (1985a). Rocking boats, blowing whistles, teaching speech communication. *Communication Education* 34: 245–258.

Redding, W. C. (1985b). Stumbling toward identity: The emergence of organizational communication as a field of study. In R. McPhee & P. Tompkins, eds., *Organizational communication: Traditional themes and new directions* (pp. 15–54). Beverly Hills, Calif.: Sage Publications.

Redding, W. C. (1991). Unethical messages in the organizational context. Paper presented at the Annual Convention of the International Communication Association, Chicago.

Redding, W. C., & Tompkins, P. (1988). Organizational communication—Past and present tenses. In G. Goldhaber & G. Barnett, eds., *Handbook of organizational communication* (pp. 5–33). Norwood, N.J.: Ablex.

Reddy, M. (1979). The conduit metaphor—a case of frame conflict in our language about language. In A. Ortony, ed., *Metaphor and thought* (pp. 284–324). Cambridge, England: Cambridge University Press.

Rehfield, J. (1994). Cited in Barnlund, D.C. *Communicative styles of Japanese and Americans.* Belmont, Calif.: Wadsworth.

Reich, R. (1991). Global business. *Wall Street Journal*, July 5.

Rheinhold, H. (1991). *Virtual reality.* New York: Summit Books.

Rheingold, H. (1993). *The virtual community.* Boston: Addison-Wesley.

Richards, I. A. (1936). *The philosophy of rhetoric.* New York: Oxford University Press.

Richards, W. (1985). Data, models, and assumptions in network analysis. In R. McPhee & P. Tompkins, eds., *Organizational communication: Traditional themes and new directions* (pp. 109–128). Newbury Park, Calif.: Sage Publications.

Richmond, V., Davis, L., Saylor, K., & McCroskey, J. (1984). Power strategies in organizations: Communication techniques and messages. *Human Communication Research* 11: 85–108.

Richmond, V., & McCroskey, J. (1979). Management communication style, tolerance for disagreement, and innovativeness as predictors of employee satisfaction: A comparison of single-factor, two-factor, and multiple-factor approaches. In D. Nimmo, ed., *Communication Yearbook* 3 (pp. 359–374). New Brunswick, N.J.: Transaction Books.

Rider, A. (1992). Wishful thinking. *Los Angeles Times* Magazine, September 15, p. 10.

Rifkin, J. (1995). *The end of work.* New York: Tarcher/Putnam.

Riley, P., & Eisenberg, E. (1991). The ACE model of management. Unpublished working paper, University of Southern California.

Rilke, R. (1984). *Letters to a young poet.* Trans. Stephen Mitchell. New York: Random House.

Robert, M. (1993). *Strategy: Pure and simple.* New York: McGraw-Hill.

Roberts, K., & O'Reilly, C. (1974). Failures in upward communication: Three possible culprits. *Academy of Management Journal* 17: 205–215.

Robertson, J. (1985). *Future work: Jobs, self-employment, and leisure after the industrial age.* New York: Universe Books.

Rogers, E., & Kincaid, D. (1981). *Communication networks: Toward a new paradigm for research.* New York: Free Press.

Rose, D. (1989). *Patterns of American culture.* Philadelphia: University of Pennsylvania Press.

Rose, H. (1983). Hand, brain, and heart: A feminist epistemology for the natural sciences. *Signs* 9: 81.

Rosen, M. (1985). Breakfast at Spiro's: Dramaturgy and dominance. *Journal of Management* 11: 31–48.

Rosen, M. (1991). Scholars, travelers, thieves: On concept, method, and cunning in organizational ethnography. In P. Frost et al., eds., *Reframing organizational culture* (pp. 271–284). Newbury Park, Calif.: Sage Publications.

Rosenberg, B., & White, D. (1957). *Mass culture.* Glencoe, Ill.: Free Press.

Rosenmann, R., Brand, R., Jenkins, C., Friedman, M., Straus, R., & Wurm, M. (1975). Coronary heart disease in the western collaborative group study: Final follow-up experience of 8.5 years. *Journal of the American Medical Association* 233: 872–877.

Ross, R. (1989). *Small groups in organizational settings.* Englewood Cliffs, N.J.: Prentice-Hall.

Rounds, J. (1984). Information and ambiguity in organizational change. *Advances in information processing in organizations* 1: 111–141.

Roy, D. (1960). Banana time: Job satisfaction and informal interaction. *Human Organization* 18: 156–180.

Rummler, G., & Brache, A. (1991). *Managing the white space in your organizational chart.* New York: Free Press.

Rushing, J. (1993). Power, Other, and Spirit in cultural texts. *Western Journal of Communication* 57: 159–168.

Sackmann, S. (1991). *Cultural knowledge in organizations.* Newbury Park, Calif: Sage Publications.

Sahlins, M. (1976). *Culture and practical reason.* Chicago: University of Chicago Press.

Said, E. (1978). *Orientalism.* New York: Pantheon.

Said, E. (1984). *The world, the text, and the critic.* Cambridge, Mass.: Harvard University Press.

Sailer, H., Schlachter, J., & Edwards, M. (1982). Stress: Causes, consequences, and coping strategies. *Personnel* (July–August) 59: 35–48.

Salancik, G., & Pfeffer, J. (1978). A social information processing approach to job attitudes and task design. *Administrative Science Quarterly* 23: 224–252.

Sartre, J. P. (1973). *Existentialism and humanism.* Trans. P. Mariet. London: Methuen.

Sashkin, M. (1991). *Total quality management.* Brentwood, Md.: International Graphics, Inc.

SCA. (1991). *Pathways to careers in communication.* Annandale, Va.: SCA.

Scandura, T., Graen, G., & Novak, M. (1986). When managers decide not to decide autocratically. *Journal of Applied Psychology* 71: 1–6.

Schaef, A. & Fassel, D. (1988). *The addictive organization.* San Francisco, Calif.: Harper & Row.

Schall, M. A. (1983). A communication-rules approach to organizational culture. *Administrative Science Quarterly* 28: 557–581.

Scheidel, T., & Crowell, L. (1964). Idea development in small discussion groups. *Quarterly Journal of Speech* 50: 140–145.

Schein, E. (1969). *Process consultation: Its role in organizational development.* Reading, Mass.: Addison-Wesley.

Schein, E. (1988). *Organizational culture and leadership: A dynamic view.* San Francisco: Jossey-Bass.

Schein, E. (1991). The role of the founder in the creation of organizational culture. In P. Frost et al., eds., *Reframing organizational culture* (pp. 14–25). Newbury Park, Calif.: Sage Publications.

Schuler, R., & Jackson, S. (1986). Managing stress through PHRM practices: An uncertainty interpretation. *Research in Personnel and Human Resource Management* 4: 183–224.

Schwartzman, H. (1993). *Ethnography in organizations.* Newbury Park, Calif.: Sage Publications.

Scott, J. (1990). *Domination and the arts of resistance: Hidden transcripts.* New Haven, Conn.: Yale University Press.

Scott, W. R. (1964). Theory of organizations. In R. Faris, ed., *Handbook of modern sociology* (pp. 485–529). Chicago: Rand McNally.

Scott, W. R. (1981). *Organizations: Rational, natural, and open systems.* Englewood Cliffs, N.J.: Prentice-Hall.

Seabright, M., Levinthal, D., & Fichman, M. (1992). Role of individual attachments in the dissolution of interorganizational relationships. *Academy of Management Journal* 35: 122–160.

Selznick, P. (1948). Foundations of the theory of organizations. *American Sociological Review* 13: 25–35.

Selznick, P. (1957). *Leadership in administration.* New York: Harper & Row.

Senge, P. (1991). *The fifth discipline: The art and practice of the learning organization.* New York: Doubleday/Currency.

Senge, P., Roberts, C., Ross, R., Smith, B., & Kleiner, A. (1994). *The fifth discipline fieldbook.* New York: Currency Doubleday.

Sennett, R. (1978). *The fall of public man.* New York: Vintage.

Shockley-Zalabak, P. (1991). *Fundamentals of organizational communication.* New York: Longman.

Shockley-Zalabak, P., & Morley, D. (1994). Creating a culture. *Human Communication Research* 20: 334–355.

Shorris, E. (1984). *Scenes from corporate life.* Hammondsworth, England: Penguin.

Sias, P., & Jablin, F. (1995). Differential superior--subordinate relations, perceptions of fairness, and coworker communication. *Human Communication Research* 22: 5–38.

Silverman, D., & Bloor, M. (1990). Patient-centered medicine: Some sociological observations on its constitution, penetration, and cultural assonance. *Advances in Medical Sociology* 1: 3–25.

Silverstein, S. (1992). Sabbaticals are costly for women. *Los Angeles Times,* January 1, p. D1.

Simon, H. (1957–1976). *Administrative behavior.* 3rd. ed. New York: Free Press.

Sink, D. (1985). *Productivity management.* New York: John Wiley and Sons.

Sivard, R. (1983). *World military and social expenditures 1983* (p. 26). Washington, D.C.: World Priorities.

Small, A. (1905). *General sociology.* Chicago: University of Chicago Press.

Smircich, L., & Calas, M. (1987). Organizational culture: A critical assessment. In F. Jablin et al., eds., *Handbook of organizational communication* (pp. 228–263). Newbury Park, Calif.: Sage Publications.

Smith, A. (1898). *Wealth of nations.* London: G. Routledge.

Smith, D. (1972). Communication research and the idea of process. *Speech Monographs* 39: 174–182.

Smith, H. (1982). *Beyond the postmodern mind.* New York: Crossroad.

Smith, H. (1995). *The three faces of capitalism.* Public Broadcasting System, May.

Smith, M., Cohen, B., Stammerjohn, V., & Happ, A. (1981). An investigation of health complaints and job stress in video display operations. *Human Factors* 23: 387–400.

Smith, R. (1990). In pursuit of synthesis: Activity as a primary framework for organizational communication. Doctoral dissertation, Department of Communication Arts and Sciences, University of Southern California, Los Angeles.

Smith, R., & Eisenberg, E. (1987). Conflict at Disneyland: A root metaphor analysis. *Communication Monographs* 54: 367–380.

Somervell, D., & Toynbee, A. (1947). *A study of history.* New York: Oxford University Press.

Spencer, D. (1986). Employee voice and employee retention. *Academy of Management Journal* 29: 488–502.

Spretnak, C. (1991). *States of grace.* San Francisco: HarperCollins.

Staimer, M. (1992). U.S. workers get little vacation. *USA Today.*

Stallybrass, P., & White, A. (1986). *The politics and poetics of transgression.* Ithaca, N.Y.: Cornell University Press.

Steelman, J., & Klitzman, S. (1985). *The VDT: Hazardous to your health.* Ithaca, N.Y.: Cornell University Press.

Steers, R. (1977). Antecedents and outcomes of organizational commitment. *Administrative Science Quarterly* 22: 46–56.

Steers, R. (1981). *Introduction to organizational behavior.* Santa Monica, Calif.: Goodyear.

Steier, F. (1989). Toward a radical and ecological constructivist approach to family communication. *Journal of Applied Communication Research* 17: 1–26.

Steier, F., & Smith, K. (1992). The cybernetics of cybernetics and the organization of organization. In L. Thayer, ed., *Organization-communication: Emerging perspectives.* Norwood, N.J.: Ablex.

Steiner, G., & Ryan, W. (1968). *Industrial project management.* New York: Crowell-Collier and Macmillan.

Stewart, T. (1991). GE keeps those ideas coming. *Fortune,* August 12, Vol. 124, p. 40(8).

Stoller, P. (1989). *The taste of ethnographic things.* Philadelphia: University of Pennsylvania Press.

Strine, M. (1991). Critical theory and "organic" intellectuals: Reframing the work of cultural critique. *Communication Monographs* 58: 195–201.

Strine, M., & Pacanowsky, M. (1985). How to read interpretive accounts of organizational life: Narrative bases for textual authority. *Southern Speech Communication Journal* 50: 283–297.

Sullivan, J. (1988). Three roles of language in motivation theory. *Academy of Management Review* 13: 104–115.

Sundstrom, E., DeMeuse, K., & Futrell, D. (1990). Work teams: Applications and effectiveness. *American Psychologist* 45: 120–133.

Sussman, G. (1976). *Autonomy at work.* New York: Praeger.

Sutton, R., & Rafaeli, A. (1988). Untangling the relationship between displayed emotions and organizational sales: The case of convenience stores. *Academy of Management Journal* 31: 461–487.

Swidler, A. (1986). Culture as action. *American Sociological Review* 51: 273–286.

Tamaki, J. (1991). Sexual harassment in the workplace. *Los Angeles Times,* October 10, p. D2.

Taylor, F. (1913). *The principles of scientific management.* New York: Harper.

Taylor, F. (1947). *Scientific management.* New York: Harper & Brothers.

Thomas, J. (1993). *Doing critical ethnography.* Newbury Park, Calif.: Sage Publications.

Thomas, L. (1975). *The lives of a cell.* New York: Penguin.

Thompson, J. (1967). *Organizations in action.* New York: McGraw-Hill.

Tichy, N. (1983). *Managing strategic change.* New York: John Wiley and Sons.

Tjosvold, D. (1984). Effects of leader warmth and directiveness on subordinate performance on a subsequent task. *Journal of Applied Psychology* 69: 422–427.

Tjosvold, D., & Tjosvold, M. (1991). *Leading the team organization.* New York: Lexington Books.

Tompkins, P. (1987). Translating organizational theory: Symbolism over substance. In F. Jablin, L. Putnam, K. Roberts, & L. Porter, eds., *Handbook of organizational communication* (pp. 70–96). Newbury Park, Calif.: Sage Publications.

Tompkins, P., & Cheney, G. (1985). Communication and unobtrusive control in contemporary organizations. In R. McPhee & P. Tompkins, eds., *Organizational communication: Traditional themes and new directions* (pp. 179–210). Beverly Hills, Calif.: Sage Publications.

Torbert, W. (1991). *The power of balance.* Newbury Park, Calif.: Sage Publications.

Tracy, K., & Coupland, N. (1990). Multiple goals in discourse: An overview of issues. *Journal of Language and Social Psychology* 9: 1–13.

Tracy, K., & Eisenberg, E. (1991). Giving criticism: A multiple goals case study. *Research on Language and Social Interaction* 24: 37–70.

Treadwell, D., & Harrison, T. (1994). Conceptualizing and assessing organizational image: Model images, commitment, and communication. *Communication Monographs* 61: 63–85.

Trice, H., & Beyer, J. (1984). Studying organizational cultures through rites and ceremonies. *Academy of Management Review* 9: 653–669.

Trist, E. (1981). The evolution of socio-technical systems. *Occasional Paper* No. 2. Toronto: Quality of Work Life Centre.

Trujillo, N. (1985). Organizational communication as cultural performance: Some managerial considerations. *Southern Speech Communication Journal* 50: 201–224.

Trujillo, N., & Dionisopoulos, G. (1987). Cop talk, police stories, and the social construction of organizational drama. *Central States Speech Journal* 38: 196–209.

Truscott, M. (1989). *Brats: Children of the American military speak out.* New York: Dutton.

Turnage, J. (1990). The challenge of new workplace technology for psychology. *American Psychologist* 45: 171–178.

Turner, B. (1990). *Organizational symbolism.* Berlin: Walter de Gruyter.

Tyson, L. (1991). U.S. needs new spending priorities. *Los Angeles Times,* November 10, p. D2.

Van Maanen, J. (1979). *Qualitative methodology.* Beverly Hills, Calif.: Sage Publications.

Van Maanen, J. (1988). *Tales of the field: On writing ethnography.* Chicago: University of Chicago Press.

Van Maanen, J. (1991). The smile factory: Work at Disneyland. In P. Frost et al., eds., *Reframing organizational culture* (pp. 58–76). Newbury Park, Calif.: Sage Publications.

Van Maanen, J., & Barley, S. (1984). Occupational communities: Cultural control in organizations. In B. Staw & L. Cummings, eds., *Research in Organizational Behavior* Vol. 6 (pp. 265–287). Greenwich, Conn.: JAI Press.

Varner, I., & Beamer, L. (1995). *Intercultural communication in the global workplace.* Chicago: Irwin.

Victor, D. A. (1994). *International business communication.* New York: HarperCollins.

Von Bertalanffy, L. (1968). *General systems theory.* New York: George Braziller.

Vroom, V. (1964). *Work and motivation.* New York: John Wiley and Sons.

Waldera, L. (1988). *The effects of influence strategy, influence objective, and leader–member exchange on upward influence.* Unpublished doctoral dissertation, George Washington University.

Waldron, V. (1991). Achieving communication goals in superior–subordinate relationships: The multi-functionality of upward maintenance tactics. *Communication Monographs* 58: 289–306.

Waller, R. (1986). Women and the typewriter during the first 50 years: 1873–1923. *Popular Culture* 10: 39–50.

Walljasper, J. (1992). At home in an eco-village. *Utne Reader* 51: 142–143.

Wanous, J. (1980). *Organizational entry: Recruitment, selection, and socialization of newcomers.* London: Addison-Wesley.

Ward, J. W. (1990). Cited in O. Zunz, *Making America corporate: 1870–1920.* Chicago: University of Chicago Press.

Watts, A. (1966). *The book: On the taboo against knowing who you are.* New York: Pantheon.

Watzlawick, P., Beavin, J., & Jackson, D. (1967). *The pragmatics of human communication: A study of interactional patterns, pathologies, and paradoxes.* New York: Norton.

Weber, M. (1946). *From Max Weber: Essays in sociology.* H. Gerth & C. Wright Mills, eds., New York: Oxford University Press.

Weick, K. (1984). Theoretical assumptions and research methodology selection. In F. McFarlan, ed., *Proceedings of the information systems research challenge* (pp. 111–132). Boston: Harvard Business School Press.

Weick, K. (1990). The vulnerable system: An analysis of the Tenerife air disaster. In P. Frost et al., eds., *Reframing organizational culture* (pp. 117–130). Newbury Park, Calif.: Sage Publications.

Weick, K. (1976). Educational organizations as loosely coupled systems. *Administrative Science Quarterly* 21: 1–19.

Weick, K. (1979). *The social psychology of organizing.* 2nd ed. Reading, Mass.: Addison-Wesley.

Weick, K. (1980). The management of eloquence. *Executive* 6: 18–21.

Weick, K. (1995). *Sensemaking in organizations.* Newbury Park, Calif.: Sage Publications.

Weil, S. (1977). *The Simone Weil reader.* George Panichas, ed. New York: McKay.

Wellins, R., Byham, W., & Wilson, J. (1991). *Empowered teams.* San Francisco: Jossey-Bass.

Wenberg, J., & Wilmot, W. (1973). *The personal communication process.* New York: John Wiley and Sons.

Wentworth, W. (1980). *Context and understanding.* New York: Elsevier.

Whalen, S., & Cheney, G. (1991). Contemporary social theory and its implications for rhetorical and communication theory. *Quarterly Journal of Speech* 77: 467–479.

Wheatley, M. (1992). *Leadership and the new science.* San Francisco, Calif.: Berrett-Koehler.

Whyte, W. F. (1948). *Human relations in the restaurant industry.* New York: McGraw-Hill.

Whyte, W. F. (1969). *Organizational behavior.* Homewood, Ill.: Irwin-Dorsey.

Wilensky, Harold. (1967). *Organizational intelligence.* New York: Basic Books.

Wilkins, A. (1984). The creation of company cultures: The role of stories and human resource systems. *Human Resource Management* 23: 41–60.

Wilkins, A., & Dyer, W. (1988). Toward culturally sensitive theories of culture change. *Academy of Management Review* 13: 522–533.

Wilkinson, L. (1995). How to build scenarios. *Wired*, May, 4–81.

Williams, M. (1977). *The new executive woman: A guide to business success.* New York: New American Library.

Williams, R. (1993). IBM's efforts to redefine its workplace compact. Presentation to the 21st issues management conference, Human Resources Institute, St. Petersburg, Fla., February 18.

Wilson, G., & Goodall, H. L. (1991). *Interviewing in context.* New York: McGraw-Hill.

Wood, J. (1977). Leading in purposive discussions: A study of adaptive behavior. *Communication Monographs* 44: 152–165.

Woods, J. (1991). The corporate closet: Heterosexual hegemony in a white-collar world. Presented as part of the panel "In or out? The ethics and politics of disclosure and exposure of sexual orientation" at the International Communication Association, Chicago.

Zedeck, S., & Mosier, K. (1990). Work in the family and employing organization. *American Psychologist* 45: 240–251.

Zeithaml, V., Parasuraman, A., & Berry, L. (1990). *Delivering quality service: Balancing customer perceptions and expectations*. New York: Free Press.

Acknowledgments

Table 2.4: adapted from Michael Jackson, *Paths Toward a Clearing: Radical Empiricism and Ethnographic Inquiry.* Copyright © 1989 by Michael Jackson. Reprinted with the permission of Indiana University Press.

Figure 3.1: adapted from Gareth Morgan, *Images of Organization.* Copyright © 1986 by Sage Publications, Inc. Reprinted with the permission of the publisher.

Figure 3.2: from *Slave Ships and Slaving* (Detroit: Negro History Press, 1969), p. 159.

Table 3.2: adapted from Dwight Conquergood, "Ethnography, Rhetoric, and Performance," *Quarterly Journal of Speech* 78 (1992): 80–97. Copyright © 1992 by Speech Communication Association. Reprinted with the permission of the publisher.

Table 3.3: from Charles Perrow, "Why Bureaucracy?" in *Complex Organizations, Third Edition* (New York: Random House, 1986). Copyright © 1986. Reprinted with the permission of McGraw-Hill, Inc.

Ethics Box 3.1: Excerpts from Mary Tryscott, *Brats: Children of the American Military Speak Out.* Copyright © 1989 by Mary Tryscott. Reprinted with the permission of Dutton Signet, a division of Penguin Books USA, Inc.

Ethics Box 3.2: contains excerpts from Earl Shorris, *Scenes from Corporate Life* (New York: Penguin Books, 1984). Copyright © 1981 by Earl Shorris. Reprinted with the permission of the author and Roberta Pryor, Inc.

Table 4.2: from Ludwig von Bertalanffy, *General Systems Theory: Foundations, Development, Applications.* Copyright © 1968 by Ludwig von Bertalanffy. Reprinted with the permission of George Braziller, Inc.

Table 4.3: adapted from Richard V. Farace, Peter R. Monge, and Hamish M. Russell, *Communicating and Organizing.* Copyright © 1977 by Richard V. Farace, Peter R. Monge, and Hamish M. Russell. Reprinted with the permission of The McGraw-Hill Companies.

Figure 4.1: from Karl Weick, *The Social Psychology of Organizing,* Second Edition (New York: Random House, 1979). Reprinted with the permission of McGraw-Hill, Inc.

Karl Weick's seven properties of sensemaking from *Sensemaking in Organizations.* Copyright © 1996 by Sage Publications, Inc. Reprinted with the permission of the publisher.

Table 5.1: adapted with permission from *The Hudson Review,* Vol. XVI, No. 4 (Winter 1963–64). Copyright © 1964 by The Hudson Review, Inc.

Table 5.3: adapted from William Ouchi, *Theory Z.* Copyright © 1981 by William Ouichi. Reprinted with the permission of The McGraw-Hill Companies.

Figure 6.1: from Stanley Deetz, *Transforming Communication, Transforming Business* (Cresskill, N.J.: The Hampton Press, 1995), p. 50. Reprinted by permission.

Figure 7.1: Nordstrom Employee Handbook. Courtesy of Nordstrom.

Table 8.1: from Vernon Miller and Fred Jablin, "Information Seeking During Organizational Entry: Influences, Tactics, and a Model of the Process," *Academy of Management Review* 16 (1991). Copyright © 1991 by the Academy of Management. Reprinted with the permission of the Academy of Management.

Figure 8.1: from Eric M. Eisenberg and P. Riley (1992), "A Closed-Loop Model of Communication, Empowerment, Urgency, and Performance" (unpublished working paper, University of Southern California). Reprinted with the permission of the authors.

Table 8.2: from H. Sailer, J. Schlachter, and M. Edwards, "Stress: Causes, Consequences, and Coping Strategies," *Personnel* 59 (July–August 1982). Copyright © 1982 by the American Management Association. Reprinted with the permission of *Personnel.*

Table 9.1: from David M. Noer, *Healing the Wounds: Overcoming the Trauma of Layoffs and Revitalizing Downsized Organizations.* Copyright © 1994 by Jossey-Bass, Inc., Publishers. Reprinted with the permission of the publisher.

Table 9.2: from Ross J. Williams, Director of Leadership and HR Development, presentation to the 21st Issues Management Conference, Human Resources Institute, St. Petersburg, Fl., February 18, 1993. Reprinted by permission.

Figure 9.1: adapted from J. Conger and R. Kanungo, "The Empowerment Process: Integrating Theory and Practice," *Academy of Management Review* 13 (1988). Copyright © 1988 by the Academy of Management. Reprinted with the permission of the Academy of Management.

Table 9.3: from Jack Hawley, "The Management/Spiritual Leader Model" from *Reawakening the Spirit in Work: The Power of Dharmic Management.* Copyright © 1993 by Berrett-Koehler Publishers, Inc. Reprinted with the permission of Berrett-Koehler Publishers, Inc., San Francisco, California. All rights reserved.

Excerpt from Gifford and Elizabeth Pinchot, *The End of Bureaucracy and the Rise of Intelligent Organization.* Copyright © 1993 by Berrett-Koehler Publishers, Inc. Reprinted with the permission of Berrett-Koehler Publishers, Inc., San Francisco, California. All rights reserved.

Figure 10.1: from Richard S. Wellins, William C. Byham, and Jeanne M. Wilson, *Empowered Teams: Creating Self-Directed Work Groups that Improve Quality, Productivity, and Participation.* Copyright © 1991 by Jossey-Bass, Inc., Publsihers. Reprinted with the permission of the publishers.

Figure 10.2: Kilmann, R. H. & Thomas, K. W.: "Interpersonal Conflict-Handling Behavior as a Reflection of Jungian Personality Dimensions," *Psychological Reports,* (1975), 37, 971–980. Copyright © by Psychological Reports 1975. Reprinted with the permission of Ralph H. Kilmann and *Psychological Reports.*

Figure 10.3: from Peter M. Senge, Art Kleiner, Charlotte Roberts, Richard B. Ross and Bryan J. Smith, *The Fifth Discipline Fieldbook.* Copyright © 1994 by Peter M. Senge, Art Kleiner, Charlotte Roberts, Richard B. Ross and Bryan J. Smith. Reprinted with the permission of Doubleday, a division of Bantam Doubleday Dell Publishing Group, Inc.

Figure 10.4: from Peter M. Senge, Art Kleiner, Charlotte Roberts, Richard B. Ross and Bryan J. Smith, *The Fifth Discipline Fieldbook.* Copyright © 1994 by Peter M. Senge, Art Kleiner, Charlotte Roberts, Richard B. Ross and Bryan J. Smith. Reprinted with the permission of Doubleday, a division of Bantam Doubleday Dell Publishing Group, Inc.

Figure 10.5: from Peter M. Senge, Art Kleiner, Charlotte Roberts, Richard B. Ross and Bryan J. Smith, *The Fifth Discipline Fieldbook.* Copyright © 1994 by Peter M. Senge, Art Kleiner, Charlotte Roberts, Richard B. Ross and Bryan J. Smith. Reprinted with the permission of Doubleday, a division of Bantam Doubleday Dell Publishing Group, Inc.

Figure 10.6: from W. Richard Scott, *Organizations: Rational, Natural, and Open Systems,* Third Edition. Copyright © 1992 by Prentice-Hall, Inc. Reprinted with the permission of the publishers.

Figures 11.1 and 11.2: from Richard D'Aveni, "Coping with Hypercompetition: Utilizing the New 7S's Framework," *Academy of Management Executive* 9, no. 3 (1995): 45–57. Copyright © 1995 by the Academy of Management. Reprinted with the permission of the Academy of Management.

Table 11.1: Jan Mouritsen and Niels Bjorn-Anderson, "Understanding Third-Wave Information Systems" in Charles Dunlop and Rob Kling, eds., *Computerization and Controversy: Value Conflicts and Social Choices.* Copyright © 1991 by Academic Press, Inc. Reprinted with the permission of the publisher.

Figure 11.3: adapted from Charles Grantham, "The Virtual Office," *At Work: Stories of Tomorrow's Workplace* 4, no. 5 (September/October 1995). Copyright © 1995 by Berrett-Koehler Publishers, Inc. Reprinted with the permission of Berrett-Koehler Publishers, Inc., San Francisco, California. All rights reserved.

Case Study 11: from *Wall Street Journal* (from *The Tampa Tribune-Times,* Sunday, August 6, 1995). Reprinted by permission of the *Wall Street Journal.* © 1995. © 1995 Dow Jones & Company, Inc. All Rights Reserved Worldwide.

Figure 12.1: from Lawrence Wilkinson, "How to Build Scenarios," 10 lines plus chart on p. 78 in *Wired Scenarios,* pp. 4–81. Copyright © 1995–1996 Wired Magazine Group, Inc. All rights reserved. Reprinted by permission of Wired Magazine, Inc.

Subject Index

Author Index